Tolley's International Personal Tax

Tolley's International Personal Tax Planning

edited by John Dixon and Malcolm Finney

Tolley
LexisNexis™

Members of the LexisNexis Group worldwide

United Kingdom	LexisNexis Butterworths Tolley, a Division of Reed Elsevier (UK) Ltd, Halsbury House, 35 Chancery Lane, LONDON, WC2A 1EL, and 4 Hill Street, EDINBURGH EH2 3JZ
Argentina	LexisNexis Argentina, BUENOS AIRES
Australia	LexisNexis Butterworths, CHATSWOOD, New South Wales
Austria	LexisNexis Verlag ARD Orac GmbH & Co KG, VIENNA
Canada	LexisNexis Butterworths, MARKHAM, Ontario
Chile	LexisNexis Chile Ltda, SANTIAGO DE CHILE
Czech Republic	Nakladatelství Orac sro, PRAGUE
France	Editions du Juris-Classeur SA, PARIS
Hong Kong	LexisNexis Butterworths, HONG KONG
Hungary	HVG-Orac, BUDAPEST
India	LexisNexis Butterworths, NEW DELHI
Ireland	Butterworths (Ireland) Ltd, DUBLIN
Italy	Giuffrè Editore, MILAN
Malaysia	Malayan Law Journal Sdn Bhd, KUALA LUMPUR
New Zealand	LexisNexis Butterworths, WELLINGTON
Poland	Wydawnictwo Prawnicze LexisNexis, WARSAW
Singapore	LexisNexis Butterworths, SINGAPORE
South Africa	Butterworths SA, DURBAN
Switzerland	Stämpfli Verlag AG, BERNE
USA	LexisNexis, DAYTON, Ohio

A CIP Catalogue record for this book is available from the British Library.

ISBN 0 7545 1337 8

Typeset by Phoenix Photosetting, Chatham, Kent
Printed and bound in Great Britain by The Bath Press, Bath

Visit Butterworths LexisNexis *direct* at www.butterworths.com

Preface

Tolley is delighted to present International Personal Tax Planning.

This title was originally part of Tolley's International Tax Planning. This year, however, that book has been divided into International Personal Tax Planning and a companion volume, International Corporate Tax Planning, providing for more in-depth coverage of the two areas of tax planning.

The editors would like to extend their thanks to each of the contributors who willingly and unsparingly gave of their time and experience in the updating and writing of their chapters.

Comments on this publication and suggestions for improvements are always welcomed.

April 2002

Table of Contents

3 Buying and Selling Residential Property in France

Eamonn McGregor FCCA ATII (Moores Rowland, Monaco)

4 Buying and Selling Residential Property in Spain

Anne McMahon BA Hons (Senior Solicitor) (Wilde Sapte) in conjunction with lawyers from Estudio Legal of Madrid and Barcelona
Material enlarged and updated by José María Gómez Tabernero de Paz (Ldo. en Derecho, U. Salamanca; LLM, Collège d'Europe, Bruges; Notary candidate)

5 Immigration Controls in the United Kingdom

Caroline Stack LLB (Reynolds Porter Chamberlain)
Updating material by Matthew Chapman LLB LLM and
Kim Vowden BA (CMS Cameron McKenna)

6 Income Tax and Capital Gains Tax Planning for Non-Domiciled Individuals

F Michael Mitchell MA (Oxon) MA (Cantab) (Withers LLP) and
Janette Cattell LLB (Withers LLP)

7   Inheritance Tax Double Taxation Agreements

Bernard Geoffrey Owen Clutton BALLB BCL ATII
(Partner, Macfarlanes)

8   Inheritance Tax Planning for Non-UK Domiciled Individuals

Caroline Kirby (Partner, Farrer & Co.)

9   Money Laundering – A Supervisor's Perspective: Guernsey

Steve Butterworth (Director of Insurance, Guernsey Financial Services Commission and Chairman of the Insurance Fraud Subcommittee of the International Association of Insurance Supervisors)

10   Money Laundering, Tax Evasion and Professional Liability

Michael Brindle QC

11   Non-Resident Entertainers

Richard Citron MA (Cantab) FCA FTII TEP (BDO Stoy Hayward)

12   Secondments in and out of the UK

Robert Maas (Blackstone Franks)

13   Sheltering Income and Gains Overseas for UK Domiciled Individuals: Problems and Solutions

David Kilshaw BA (Oxon) and Carolyn Steppler MA DPhil (KPMG)

Table of Contents

14 Tax Havens: A Comparative Study

Ian Ferrier

15 The Taxation of UK Source Income in the Hands of Non-Residents

John Dixon and Phil Barrett (Ernst & Young)

16   UK Self-Assessment for Non-Residential Individuals and Trustees

Andrew Roycroft ATII (Solicitor)

17   Use of Trusts in International Tax Planning

Andrew Penney BA Hons TEP (Solicitor) (Partner, Speechly Bircham, London)

Abbreviations and References

APT	=	Asset Protection Trusts (UK)
CA	=	Court of Appeal (UK)
CC	=	Spanish Civil Code (Spain)
CGI	=	*Code Générale des Impôts* (France)
Ch D	=	Chancery Division (UK)
CNR	=	Inland Revenue Centre for Non-residents (UK)
CPT	=	Creditor Protection Trusts (UK)
DGRN	=	*Dirección General de los Registrosy del Notariado* (Directorate General for the Public Registries and the Notaryship) (Spain)
EC	=	European Commission
EEA	=	European Economic Area
EFTA	=	European Free Trade Association
ESC	=	Inland Revenue Extra-Statutory Concession (UK)
FAPI	=	Foreign Accrual Property Income (Canada)
FATF	=	Financial Action Task Force
FEU	=	Inland Revenue Foreign Entertainers Unit (UK)
FICO	=	Inland Revenue Financial Intermediaries & Claims Office (UK)
FIRPT	=	Foreign Investment in Real Property (Canada)
FSF	=	Financial Stability Forum
FIS	=	Financial Intelligence Service (Guernsey)
FIU	=	Financial Intelligence Units (UK)
GST	=	Generation Skipping Tax (US)
HL	=	House of Lords (UK)
HND	=	Higher National Diploma (UK)
IAAPR	=	Immigration and Asylum Appeals (Procedure) Rules (UK)
IAIS	=	International Association of Insurance Supervisors
IBC	=	International Business Company (Bahamas)
ICTA	=	Income and Corporation Taxes Act (UK)
IHTA	=	Inheritance Tax Act (UK)
IRC	=	Inland Revenue Code (US)
ISF	=	*Impôt de Solidarité sur la Fortune* (Wealth Tax) (France)
IVA	=	*Impuesto sobre el Valor Añadido* (Value Added Tax) (Spain)
LGT	=	*Ley General Tributaria* (Spain)
LPH	=	*Ley Sobre Propiedad Horizontal* (Law of Horizontal Ownership) (Spain)
NIF	=	*Numero de Indentification Fiscal* (Fiscal Identification Number) (Spain)
OECD	=	Organisation for Economic Co-operation and Development
PAYE	=	Pay As You Earn (UK)
QB	=	Queen's Bench Division (UK)
RTP	=	Reduced Tax Payment (UK)
SCI	=	*Société Civile Immobilière* (Real estate partnership) (France)
SP	=	Inland Revenue Statement of Practice (UK)

TCGA	=	Taxation of Chargeable Gains Act (UK)
TMA	=	Taxes Management Act (UK)
TWES	=	Training and Work Experience Scheme (UK)
VATA	=	Value Added Tax Act (UK)

Table of Cases

Y

Table of Statutes and Regulations

Table of Double Taxation Agreements

Part III

Other Agreements

United States

Table of EC Legislative Material

1 Acquiring and Retaining Non-Residency

Stephen Arthur LLB ATII TEP
(Solicitor)

Introduction

1.1   The purpose of this chapter is to explain how an individual can acquire and retain non-resident status for the purposes of United Kingdom taxation.

1.2   Before considering tax efficient ways of leaving the United Kingdom, it is necessary to have an understanding of the rules that determine whether an individual is resident and/or ordinarily resident in the United Kingdom. Being resident and/or ordinarily resident in the United Kingdom has a major bearing on an individual's income tax and capital gains tax (CGT) liabilities.

This is one of those subjects where it is more important to know what *not* to do, rather than what pro-active steps to take.

Non-resident status for varying periods can be crucial to United Kingdom tax liability:

(*a*)   for a minimum period of 12 months, income tax liability may be avoided during that period;

(*b*)   for a minimum period of 3 years in any 20-year period, inheritance tax liability may permanently be avoided on non-United Kingdom assets;

(*c*)   for a minimum period of 5 years (since 5 April 1998) UK CGT liability may be avoided from the date of departure from the United Kingdom.

Residence and ordinary residence

Introduction

1.3   For the purposes of UK income tax and CGT there is no precise statutory definition of 'residence'. The law relating to residence (and the additional concept of being 'ordinarily resident') has become part of United Kingdom law almost by accident. The law on the subject can be distilled only from a mixture of statute (since 1799), case law and Inland Revenue practice. The present rules are complicated to understand and not easy to explain, and may often be capricious in their operation. Unfortunately, it is necessary to be fully aware of the detail of these rules if an individual wishes to acquire the status of being neither resident nor ordinarily resident in the United Kingdom for tax purposes.

1.4   In the absence of a statutory definition of these terms, one of the best starting points for discussion is the Inland Revenue Booklet IR20 'Residents and Non-Residents: Liability to Tax in the United Kingdom'. The most recent edition of IR20 was published in December 1999. A further summary of the existing law is set out in the Inland Revenue Consultative Document published in July 1988 (but shelved by the government of the day) entitled 'Residence in the United Kingdom – the Scope of UK Tax for Individuals'. These two publications, the first published by the Inland Revenue and the second by HM Stationery Office, together contain probably the most concise, accurate and understandable distillations of current law and practice with regard to United Kingdom tax residence status.

1.5   An analysis of court decisions, over the last 100 years or so, makes it clear that the terms 'residence' and 'ordinary residence' should be given their normal everyday meaning. No special technical meaning should be attributed to the words for tax purposes. In the wider sense this is true, but when analysing the operation in practice of the general rules, some technical administrative detail has to be applied over and above the tests of everyday meaning.

Residence

1.6   Residence in the United Kingdom for tax purposes is determined almost invariably as a simple matter of fact. The main factual tests can be summarised as follows:

(*a*)   if an individual is physically present in the United Kingdom for more than six months (183 days) in any year of assessment he will be resident in the United Kingdom;

(*b*)   if an individual visits the United Kingdom for more than three months (90 days) on average a year over any four-year period, he will be resident in the United Kingdom;

(*c*)   since 6 April 1998 if an individual who has been United Kingdom resident leaves the United Kingdom and is not resident within (*a*) or (*b*) above but then within five tax years (April 6 to April 5) again becomes United Kingdom resident within (*a*) or (*b*) above, he will be treated for CGT purposes as always being resident in the United Kingdom. [*TCGA 1992, s 10A*; *FA 1998, s 127*]. This legislation introduced the residence category of 'temporary non-residence'.

For all years prior to 6 April 1993, there was an alternative factual test: if an individual was physically present in the United Kingdom for less than six months (183 days), but during that year of assessment he had accommodation available for his use in the United Kingdom at a time when he was not working full time abroad, he was resident in the United Kingdom.

This rule could often work harshly in practice. In an effort to bring United Kingdom tax residence more closely into line with other European countries, and to make the United Kingdom an attractive business location, this rule was abolished with effect from 5 April 1993, by the *Finance Act 1993*.

1.7 In determining whether an individual is physically present in the United Kingdom, days of arrival in and departure from the United Kingdom are ignored. The only exception to this practice is when an individual arrives in or leaves the United Kingdom to change residence status part way through a tax year (splitting the year of assessment – 1.15 below). Ignoring days of arrival in the United Kingdom is entirely a matter of Inland Revenue practice and has no statutory basis. Ignoring days of departure from the United Kingdom has statutory basis only for the purposes of contracts of employment outside the United Kingdom. [*ICTA 1988, Sch 4 para 2*]. The Inland Revenue practice has now become so widely publicised and acknowledged (Booklet IR20 1.2) that it would be difficult for the Inland Revenue now to argue differently before the courts, although there is a court decision dating from 1951 which specifically held that hours can be taken into account when calculating periods of presence in the United Kingdom (*Wilkie v IRC (1951) 32 TC 495, Ch D*). In that case the taxpayer avoided becoming resident in the United Kingdom by four hours.

1.8 For the first time, the 1996 edition of IR20 made public what was previously an unpublished matter of practice – when counting the 91 days a year (1.6(*b*) above), any days spent in the United Kingdom for exceptional reasons are not normally taken into account – for example, illness of the (non-resident) taxpayer or his immediate family (IR20 2.8, 2.9).

1.9 The courts have made it clear that Inland Revenue concessions and practice may not be abused (see, for example, *R v Inspector of Taxes (ex p Fulford-Dobson) (1987) 60 TC 168, QB*). An individual who places too 'aggressive' a reliance on existing Inland Revenue practice with a view to avoiding United Kingdom taxation solely by counting (or rather by not counting) days of arrival in the United Kingdom, may find his best laid plans coming to nought, and a United Kingdom tax liability arising. The inside cover of the Inland Revenue Booklet 'Inland Revenue Extra-Statutory Concessions' contains the following warning:

> 'The concessions described within are of general application, but it must be borne in mind that in a particular case there may be special circumstances which will require to be taken into account in considering the application of the concession. *A concession will not be given in any case where an attempt is made to use it for tax avoidance.*' [Emphasis added.]

Ordinary residence

1.10   An individual will be *ordinarily resident* in the United Kingdom if he is habitually resident in the United Kingdom. If an individual is resident in the United Kingdom year after year, he will be ordinarily resident in the United Kingdom. The exception to this general statement is the operation of ESC A78. This extra-statutory concession may, in certain circumstances, operate to give 'not ordinarily resident' status, despite the fact that an individual may be technically resident because of the available accommodation test. It is possible to be ordinarily resident but not resident in the United Kingdom for any year of assessment – a student who spends twelve months abroad, for example. Conversely, it may be possible for an individual to be United Kingdom resident without being ordinarily resident – for example, a temporary visitor to the United Kingdom.

1.11   As a general rule an individual will be ordinarily resident in the United Kingdom if he is present in the United Kingdom on average for more than three months a year over any four-year period. As noted in 1.8 above, the Inland Revenue operates a practice whereby it applies some flexibility in the operation of this rule. Exceptional visits to the United Kingdom in excess of 91 days (e.g., for medical reasons) may be ignored. Also, in some cases, the Inland Revenue may look at separate years rather than apply an average over four years – e.g., visits to the United Kingdom of ten days in each of two years, and 160 days in the third year. The Inland Revenue might, in practice, agree not ordinarily resident status for the first two years, notwithstanding the published IR20 'averaging' rule. More often than not this works to the taxpayer's advantage.

1.12   Inland Revenue Statement of Practice SP17/91 and Press Release dated 16 March 1993 (Temporary Residents in the United Kingdom – available accommodation) indicate that the Revenue has some standard rules which can operate harshly in practice. These rules will be applied to determine when ordinary residence commences for an individual who comes to the United Kingdom intending originally to stay for less than three years. If such an individual changes his intentions, or purchases or acquires on lease for three years or more any accommodation in the United Kingdom, he will be treated as ordinarily resident in the United Kingdom with effect from the beginning of the tax year when the property was acquired or the intentions altered. Adequate proof of a changed intention can be practically difficult to obtain, except by inference. This published practice remains in force, notwithstanding the abolition (by statute) of the 'available accommodation' rule from 5 April 1993. [*FA 1993, s 208*]. Could the practice now be challenged?

Temporary non-residence

1.13   This category of 'residence' was introduced by the *Finance Act 1998* (see 1.6). For purposes of United Kingdom CGT an individual who leaves the United Kingdom but returns as a resident within the next five years of assessment falls into this category. Disposals of capital assets made within the period of temporary non-residence will be treated as made immediately on the individual's return to the United Kingdom as a resident. There are exceptions, subject to special rules, for some assets acquired and disposed of during the period of temporary non-residence. A limited number of double taxation treaties to which the United Kingdom is a party may in certain circumstances alleviate the effect of this legislation, either because of specific provisions exempting capital gains from double taxation, or because of domestic rules regarding fiscal residence (e.g., Mauritius) which are automatically imported into double taxation treaties and may perhaps provide exemption. It is to be expected that these anomalies may be short-lived as double taxation treaties are periodically reviewed and updated to take account of changes in domestic legislation.

Available accommodation – prior to 6 April 1993

1.14   Although this rule was abolished with effect from 6 April 1993, it may still be relevant when dealing with the historic tax affairs of taxpayers based outside the United Kingdom who own, directly or indirectly, United Kingdom residential property; or generally for inheritance tax purposes (see 1.30 below). The rule may also be relevant to individuals who left the United Kingdom prior to 6 April 1993 but who have not agreed their non-resident status with the Inland Revenue.

If accommodation was in fact available to be used by an individual in the United Kingdom, case law has decided, with some statutory corroboration [*ICTA 1988, s 335*], that *ownership* of relevant accommodation by the individual is immaterial. All that is relevant is whether or not accommodation was *as a matter of fact* available to the taxpayer. It is irrelevant whether or not that taxpayer made use of the accommodation when he visited the United Kingdom (see *In Re Young (1875) 1 TC 57*; *Cooper v Cadwalader (1904) 5 TC 101*; *Bayard Brown v Burt (1911) 5 TC 667, CA*; *Loewenstein v De Salis (1926) 10 TC 424, KB*; *Levene v IRC (1928) 13 TC 486, HL*; *Lysaght v IRC (1928) 13 TC 511, HL*; *Robson v Dixon (1972) 48 TC 527, Ch D*).

Traditionally, the best advice was that parents should not keep bedrooms exclusively available for use by their adult children who were trying to establish tax residence outside the United Kingdom. However, it is understood that the Inland Revenue does not usually argue that a house owned by parents or parents-in-law, is 'available accommodation' in the United Kingdom for adult children who have, by and large, fled the nest; nor did it accept this argument when put forward by an individual who claimed to be United Kingdom resident on this basis alone. Where a husband is not resident because he is working abroad under a contract of employment, it was not unusual for his wife to claim that she remained resident in the United Kingdom by spending some time in the United Kingdom (in order, for example, to offset her personal allowances against rental income from the marital home). The fact that she stayed with her parents or parents-in-law was not often by itself thought to persuade the Inland Revenue to accept a residence claim. Extra-statutory concession A78 clarifies Inland Revenue practice in this area. In line with existing practice, ESC A78 confirms that, for the purposes of residence status, years of assessment can be split so that, for example, an individual can be treated as not resident with effect from, say, 31 May, notwithstanding that date is not the end of a tax year of assessment.

Each case will ultimately depend on its own facts and circumstances. However, it is accepted that if the marital home was let to tenants, it was no longer 'available accommodation'.

Splitting the year of assessment

1.15   The legislation refers only to individuals being resident or ordinarily resident during or throughout a year of assessment. There are no statutory provisions which sanction the splitting of years of assessment. Where an individual leaves the United Kingdom to take up residence abroad, as a matter of practice and extra-statutory concession (ESC A11) the Inland Revenue will treat the period of non-residence as commencing on the day the individual leaves the United Kingdom – i.e., by splitting the year of assessment. Undue reliance should not be placed on this practice, which is published only in extra-statutory concessions and is not enshrined in statute. Again, the warning sounded in *R v Inspector of Taxes (ex p Fulford-Dobson)*, where the taxpayer attempted to exploit ESC D2, is salutary. The converse applies when an individual arrives to live in the United Kingdom for at least two years.

ESC A11 contains two important points to be noted:

(*a*)   it confirms that years of assessment can in some circumstances be split for residence purposes even where a taxpayer leaves the United Kingdom for a temporary purpose for full time service under a contract of employment outside the United Kingdom; and

(*b*)   there is a clear implication that 'not ordinarily resident' status can be achieved immediately on departure from the United Kingdom, provided that there is no resumption of United Kingdom residence before the end of one complete tax year after departure (i.e., normally the second 5 April following departure from the United Kingdom).

ESC D2 was amended as a result of the CGT legislation for temporary non-residents introduced in April 1998 (see 1.6 and 1.13). In certain circumstances, notwithstanding split year treatment for income tax purposes, an individual may still be regarded as United Kingdom resident for CGT purposes for a whole tax year or more – i.e., at least until the next 5 April following his departure from the United Kingdom.

Contracts of employment and periods of absence abroad

1.16   This is one of the few topics relating to fiscal residence where statute contains specific provisions. [*ICTA 1988, Sch 12*]. Until 17 March 1998 *ICTA 1988, s 193(1)* specifically relieved Schedule E income from the charge to United Kingdom income tax where 'qualifying periods' of varying lengths are spent outside the United Kingdom performing the duties under any contract of employment. *Section 193(1)* was repealed with effect from 17 March 1998 for all employees except seafarers, who are now governed by a separate new provision. [*ICTA 1988, s 192A*]. Although the legislation does not itself define the terms 'residence' or 'ordinary residence', there is specific guidance on how periods of absence from the United Kingdom should be measured for the purposes of Schedule E taxation. *ICTA 1988, Sch 4 para 12* provides specifically that 'a person shall not be regarded as absent from the United Kingdom on any day unless he is so absent at the end of it'. The legislation refers only to the specific purposes of *Schedule 12* in relation to foreign contracts of employment (or contracts of employment performed outside the United Kingdom). There is no statutory reference whatsoever to days of arrival in the United Kingdom – by corollary it might perhaps be assumed that the day of arrival in the United Kingdom should be counted. However, it is understood that generally accepted Inland Revenue practice is to ignore completely days when taxpayers arrive in the United Kingdom.

1.17   Prior to the introduction of self-assessment on 5 April 1997, for 1996/97 onwards, the Inland Revenue operated a long-standing practice for income tax purposes (extended for CGT purposes) whereby an individual who left the United Kingdom to take full-time employment outside the United Kingdom for even a limited period (provided that limited period was intended at the outset to include a complete tax year) was immediately accorded a provisional status of being neither resident nor ordinarily resident in the United Kingdom. Provided all (except incidental see 1.23) duties are performed abroad, and the full-time employment outside the United Kingdom straddles a complete tax year of assessment, an individual may return to the United Kingdom (on leave or for whatever purposes he wishes other than fulfilling duties of his employment which are not regarded only as 'incidental'), for up to six months in a year, or on average not exceeding three months a year, without the Inland Revenue overturning the initial ruling regarding residence status. ESC A78 extends similar treatment to spouses who accompany their partners who are working full-time outside the United Kingdom for a limited period. The initial ruling was given, usually, at or about the time the taxpayer left the United Kingdom to take up residence abroad. The judicious use of employment contracts with non-resident tax haven companies can sometimes be of assistance to taxpayers temporarily absent from the United Kingdom, but it is to be expected that the Inland Revenue will seek full information and justification for such arrangements.

1.18   The self-assessment legislation no longer permits the Inland Revenue to make provisional rulings about an individual taxpayer's residence status – the onus is clearly on the taxpayer to file returns on the basis of his own conclusions about residence status. However, in practice, the Inland Revenue acts in a way which achieves the same result as prior to self-assessment. If a taxpayer completes Form P85 (see 1.22) when leaving the United Kingdom, the Inland Revenue will make all appropriate adjustments to PAYE coding and Schedule D assessments/repayments (cessation of trade or vocation), based on the P85 information. If the taxpayer's circumstances subsequently do not match the P85 information, formal enquiries and, if appropriate, compensating assessments will be raised.

1.19   Tax Bulletin Issue 6 (February 1993) and Booklet IR20 2.5 contain guidance as to Inland Revenue interpretation of 'full-time' employment abroad. The Inland Revenue accepts that circumstances may vary, but regard 35 to 40 hours a week as the norm. However, see also Revenue Interpretation, April 1999 (1999 STI 832) with regard to 'full-time' employment in the context of CGT retirement relief, and *Palmer v Maloney and Shipleys [1998] STC 425*. Legislation and Inland Revenue interpretations on this topic are, generally speaking, consistent. The first instance court decision does not sit comfortably with previous practice on this point.

This applies also to self-employed individuals or to individuals who work partly as employees, and partly on a self-employed basis.

1.20   In practice, it may be more difficult for self-employed taxpayers to convince the Inland Revenue that they are working full time abroad. On the one hand, many companies are increasingly 'employing' individuals on short-term consultancy contracts – this is particularly prevalent in the computer software industry. On the other hand, as a self-employed consultant, it may be easier for a taxpayer to determine where and when he works. Historically, the Inland Revenue deferred making a definitive (ordinary) residence ruling for self-employed taxpayers until it had the benefit of three years' history after the taxpayer first left the United Kingdom. The introduction of self-assessment required a revision of this practice, so that self-employed contractors are now treated on an equal basis with employees – if a self-employed individual leaves the United Kingdom with the declared intention of working abroad for three years – or at least a complete tax year – an appropriate tax adjustment will be made. An early approach to the Inland Revenue is always recommended.

1.21   *ICTA 1988, s 334* provides that 'occasional' residence abroad is ignored when computing United Kingdom tax liabilities in the case of Commonwealth and citizens of Ireland who have been ordinarily resident in the United Kingdom. The courts have now decided that complete absence from the United Kingdom for a period in excess of one year is sufficient to break the normal habitual residence cycle. A one-year (complete) absence is not 'occasional' (see *Reed v Clark [1985] 58 TC 528, Ch D*).

Leaving the United Kingdom

1.22   An individual should notify his Inspector of Taxes of his intention to leave the United Kingdom on a certain date to take up residence elsewhere. He should give an indication of the minimum period he expects to be absent from the United Kingdom. This notification can best be effected by completing Inland Revenue Form P85, obtainable from any tax office. Normally, if the Inland Revenue are satisfied on the information given that the individual has the intention of leaving the United Kingdom for a period of at least three years, the individual will be treated as neither resident nor ordinarily resident in the United Kingdom from the day following his departure. Despite the fact that non-residence status may begin at any time during the assessment year, individuals are required to complete a return of income for the complete year of assessment during which they leave the United Kingdom. All personal allowances and reliefs for that year of assessment are available to offset United Kingdom taxable income.

As a general practice the Inland Revenue will review the residence status of an individual some time after he has left the United Kingdom. In the case of individuals who go abroad to work under a contract of employment the Inland Revenue will normally review the facts after an individual has been abroad for a complete tax year. For example, if an individual left the United Kingdom on 1 September 2001 to work as an employee outside the United Kingdom, the Inland Revenue will make a formal enquiry about residence status shortly after 5 April 2003. In the case of other individuals who claim to leave the United Kingdom on a permanent basis (i.e., not under a contract of employment), the Inland Revenue will normally review the non-residence claim anything up to three years after the date of departure from the United Kingdom. The self-assessment system now requires that what used to be a review of a provisional ruling on residence status now has to be conducted by the Inland Revenue issuing a formal enquiry notice. Only when enquiries are satisfactorily answered will the Inland Revenue formally accept that the individual has severed his ties with the United Kingdom to such an extent that he will be treated as neither resident nor ordinarily resident in the United Kingdom with effect from the date of his departure. In general, whenever the Inland Revenue reviews the circumstances of individual cases it will have regard to the conditions set out in paragraphs 2.9 and 2.10 of Inland Revenue Booklet IR20. It is, therefore, important that the individual who wishes to acquire non-resident status does not return too frequently to the United Kingdom after he has informed the Inspector of Taxes that he intends to become non-resident. Records should be maintained of visits to the United Kingdom.

The onus of reporting visits to the United Kingdom, and taking an informed view of the consequences of those visits after claiming to have left the United Kingdom, is now unequivocally placed on the individual tax-payer, as a result of the introduction of self-assessment in 1996/97.

As a matter of administration, an individual may have to deal with one or more offices of the Inland Revenue before the Inland Revenue accepts that he is neither resident nor ordinarily resident in the United Kingdom. Correspondence should be addressed in the first instance to the taxpayer's usual Inspector of Taxes. Individuals who are sent abroad under a contract of employment will normally have their non-residence claim dealt with by the local Inspector who handles PAYE affairs. If the foreign posting is planned to be longer than one complete year of assessment, the Inspector will probably refer the matter directly to Inland Revenue Financial Intermediaries and Claims Office (International) – commonly known as FICO – in Bootle. If an individual is simply moving abroad for the purposes of retirement and will receive no United Kingdom income other than pension from his former employer, in the majority of cases FICO (International) in Nottingham – formerly the Inspector of Foreign Dividends – will deal with the adjudication of the non-residence claim. Where an individual who leaves the United Kingdom to take up residence abroad is likely to receive United Kingdom income other than pension income, Inland Revenue Claims Branch in Bootle may be involved in adjudicating a non-residence claim. The involvement of FICO in Bootle may either be direct or in conjunction with FICO (International) in Nottingham. The addresses of these two central Inland Revenue offices are:

Financial Intermediaries and Claims Office (International),
Fitz Roy House,
PO Box 46,
Nottingham, NG2 1BD
Telephone: 0115 974 2000

Financial Intermediaries and Claims Office (International),
Residence Section,
St John's House,
Merton Road,
Bootle,
Merseyside, L69 9BB
Telephone: 0151 472 6196

In practice, as far as individual taxpayers are aware, approximately 95 per cent of non-residence claims are dealt with by the Inland Revenue at local district level.

Return visits to the United Kingdom

1.23   Since the abolition of the 'available accommodation' test of residence in 1993 it is easier for some non-residents to make temporary visits to the United Kingdom without prejudicing their non-resident status. If prolonged or frequent visits are made to the United Kingdom, the first two main factual tests of residence (see 1.6) will become relevant.

With regard to contracts of employment for working outside the United Kingdom, *ICTA 1988, s 132(2)* provides that 'incidental' duties performed in the United Kingdom will be ignored. In determining whether duties are 'incidental' the Inland Revenue considers the nature of United Kingdom duties and their relation to the duties abroad. If United Kingdom duties amount to little more than simple reporting or receiving fresh instructions the United Kingdom duties are normally treated as being incidental. However, a company director who attends board meetings in the United Kingdom will not normally have his duties as a director treated as being incidental. It is, therefore, advisable to resign all United Kingdom company directorships (other than, perhaps, non-executive appointments, although for company law purposes there is no distinction of responsibility between executive and non-executive directors) if an individual is likely to visit the United Kingdom after leaving to become resident elsewhere. The Inland Revenue's view is that it is the importance of the duties in relation to commercial reality which matters, rather than the time spent in the United Kingdom. Duties in the United Kingdom will not be regarded as incidental if they require an individual to be in the United Kingdom for a period which exceeds three months in any year. The three-month rule is applied also to periods of training spent in the United Kingdom even if no formal duties of employment are undertaken during that period.

1.24   Where an individual is not employed under a full-time contract but is self-employed, or where he does not have any commercial activities (because, for example, he has retired or is involved only in the management of investments), the best advice would be for him not to set foot in the United Kingdom for one complete tax year (6 April to 5 April) immediately following his departure from the United Kingdom. The reason for this is to establish an habitual pattern by remaining outside the United Kingdom and so breaking the four-year period which the Inland Revenue will look at when determining whether an individual is ordinarily resident in the United Kingdom. The test is whether an individual has spent more than three months a year on average in the United Kingdom in any four-year period. The need for this advice is that, as has been explained, the rules regarding residence and ordinary residence are founded principally on Inland Revenue practice in areas of detail. Employments with tax haven companies can be useful if carefully documented, and if substance to the employments can be demonstrated to the Inland Revenue. However, it is not advisable to court arguments with the Inland Revenue by flouting its well-published general practice for any reason.

Notwithstanding 'best advice', many individuals who leave the United Kingdom (for retirement, or for tax or health reasons) will often want to make return visits to the United Kingdom to visit family and friends, or to take regular holidays. Despite the fact that passports are no longer stamped as a matter of course at ports of entry into the United Kingdom (particularly when travelling from one EU country to another), it is advisable to keep careful records of visits to the United Kingdom after a claim for non-resident status has been submitted. When the Inland Revenue requests proof that visits to the United Kingdom are as few as a taxpayer claims, it will be far more impressed by detailed lists of visits to the United Kingdom which in aggregate total less than 90 days (three months) than by general statements that specific records have not been maintained, but visits to the United Kingdom are well below three months a year in aggregate. The sceptical Inland Revenue response to the latter claim is: how can you be so sure in the absence of detailed records? You obviously are aware of the three month tax (practice) rules – therefore why did you not keep records? The Inland Revenue must assume the worst! Diary entries are, however, normally sufficient to satisfy the inquisitiveness of most Inspectors of Taxes. Receipts and copy credit/charge card vouchers for staying in hotels are the best possible records. The Inland Revenue is forced to rely on taxpayers' honesty on this topic – but the trail left by credit/charge card vouchers has been the downfall of many taxpayers who claimed not to be in the United Kingdom and were then found, on enquiry by the Inland Revenue, to have purchased goods by credit card in United Kingdom airport duty-free shops.

Husband and wife

1.25   The normal CGT rule is that disposals of assets between husband and wife are ignored and do not give rise to CGT liabilities. A wife will inherit her husband's CGT acquisition costs if her husband disposes of chargeable assets to her, and vice versa.

Where one spouse leaves the United Kingdom and is accorded non-resident status by the Inland Revenue, this normal rule is displaced unless both spouses acquire non-resident status at the same time (see *Gubay v Kington [1984] STC 99, HL*, where a spouse left the United Kingdom to take up residence abroad some six months before her husband finally left the United Kingdom to join her on a permanent basis).

1.26   Similar problems may arise for the purposes of income tax where a husband may often leave the United Kingdom to take up a foreign posting leaving his wife and children behind for a few months pending the end of the school year. If the husband is working full time abroad under a contract of employment he may find it difficult as a matter of evidence to satisfy the Inland Revenue that he is working 'full time' if he spends time returning to the United Kingdom to visit his family. ESC78 affords non-resident status to a (non-employed) spouse of an employee working abroad, unless return visits to the United Kingdom by the spouse exceed 183 days a year, or more than 90 days a year on average (see 1.6 above).

Special cases

1.27   Most double tax treaties have special provisions for students and teachers who visit foreign countries on a temporary basis. Residence status for tax purposes may not always be practically important for those taxpayers, unless they are entitled to savings or investment income which would result in higher taxes becoming payable. Professors or teachers at a university, college, school or other educational institution may be exempted from foreign taxation on their earnings from a temporary teaching post which does not exceed two years. Some double taxation treaties provide that the exemption is conditional on United Kingdom taxation being levied on the relevant earnings. Where this condition is not present, it may be possible for teachers and professors to avoid paying income tax on their earnings provided they have a valid contract requiring them to perform their duties outside the United Kingdom.

Students or business apprentices working abroad solely for the purpose of full-time education or training may also be able to escape local and United Kingdom taxation dependent upon the length of sojourn outside the United Kingdom and the provisions of the relevant double tax treaty.

Miscellaneous

1.28   Individuals who plan to leave the United Kingdom to take up residence abroad will normally incur professional fees in connection with the obtaining of agreement with the Inland Revenue as to their United Kingdom tax status. For VAT purposes in the United Kingdom, it is relevant to consider where the individual has his usual place of residence. Depending on the timing of invoices, where the individual is actually residing, and the capacity in which he receives advice given (business or private capacity), it may be possible for accounts for professional advice given to be delivered without levying VAT. [*VATA 1983, Sch 5, Group 9, para 6*]. This VAT saving is not possible if the country of residence is an EU Member State.

1.29   Individuals who cease to be resident in the United Kingdom, and who are entitled to a refund in respect of an overpayment of United Kingdom tax, may be entitled to claim repayment supplement (effectively non-taxable interest on overpaid tax). *ICTA 1988, s 824* and ESC A82 provide that repayment supplement can be paid to an individual, partner, trustee, or personal representative who is resident in an EU state when the claim is made. Without ESC A82, no repayment supplement can be made to individuals not resident in the United Kingdom.

Inheritance tax

1.30   Technically liability to United Kingdom inheritance tax depends only on the domicile status of an individual. However, there is a 'deemed domicile' rule [*Inheritance Tax Act 1984, s 268*] which imposes inheritance tax liability on worldwide assets dependent on the number of years an individual has or has not been resident for tax purposes in the United Kingdom (see 1.2). For the purposes of this chapter it is worth noting that, if an individual has left the United Kingdom and become resident for more than three years in a jurisdiction where civil (rather than common) law applies, or otherwise satisfies the '17 out of 20-year rule', it may be difficult to claim exemption from United Kingdom inheritance tax on non-United Kingdom assets. The reason for this is twofold. Civil law jurisdictions (e.g., Italy) do not have the same fundamental concept of 'domicile' as the United

Kingdom, and it is not usually sufficient to show that a taxpayer is no longer domiciled in the United Kingdom – the Inland Revenue may require evidence (e.g., a local legal opinion) that the taxpayer has become domiciled outside the United Kingdom as a matter of local domestic law – fiscal residence may be of only partial assistance. Further, notwithstanding the United Kingdom rule about '17 years residence over 20 years', double tax treaties since 1974 (when this rule was first introduced) may treat an individual as domiciled in a country where he has been fiscally resident for 7 years in any 10-year period.

When looking at a 20-year residence period, and the relevance of the available accommodation rules as they were prior to April 1993, see the exchange of correspondence between a Technical Committee of the Chartered Institute of Taxation and the Inland Revenue, published in Taxation Practitioner, May 1999 at page 8. In short, for years prior to 1993/94 the available accommodation rule is ignored when considering the deemed domicile '17 out of 20 years' rule for IHT purposes.

2   Asset Protection and Offshore Creditor Protection Trusts

Tim Bennett LLB TEP
(Solicitor) (Managing Director, Belgrave, S.A. Switzerland)

Introduction

2.1   'Asset Protection' can best be defined as the process of organising one's assets and affairs so as to guard them against future financial risks. As used in relation to offshore trusts, the expression 'asset protection' is a confusing concept, meriting further definition.

Traditional offshore trust planning is generally passive and long-term in nature, and designed to last for two or more generations. Protection against political risks has also been a common theme in the establishment of offshore trusts for the last several decades.

By contrast, the expression 'asset protection trusts' (APT) is of recent coinage, and refers specifically to a form of highly focused and pro-active trust planning that is designed to place specific assets beyond the reach of future creditors. This type of planning became popular during the late 1980s, largely in response to the problems certain groups of high risk professionals experienced in the United States in obtaining affordable professional liability/malpractice cover.

If used in the right circumstances, this type of offshore trust will protect and provide a nest egg against the financial 'rainy day' that would otherwise follow a substantial adverse judgment in the countries of the professional's residence and domicile (referred to herein as the 'home' country).

The law is stated as at 15 January 2002.

2.2   To emphasise the distinction between offshore trusts in general and this type of planning in particular, this chapter will use the expressions 'creditor protection planning' and 'creditor protection trusts' (Cpts).

The offshore dimension is a key ingredient in CPT planning. Although the existence of a CPT cannot prevent creditors from bringing proceedings in the professional's home country, they invariably affect the outcome. It is the deliberate arbitraging of two legal systems whose laws differ that produces this effect, and ensures there is some form of (albeit reduced) financial life once the home country proceedings have been concluded.

In its simplest terms, the laws of the professional's home country (being also the creditor's home country), are of no effect in the offshore jurisdiction. Likewise, judgments of the home country's courts are generally unenforceable in the offshore jurisdiction. The trust fund thus remains secure in the offshore jurisdiction (referred to also as the 'host' country) for the benefit of the individual concerned, and his family.

2.3   The rest of this chapter will review in some detail:

(*a*)   the economic and business context that created the need for CPT planning;

(*b*)   the different types of CPT planning that may be encountered;

(*c*)   the historical evolution of the legal rules and restrictions protecting creditors;

(*d*)   legal limits to the scope of CPT planning, both in the home and host jurisdictions;

(*e*)   offshore jurisdictions that encourage CPT planning;

(*f*)   the different legislative frameworks offshore jurisdictions have adopted in relation to CPTs;

(*g*)   CPT structures involving the use of offshore trusts; and

(*h*)   planning issues, and procedural safeguards.

2.4   As creditor protection planning also raises important ethical and judgmental issues, these will be highlighted in the course of the overall discussion.

Creditor protection planning is one of the current areas of concern in the offshore world. In the last decade or so, CPTs have been increasingly marketed by American law firms, as well as by international financial service businesses and offshore trust companies.

This chapter will explore the issues relating to CPTs in detail, enabling those involved with CPTs to understand and identify the kind of business they wish to attract, and thereby avoid taking unnecessary or undesirable risks in their *own* business.

Creditor protection planning in context

2.5   Persons of means invariably undertake some form of estate planning during their lifetime. This is usually designed to take effect only after their death, and usually involves a combination of wills, will trusts and living (or *inter vivos*) trusts.

Creditor protection planning may be regarded in a general sense as nothing more than a precursor of estate planning. The distinction is that in creditor protection planning, the arrangements made during the individual's lifetime are immediately effective to restructure and protect the ownership of specific assets, and do not merely take effect on death.

The groups of high risk professionals in the United States that have faced the worst escalation in their professional liability insurance premiums include surgeons, obstetricians/gynaecologists and anaesthetists. But the accountancy/audit and legal professions, civil engineers, architects and many other professions are also within the 'high risk' list, as they too have all too frequently been drawn into their own types of high stakes litigation.

2.6   The litigation explosion in the United States is a well-documented phenomenon, and its causes need only be briefly identified here. It results from a combination of factors, including a rapid proliferation in the size of the legal profession; the 'contingent fee' system; continuously expanding theories of legal liability; the setting of damage awards by juries; and a tendency for juries to make 'punitive' awards. Successful plaintiffs can literally win a jackpot.

The US Government's Tort Policy Working Group issued reports in 1986 and 1987 on the crisis in insurance availability and affordability. In successive annual reports, the Chairman of Lloyd's also commented on the effect of this on underwriting in the London insurance market. Former Vice-President Dan Quayle referred to these issues in his address to the American Bar Association on 13 August 1991; and the American Institute of CPAs passed a resolution in November 1992 calling for reforms in the law of tort and jury awards. Since then, the issue of 'tort reform' was taken on by the Clinton Administration, and Congress has recently considered draft legislation.

This explosion of litigation and high damage awards caused underwriters to introduce sky-rocketing increases in professional liability insurance premiums. Professional insurance became barely affordable. Some groups of professionals opted for self-insurance. Other professionals continue to practice, albeit 'naked' (i.e., without insurance), and yet others have simply ceased to practice.

Those who continue to practice do so fully aware of the risk that one claim against them that is successfully litigated may wipe them out. Indeed, enforcement of the jury award might also lead to personal bankruptcy in the home jurisdiction.

In this context, creditor protection planning can be highly attractive. It offers such professionals the possibility of placing the 'nest egg' part of their savings into a reserve fund, immune from potential claimants. A portion of their life savings can be immunised from ruinous 'jackpot' jury awards in future lawsuits brought by patients or clients. As a result, the professionals continue in practice safe in the knowledge that, whatever litigation may arise in the future, they will not be totally wiped out.

2.7   There are, of course, many different motives for establishing CPTs. At one end of the spectrum is the type of planning which is undertaken by such wealthy professionals at a time when seas are calm. They are not being sued. They are not in dispute with clients or patients. They are solvent. They have no immediate worries. They are ideal CPT clients, who simply wish to put a portion of their assets aside for a rainy day.

Moving across the spectrum, one finds a second wave of CPT clients, who emerged as a result of the economic downturn of the late 1980s and early 1990s. Numbers of businessmen, property developers, Lloyd's Under-writers and others gave personal guarantees to banks and other lenders at times when markets seemed to be going upwards forever: at the time such guarantees were given, the guarantors never considered they were putting their entire wealth at risk. But the businesses and markets then fell into dif-ficulty. There were major declines in property values across the board, and many banks were ruthless with their loan portfolios. As a result, many of these individuals faced calls under their guarantees. Due to the overall reduction in their personal financial statements, such calls led, in many cases, to their financial ruin.

Moving further across the spectrum, one finds trusts established in contem-plation of imminent matrimonial break-up. The sole purpose of these arrangements is to shelter or conceal assets from the ensuing financial settle-ment, and confound the application of home country laws and public policy rules. CPT planning for these types of clients is more difficult, and can be controversial.

At the extreme end of the spectrum one finds the most controversial type of CPT planning, where the motive is actively to hinder existing creditors: this is discussed more fully at 2.56.

As noted above, offshore trusts are often the preferred vehicles for such planning, as the incompatibility of the legal systems of the home and host country reinforces the untouchability of the offshore assets. But offshore trusts do not provide a simple solution to all perceived problems. If they are essentially being used just to hide assets, some of the types of CPT planning will be unsuccessful in both the home jurisdiction and the offshore host jurisdiction, for reasons given below.

It is interesting to note the existence of a loose-leaf reference work entitled *Asset Protection: Domestic and International Law and Tactics* (Clark Board-man Callaghan, New York, NY). Clearly this subject area attracts great interest in the United States.

Creditor protection planning and trusts

2.8   The simplest type of creditor protection planning involves nothing more complex than transferring assets out of one's name, and placing them in someone else's hands and name. Such a transfer is usually gratuitous and without any consideration.

As a first level solution, a transfer of assets to a spouse is quite common, but this may be an unsatisfactory approach for a number of reasons. These include perceived or actual loss of control in a relationship, and the ever-present possibility of marital dispute. Thus, wherever possible, it is more appropriate to transfer assets to a neutral third party, such as a trustee, who is independent and can be relied on in the future. A trust agreement can be drawn up to confirm and regulate the arrangement.

Of course, such a trust agreement must be strong enough to withstand challenge by creditors. If the settlor (transferor) has or retains clearly identifiable rights under the trust, the creditors will simply take over those rights, as judgment creditors stand in the same relation to those rights and assets as does the settlor. For example, if the transferor retains a life interest in the income, the creditors may seek to attach the income stream.

2.9   Discretionary trusts are, therefore, ideal instruments for creditor protection planning. Under a discretionary trust, the settlor/transferor gives up control over the assets to the trustees, whilst the beneficiary group have no rights or entitlement over the trust fund. The decision and timing as to which of the group of beneficiaries may receive a payment from the trust is entirely up to the trustees.

The settlor/transferor will usually (but not always) be included in the class of beneficiaries. As such, he has no 'rights' or 'interests' capable of attachment. However, as a beneficiary, the transferor will still be able to receive benefit from the trust in the future, subject always to the trustees' decision. But the argument in support of the planning is that, from the creditor's standpoint, as the settlor/transferor has no definable interest in the trust, so neither can his creditors (*Estate of German v United States 7C Ct 641 (1985)*). There are, of course, contrary arguments based on the *Estates Powers and Trusts Law* (and see *Vanderbilt v Chase Manhattan 100 App Div Rep 544 (1984)*).

Thus, on the face of it, once the portion of the settlor/transferor's assets for which protection is desired has been properly transferred into the discretionary trust, the transferor's worries should be over; but the key to successful CPT structuring lies in ensuring that the actual transfer itself by the settlor is valid and unimpeachable. In this regard, there are important legal provisions in the transferor's home jurisdiction which creditors may try to invoke in order to 'undo' the original transfer of assets into the trust. These are the laws relating to insolvent or fraudulent transfers, and bankruptcy. Trust provisions may also be void to the extent that they are contrary to the policy of bankruptcy law, although 'protective trusts' are a permissible exception to this. The next part of this chapter looks at those laws in greater detail.

Laws relating to transfers into trust: a historical perspective

Introduction

2.10   Transfers of assets may be open to challenge under two sets of legal rules. The first set of rules are known as 'fraudulent conveyance' rules. The second set of rules relate to bankruptcy. The legal provisions applicable in these two scenarios are considered separately below.

Fraudulent conveyance rules

2.11   The earliest United Kingdom statutory provisions relating to transfers of assets generally are found in the '*Statute of Elizabeth*', enacted in England in 1571. Most common law countries, including the United States, have adopted similar legal rules as a result of their common legal heritage.

The *Statute of Elizabeth* is entitled 'An Act against fraudulent deeds, alienation, etc.' – it is also known as the *Fraudulent Conveyances Act 1571*. The *Act* declares to be 'clearly and utterly void' any conveyance of land goods or chattels made with the purpose or intent of hindering or defrauding creditors and others of their just and lawful debts.

Subsequent case law clearly expanded the scope of the *Statute* to include future creditors. The inclusion along with 'creditors' of the undefined category of 'others' was held to allow a future creditor, whose debt was not in existence at the time of the transfer, to apply under the statute to set aside the transfer, by showing that his subsequent claim is also delayed or hindered by the transfer. The creditor/applicant has the burden of proof of establishing that one of the transferor's objectives in making the transfer was to delay or hinder or defraud the creditors and others. But the tendency through the case law has been for judges to be relatively easily swayed by arguments in the public interest. In addition, the expression 'intent to defraud' was given a broad meaning, not requiring anything like a criminal intent. (*MacKay v Douglas (1872) LR 14 Eq 106; Re Butterworth, ex p Russell (1882) 19 Ch D 588; Re Wise (1886) 17 QBD 290; Cadogan v Cadogan [1977] 1 All ER 200.*)

The *Statute of Elizabeth* contained no limitation period: thus, actions to set aside a given transfer could be brought *at any time*, and the length of time between the transfer and the aggrieved creditor's claim (or the application to court) was of no consequence.

If the court made an order under the *Statute* setting aside the transfer, then the transfer was held void *ab initio*, and of no effect. If the transfer created a trust, and remained its only funding, then it followed that the trust would also be voidable or void. (*Smith v Dresser (1866) LR 1 Eq 651; Ideal Bedding Co v Holland [1907] 2 Ch 157.*)

The United Kingdom provisions are now contained in the *Insolvency Act 1986, ss 423–425,* replacing the old *section 172* of the *Law of Property Act 1925.* These provide that if the court is satisfied that the transfer into trust was made for the purpose of putting assets beyond the reach of a person who is making, or may at some time make a claim against the settlor, or otherwise prejudices the interests of such claimant or potential claimant, the court can order that the transfer be set aside.

Underhill & Hayton on Trusts & Trustees (15th edition) states in article 18 (page 266), on the effect of settlements intended to prejudice creditors apart from bankruptcy, the following:

> 'Thus, if a professional man about to become a partner is worried that the amount of professional indemnity assurance cover may prove insufficient for possible future claims so that he had better preserve his house as his major asset, and so vests it in his wife . . . then it seems that the transaction will be impeachable, irrespective of any time limits, or of the man being adjudged bankrupt . . .'.

As a comparative note, similar rules also exist in civil law jurisdictions, deriving from Roman law. These rules provide for a legal action called *action revocatory* or *action paulienne.* The effect of the rules is broadly similar, enabling creditors to recover property disposed of by a debtor with fraudulent intent.

Bankruptcy laws

2.12   Bankruptcy legislation is also of critical importance. The earliest provisions relating to official collection and realisation of a debtor's estate under English law date from 1542 – 'An Act against such persons as do make bankrupt,' applying only to traders. Prior to 1542, falling into debt was considered a mortal sin. The *Bankruptcy Act 1861* extended the legislation to non-traders. Warrants of arrest for debtors are still issued in some parts of the world.

The United Kingdom provisions are now contained in the *Insolvency Act 1986, ss 339–342,* replacing the old *section 42* of the *Bankruptcy Act 1914.* These provisions enable existing, future or contingent claimants to set aside transfers (voluntary settlements) made gratuitously or at an undervalue, if the settlor is adjudged bankrupt within a defined period (of up to ten years) of the transfer.

Contingent creditors are protected, such as a victim of the transferor's torts who has not yet obtained judgment or even commenced proceedings against the transferor. A future victim would not, however, be protected. (*Crossley v Elworthy (1871) LR 12 Eq 158; Re Ridler (1882) 22 Ch D 74; Official Receiver v Saebar (1972) ALR 612.*)

The distinction between the settlor's solvency and insolvency is critical as to limitation. If the settlor was insolvent at the time of the transfer, the transfer can be set aside up to five years prior to the commencement of the bankruptcy. However, if the settlor was solvent at the time, the transfer can only be set aside if made within two years prior to the commencement of the bankruptcy.

In the UK *Insolvency Act 1986*, 'insolvent' is defined as either being 'unable to pay debts as they fall due' or having less assets than liabilities.

There is also a presumption of insolvency where the transfer is to an 'associate' of the transferor. Under *section 435*, a trustee is an 'associate' if the beneficiaries of the trust include the settlor, or the trust terms confer a power that may be exercised for the benefit of the settlor or an 'associate' of the settlor.

Thus, a potential settlor will not be able to make a valid transfer of assets to a trustee unless he can show that at the time of the transfer he was *not* insolvent, and was not transferring the assets with the intention of defeating debts or liabilities due to known and identifiable claimants. (For these purposes it is assumed that a bankruptcy occurs within five years of the transfer.)

Conversely, if the transfer was made at a time when the transferor *was* solvent, and as a result of the transfer the transferor remained able to pay all of his actual or contingent liabilities known to exist at the time, then the transfers *cannot* be invalidated under the *Insolvency Act* provisions unless the settlor/transferor becomes bankrupt within two years.

Protective trusts

2.13   Protective trusts are a statutory exception [*Trustee Act 1925, s 33*] to the common law rule that a beneficiary's interest under a trust may not be subject to conditions or provisos excluding them from claims of creditors. A distinction must be drawn between trusts created by a third party, and trusts where the settlor is also the protected beneficiary: in the latter case, the settlor/beneficiary will not be protected from creditors in the event of his own bankruptcy.

Why offshore?

2.14   As the rules seem fairly clear-cut, why then is there a need to 'go offshore' at all if the legal system in the home jurisdiction upholds the validity of the transfer into trust, provided the transfer took place in all of the right circumstances? The simple answer seems to be that, by moving the assets offshore, it becomes more difficult, or too difficult, for creditors to re-possess the trust assets. The transferor may be able to select a jurisdiction whose legal system has narrower provisions protecting creditors than those in his home country. From the transferor's point of view, there is thus a higher degree of certainty about the favourable outcome of a possible dispute than there would be in the home country.

The offshore dimension

2.15   Individuals with international assets have traditionally used offshore trusts as will substitutes, thereby achieving effective asset transmission. As noted at 2.1, offshore trusts have for decades been a successful way of protecting against political risk. The effectiveness, confidentiality and favourable tax status of offshore trusts make them attractive vehicles for these purposes. In response to this need, the offshore trust industry has expanded enormously in the last 30 years.

However, the full range of possible benefits of offshore trusts are by no means automatically available to everybody. Most countries with sophisticated tax and estate duty laws have limited the scope for their own citizens or residents to use offshore trusts.

For example, in the United States, amendments to the *Internal Revenue Code* passed in 1976 rendered it disadvantageous for 'US persons' (namely, US citizens and 'resident aliens') to use offshore trusts for income tax planning purposes.

On 30 August 1996 President Clinton signed into law the *Small Business Job Protection Act 1996* which is aimed at curbing so-called abuses in relation to offshore trusts and gives rise to reporting requirements by a US person creating an offshore trust of transferring property to it; and on the part of US persons being beneficiaries who receive income from any foreign trust. These provisions are of major significance in the offshore and international tax planning field, and will impact not only CPT planning but virtually all forms of offshore trust planning relating to the United States.

In the United Kingdom, changes introduced in 1991 and 1998 severely curtailed the use of offshore trusts for capital gains tax planning purposes (see also 2.18).

As the typical CPT client might be a US professional, two questions naturally arise. The first is 'why use offshore?' if transfers into trust may be upheld anyway onshore? The second is 'are there any tax implications in the home country?'.

In answer to the first question, if the initial transfer of assets is to a trust established in an offshore jurisdiction, then the party seeking to set aside the transfer needs to consider *two* sets of laws; not only those of the home jurisdiction, but also those of the host trust jurisdiction. This means two sets of attorneys, with the added costs entailed.

American plaintiffs begin to feel distinctly uncomfortable when confronted with what to them are 'foreign' laws. Also, as a preliminary matter, the necessity for plaintiffs to obtain evidence within the offshore jurisdiction relating to the CPT and its assets may present further hurdles in terms of privacy, confidentiality or secrecy laws.

'Domestic' proceedings, brought in the transferor's own jurisdiction, may well establish that – under local law – the transfer was invalid; but unless the home country judgment can be enforced against the trustee, and the trustee compelled to release the assets to the creditor, the domestic judgment will be of no practical effect. Nor can the home country court order the individual transferor (on pain of contempt) to re-transfer the assets, as the transferor no longer has the power to do so. Only the trustees can take that decision, and, being in a foreign jurisdiction, they are not directly responsive to orders made by a US court.

2.16   The question of location of trust assets may be of critical importance in relation to enforcing a home country judgment. If it transpired that part of the trust fund were 'within the jurisdiction,' then the local court could make orders in respect of the asset or assets in question (see also 2.47). The creditor may therefore need to proceed against the offshore trustee *in the offshore jurisdiction* to obtain a judgment that will be binding on the offshore trustee.

Many of the offshore jurisdictions have taken initiatives, and amended their laws so as to limit the scope of *both* their fraudulent transfer rules *and* their bankruptcy legislation in relation to CPTs. These legislative innovations are discussed at 2.22–2.35.

On the second question, the income tax provisions of the *Internal Revenue Code* did not per se prevent a US person from setting up and being a beneficiary of an offshore trust, and if the trust is 'tax neutral' for income tax purposes (and properly reported) it can be advantageous for non-tax reasons. The US income tax and federal estate and gift tax aspects, including the 1996 legislative amendments, are further considered at 2.43 and 2.45.

The next part of this chapter explains the relevant US provisions relating to transfers into trust. This is essential, as it is assumed throughout this chapter that the typical CPT settlor/transferor is from the United States.

Creditor enforcement in the US (the transferor's 'home' country)

2.17   Within the United States, creditor enforcement against transfers into trust broadly follows the UK model, with statutory provisions barring both 'fraudulent conveyances' and 'pre-bankruptcy transfers'. In addition, there is legislation at both Federal and State level.

The *Federal Bankruptcy Code* (*11 USC*) contains provisions on both fraudulent conveyances, and pre-bankruptcy transfers. *Section 544(b)* of the

Bankruptcy Code allows a trustee in bankruptcy to invalidate a fraudulent conveyance (transfer), but contains a *renvoi* (or referral) to State law to determine if the transfer is voidable: if it is voidable, then the trustee in bankruptcy can also avoid it.

Section 548 of the *Bankruptcy Code* allows the trustee in bankruptcy to set aside all transfers made within one year of filing of the petition in bankruptcy if the transfer was made at a time when the debtor received less than reasonably equivalent value, and if the debtor was insolvent at the time of the transfer, or was rendered insolvent as a result of the transfer. Insolvency is measured by comparing debts to 'non-exempt' property. Future creditors (i.e., those arising after the transfer) can also seek to satisfy the transfer.

Creditors rights are generally governed by the settlor's local State law. The applicable State law is determined by many factors, including the residence of the settlor, the situs of the disputed property and the place of the transfer.

On 'fraudulent conveyances', the model law, the *Uniform Fraudulent Transfer Act 1984* (*UFTA 1984*) may be applicable. *UFTA 1984, s 4* defines a 'fraudulent conveyance' as one made 'with the actual intent to hinder, delay or defraud any creditor of the debtor', irrespective of whether the creditor's claim arose before or after the transfer was made.

Transfers made with actual intent to defraud are *voidable* by both existing and future creditors. 'Actual intent' is defined broadly, and the *section* enumerates the activities that constitute it. A transferor who only places a portion of his wealth in a CPT should be able to avoid the conclusion that there was 'actual intent'.

Under *UFTA 1984*, a transfer made when the transferor was insolvent is also characterised as a 'fraudulent conveyance', and creditors (both existing and future) may be able to set it aside. This also extends to transfers when the transferor was rendered insolvent as a result. The general rule is that transfers will only be upheld if made when the transferor was not 'insolvent' or rendered 'insolvent' as a result of the transfer. 'Insolvent' is measured by the excess of liabilities over assets (other than excluded assets – see 2.46), or the inability to pay debts as they fall due.

Under *UFTA 1984, s 5*, a transfer is deemed to be 'fraudulent' if it is made for less than full value at a time when the transferor is insolvent. Such a conveyance is *voidable* by the existing creditors of the transferor.

States that have not yet adopted *UFTA 1984* may be governed by provisions of the older *Uniform Fraudulent Conveyances Act* (*UFCA*).

Also, some States (e.g., Florida) have statutory provisions permitting existing creditors to seek to attach property on a debt *not* due if the debtor is removing his property out of State, or secreting it to avoid payment of his debts.

The next part of this chapter will look at direct and indirect enforcement of creditor claims in the offshore jurisdiction.

Creditor enforcement in the United Kingdom (a comparison)

2.18   It is appropriate also to consider the UK provisions pertaining to transfers of assets into trust. There are three principal ways of attacking such transfers, each of which will be considered below.

First (as noted at 2.11), *section 423* of the *Insolvency Act 1986* enables the court to set aside transactions undertaken for the purpose of putting assets beyond the reach of a person who is making or may at some time make a claim against him, or otherwise prejudicing the interests of such a person. The *section* relates to transactions entered into at an undervalue, where the dominant purpose of the transaction was to avoid the claim of a creditor (see *Chohan v Saggar [1992] BCC 306*). The 1882 case of *Re Butterworth* enables future unknown creditors to bring such claim: this Court of Appeal decision effectively rules out the use of CPTs in the UK. Furthermore, the six-year civil limitation period may not apply, or may be capable of extension in these circumstances. On the ethical aspects (see 2.56), solicitors and accountants cannot raise professional privilege against a trustee-in-bankruptcy.

Second, *sections 339* and *340* of the *Insolvency Act 1986* also apply to transfers at an undervalue, but where a trustee-in-bankruptcy has already been appointed. *Section 340* relates to preferences. The *Act* defines the concept of 'insolvent'. Transactions at an undervalue with an 'associate' (defined in *section 435*) shift the burden of proof.

Third, there are also grounds for attacking the transfers at common law on the basis of fraud. In *Cadogan v Cadogan [1977] 1 WLR 1041*, the Court of Appeal confirmed that a transfer could be set aside if the claimant could prove the transferor's intent to defeat a claim.

It is also worth noting *section 357* of the *Insolvency Act*, which establishes a criminal offence of making or causing to be made any gift or transfer of property within five years prior to bankruptcy. Given the wide scope of this *section*, there is a clear possibility that professional advisers who assist a transferor with knowledge of the essential facts could be charged with aiding and abetting the criminal offence.

Enforcement offshore (in the trust's 'host' country)

2.19   Here there are two aspects to consider. First, whether the courts in the offshore jurisdiction will grant reciprocal enforcement (over trust assets) of an insolvency award of a US court setting aside a transfer into trust on either of the grounds explored at 2.17. Second, whether the creditor will be able to commence proceedings direct in the courts of the trust jurisdiction seeking to set aside the transfer into trust, and thereby obtain direct enforcement over the trust fund.

On the question of reciprocal enforcement, it is a long-standing rule of private international law that foreign penal or revenue laws will not be enforced (*Government of India v Taylor [1955] AC 491*; but see *Bullen and Garner v United Kingdom 533 So 2d (Fla App 4 Dist 1989)*). Thus, only purely civil (i.e., non-penal or revenue) awards may be enforceable under common law principles of comity, or under reciprocal civil judgments conventions.

The United Kingdom position on enforcement of foreign judgments is explained in *Dicey and Morris on The Conflict of Laws* (11th edition) in Chapter 14 (and see further *International Corporate Tax Planning* (5th edition) in the chapter entitled 'Transnational Enforcement of Tax Liabilities'.

Reciprocal recognition of bankruptcy in Commonwealth (or ex-Commonwealth) jurisdictions is provided for under *section 426* of the *Insolvency Act 1986*. The list of some 17 jurisdictions covered include the Channel Islands, Isle of Man, Anguilla, Bermuda, Cayman, Gibraltar, Bahamas, Turks & Caicos and the BVI. Either the English courts (or the offshore courts) could apply English law, including the insolvency tax provisions setting aside transactions defrauding creditors. This is clearly an area of conflict.

Many jurisdictions also have legislation relating to evidence and recognising and enforcing foreign judgments. In the UK, relevant provisions include: the *Administration of Justice Act 1920*; the *Foreign Judgments (Reciprocal Enforcement) Act 1933*; the *Brussels Convention 1968*; the *Convention in the Taking of Evidence Abroad in Civil or Commercial Matters 1970*; and the *Lugano Convention 1988*. Again, the *Evidence Convention* has been extended by Cayman, the Channel Islands, Gibraltar and the Isle of Man.

2.20   Enforcement of United States judgments in foreign countries is primarily dependent upon the comity (generosity) of the foreign jurisdiction, as the United States is not a party to *any* treaties of enforcement of foreign judgments (other than the Inter-American Agreement dealing with South America).

The offshore jurisdiction may treat a United States judgment in one of three possible ways. First, it may as a matter of internal law or policy totally preclude the enforcement of foreign judgments (unless there is a mutual enforcement treaty with the United States, which, as noted above, is unlikely). Second, there may be a limited recognition short of granting the US judgment a conclusive or binding effect: in this situation, the US judgment may be wholly or partly reopened and its issues subjected to further findings of fact and law. Third, some jurisdictions will readily recognise the US judgment, on being satisfied that their own judgments will be similarly recognised in the US.

2.21   Proceedings may be commenced under the substantive laws of the offshore jurisdiction either under its fraudulent conveyance or its bankruptcy laws. Fraudulent conveyance proceedings may be available if the creditor can establish the transferor's intent to defraud. Jurisdiction to commence bankruptcy proceedings is generally narrower, requiring either the transferor to be resident or domiciled in the offshore jurisdiction, or an 'act of bankruptcy' to be committed there. The detailed provisions relating to both aspects are considered further at 2.22–2.35 for various of the offshore jurisdictions.

Selection of the offshore jurisdiction to site the CPT is thus of critical importance, as different offshore jurisdictions will lead to different results in terms of offshore enforcement of a foreign judgment.

Listed below (2.36–2.40) are the offshore jurisdictions that have *not* (or not yet) introduced new laws relating to creditor protection trusts. It is possible that some of these may well 'give aid' and enforce a foreign judgment containing a purely civil damages award.

Conversely, the offshore jurisdictions that *have* introduced laws relating to creditor protection trusts, it is unlikely that the courts of any of these offshore jurisdictions would contradict their new laws and 'give aid' or enforce a foreign judgment (although see 2.27 in the case of the Bahamas), as to do this would run counter to the policy and intent of their own tailor-made legislation. Indeed, some of this latter group of jurisdictions have gone further, and given statutory effect to the 'ouster' of foreign judgments (e.g., Cook Islands, see 2.23). Clearly, from the settlor's point of view, it is most desirable to select an offshore jurisdiction where enforcement of a US judgment is a near-impossibility. If the offshore jurisdiction is *not* one that will recognise or enforce a US judgment, then the only alternative may be to commence proceedings in the offshore jurisdiction.

If a trustee-in-bankruptcy is acting, then the 'doctrine of universality' may apply. This operates to pass all movable property of the debtor, wherever located, to the trustee in bankruptcy. Many of the offshore jurisdictions recognise and apply the doctrine of universality in respect of property of a debtor located in their jurisdictions. However, assets held in a CPT will not be subject to the doctrine, as the debtor (the settlor) does not normally retain any interest in the trust fund.

The detailed provisions relating to these aspects are considered further at 2.22–2.35.

The offshore jurisdictions that attract CPT business

Introduction

2.22   The following part of this chapter looks at the legislation of some of the offshore jurisdictions, and considers in detail the provisions in the jurisdictions that have introduced specific amendments designed to attract CPT business. A number of other jurisdictions are currently considering amendments.

These provisions vary considerably in approach, as the legal systems in these jurisdictions have evolved differently. The Cayman Islands and Bahamas have focused on amending their equivalent of the *Statute of Elizabeth* provisions on fraudulent transfers. (At the same time, they have left untouched their bankruptcy provisions, based on the *Bankruptcy Act 1914*.) Gibraltar has, on the other hand, specifically amended its bankruptcy provisions in relation to transfers into trust.

The offshore jurisdictions are tending to introduce as a common theme what are sometimes referred to as 'guillotine' statutes, the effect of which is to cut off the possibility of legal action being brought after a stated period of time.

Offshore jurisdictions introducing CPT legislation tend to adopt provisions, or parts of provisions, already in force elsewhere. This phenomenon, which has sometimes been criticised as 'designer legislation', is understandable in light of competitive pressures. However, it does not necessarily follow that a settlor/transferor should simply select the jurisdiction with the most attractive laws. A detailed examination of the various provisions follows.

Cook Islands

2.23   The Cook Islands was the first offshore jurisdiction to adopt specific CPT legislation: this is contained in the *International Trusts Amendment Act 1989,* passed on 8 September 1989, and effective the same day. *Section 6* of the *1989 Act* inserts new sections into the principal *Act*, in particular new *sections 13A–13I*. The *Act* was further amended in December 1989, and again in December 1991.

The *Act* applies specifically to transfers to 'international trusts' (as defined). *Section 13A* provides that an international trust shall not be void or voidable in the event of the settlor's bankruptcy, or in any action or proceeding at the suit of creditors of the settlor: however, the 'fraud' provisions of *section 13B* may apply.

Section 13B provides a remedy in cases of fraud. The burden is on the creditor to prove that an international trust was settled 'with principal intent to defraud that creditor of the settlor', and that the transfer rendered the settlor insolvent or without property by which that creditor's claim could (if successful) be satisfied. If the creditor does succeed in showing this, then the trust fund is made available to satisfy the creditor: the transfer (hence the trust itself) is *not* made void or voidable.

The expression 'insolvent' is not specifically defined, but *section 13B* provides that in determining whether a transfer has rendered the settlor insolvent, regard is to be had to the fair market value of the settlor's remaining property immediately *after* the transfer, and if such fair market value exceeded the value of the creditor's claim at that time, then the transfer is deemed not to have been made with fraudulent intent.

There are other restrictions. A transfer is deemed not to be fraudulent if made *more than two years after* the creditor's cause of action 'accrued', or where the creditor fails to bring an action *within one year* of the transfer. Conversely, a transfer is not deemed fraudulent just because it is made within two years of the creditor's cause of action accruing. Also, by virtue of amendments passed in December 1991, the action must be commenced in the Cook Islands within *two years of the transfer*.

The *International Trusts (Amendment) Act* has amended *section 13B* in an attempt to reverse the effect of the two *Orange Grove* judgments (of 6 November 1995 and 2 December 1996), being important decisions on the two-year time limit and the concepts of 'accrued' and 'arisen'.

As noted, the burden of proof is on the creditor: in addition, the *Act* requires creditor claimants to prove their claim 'beyond a reasonable doubt'.

Where the trust fund is held liable to satisfy a creditor's claim but is unable to do so by reason of the fact that the property has been distributed to a beneficiary, then the distribution to the beneficiary is itself held void. In the absence of a 'good faith' test the effect of these provisions may be impracticable, especially if the beneficiary has spent or consumed the funds distributed.

As noted above, *section 13D* provides for the non-recognition of a foreign judgment against an international trust, its settlor, trustee or protector.

Cayman Islands

2.24   The Cayman Islands were next to introduce CPT legislation: their *Fraudulent Dispositions Law 1989* was passed on 6 November 1989 (less than two months after the Cook Islands' Laws) and became effective on 1 May 1990.

Under *section 4(1)* of the Cayman provisions, a transfer into trust is *voidable* at the instance of the creditor thereby prejudiced if made within an 'intent to defraud' *and* at an undervalue. 'Intent to defraud' is defined as an intention of a transferor wilfully to defeat an 'obligation owed' to a creditor. It is not sufficient to show that a creditor was merely delayed or hindered. 'Obligation' means an obligation or liability (including a contingent liability) which existed on or prior to the date of the transfer, and of which the transferor had notice. Under *section 4(2)* the burden of establishing 'intent to defraud' is on the creditor seeking to set aside the transfer.

Under *section 4(3)* there is a limitation period of six years, measured from the date of the transfer. Thus, a creditor can effectively challenge a trust only *during the first six years* from its creation. Contrast this with the two-year rule in the Bahamas, described at 2.27.

If a transfer is set aside pursuant to these provisions, the creditor obtains a first charge over the property, but subject to the rights of any beneficiary receiving a distribution in good faith. Thus, a beneficiary to whom trust assets have been distributed may retain them in the absence of the beneficiary having acted in bad faith.

The trustee, as transferor, is awarded its costs of defending the litigation if the court is satisfied that it has *not* acted in bad faith. Likewise, a beneficiary to whom trust assets have been distributed may also retain them if the court is satisfied that the beneficiary has not acted in bad faith. The onus is placed on the trustee and/or the beneficiary to establish an absence of bad faith.

The *1989 Law* did not alter the pre-existing bankruptcy legislation in the Cayman Islands. Cayman Islands bankruptcy law can be applied on jurisdictional grounds either if the debtor is a resident of the Cayman Islands, or if the debtor (being resident anywhere) commits an act of bankruptcy in the Cayman Islands. The first jurisdictional ground (the debtor being a Cayman Island resident) is unlikely to apply as regards CPTs, as the settlor/transferor of these will normally be resident in the United States.

Thus, if there is an act of bankruptcy in the Cayman Islands and the settlor becomes bankrupt within two years of creating a trust, it may be set aside by his trustee in bankruptcy. Alternatively, if the settlor becomes bankrupt within twelve years of the settlement, the trustee in bankruptcy may apply to have the settlement set aside unless the persons who claim the benefit under the settlement can establish that at the date of the settlement, the settlor was able to pay all his debts without taking the settled property into account, and that the interest of the settlor in the property passed to the trustee thereof.

Gibraltar

2.25   Gibraltar passed CPT legislation by way of amendments to its *Bankruptcy Ordinance* on 8 March 1990. The legislation aims specifically at transfers into trusts made by non-resident individual settlors, and provides for a system of confidential registration with the Gibraltar authorities.

If a transfer to a trust made by an individual is duly registered, and at the date of the transfer the individual transferor is not insolvent *and* does not thereby become insolvent, the transfer is not voidable. *In any other case, the transfer is voidable.*

'Insolvent' is defined as where liabilities exceed assets. Note that the definitions of 'insolvent' in relation to a settlor/transferor includes any of his liabilities, both actual, contingent or prospective. This is mitigated by the proviso that a claim is only deemed a contingent or prospective liability of the settlor/transferor if he had (at the time of the transfer) actual notice of the claim, or of the facts and circumstances which may render him liable. The details of the registration and authorisation requirements are contained in the *Bankruptcy (Register of Dispositions) Regulations 1990*. These are designed to safeguard the way in which trusts are established, and by whom. In addition to the normal licensing requirements for trust companies under the *Gibraltar Financial Services Ordinance*, the legislation requires any proposed trustee of a CPT to be specifically authorised by the Gibraltar authorities as having adequate financial and administrative resources.

It is further a requirement that any such trustee must obtain the approval of the authorities to the trustee's 'forms of enquiry' with regard to solvency, which must be administered to the settlor. The trust company furthermore should have a level of professional indemnity insurance considered adequate by the Gibraltar authorities, and in any event not less than the sum of £1 million sterling.

Any transfer into trust that seeks to acquire the benefit of the legislation must be registered in a confidential register established for such purposes. There is an application fee of £300, and an annual fee of £100 in respect of such trusts. The transfer itself is what is registerable: any additions to the trust fund require separate notifications, as the criterion of not making the settlor insolvent is on-going.

The Gibraltar provisions specifically make the *Statute of Elizabeth* inapplicable to trusts that are duly registered. The Gibraltar provisions do not, however, include any requirement or test of the transferor's intent. They also do not deal with the treatment of distributions to a beneficiary in the event the initial transfer to the trust is held voidable.

The enactment of Gibraltar's CPT legislation promoting confidentiality and stating that only insolvency would render a transfer voidable proved to be attractive factors for the defendant in *Securities and Exchange Commission v Robert Brennan* (US Court of Appeals for the Second Circuit 26 Oct 2000) – (see 2.56).

Turks & Caicos

2.26   Turks & Caicos' CPT legislation is contained in the *Trusts Ordinance 1990* and the *Voidable Dispositions Ordinance 1998*. The *Trusts Ordinance* is extensive, dealing with a broad range of trust issues, including specific provisions on creditor protection trusts created by individual settlors.

The CPT provisions state that a transfer is not voidable by a creditor unless the settlor was insolvent at the time of the transfer, or became insolvent by reason thereof. 'Insolvent' is defined in *section 2* as 'being subject to liabilities, whether actual, contingent or prospective, of which the value exceeds that of the assets available to meet such liabilities as they become due'. The creditor has the burden of proving insolvency, and no limitation period for actions is stipulated.

The *Voidable Dispositions Ordinance* abolishes all vestiges of the *Statute of Elizabeth* (previously curtailed in 1990); and provides a six-month transition period during which actions may still be brought under existing law, but not thereafter. In order to justify setting aside a transfer into trust, the relevant debt or cause of action must have arisen within two years after the date of the transfer, proceedings to set aside must be commenced within six years after the transfer; and a creditor must prove that the transferor wilfully intended to defeat an obligation owed to the creditor, as well as that the transfer was at less than full value.

Bahamas

2.27   Bahamas adopted CPT legislation with its *Fraudulent Dispositions Act 1991*, which came into effect on 5 April 1991. These provisions are based on the Cayman Islands' legislation (see 2.24), but are not as detailed. On the other hand, they are generally more favourable to transferors.

Section 4(1) provides that every disposition of property made with an intent to defraud and at an undervalue shall be voidable at the instance of a creditor thereby prejudiced. 'Intent to defraud' is defined as meaning an intention of a transferor wilfully to defeat an obligation owed to a creditor, and 'obligation' means an obligation or liability (including a contingent liability) which existed on or prior to the date of a relevant disposition, and of which the transferor had actual notice.

Under *section 4(2)* the creditor has the burden of establishing the transferor's 'intent to defraud'.

There is a limitation period for commencing proceedings of *two years* from the date of the relevant disposition. Contrast the Cayman Islands' six-year limitation period (see 2.24).

If a disposition is set aside, then beneficiaries who have already received distributions may retain them unless the court is satisfied that a beneficiary has acted in bad faith. The trustee is also given a first charge over the trust fund for its own costs, again unless the court is satisfied that the trustee has acted in bad faith. The burden of proving that either the trustee or a beneficiary has acted in bad faith is placed upon the person making the allegation. This may be contrasted with the Cayman Islands provisions, where the burden is placed on the trustee/beneficiary to establish they were not acting in bad faith.

Trustees are therefore subject to a degree of uncertainty as to what, in the circumstances, will amount to 'bad faith'. The trustee would seem to have to take certain pro-active steps in order to establish the settlor's solvency.

The Bahamas Supreme Court held in its Ruling of 1 September 1995 in the Civil Action *Grupo Torras SA v Sheikh Fahad Al Sabah* that the *Fraudulent Disposition Act* should be construed in a restrictive way, so that only persons alleged to have intent to defraud or actual notice of a possible claim could claim the two-year statutory protection. The judge in the decision specifically criticised the Legislature's intention of allowing the Bahamas' position 'as a legitimate tax haven to be used as a cover for fraudulent activity which has little or nothing to do with the minimisation of taxes or the protection of honestly acquired assets . . .'.

Note that the Bahamas extensively consolidated and updated its trust legislation by virtue of the *Trustee Act 1998* (effective 22 July 1998).

The bankruptcy legislation of the Bahamas remains unchanged. Jurisdiction for *Bankruptcy Act* purposes does not require the debtor to be resident in the Bahamas, but exists irrespective of his domicile or residence simply if one of the 'acts of bankruptcy' enumerated in the *Act* is committed. These include commission of a fraudulent conveyance.

The territorial scope of the *Bankruptcy Act* limits its jurisdictions in regard to acts of bankruptcy committed outside the Bahamas to debtors who are citizens of the Bahamas, or foreign persons who are resident in the Bahamas. Some professionals advise settlors of a Bahamas CPT to execute any disposition of property into trust *outside the Bahamas*, so as to avoid the possibility of an 'act of bankruptcy' being committed within the jurisdiction of the Bahamas.

An alternative practice is for the Bahamian trustee to have the assets vested in a Bahamian international business company (IBC); Bahamian IBCs are exempt from Bahamas exchange controls, do not need to file annual returns, and their shares can be issued in bearer form.

Cyprus

2.28 Cyprus' CPT legislation is contained in the *International Trusts Law 1992* (effective 24 July 1992). This provides that a trust shall not be void or voidable in the event of the settlor's bankruptcy, unless made with intent to defraud creditors. The onus of proof of such intent is placed on the creditor(s). An action against the trustees to avoid the trust on grounds of fraud must be brought within two years from the date of the transfer.

Belize

2.29 The *Belize Trusts Act 1992* contains APT provisions in its *section 7*, cross-referenced also in *sections 2, 4, 9, 16, 57* and *64*.

Under the *Belize Act* a settlor can create a trust under which he is entitled to the income until he becomes bankrupt and thereafter he becomes one of a class of beneficiaries under a discretionary trust. The settlor can have virtual full control of his assets until there is some legal, administrative or forfeiture action against the assets, at which point the trust converts itself into a fully protective discretionary trust. The *Belize Act* abolishes the doctrine of fraudulent conveyance, so that once a person has transferred property to another person, his responsibility for it is ended.

In addition, under the *Act* the Belize court cannot set aside a Belizian trust, nor recognise the validity of any claim against the trust property, pursuant to the law of another jurisdiction or the order of a foreign court in respect of marriage or divorce, succession or claims by creditors in an insolvency, notwithstanding the law relating to fraudulent transfers, the *Bankruptcy Act* and the *Reciprocal Enforcement of Judgments Act*.

Mauritius

2.30   In Mauritius, the *Offshore Trusts Act 1992* makes similar provision for 'offshore trusts' (as defined) to be set aside as fraudulent by creditors' action within two years from the transfer into trust, but unlike Cyprus the creditors have the burden of proving this *beyond reasonable doubt* (the higher standard of proof, as in the Cook Islands). The trust is not void or voidable in the event of the settlor's bankruptcy or liquidation of his property or in any action brought against the settlor by a creditor, except where made with intent to defraud his creditors at the time of the transfer of assets.

Bermuda

2.31   *Section 11* of the *Trusts (Special Provisions) Act 1989* states, in relation to enforcement claims by foreign creditors, that:

> 'Where a Trust is validly created under the Law of Bermuda the Court shall not vary it or set it aside pursuant to the law of another jurisdiction in respect of . . . (c) the protection of creditors in matters of insolvency, unless the law of Bermuda has corresponding laws or public policy rules'.

Bermuda's *Conveyancing Act 1983* (based on the *Law of Property Act 1925, s 172*) was amended in 1994 to render voidable any disposition made with the dominant intention of putting property beyond the reach of a person who is making (or may at some future time make) a claim. The persons who may seek to avoid the disposition are: a person then or within two years afterwards owed an obligation; a person then owed a contingent liability which has since matured; or a person owed an obligation from a cause of action accruing before the disposition or within two years thereafter. A test of reasonable foreseeability is imposed in respect of contingent and future creditors, and there is a limitation period of six years for claiming to set aside a disposition. As previously, trusts are not required to be disclosed to, filed, or registered with any government body.

Nevis

2.32   The *Statute of Elizabeth* is not applicable to an international trust. A creditor who brings an action against any trust property is required to first deposit a bond with the Ministry of Finance. A register of international trusts is maintained, but is not open for inspection except where a trustee of the trust, by written authorisation, allows a person to inspect the entry of that trust.

Nevis passed legislation in 1994 to protect international trusts against creditors. A time limit is imposed within which a cause of action based on fraud must be brought. Under the new Nevis law, an international trust or disposition shall not be void, voidable, liable to be set aside or defective in any fashion because a foreign jurisdiction does not recognise the concept of a trust or because it contravenes any rule in a foreign law. No trust or any aspect of it shall be declared void, voidable, or defective, nor is the capacity of the settlor to be questioned by reason that the trust may avoid or defeat heirship rights or the interests of a person held by reason of a personal relationship to the settlor. This aspect of Nevis law is considered in a recent US case *Securities and Exchange Commission v Robert Brennan* (US Court of Appeals for the Second Circuit 26 Oct 2000) concerning the actions of a US Court over a 'flight clause' where a trust relocated from Gibraltar to Mauritius and then onto Nevis (see also 2.56). Attempts to recover the assets by the settlor's bankruptcy trustee in 1998 were unsuccessful when the High Court of Nevis dismissed the action due to the failure to state a claim under Nevis law.

Niue

2.33   The *Niue Trusts Act 1994* essentially copies the provisions of the *Belize Trusts Act 1992* (see 2.29).

Anguilla

2.34   Anguilla's *Trusts Ordinance 1994* and *Fraudulent Dispositions Ordinance 1994* came into force on 1 January 1995. The *Trusts Ordinance* permits asset protection trusts. The provisions ensure that an Anguillian trust may not be varied or set aside pursuant to the order of the court of another jurisdiction in respect of *inter alia* the claims of creditors in an insolvency. Registration of a trust is optional. The *Fraudulent Dispositions Ordinance* (similar to those of the Cayman Islands – 2.24, and Bahamas – 2.27) complements the *Trusts Ordinance*, and provides that a fraudulent disposition (i.e., a disposition made with intent wilfully to defeat a liability (actual or contingent) existing at the time of such disposition owed to another person) is voidable by a creditor provided that the settlor was insolvent at the time of the disposition or became so as a result thereof. The creditor must commence his action within three years of the date that the assets were settled into trust. The burden of proving that the settlor was or became insolvent as a result of the transfer is on the creditor.

The need for confidentiality in ordinary business dealings is already protected by the *Confidential Relationships Ordinance 1981*.

Barbados

2.35   The recently enacted *International Trusts Act 1995* provides for the use of trusts for protection of assets from future personal liability. An international trust means 'a trust' in respect of which the settlor is resident outside of Barbados at the time of the creation of the trust and at such times as the settlor adds new property to the trust; at least one of the trustees is resident in Barbados; no beneficiary other than otherwise specified in the *Act* is a resident of Barbados at the time of the creation of the trust and at such times as the settlor adds new property to the trust; and the trust property does not include any immovable property situate in Barbados or an interest in any property so situate.

Under the *Act*, every disposition of property made with an intent to defraud or at an undervalue shall be voidable at the instance of a creditor thereby prejudiced. The burden of establishing an intent to defraud for the purposes of this *Act* shall be upon the creditor seeking to set aside the disposition. No action or proceedings shall be commenced later than three years after the date of the relevant disposition. The *Act* provides for full confidentiality of the trust, and there is no requirement for the registration of international trusts.

Offshore jurisdictions that do not have specific CPT legislation

British Virgin Islands

2.36   The British Virgin Islands considered introducing comprehensive CPT amendments in their trustee ordinance and bankruptcy legislation. CPT proposals were in the draft *Trustee Amendment Act*, but were removed from the final text of the *Trustee (Amendment) Act 1993* (which amended the *Trustee Ordinance 1961*), as a result of comments received. The BVI Ministry of Finance wrote in December 1991 that 'in our opinion, it is perhaps prudent for us to proceed with the draft less the particular *sections*, and then (if necessary) address the issues later if not by way of amending the principle Statute, then through a different Act'.

A draft law of creditor protection trusts (entitled the *Fraudulent Dispositions and Validity of Settlements Act*) was subsequently circulated: this was intended to be the state-of-the-art in creditor protection legislation. However, the BVI has not enacted any CPT provisions.

Guernsey

2.37   There is no equivalent in Guernsey to the *Statute of Elizabeth*. The Guernsey courts will nevertheless not uphold a trust created for the purpose of defeating known existing creditors. However, as regards trusts created in anticipation of future creditors or litigation, the position is not quite so clear. A transfer would be deemed to be a fraudulent conveyance under Guernsey law only if the settlor already had knowledge or should reasonably have had knowledge of circumstances giving rise to a claim by creditors, and if as a result of such transfer the settlor put the assets outside his power to satisfy a judgment against him. If he had no such knowledge, the courts would not regard such a transfer as fraudulent.

There are no limitation periods in Guernsey: all that can be said is that the longer the period between the creation of the trust and the date when the settlor had knowledge of the claim, or circumstances of which could potentially lead to a claim, the more likely it is that the trust would be upheld.

There are no provisions in the *Trusts (Guernsey) Law 1989* or the *Trusts (Amendment) (Guernsey) Law 1990* relating to enforcement of claims by foreign creditors.

Proposals under discussion in Guernsey on draft legislation entitled the *Rights of Creditors (Guernsey) Law 1992* were dropped in favour of fine tuning and minor adjustments to make the position in law more certain.

Isle of Man

2.38   The Isle of Man is not a signatory to any reciprocal agreement with the United States on enforcement of US judgments. The US creditor will have difficulty in invoking Manx bankruptcy laws on jurisdictional grounds, as the transferor will usually not be domiciled in, or a resident of the Isle of Man.

The Isle of Man's fraudulent conveyance laws may, on the other hand, be available. *Section 4(4)* of the *Evidence Act 1736* (also called the *Fraudulent Assignments Act*) provides that fraudulent transfers are void against creditors. 'Fraudulent' is not defined. The *Evidence Act* does not apply to future creditors. (*Re Corin's Bankruptcy, Kermode v Craig (1902), unreported; Lloyds Bank Ltd v Marcam [1973] 2 All ER 359.*)

The *Trusts Act 1995* introduced provisions similar to those in Jersey's law [*Art 8A*] and Guernsey's law [*section 11A*], deeming persons lacking capacity to transfer into trust under their personal law the full capacity for effecting the transfer. Until implementation, the Isle of Man remains a problematic jurisdiction for establishing CPTs.

Jersey

2.39   The position in Jersey is broadly similar to that in Guernsey (see 2.37). Jersey law prohibits fraudulent transfers, although the provisions are not incorporated in any statute other than in relation to bankruptcy proceedings.

The *action paulienne* (referred to at 2.11) is part of Jersey customary law, and enables creditors who have been defrauded to have the relevant transfer set aside. (*Golder v Société des Magasins Concorde Ltd 1JJ 721.*) The action may be brought by any creditor whose debt is in existence at the date of the transfer. Subsequent creditors may also benefit where there has been a bankruptcy. The debtor must be insolvent at the time of the transfer, or if the transfer is gratuitous must render himself insolvent thereby.

There are no statutory provisions in the *Trusts (Jersey) Law 1984*, or the *Amendment Laws 1989* or *1991* relating to enforcement of claims by foreign creditors.

Conflict of laws

2.40   It is noted above (2.15–2.16) that although under the transferor's own 'domestic' law the transfer may be invalid, the transfer may nevertheless be upheld by the law of the offshore jurisdiction. It is, however, worth noting that there are conflicting arguments as to whether the law of the offshore jurisdiction or the law of the settlor/transferor's domicile should be applied to consider whether a given transfer was fraudulent. It would avail the transferor little to find an offshore jurisdiction in which the laws are more lax than are the laws of his own domicile if the courts of the offshore jurisdiction are going to apply the law of the transferor's domicile in any event.

Structures and planning issues

Introduction

2.41   At simplest, a trust can be used by itself. It will be formed in an offshore low tax jurisdiction, outside the United States, with an independent trust company appointed as trustee.

The trust will be irrevocable and discretionary. The settlor will be capable of benefiting from the trust fund at some future time when liability to creditors is no longer an issue. This can be achieved in either of two ways:

(*a*)   either by the settlor receiving assets as a distribution to him as a beneficiary;

(*b*)   or by the trust becoming revocable after a certain period and the settlor then exercising his power to revoke it.

It is also possible for the settlor/transferor to create a discretionary trust of which he is *not* named as a beneficiary (and will not be added as a beneficiary in the future): the named beneficiaries would typically be other family members, such as the children. This type of arrangement is less usual, as the settlor normally wishes to be capable of benefiting in the future, but has the advantage of eliminating arguments based on *section 7–3.1* of the *Estates Powers and Trusts Law* and the *Vanderbilt* case (see 2.9).

The settlor may retain the power of appointing new/successor trustees, but he will be excluded from being so appointed. As a further refinement, this power can be vested in a Protector, or a Committee of Protectors.

Underlying companies

2.42   In addition, the trust may incorporate a new offshore company to act as its underlying investment holding company. This wholly-owned subsidiary of the trust would open bank and brokerage accounts, and thus hold the trust fund indirectly for the trustees.

US income tax issues

2.43   The US income tax treatment of the trust is of critical importance. In general, the trust should be tax neutral. There are two alternatives:

(*a*)   either the trust can be configured as an offshore grantor trust for US income tax purposes under *IRC, ss 671–679*, in which case the settlor remains liable for all reporting and taxation issues (and see 2.52); or

(*b*)   the trust can have two or more co-trustees who are US residents or citizens, in which case the trust is classified as a 'US trust', and is taxable in the US on its income and gains.

The first 'wholly offshore' alternative is generally preferable for jurisdictional reasons, as the entire structure is thereby outside the jurisdiction of the US courts though since 20 August 1996 there are significant reporting requirements (see 2.52).

If the second alternative is used, the trust will contain 'anti-duress' provisions, enabling the offshore co-trustee to fire the US co-trustees in the event the latter become subject to court orders in the home country directing them to take particular action with regard to trust assets. The trust thereby becomes 'wholly offshore', so the same result is achieved. The purpose of an anti-duress clause is, of course, to protect the settlor against coercion by the courts of his jurisdiction, and consequent exposure to perjury charges for failure to comply therewith. A specimen clause is attached as Appendix 2:1.

Also in relation to the second alternative, if a US trust is used, it might have a wholly-owned subsidiary incorporated in Delaware. The Delaware holding company would elect for taxation in the US as a *Sub-Chapter S* corporation. See also 2.42.

Reportings and filings are discussed at 2.52 below.

Federal estate and gift tax issues

2.44   In order to avoid the gift tax provisions of *Code sections 2501* and *2511*, the transferor/settlor should make an incomplete gift. This can be accomplished by the settlor reserving a power in the trust agreement such as the power to add or delete persons as beneficiaries, with the consent of the trustees, or, alternatively, a power to remove and appoint trustees. The settlor should also file a gift tax return in respect of the incomplete gift, disclosing all relevant facts including a copy of the trust agreement. [*Treasury Regulations on Gift Tax, s 25.2511* and *s 25.6019*].

Federal excise tax

2.45   *Code section 1491* excise tax does not apply on a transfer of appreciated assets to an offshore trust if the trust is configured as a grantor trust (see *Revenue Ruling 87–61*).

Types of assets

2.46   In theory, the settlor is free to transfer to the trust any and all assets that he wishes to have protected by the trust. In practice, offshore trustees prefer to receive, and may insist on only receiving financial assets, such as bank deposits and cash equivalents. These will be transferred to newly-opened accounts in one or more offshore banks in the name of the trustee. Investment portfolios and brokerage accounts are generally acceptable and are subject to the same procedure.

Offshore trustees will have difficulty in accepting shares of stock in privately-held US corporations – and must be circumspect about accepting title to real estate assets in the United States. Why? Because these categories of assets are by definition 'US situs' assets. As such they remain within the jurisdiction of the US courts, hence liable to attachment by order of a US court on successful suit by a creditor claimant. This involves consideration of jurisdictional issues, both in relation to the trust fund, and to the trustee itself (see 2.47).

Depending on the State of the settlor, a range of assets are not attachable in a bankruptcy (e.g., the homestead). Florida and Texas place no limits on the value of the home. Pennsylvania excludes insurance policies in favour of the spouse or children. Normally in creditor protection trusts, these 'exempt' assets are not among those transferred to the trust.

Jurisdictional issues and location of assets

2.47   In relation to jurisdiction over trust assets, the trustee must be mindful of extra-territorial jurisdictional aspects in relation to opening accounts for the trust with banks or brokers within the United States (see the *Perez–Rubio* case (*84 CIV 8229, US District Court, Southern District of NY, 1989*).

Effectively it is open to a judge in the onshore proceedings to disregard the structure created by the settlor vis-à-vis assets remaining in the United States, and order direct attachment of the US assets (a robust 'substance over form' approach). In this regard two decisions should be noted. The case of *Duttle v Bandler & Cass 82 Cir 5084 (KMW, 1992)* involved an American lawyer living in New York attempting to defeat the interests of his creditors by creating a Liechtenstein trust. And the more recent case of *In Re Larry Portnoy 201 Bank 685 (1996)* involved a New York clothing manufacturer placing loan proceeds in a Jersey trust. In both cases the US court found that it had jurisdiction over the foreign trust.

Some US advisers recommend against the CPT holding US dollar deposits, which, by their very nature, are always (ultimately) onshore US assets. On the other hand, it is possible for US situs property such as real estate, section 144 stock, or accounts receivable to be sold or mortgaged for cash, and the resulting liquid assets transferred to the offshore trustees.

For best security, it is important that trust assets are located outside the settlor's home jurisdiction, outside a Hague Convention country, outside a jurisdiction likely not to apply protective legislation, and advisedly in a trust located in one of the jurisdictions whose laws support CPTs by protective legislation. These considerations are most relevant at the date of the disposition which may be attacked.

In relation to jurisdiction over the trustee itself, if the offshore trustee is a subsidiary of an onshore parent, then creditors may try to 'short circuit' enforcement against the offshore structure by a direct attack against the onshore parent. This further jurisdictional aspect of the trustee itself having a US branch, subsidiary or presence is also critically important, but a detailed consideration of this is beyond the scope of this chapter.

It should be noted that most US banks/trust companies do not accept US persons as clients of their international private banking divisions, which generally include their offshore trust companies.

Limited partnerships

2.48   There are other apparently more sophisticated structures, involving the use of US limited partnerships. In these, the settlor becomes the general partner of the partnership, and the offshore trust is the limited partner: the settlor, as general partner, usually has a 5 per cent or less interest in the assets of the partnership, and the offshore trust has a 95 per cent or more interest. The settlor transfers his assets to the limited partnership, and continues to manage them. This type of planning takes advantage of the provisions of *Article 7* of the *Uniform Limited Partnership Act 1976* (as amended) relating to the nature of a partnership interest, assignment thereof, and rights of creditors.

If a creditor obtains an 'onshore' judgment against the limited partnership, he cannot under present law force the limited partnership to make cash distributions or to sell the assets of the partnership to satisfy the judgment. The creditor's claim is thus satisfied by a charging order, the effect of which is normally held in suspense, although this principle may be being eroded. (*Centurion Corpn v Crocker National Bank 255 Cal Rep 794 (1989).*) Meanwhile, the creditor becomes a substituted limited partner for US income tax purposes, and must report and pay tax on the phantom income of the partnership. The creditor is thus responsible in law for income tax on the asset of which he is not yet the legal owner: there is thus a deterrent effect on the creditor.

The offshore trust remains in a back-up role, until such time as the partnership is wound up, at which point the assets are owned direct by the offshore trust. An offshore trust can of course own interests in a series of limited partnerships, each of which would have different types of underlying assets.

Insurance

2.49   The trustee should also check with its own insurers that its normal policy will remain effective in relation to CPTs. Many proposal trusts now require specific disclosure of whether the trust company is in the business of creditor protection trusteeship! Many trustees have ended up declining certain types of CPT business for this reason, which has become a limiting factor in the growth of this market.

Procedural safeguards

'Know your client'

2.50   As a result largely of anti-money-laundering legislation, the 'know your client' rule has for some years now been standard operating procedure in the financial services industry. Trustees (whether onshore or offshore) must always obtain background information on proposed clients, or insist on professional references/introductions. This procedure is doubly important in relation to CPTs.

The proposed offshore trustee needs to be sure that the transfer into trust cannot be impugned. It must therefore be satisfied that the settlor:

(*a*)   is not presently subject to demands claims or legal actions from purported creditors; and

(*b*)   has no fraudulent intention or plan behind the establishment of the trust.

The biggest difficulty for the proposed offshore trustee is that it has neither the financial nor human resources to enable it to assess or verify either of these to any level of sophistication or accuracy. But the proposed trustee needs to be able to make an informed determination regarding what type of business to accept.

In practice, (and necessarily) the offshore trustee has to rely almost entirely on information provided by the professional intermediary (usually either an attorney or CPA) who is acting for the settlor and is introducing the business. At one end of the spectrum, the settlor will have good and legitimate planning needs. At the other end of the spectrum, the settlor may have an imminent lawsuit, or a divorce looming, and want only to protect against that eventuality. One of the central issues will be the intent of the settlor.

The onshore advisers must screen their client carefully to see if there are any outstanding malpractice suits, or other events such as a divorce pending. If necessary, the adviser should obtain affidavits from the client on these, and other points (see Appendix 2:2). This information must be shared with the proposed trustee. The trustee will thereby be able to make an informed appraisal of the situation, and satisfy itself both as to the factual background, and to the settlor's intentions and motivation in relation to the planning.

A thorough trustee will ask searching and probing questions on these issues. If it is not satisfied, it must decline the business. All normal trustees will be very careful with their reputation, and should also have a sensitivity to the plight of creditors. The trustee should not accept trusteeship of a CPT on the basis of possible resignation later: this may be difficult, as once the trust becomes enmeshed in litigation, it may be impossible to find a willing successor trustee.

Solvency

2.51   The other central issue is the settlor's solvency at the time of the transfer. This is another key aspect of the trustee's appraisal. To ensure that the transfer into trust cannot be impugned, the settlor must neither be insolvent at the time of transfer, nor rendered insolvent by the transfer. In order to substantiate this, the settlor should arrange with his accountant to provide a 'certificate of solvency'.

As an alternative, or in addition to the certificate of solvency, where the adviser provides certified copies of affidavits received from the client on his personal background, these should also depose as to his financial status, including a clear statement as to his solvency at the time.

The trustee might also consider establishing an internal policy that settlors may not put into trust more than a certain predetermined percentage of their net worth; around 50 per cent, or up to 66 per cent would be an acceptable working range.

US Treasury and tax filings

2.52   The settlor's accountant or tax attorney must also assume responsibility for initial and ongoing Treasury Reports, IRS tax filings and compliance. This will include all tax issues relating to creation of the trust, and creation of any non-US companies, and currency control transactions.

Relevant Treasury/IRS Forms include:

(*a*)   Form 1040, Schedule B, Part 111, to report foreign accounts and foreign trusts (annually);

(*b*)   Treasury Information Return – Form 3520 – creation or transfer to foreign trust (and see below);

(*c*)   Treasury Information Return – Form 3520A – annual return of foreign trust with US beneficiaries (and see below);

(*d*)   Treasury Form 90–22.1 – report of foreign bank/financial account;

(*e*)   Form 56 – notice concerning fiduciary relationship;

(*f*)   Form 709 – gift and generation-skipping tax return (for completed gifts);

(*g*)   Form 926, return by a transferor of property to a foreign corporation, foreign estate or trust, or foreign partnership (not applicable if the transfer is to a foreign grantor trust); and

(*h*)   W8/W9 Reporting.

As noted in 2.43, the foreign trust provisions in the *Small Business Job Protection Act 1996* give rise to a series of reporting requirements on the part of transferors and of US beneficiaries. The *Act* defines 'reportable event' as the creation of any foreign trust by a US person, and the transfer of any money or property direct or indirectly to such a foreign trust. Transferors are required within 90 days to file with the IRS details of the amount of money or other property transferred and the identity of its trustees and each of its beneficiaries. Failure to file will lead to a penalty equal to 35 per cent of the gross reportable amount, plus a further penalty of US$10,000 for each 30-day period during which the failure continues.

As regards US beneficiaries, the *Act* requires all such beneficiaries who receive a distribution after 20 August 1996 to report annually their total distributions, and to produce adequate information to determine the proper treatment of any such distribution exceeding US$10,000 per annum (failure to do so resulting in it being treated as income, and triggering the same penalties noted above). The *Act* also requires the offshore trust to appoint someone in the United States as its 'limited agent' for service of process upon the trustee.

Indemnity for costs

2.53   The trustee must consider taking a personal indemnity from the settlor for any and all legal costs incurred in the future in connection with the trust. Of course, in the event of the settlor's future bankruptcy, the indemnity will be of little use.

In addition, (and of greater value), the trust agreement must also indemnify the trustee out of the trust fund against all costs incurred in obtaining legal advice for the trust, and/or the trust being involved in litigation. For this indemnity to be of real value, the trust fund must be in the hands of the trustee and under its direct control. Assets held in the United States, or through sub-custodians elsewhere, are open to seizure in satisfaction of the US judgment, and be unavailable to satisfy the trustee's indemnity.

This may become a very real problem in practice, if the creditor or trustee in bankruptcy obtains injunctions in the offshore jurisdiction freezing the trust fund. The trustee may face having to make an application for an order lifting the injunction to the extent of allowing the trustee to have recourse to the trust fund in order to pay legal fees to defend the proceedings. If no order is forthcoming the trustees would have to use their personal (or corporate) assets. The relevant provisions in Cayman Islands and Bahamas law are referred to at 2.24 and 2.27 respectively.

Insurance cover

2.54   A possible refinement on the normal indemnity for costs etc. (see 2.53) involves the trustees purchasing insurance cover to indemnify them from the cost of defending such litigation as may subsequently be brought by persons wishing to set aside the trust. Upon the occurrence of the assured event, the monies payable under the policy would belong not to the settlor but to the trustees. The costs of such a policy might be fairly high, even assuming it is possible to get underwriters to quote on this type of risk. Indeed, a possible limit to the growth of offshore CPT planning may be the unavailability of affordable insurance cover against just this type of risk.

Checklist

2.55   The checklist, reproduced as Appendix 2:3 to this chapter, sets out in summary form the procedural safeguards referred to above.

Abuses of CPT planning, and ethical considerations

2.56   The undesirable side of offshore creditor protection planning is where litigation is actively contemplated or is under way at the time the Trust is established. The US courts have drawn a distinction between what they call 'bankruptcy planning' (which is generally acceptable), and actively hindering creditors (which is not) (*Oberst v Oberst 91 BR 97, Bankr L Rep 72 (1988)*).

This planning invariably depends for its success on a succession of changes of jurisdiction. Thus, as soon as the claimant/plaintiff has commenced proceedings in (say) the Cayman Islands, the debtor/settlor will arrange for the trustees in Cayman to be replaced by trustees in (say) the Cook Islands. This international 'pass-the-parcel' can continue virtually ad infinitum, with the jurisdiction of the trust being moved around the world every time the claimants get close to the assets.

This type of CPT is popular, and has been highly successful as new strategy for US litigation attorneys. After all, it increases pressure on the plaintiff creditor to accept a greatly reduced out-of-court settlement. In this context, the CPT becomes nothing more than a procedural aspect of purely US domestic litigation: a 'bargaining chip'.

However, as transfers in such circumstances invariably breach the fraudulent conveyance rules in the home jurisdiction, a trust is created which has an almost 100 per cent certainty of involving litigation. This is not one of the normal characteristics of offshore trusts, which are usually passive and always try to be non-controversial during their existence.

The concept of a controversial 'flight clause' was highlighted in a recent US case *Securities and Exchange Commission v Robert Brennan* (US Court of Appeals for the Second Circuit 26 Oct 2000) in which the trust provided for relocation of trust assets on the occurrence of 'an event of duress'. The trust had switched from its established location of Gibraltar to Mauritius and then onto Nevis after a 1995 judgment requiring the defendant to 'disgorge ill-gotten gains'. Attempts to recover the assets by the settlor's bankruptcy trustee in 1998 were unsuccessful when the High Court of Nevis dismissed the action due to the failure to state a claim under Nevis law. Moreover, the US Court ruled against repatriation of the trust assets as being a violation of an automatic stay under the Bankruptcy Code. However, the subsequent trial led to the defendant being found guilty in April 2001 of seven (out of 13) charges of bankruptcy fraud and money laundering.

Professional advisers in the US involved in implementation of such trusts must consider two aspects relating to their own liability. First, whether they might be held liable for their role in a transaction deemed to be a fraudulent conveyance: liability as a joint tortfeasor or as an aider and abettor would require proof of the adviser's intention, namely their knowing assistance or participation in the commission of a fraud. As it is nearly impossible to eliminate potential exposure to a lawsuit, the adviser should beware of actively encouraging clients to make a fraudulent conveyance.

Second, if the adviser is an attorney, he is bound by ethical rules, such as a *Rule 1.2(d)* of the American Bar Association *Model Rules of Professional Conduct*. Under these, attorneys are prohibited from assisting clients in conduct that the attorney knows is fraudulent. Violation of such ethical rules may lead to sanctions by a Bar Association. The attorney should practice due diligence as regards the client and his financial status, including independent verification and documentation thereof. Note that no amount of due diligence will ensure that an action against the attorney will not be brought if fraud is involved. (*South Carolina Bar Ethics Advisory Committee Opinion 84/02 [1984].*)

As regards fraud or crime generally, it is also worth noting the provisions of the *US Crime Control Act 1990*, which contains banking law enforcement provisions (the *Comprehensive Thrift and Bank Fraud Prosecution and Tax Payer Recovery Act*). These create criminal offences in relation to transferring or concealing assets deriving from failed banks or savings and loan institutions (including loans therefrom).

From an offshore (US) perspective, a CPT may be an effective litigation device, but in view of the US courts' continuing jurisdiction over the transferor, it may be realistic only to regard this type of CPT as fully 'effective' from an offshore perspective if the transferor is prepared to leave his country permanently, and go and live somewhere else. There is little point in having trustees make distributions to him if they will then have to be paid directly to his trustee in bankruptcy!

CPTs are only designed to protect against civil law risks. Unlike settlors of 'political risk' trusts, settlors of CPTs invariably remain living in the same place, and subject to the jurisdiction of their State and Federal courts. It is therefore open to those courts to order the settlor to re-transfer the assets, or give other instructions to the trustee in the offshore jurisdiction to ensure compliance with the order. Such an order may be backed up by contempt sanctions, daily fines or imprisonment.

It is not difficult to imagine a judge in the US simply determining that the transferor has acted outrageously, that the trust arrangement is a sham, and that the defendant had better get the assets sent back over to the US 'or else' (see 2.47). Nor may the existence of an 'anti-duress' clause cut much ice with the judge (see 2.43). Also note that a bankruptcy judge may exercise his discretion and *not* put the debtor into bankruptcy at a time when the debtor may have counted on the suspensive effects of the bankruptcy coming to his aid.

This type of planning has already given the offshore industry a bad name, at a time when 'offshore' is already, in some people's minds, a dirty word. It has only fees to offer the offshore world in the short term, and nothing but trouble in the medium term. The offshore world by its very nature attracts the Bad and the Ugly as well as the Good. But it is worth remembering that the onshore centres are the spawning grounds for most of the fraudulent and dirty money activities that end up offshore. There have been plenty of financial scandals in recent years involving the offshore scene: why invite more, through indifference or unpreparedness?

Regulations passed onshore tend to have a direct effect offshore (e.g., 'money laundering' rules). Offshore trustees must take great care over the types of CPT planning they accept. To do otherwise is to provoke or invite further legislative intervention in the onshore jurisdictions, which will inevitably adversely impact the offshore industry as a whole.

It may also not be too far-fetched to imagine claims by creditors being brought under the United States' *Racketeer Influenced Corrupt Organisations Act* (*RICO*), and upheld by sympathetic courts in the United States in respect of flagrant and abusive examples of CPT planning. Indeed, one US adviser has gone even further, and suggested that the mass-marketing of CPT arrangements via US attorneys working together with offshore trustees, with model documents and supporting literature, may constitute an offer of a 'security' and trigger the jurisdiction and registration requirements of the US Securities and Exchange Commission.

Recent trends

2.57   The 'Review of Financial Regulation in Anguilla, Bermuda, British Virgin Islands, Cayman Islands, Montserrat, and Turks & Caicos Islands' (known as 'The KPMG Report'), published in November 2000 criticised the use of flight clauses.

And, on 1 February 2001, the FATF published its *Report on Money Laundering Typologies 2000–2001*, also referred to as 'FATF-XII'. The Report deals in paras 19–30 with Trusts, other non-corporate vehicles and money laundering. Para 28 is worth quoting *in extenso:*

> 'In recent years, changes to the trust laws in many jurisdictions have helped to increase their attractiveness for concealing the identity of the persons involved in such legal arrangements and thus facilitating the work of money launderers and the perpetrators of other criminal activity. The trusts established using these new laws often bear little or no resemblance to the trusts formed in traditional common law contexts. Some jurisdictions now offer what are termed "asset protection trusts" that may permit the settlor to keep control over the trust assets by being named as the beneficiary of such an arrangement. Other jurisdictions have permitted trusts to be formed with what are known as "flee clauses". These provisions in the trust document provide for the automatic transfer of the trust to another jurisdiction if the trust becomes the subject of any sort of enquiry.'

The FATF Report goes on to propose possible counter-measures in Para 29, including recommendations to '*Regulate the form of trusts*' and goes on to note that:

'establishing norms in this area could mean imposing a standardised documentation requirement for trusts that could vary according to the types of trusts and might also include abolishing or banning certain types of particularly abusive forms of trust (i.e. the "blind" or "black hole" trusts, etc.) or certain harmful aspects such as "flee clauses" or the possibility for a settlor to retain control of assets (i.e., the asset protection trust).'

The suggestion of imposing a standardised documentation requirement for trusts would be almost laughable, were it not so seriously put. The abolition or banning of 'harmful aspects' such as 'flee clauses' indicates a misunderstanding of the purposes of such clauses; the Courts have recently started to intervene to cut down possible abuses. Abolishing or banning 'the possibility for a settlor to retain control of assets' through an asset protection trust is already so clearly circumscribed by both creditor protection legislation and rules of professional conduct as to require no further comment. (See *Grupo Torras v Sheikh Fahad Al Sabah*, Bahamas at 2.27 above, where the Judge interpreted the Bahamas' creditor protector legislation on the basis that the Bahamas legislature could not possibly have intended the Bahamas to become a refuge for persons trying to evade their lawful creditors, and accordingly granted a freeze order (a 'Mareva injunction') to prevent the flee clause from being acted on.)

Nevertheless, the degree of interest from the supranationals and regulators may lead to some form of preventative legislation in the near future.

Conclusions and caveats

2.58   Offshore creditor protection trusts are a popular and legitimate way of separating off part of an individual's total assets, and placing these in a financially safe haven away from possible attack. Effective creditor protection trusts do not depend on secrecy, nor are they necessarily designed to produce any tax savings.

It is possible, through careful planning, for a settlor to transfer assets to a CPT at a time when he is fully solvent, and when such transfer is not rendered invalid as a 'fraudulent conveyance', and is not made as part of a course of fraudulent behaviour.

The following 'caveats' must also be borne in mind.

1.   No jurisdiction protects a disposition where the settlor was not, in law, the owner of the property. 'Constructive trustee' issues will be raised, as well as possible criminal action.

2.   No jurisdiction prevents a transfer from being set aside on the basis that it was established under mistake, duress, misrepresentation or undue influence.

3.   Few jurisdictions limit a creditor's ability to enforce his judgment(s) obtained elsewhere under reciprocal enforcement statutes.

4. Nearly all jurisdictions prohibit self-settlements 'until bankruptcy' and thereupon the purported alienation to third parties.

5. Nearly all jurisdictions recognise the 'universality' of powers of a trustee-in-bankruptcy as being the settlor's personal representative, and being able to exercise all his personal powers, including waiver of secrecy laws or professional privilege, and thus entitled to all records and documentation.

Trustees and others involved in CPT planning must take great care, as it is still not proven CPT planning is effective, in the sense of being immune from successful attack by creditors. For this reason, it is best to err on the side of caution and conservatism, and only accept CPTs where it is reasonably certain that all necessary safeguards are in place.

The safeguards outlined in this chapter may assist trustees in selecting trusteeships of CPTs which will effectively shelter the assets placed in trust from creditor risk, and at the same time prevent the trustees themselves from being drawn into time-consuming litigation.

Appendix 2:1

Anti-duress provision

'Notwithstanding any other provision of this Settlement, the Trustee may ignore any advice instructions and/or commands to act by the Settlor or the Protector or any beneficiary (even if any such individual has the power and authority pursuant to this Settlement to give such advice, instructions and/or command the Trustee to so act) if such advice, instructions and/or commands to act are given under compulsion, including but not limited to any such advice instructions, and/or commands to act given pursuant to an order directive, or otherwise, of a court of any other government or government-related organisation or entity, or a court officer or any other government official from any jurisdiction. In addition, notwithstanding any other provision of this Settlement, the Trustee may ignore a decision to discharge or replace such Trustee if such a decision is made under compulsion including but not limited to decisions made pursuant to an order, directive or otherwise, of a court of any other government or government-related organisation or entity, or a court officer or any other government official from any jurisdiction.'

Appendix 2:2

Affidavit

The settlor should represent, state and affirm:

1. that the settlor has no pending or threatened claims;

2. that the settlor is not presently under any investigation of any nature, and that the settlor is not involved in any administrative proceedings;

3. that no situation has occurred which the settlor has reason to believe will develop into a legal problem in the future;

4. that following any subsequent transfers to the CPT, the settlor intends to remain solvent, and able to pay his reasonably anticipated debts as they become due;

5. none of the assets which the settlor may transfer was derived from or relate to any of the activities specified in the *Money Laundering Control Act* of 1986.

Furthermore, to the extent that a legal dispute or other problem presently exists, it should be disclosed in the affidavit, which should provide that either sufficient assets have been retained with which to satisfy the problem, or the settlement should be drafted with a provision requiring the trustees to satisfy out of the CPT's assets any liability which may result from the disclosed problems.

Appendix 2:3

Checklist

1. Minimise the risk of litigation by appropriate planning and proper legal advice.

2. Onshore and offshore counsel to review the trust agreement.

3. Ensure that assets to be settled into the CPT do not represent a majority of the settlor's net worth. The trustee may apply a percentage criterion (say 50 per cent to 66 per cent) as a policy.

4. Obtain affidavit as to settlor's intent in undertaking the planning (see Appendix 2:2).

5. Obtain certificate of solvency (and/or affidavit to same effect).

6. Transfer the assets to the offshore jurisdiction, where they are under the control of the trustee.

7. If an underlying company is to be formed to hold the assets, ensure trustees also provide directors for the underlying company, to ensure the trustee has full control over all of the trust assets.

8. Do not accept underlying assets located in the United States.

9. Ensure trust agreement contains adequate indemnities for legal costs in favour of the Trustee, supported by assets over which the trustee has direct control. Consider insuring this risk.

10. Ensure trustee is satisfied as to the continuing good reputation of the settlor: also that settlor will maintain good business practice as regards those assets not transferred to the trust.

3 Buying and Selling Residential Property in France

Eamonn McGregor FCCA ATII
(Moores Rowland, Monaco)

Introduction

3.1 France is a very attractive country and many foreigners decide to buy a house or apartment there either as their permanent home or as a secondary residence.

Advisability of obtaining local professional advice

3.2 In France, notaries, who are semi-governmental officials, have a monopoly in conveyancing matters. Many people are under the impression that a purchase of property must be handled by a notary in the locality of the residence. This is not correct. Any notary in France can handle the purchase or sale of real property anywhere in France. In the case of foreigners who do not speak French it is usually advisable to consult a notary who has a knowledge of English, or of the purchaser's own language, most of whom are to be found in Paris. The vendor will often endeavour to persuade the purchaser to employ the vendor's own notary. While this is perfectly legitimate, it is felt that, as in England, it is generally preferable for the purchaser to be represented by his own notary. This does not cost the purchaser anything because, if the purchaser uses a notary of his own choice, the seller's notary must share his scale fee, which is always payable by the purchaser, with the purchaser's notary.

3.3 In addition to consulting a French notary of his own choice, the purchaser is normally well advised also to consult a local lawyer who is familiar not only with French conveyancing but who also understands the purchaser's tax situation and powers of testamentary disposition in his own country. This is something with which the average French notary is unfamiliar.

Expenses of purchase

Registration and similar taxes

3.4 The normal taxes payable on the purchase of residential real estate in France are as follows:

(*a*)	departmental registration tax:	3.6%
(*b*)	local tax:	1.2%
(*c*)	supplementary tax of 2.5% based on the amount of the departmental registration tax:	0.09%
(*d*)	tax on the registration of deeds:	0.1%
		4.99%

New buildings: VAT

3.5   If the residence acquired is a new building then the sale is gener-ally subject to VAT at a rate of 19.6 per cent. The local tax is not payable but the departmental registration tax (*taxe de publicité foncière*) is reduced to 0.6 per cent, to which the supplementary tax of 2.5 per cent is applied, resulting in a total of 0.615 per cent which is chargeable on the purchase price excluding VAT. The sale of a new building is subject to VAT provided:

(*a*)   the sale takes place within five years from the date on which the build-ing was completed; and

(*b*)   the sale has not been preceded by another transfer for valuable consid-eration since the building was completed to a person not considered to be a *marchand de biens*, i.e., a person engaged in the business of buying and selling real property.

[*Code Générale des Impôts (CGI), Art 257–7*].

This VAT is normally included in the price quoted by the seller.

Building land acquired by individuals on or after 22 October 1998 in order to construct a dwelling is no longer subject to VAT but to registration duties at a rate of 4.99 per cent.

Notary's fees

3.6   Notary's fees are fixed by law according to a decreasing scale which, in the case of sale of real property starts at 5 per cent on sales of up to €3,050 and drops to 0.825 per cent on sales exceeding €16,770. VAT at 19.6 per cent is added to the notary's fees.

On a sale of €16,770, the notary's fee amounts to €429.20 increased by 0.825 per cent on any amount by which the sale price exceeds €16,770, plus VAT at 19.6 per cent.

Annual taxes

Taxe foncière or impôt foncier

3.7   This is an annual tax payable to the commune by the person who was the owner on 1 January of the tax year. The owner on 1 January is responsible for the whole tax for the year.

Taxe d'habitation (residence tax)

3.8   This is a tax on furnished property calculated on the rental value of the property. It is payable by the owner if he occupies the property. If let, the tax is payable by the tenant.

The matrimonial regime of the purchaser

3.9   The notary representing a purchaser who is married will always enquire as to his matrimonial regime.

In France there are basically two matrimonial regimes, namely: the regime of separate property and the regime of community property. If parties domiciled in France marry in France without concluding a marriage contract drawn up by a notary before the marriage, the matrimonial regime applicable will be the regime of community property. This basically means that all property of both the husband and the wife acquired since the date of the marriage is community property. In most common law countries there is no matrimonial regime as such. When, for example, persons resident in England marry, there is no special regime and each party retains his own property so that the position is analogous to the French regime of separate property.

However, if the parties, wherever they may be resident, marry in England, for example, but intend to take up residence immediately after the marriage in some civil law country such as France, it may well be that the matrimonial regime is that applicable according to the law of France which, in the absence of a prior marriage contract, brings about the automatic application of the community property regime.

Obligation to disclose the full purchase price in deed of purchase

3.10   In France the seller often tries to persuade the purchaser to economise on the purchase expenses by not declaring the full purchase price in the purchase deed. They are not trying to reduce their own legal expenses as, in France, these are all paid by the purchaser. What they are normally trying to do is to reduce their own liability to capital gains tax and place this potential burden on the shoulders of the purchaser.

Any such suggestion is something that should be resisted. In the first place it will decrease the purchaser's base price and thus give rise to higher capital gains tax when the purchaser resells the property.

Furthermore under-declaration of the purchase price is liable to criminal sanctions. In addition, the secret agreement is void and interest and a 50 per cent penalty are charged on the underpaid registration taxes.

Forced heirship rules

3.11   It is important to realise that any real property situated in France devolves on death according to the French rules of forced heirship, irrespective of the country of residence or domicile of the owner.

Under the provisions of the French *Civil Code* (which are similar to those in many other civil law countries), reserved rights exist in favour of ascendants and descendants on the death of a child or parent as the case may be. This chapter only deals with the reserved rights of children, which is by far the more common.

One child is entitled to one-half of the property of the deceased, two children are entitled, in equal shares, to two-thirds of the property and three or more children are entitled, in equal shares, to three-quarters of the property.

The part of the estate not covered by the forced heirship rules (*quotité disponible*) may be disposed of as the individual pleases, for example, by will (see 3.17).

3.12   Where the deceased dies with a legal domicile (i.e., civil domicile) outside France, the French rules of forced heirship rights will only apply to any real property in France. Where the legal domicile on death is French, then the forced heirship rules apply to the worldwide property of the deceased with the exception of any real property situated outside France, the devolution of which will be determined in accordance with the laws of the country in which the real property is situate: the *lex situs*. Legal domicile is defined in *Article 102* of the French *Civil Code* broadly as follows: 'The domicile of any Frenchman, as regards the exercise of his civil rights, is at the place where he has his principal establishment'.

According to a judgment of the Cour de Cassation – the highest French Court (*Cassation civile I*, 20 December 1995; JCP 56.II.9173):

> 'A foreigner is deemed to be domiciled in France if he maintains there an effective residence of a stable and permanent character which coincides with the centre of his family ties and business activities'.

3.13   However, the situation is not as restrictive as it might appear.

First, children may renounce their reserved rights but only as from the date of death of their parent.

Secondly, the surviving spouse, who was not really protected by the law until now, will see her rights increased from the 1 July 2002, for example:

(*a*)   in the presence of descendants of the deceased, the surviving spouse will have the choice between a life interest in the whole of the estate, or one-quarter absolutely;

(*b*)   in the presence of descendants of the deceased, from a previous marriage, the surviving spouse will receive one-quarter absolutely;

(*c*)   in the absence of any descendants or ascendants of the deceased, the surviving spouse will inherit the whole of the estate.

In whose name should the property be bought?

3.14   In most cases, the best arrangement is for the purchaser to buy in his own name or, if he is married, in the joint names of himself and his spouse. This is the simplest and cheapest arrangement, and if the owner or owners are resident in France and this is their principal place of residence, there will be no capital gains tax to pay when the property is finally sold.

3.15   According to *The Hague Convention* of 1978, it is possible to change one's matrimonial regime in respect of real estate situated in another country. Therefore, non-residents of France could opt for the *Community Property Regime* existing in France.

This seems the best way when the principal aim is the protection of the surviving spouse. On the death of the first spouse, all real estate will belong absolutely to the surviving spouse and the heirs of the predeceased spouse will not be able to claim any rights. Furthermore, at this stage, no inheritance tax is due.

A change of matrimonial regime has to be made before a public notary. It should be noted that an election for this regime cannot be made if there are children from a previous marriage.

3.16   In certain cases it may be advisable for residential property to be bought in the name of some kind of French company. This subject is dealt with at 3.46–3.47.

Advisability of making a French will

3.17   Although French real property may be disposed of by a will made in a foreign country and in a foreign language, this is inconvenient in practice; it involves substantial expense, and may give rise to a claim or claims for French succession duties which could otherwise be avoided.

It is much more convenient to make a will in the French language and in one of the French forms dealing exclusively with real property, or preferably all property, of the testator located in France. French wills are normally very short and simple.

3.18   In France the concept of personal representatives of a deceased person does not exist. On death, the deceased's property passes directly to his heirs or beneficiaries. Trusts are unknown in French law and even when an executor is appointed (which only rarely happens when the testator is French) the deceased's property does not vest in the executor. Any attempt to achieve this is ineffective and may result in a claim for succession duties at the rate of 60 per cent applicable to a stranger in blood.

3.19   Similarly, care must be taken not to include in a will relating to real or personal property in France any bequest or legacy to strangers in blood or remote relatives or, if the will covers not only property in France but also property outside France, any disposition which the French tax authorities may consider does amount to a bequest or legacy of property in France. A common instance of this arises where there is a residuary legacy or bequest.

The date and place of death, and the names of the deceased's heirs (or beneficiaries) are recorded in a deed known as an *acte de notoriété* drawn up by a notary.

If the deceased left a will, which in the case of French nationals is the exception rather than the rule, the *acte de notoriété* will either summarise the effects of the will or will have a copy of the will, or in the case of a foreign will a sworn French translation, annexed.

3.20   Where a testator has made a will dealing with real property in France which contains provisions that are not in accordance with French law, then before making his *acte de notoriété*, a French notary will usually require a *certificat de coutume* (corresponding to a certificate of law) to be drawn up by a lawyer familiar with the provisions of French law and the system of law which the testator intended to apply. This *certificat de coutume* will state the lawyer's opinion as to the correct devolution of the deceased's real property in France taking into account the mandatory provisions of French law and any conflict between such law and the provisions which the testator intended to apply.

Income tax

3.21   The French notion of fiscal domicile is very wide [*CGI, Article 4B*] and a person is now considered as being fiscally domiciled in France if any one of the four following conditions are fulfilled:

(*a*)   he has his *foyer* (home or household) in France, or

(*b*)   he has his principal place of residence in France, or

(*c*)   he carries on a business or professional activity in France, whether salaried or not, unless he can show that the activity is incidental to another activity carried on outside of France, or (*d*)   he has the centre of his economic interests in France.

If a person is fiscally domiciled in France this governs his situation as regards income tax, tax on capital gains, gift taxes, succession duties on death and the French wealth tax, *Impôt de Solidarité sur la Fortune* (ISF).

3.22   If he is fiscally domiciled in France then he will become liable to all the taxes mentioned above on his worldwide property, subject to the provisions of any applicable tax treaties. If the person concerned does not fall within the definition of fiscal domicile, the general rule is that he will be subject to French income tax on a notional income equal to three times the annual market rental value of any property in France which he may own, lease or have at his disposition. [*CGI, Art 164C*]. However, this particular provision does not apply to individuals resident in a country which has concluded a comprehensive double taxation treaty with France and such persons will not be subject to French income tax on a notional French income.

Tax on capital gains

3.23   The taxation of capital gains derived from real estate varies depending on whether the gain is realised by an individual or by a company subject to corporation tax (*impôt sur les sociétés*) and whether the gain is of a short-term or long-term nature. Gains realised within a period of less than two years are generally treated as short-term gains and taxed as normal income. The profits of companies not subject to corporation tax are taxed at the shareholder level.

Individuals

3.24   The regime applicable to individuals is generally more favourable than that applicable to companies.

Gains realised by individuals fiscally domiciled in France are added to their annual income and subject to income tax at normal rates. Where the gain realised is a long-term gain there are provisions for top slicing relief. Gains realised by non-residents in respect of occasional profits are subject to a withholding tax at the rate of 33⅓ per cent. [*CGI, Art 244 Bis A*]. This represents a final tax. Indexation of acquisition costs is granted provided the property has been owned for at least two years. In addition, for each year of ownership beyond the second year a deduction equal to 5 per cent of the gain is granted. Consequently, after 22 years of ownership there is a total exemption from tax. Other deductions allowed include 10 per cent of the acquisition cost, costs of improvements and repairs, interest on certain loans contracted for acquisition or improvements and tax advisory fees.

3.25   If the gains realised are considered to be business profits and they are not realised through a French permanent establishment, then a withholding tax of 50 per cent is levied on the net profit. [*CGI, Art 244 Bis*]. This provision would cover, for example, a dealer in real estate. Again, the withholding represents a final tax. However, if the vendor is a resident of a country which has signed a double taxation treaty with France then generally he would not be subject to this withholding.

3.26   There is an exemption for the sale of a principal private residence which is defined as either:

(*a*)   a property which has constituted the habitual residence of the owner since its acquisition, completion or during a period of at least five years; or

(*b*)   a property which constitutes the residence in France of French nationals resident abroad to the extent of one residence provided that the French national must have been fiscally domiciled in France for a continuous period of at least one year at some time prior to the disposal of the property and had free use of the property since its acquisition, completion of construction or during a period of at least three years. [*CGI, Art 150 C 1*].

3.27   There is also an exemption for the first sale after 1 January 1982 of a secondary residence where the owner or his spouse are not the owner of their principal private residence and the sale takes place at least five years after acquisition or completion of construction provided, however, that in the event of a sale by a non-resident, in order to benefit from the exemption the non-resident must have been fiscally resident in France for a continuous period of at least one year at some time prior to the sale. [*CGI, Art 150 C II*].

3.28   Taxpayers whose net real estate assets do not exceed FF400,000 (increased by FF100,000 per child from the third child onwards) are exempt from tax on any gain derived from the sale of real estate. [*CGI, Art 150 B*].

3.29   Any gains realised by a non-resident on the sale of movable property contained in a residence are generally exempt from tax. However, the sale of works of art and antiques are subject to a tax of 4.5 per cent based on the sales price when the price exceeds €3,050. [*CGI, Art 150V Bis*].

Companies

3.30   The withholding taxes of 33⅓ per cent and 50 per cent which apply to non-resident individuals also apply to non-resident companies. However, these withholding taxes do not represent a final tax for companies but may be used as a credit against any corporation tax finally due. The calculation of the capital gain subject to withholding tax for companies is less favourable than that for individuals. The gain is determined by taking the difference between the sales proceeds and the acquisition cost as reduced by 2 per cent for each complete year of ownership.

3.31   Gains are treated as normal income and currently taxed at the standard rate of 33⅓ per cent plus surcharges. If a deduction for depreciation has already been taken then the amount of this deduction is included in the gain. In calculating the gain no allowance is made for the effects of inflation and there is no annual 5 per cent deduction as there is for individuals.

3.32   There is also a provision in the tax code whereby profits, which term includes gains, realised in France by foreign companies are deemed to be distributed. [*CGI, Art 115 quinquies*]. In the absence of a double taxation treaty the deemed distributed profits are subject to a withholding tax of 25 per cent. EU residents are exempt from this tax provided they are subject to tax without the possibility of an option or of being exempt.

Shares in real estate companies

3.33   Gains derived from the sale of shares in real estate companies are taxed according to the same regime as gains derived from the sale of real estate. A real estate company is one whose assets are principally invested in real estate which is not used for business purposes.

Tax representative

3.34   If the vendor of the French real estate is a non-resident then he is obliged to appoint a French resident as his tax agent. The liability of the representative extends to the 33⅓ per cent withholding tax and the annual 3 per cent tax, which is discussed further at 3.44–3.45.

Succession duties

3.35   In cases where a deceased person was not fiscally domiciled in France at the date of death, then only those assets, both real and personal, situate in France will be subject to French succession duties unless the beneficiary is fiscally domiciled in France, in which case duty will also apply to assets situate outside France.

The definition of situate in France has been extended by the *Finance Act 1999*. Where an individual either alone or together with his spouse, their ascendants, descendants, brothers or sisters controls a foreign structure that owns real estate in France then that individual will be deemed to be the owner of the real estate.

Where the deceased is fiscally domiciled in France at the date of death then, subject to the provisions of any applicable tax treaty, succession duties are chargeable on the worldwide estate.

3.36   In some cases, a doubt can exist as to whether the fiscal domicile was in France or some other country. It is then necessary to look at the provisions of any death duty treaty between the two countries concerned as such treaties normally contain provisions as to what happens if a deceased person is deemed to be resident in both countries. France has concluded death duty treaties with 37 countries. In the case of the UK, the question of fiscal domicile is determined as follows.

(*a*)   Where did the deceased have his permanent home?

(*b*)   Where a permanent home was available in both countries, then in which country were his personal and economic relations the closest?

(*c*)   If this question cannot be determined, then where did the deceased have his habitual abode?

(*d*)   Where a habitual abode existed in both countries, then in which of the countries was the deceased a national?

(*e*)   If the deceased was a national of both countries, or neither of them, then the authorities of both countries shall determine the question of domicile by mutual agreement.

The purpose of such treaties is to make sure that death duties are not levied on the same asset in both countries or, if they are, that the duty paid in one country is deductible from the duty paid in the other country.

This question is, of course, of prime importance where, for example, property passing to a surviving spouse is exempt from death duty in one country whereas in the other country it is not.

3.37   French succession duties are not chargeable on the estate as a whole but on the amount of the share of each beneficiary at rates depending upon the relationship of the beneficiary to the deceased. This is the case in most countries in Continental Europe and Latin America.

In the case of a surviving spouse there is an exemption from duty on the first €76,000 and in the case of direct descendants (on the share of living children or representatives of deceased children) or ascendants €46,000.

Thereafter the excess over €76,000 or €46,000 of each share will be taxed as follows.

(i)   *Surviving spouse*

Up to	€7,600	5%
Between	€7,600 and €15,000	10%
Between	€15,000 and €30,000	15%
Between	€30,000 and €520,000	20%
Between	€520,000 and €850,000	30%
Between	€850,000 and €1,700,000	35%
Over	€1,700,000	40%

(ii)   *Ascendants and descendants*

Up to	€7,600	5%
Between	€7,600 and €11,400	10%
Between	€11,400 and €15,000	15%
Between	€15,000 and €520,000	20%
Between	€520,000 and €850,000	30%
Between	€850,000 and €1,700,000	35%
Over	€1,700,000	40%

Subject to certain conditions a brother or sister is entitled to an exemption of €15,000. In all other cases there is an exemption of only €1,500 for each beneficiary.

(iii)   *Brothers and sisters*

Up to	€23,000	35%
Over	€23,000	45%

(iv)   *Relations up to the fourth degree*   55%

(v)   *All other relations and strangers in blood*   60%

Thus, whereas in most Anglo-Saxon countries, a legacy to a friend or employee will not be penalised, the same legacy in France will attract duty at the rate of 60 per cent on the excess over €1,500.

3.38   If a loan was obtained to purchase real property in France then the amount of the loan, if bona fide, is considered as a debt which can be set off against the value of the property. Ideally, the loan should be secured on the property itself. Succession duties must be paid within six months where the death occurs in France and within twelve months if the death occurs abroad and non-payment within these periods involves a penalty.

Wealth tax

3.39   After an absence of three years, wealth tax was reintroduced by the Rocard Government with effect from 1 January 1989.

It is very similar to the wealth tax that was in force during the period 1982 to 1986. The principal differences are the higher threshold, lower rates of tax, the definition of shares for the business assets exclusion and the linking of wealth tax to income tax.

Taxable persons/taxable base

3.40   Wealth tax applies to individuals fiscally domiciled in France on their worldwide assets and to non-resident individuals on assets situated in

France subject to the provisions of double taxation agreements. Consequently, French *situs* real estate (including the extended definition in 3.35) as well as shares in real estate companies (as previously defined in 3.33) fall within the scope of the tax. An individual is taxable on the assets of his spouse or cohabitant and minor children. The tax is assessed on a net asset basis so that debts subject to certain conditions may be deducted. The tax is assessed on the value of assets held on 1 January in each year.

Rates and payment of tax

Net wealth (€)		%
Not exceeding	720,000	0
Between	720,000 and 1,160,000	0.55
Between	1,160,000 and 2,300,000	0.75
Between	2,300,000 and 3,600,000	1.00
Between	3,600,000 and 6,900,000	1.30
Between	6,900,000 and 15,000,000	1.65
Over	15,000,000	1.80

For individuals fiscally domiciled in France the total of wealth tax and income tax may not exceed 85 per cent of total income.

Individuals with net wealth in excess of €720,000 are obliged to file a return and pay the tax due by 15 June of each year.

Valuation

3.41   The basis of valuation is the market value of assets on 1 January in each year.

As far as real estate is concerned the method of valuation most favoured by the French tax authorities is the method known as *evaluation par comparaison*. This method seeks to evaluate a particular residence by looking at recent sales of similar residences in the same geographical sector. As far as furniture contained in a residence is concerned (with the exception of antiques, works of art and collections which are excluded) this may be valued at 5 per cent of the value of the residence. The taxpayer may, if he so wishes, elect to value furniture on an item by item basis and file an inventory with the tax authorities.

Double taxation treaties

3.42   France has concluded treaties covering wealth tax with the following countries:

Argentina	Malta
Austria	Mauritius
Bahrain	Mongolia
Bolivia	Namibia
Canada	Netherlands
Cyprus	Norway
Czechoslovakia	Poland
Denmark	Qatar
Egypt	Romania
Finland	Russia
Germany	Saudi Arabia
Hungary	South Africa
India	Spain
Indonesia	Sweden
Israel	Switzerland
Italy	UAE
Ivory Coast	Ukraine
Kazakhstan	United States
Kuwait	Vietnam
Luxembourg	Zimbabwe

Generally these treaties give France the right to tax non-residents on real estate situated in France, leaving the right to tax movable property situated in France to the other treaty partner.

In certain treaties France is given the right to tax shares in foreign companies whose principal assets are comprised of French real estate and movable property located in French real estate.

Substantial participations (25 per cent) in French companies may also give France the right to tax, as in, for example, the treaties with Norway and Sweden.

3.43   The United States treaty calls for particular comment in that US citizens taking up residence in France are exempt from the wealth tax on non-French *situs* assets for the five years following the year in which they acquire their French residence status.

The annual 3 per cent tax [CGI, Articles 990D–990H]

3.44   The 3 per cent tax applies to companies both French and foreign which directly or indirectly own real estate situated in France. The tax covers the situation where French real estate is held through a chain of companies. The tax is levied on the gross value of the real estate held on 1 January in each year. The tax accompanied by a declaration must be paid by 15 May each year. The tax may be described broadly as a tax on passive investment by companies in French real estate.

3.45   There are six exemptions from the tax.

(*a*)   Companies whose French real estate represents less than 50 per cent of their total French assets. Note that French real estate used for business purposes, with the exception of real estate used in a real estate business, such as a property developer or dealer, is not included in the definition of French real estate. However, the stock in trade of a property dealer or developer is not actually subject to the 3 per cent tax.

(*b*)   Companies whose place of effective management is situated in a country which has signed a double taxation treaty with France which includes an administrative assistance clause for the purposes of preventing tax fraud and evasion, provided that they file a return each year by 15 May which discloses details of the real estate held and the identity, address and number of shares held by each shareholder. The French tax authorities have released a list of qualifying countries (see Appendix 3:1).

(*c*)   Companies which have their place of effective management in France and other companies which by virtue of a treaty must not be subject to a more burdensome taxation, provided they notify each year or alternatively undertake to notify at the tax authorities request details of the real estate held and the identity, address and number of shares held by each shareholder and furnish proof of their fiscal residence. The French tax authorities have released a list of qualifying countries (see Appendix 3:2).

(*d*)   Companies whose shares are quoted on the French stock exchange (*cote officielle* or *second marché*) or on a similarly-regulated foreign stock exchange.

(*e*)   International organisations, sovereign states and public institutions.

(*f*)   Pension funds and charitable institutions provided that they can establish that their activities justify the ownership of French real estate.

Investment through a Société Civile Immobilière

3.46   In certain circumstances it may be advantageous to hold French real property through a *Société Civile Immobilière* (SCI). An SCI which may loosely be described as a 'real estate partnership' has a separate legal identity and the partners have unlimited liability. It is sometimes a suitable vehicle for investment in French residential property provided the property is not to be let furnished, its partners are individuals and the SCI does not become involved in any other industrial or commercial activity. Subject to the foregoing conditions, it is transparent for income tax and corporation tax in that profits and gains are taxed at the shareholder or partner level.

3.47   Its advantages may be listed as follows.

(*a*)   The favourable tax regime applicable to capital gains realised by individuals still applies as any capital gains realised by the SCI are taxed at the shareholder level.

(*b*)   The use of an SCI avoids the French forced heirship rules which apply to the devolution of real estate in France even if owned by foreigners, as shares in an SCI are regarded as movable and not immovable property.

(*c*)   In the event of ownership by several parties it provides greater flexibility if one party should wish to sell his share.

Renting out the property

3.48   If the property is rented out then any profit derived from the letting will be subject either to income tax at a minimum rate of 25 per cent in the case of a non-resident individual, or corporation tax at a rate of $33\frac{1}{3}$ per cent plus surcharges in the case of a company. *Inter alia*, interest on borrowings is allowed as a deduction against rental income. However, depending on the particular facts, restrictions on the quantum of interest deducted may arise. For income tax purposes where the total annual rental income does not exceed €15,000, the provisions for filing and calculation of the tax are simplified.

3.49   A foreign company, which owns furnished residential property in France and which allows a third party to stay in the property rent-free, may, following French case law, have income imputed to it on the basis of the annual market rental value of the property. This income is in turn deemed distributed to the shareholders of the company and subject to a withholding tax of 25 per cent or such lower rate as provided by any applicable double taxation treaty. (See also the exemption for EU residents in 3.32.)

Sociétés immobilières de copropriété

3.50   Unlike *Sociétés Civiles Immobilières*, which are only transparent for the purposes of income tax and corporation tax, *Sociétés immobilières de copropriété* (co-owned real estate companies) are truly transparent for all forms of tax including registration duty in particular.

3.51   A company, irrespective of its form, qualifies as a *Société immobilière de copropriété* if it has as its sole object one of the following activities. [*CGI, Art 1655 TER*].

(*a*)   The construction or acquisition of buildings with a view to dividing the building into separate parts for the use of each shareholder, e.g., a block of flats.

(*b*)   The management of such divided buildings.

(*c*)   The rental of such buildings for the benefit of the shareholders.

One of the disadvantages of these companies is that a sale of shares is treated as a sale of the underlying asset so that the lower rate of registration duty applicable to the sale of shares (4.8 per cent) does not apply.

Appendix 3:1

Countries with which France has signed a double taxation treaty which includes an administrative assistance clause for the purposes of preventing tax fraud and evasion:

Algeria	Malawi
Argentina	Malaysia
Australia	Mali
Austria	Malta
Bangladesh	Mauritania
Belgium	Mauritius
Benin	Mayotte
Brazil	Monaco
Bulgaria	Morocco
Burkina-Faso	Mexico
Cameroon	Netherlands
Canada	New Caledonia
Central African Republic	New Zealand
China	Niger
Comoro Islands	Nigeria
Congo	Norway
Cyprus	Pakistan
Czech Republic	Philippines
Denmark	Poland
Egypt	Portugal
Ecuador	Romania
Finland	Senegal
Gabon	Singapore
Germany	Slovakia
Greece	South Korea
Hungary	Spain
Iceland	Sri Lanka
Indonesia	St Pierre & Miquelon
Iran	Sweden
Ireland	Thailand
Israel	Togo
Italy	Trinidad & Tobago
Ivory Coast	Tunisia
Japan	Turkey
Jordan	United Kingdom
Kuwait	United States
Lebanon	Yugoslavia
Luxembourg	Zambia
Madagascar	

(List issue by the French authorities, 1 October 1993.)

Appendix 3:2

Countries with which France has signed a treaty comprising a qualifying non-discrimination clause:

Argentina	Lebanon
Austria	Madagascar
Bangladesh	Malawi
Brazil	Malta
Bulgaria	Morocco
China	Mauritius
Congo	Netherlands
Cyprus	Nigeria
Czech Republic	Norway
Egypt	Poland
Ecuador	Portugal
Finland	Romania
Germany	Slovakia
Greece	South Korea
Hungary	Spain
Iceland	Sri Lanka
Iran	Switzerland
Ireland	Thailand
Israel	Trinidad & Tobago
Italy	United Kingdom
Japan	Yugoslavia
Jordan	Zambia

(List issued by French tax authorities, 1 October 1993.)

4 Buying and Selling Residential Property in Spain

Anne McMahon BA Hons
(Senior Solicitor) (Wilde Sapte) in conjunction with lawyers from Estudio Legal of Madrid and Barcelona

Material enlarged and updated by José María Gómez Tabernero de Paz (Ldo. en Derecho, U. Salamanca; LLM, Collège d'Europe, Bruges; Notary candidate)

Background information

General

4.1 Many restrictions which previously governed foreign investment have been progressively liberalised as Spain adapts its law to the European Community Directives concerning the movement of capital and right of establishment. As a result, the acquisition and disposal of property in Spain by non-residents has become a more straightforward procedure.

Nonetheless, a British purchaser of Spanish property should acquaint himself with the basic concepts of property purchase and the likely tax implications and proceed with the same caution as when buying property in England. A totally different system of law, as well as language, is involved, therefore, as in England, proper legal advice is highly advisable.

It should be noted that the national legislation referred to might have been modified by particular legislation passed by the relevant autonomous community. The references to such national law are therefore a starting point, rather than a definitive reference.

Ownership

Ownership, co-ownership, horizontal property, complejos inmobiliarios/ urbanizaciones privadas and time-sharing

4.2 Ownership is defined by *Article 348* of the *Spanish Civil Code* (the CC) as the right to enjoy and dispose of a thing without further limitation than that provided by law. The owner has the right to take action against the holder or possessor of the thing in order to recover it. According to *Article 350* of the CC, the owner of land owns its surface and that which lies underneath it and may undertake any construction, sowing and excavations he deems fit, taking into account any possible easements existing over the property.

Ownership may be the subject of individual or co-ownership. *Article 392* of the *CC* establishes that co-ownership exists if a thing or right belongs *pro indiviso* (on an undivided basis) to several persons.

Spanish law also recognises so-called 'horizontal ownership', which may be defined as ownership of a complex or special nature, resulting from the sum of private and common ownership elements existing in the same building. Currently, this form of ownership is regulated by the *Ley Sobre Propiedad Horizontal* (Law of Horizontal Ownership) of 21 July 1960 (the *LPH*) (some aspects of this law have been recently amended by the *Law* of 6 April 1999). Apartments, flats and business premises are examples of such property.

The *casas adosadas* (houses linked by common walls) are examples of so-called *complejos inmobiliarios* (real estate groups). The object of the complex consists of:

(*a*)   several architectural units;

(*b*)   is likely to belong to different owners; and

(*c*)   are linked to one another by common elements which are attached *ob rem* to every single private property.

Up until 1999, there existed no legal regime concerning these *complejos* and their legal articulation had been provided by notarial practice. In order to fill this normative gap, the aforementioned *Law* of 6 April 1999 introduced *Article 24* in the *LPH*. In accordance with *Article 24*, the *complejos inmobiliarios* will be subject to the regime of the *LPH* if they fulfil the following requirements:

(i)   they must be integrated by two or more independent plots or buildings mainly aimed at housing or business premises; and

(ii)   the owners of these properties ought to participate *pro indiviso* over common elements such as services, roads, installations and equipment.

They can be legally shaped both under a single *comunidad de propietarios* (community of owners) or an *agrupación de comunidades de propietarios* (grouping of communities of owners), following the details provided by the *LPH*.

However, it must be borne in mind that the regime of *Article 24* is not compulsory. The *LPH* will be applicable on a subsidiary basis in the absence of relevant agreements entered into by the owners to regulate their interests.

Time-sharing schemes are also specifically recognised by Spanish Law through *Law 42/1998* of 15 December on *Aprovechamiento por turno de bienes inmuebles* (instrument of implementation of *Directive 94/47/CE* of the Parliament and the Council of 26 October 1994). The minimum time period of the regime is three years and the maximum 50. Execution of *escritura pública* (public deed) before a Notary and registration in the *Registro de la*

Propiedad (Land Registry) is required for the valid constitution of the regime. Following the prescriptions of the *Directive*, the Law of 15 December 1998 grants the consumer a unilateral desisting right during the following ten days after the contract has been concluded.

Property leases

4.3   Spanish property law distinguishes between rural and urban property leases. With regard to urban property, the applicable law is the *Law* of 24 November 1994 on *Arrendamientos urbanos* (urban leases). Although the general rule is that the parties are free to negotiate the terms of leases, the new legislation introduces various new requirements which apply depending on whether the lease is for residential or business purposes.

The most significant requirements on urban residential leases are as follows:

(*a*)   The term of the lease can be freely negotiated, subject to a minimum term of five years. Should the term be for a shorter period, then it must be renewed annually for five years unless the lessee gives notice not to renew;

(*b*)   Rent may be adjusted annually in line with the Retail Price Index;

(*c*)   In the event of death of the lessee, the partner of the lessee may be sub-rogated to the rights of the lessee if the couple have lived together continuously for at least two years prior to the date of death or if they have children; and

(*d*)   A security deposit equal to the rent of one month is required at the beginning of the lease. The place where the deposit is to be lodged is determined by the regional authority.

The most significant provisions relating to urban business leases are the following:

(i)   The term of the lease and the rent are to be freely negotiated;

i(ii)   The outgoing tenant will have the right to be indemnified if the premises are rented within one year to a person engaged in a business that is the same or similar to the one he engaged in;

(iii)   Contracts entered into prior to 9 May 1985: the outgoing tenant has a preferential right to a new lease within one year of the expiry of the old lease on the same terms as those offered to or agreed with a third party;

(iv)   The tenant may sublet or assign the lease without the landlord's consent; however, the landlord must be properly informed of the assignment or sublease and he will have the right to raise the rent; and

(v)   A security deposit equal to the rent of two months is obligatory.

Types of property

4.4   The choice will generally lie between a villa, an apartment (ready for occupation or partly built) or a building plot. Points to bear in mind include the following.

4.5   Villa: on a new development, a liability may initially arise in respect of the cost of e.g., road repairs, street lighting, maintenance of communal lawns. Once the development is complete, these items will become the property of the *ayuntamiento* (town hall) and such costs will form part of the local taxes (see 4.47).

4.6   Apartment: the *LPH*, referred to in 4.2, governs the ownership of apartments. The common parts including the entrances, stairways, gardens, roof and drains are owned by the *comunidad de propietarios* (community of owners) and each apartment or house is owned by the individual owner. A *cuota* (annual service charge) is payable to the *comunidad* representing the owner's share of the cost of maintenance of the common parts. The *comunidad* is organised formally with a constitution and prepares proper accounts and makes decisions in general meetings of the owners.

4.7   Plots or property in the course of construction: if the purchaser decides to buy his own plot and build a villa to his specification, then he must concern himself with various requirements and precautions as follows.

(*a*)   *Legal enquiries:* A Land Registry certificate should be obtained as described in 4.18(*b*) below, which will confirm the vendor's ownership and disclose prior charges and encumbrances. Prior charges should be paid off by the vendor. Often, the creditor will sign a discharge document before a Notary in respect of the monies owing. This document must be taxed and registered. It is unusual for plans to be filed in the Land Registry which physically identify the property and it is therefore advisable to ascertain at an early stage the present owners of the neighbouring land in order to record their names in the new *escritura de compraventa* (purchase deed). Identification of the present boundaries should also help to avoid subsequent boundary conflicts with neighbours;

(*b*)   *Planning enquiries:* these are equally important and they should be addressed to the *ayuntamiento* (town hall). It is necessary to ascertain from the *ayuntamiento* whether all amenities of the development (i.e., water, electricity, roadways etc.) have been completed and approved by the municipality and the technical department of the appropriate autonomous community, together with the nature and extent of building regulations governing e.g., the permitted number of storeys, building volume and any special construction requirements. In pursuance of the urban development legislation, namely the *Law* of 13 April 1998, (*Ley del régimen del suelo y valoraciones*) the owner of non-consolidated urban surface is obliged to transfer relevant elements (e.g., ground to open green areas, roads, etc., or a percentage of the *aprovechamiento urbanístico*) to the *ayuntamiento*. They are also subject to the completion of the urbanization process in compliance with the relevant system of equal distribution and within the timetable established by the *planeamiento* (local urban regulations).

At this point, the purchaser will sensibly wish formally to acquire title to the land before incurring the further expense of architects' plans. He will certainly need to acquire title before building works commence. Details of the appropriate transfer documentation and execution formalities are given in 4.21–4.29;

(*c*)   *Building permit:* an architect will prepare a building plan complying with any building requirements. It must be *visado* (approved) by the Provincial College of Architects, prior to submission to the *ayuntamiento*, with the application for the *licencia de obras* (building licence) and the required fee. Building licences are issued 'without prejudice to third parties'. The *ayuntamiento* takes no responsibility for infringement of third party rights, as a consequence of the building work, such as, for example, intrusion into neighbouring land;

(*d*)   *The building contract:* the contract to build the property should be negotiated with a reputable local constructor. The building contract will normally provide for stage payments based on progress certificates issued by the architect on a fortnightly or monthly basis. A retention of between 5 per cent and 10 per cent of each certificate is usually agreed, against any possible defective workmanship. This retention is normally released on issue of the architect's 'final works' or 'completion certificate';

(*e*)   *Technical supervision:* the building works must be supervised by an architect and an *aparejador* (similar to a UK building supervisor) must supervise and check the builders' work as it proceeds and record in the *libro de órdenes* (instruction book) instructions given to the builder and any matters which arise during the building works;

(*f*)   *Administrative documents:* on completion of the building, a *certificado de habitación* (habitation certificate) must be obtained in order that permanent water, gas and electricity supply companies may enter into permanent supply contracts (*Article 5* of *Royal Decree* of 24 February 1972). Prior to and as a condition for, the issue of a habitation certificate, the *ayuntamiento* must issue the *licencia de primera ocupación* (first occupation licence). (See *Article 1* of *Royal Decree* of 23 June 1978 and *Royal Decree* of 24 February 1972); and

(*g*)   *Guarantees for material damage due to building defects*: the *Law* of 5 November 1999 on the *Ordenación de la Edificación* imposes on the builder the obligation, with regard to buildings to be used for housing purposes, to subscribe to a caution or damage insurance for a one-year period. The *Law* provides on the same terms, that the promoter is also required to subscribe to an insurance contract for damages to habitation conditions. In these cases, no public deed of *declaración de obra nueva* will be executed or registered in the Land Registry until evidence of the referred guarantees is duly provided.

4.8   For an English purchaser not residing in Spain, the handling of all this complex documentation will be virtually impossible. It is therefore advisable, especially in view of any specific requirements and peculiarities of the various autonomous communities, and in view of some doubt as to the legal obligations of a builder to provide such documents, to include a clause in the building contract stating that the builder is required to obtain the habitation certificate, electrical and plumbing certificates, and in general all documentation required for the lawful occupation of the property.

Protection for purchaser buying property in the course of construction

Guarantees under Law 57 of 27 July 1968

4.9   In addition to any contractual remedies available to a purchaser, *Law 57* of 27 July 1968 was introduced to palliate the adverse effects of work being halted or not completed and to regulate the receipt of money advanced for the construction and sale of residential property. It requires any person or company promoting the construction of residential property (other than officially protected housing) and who proposes to obtain payments from the purchaser before commencement or completion of building, to comply with the following requirements.

(*a*)   To secure the repayment of the amounts paid, plus 6 per cent interest per annum, by an insurance policy issued by an insurance company, or by a joint and several guarantee issued by a bank or *caja de ahorros* (savings bank) in the event that construction is not started or completed in the time agreed or the habitation certificate is not obtained. It is also advisable that the bank guarantee should cover the obligation to execute the *escritura pública* (public deed) in favour of the purchaser, free of charges and encumbrances, and in addition any departure by the builder from the plans upon which the building licence was granted.

(*b*)   To receive the monies advanced by the purchasers through a bank or *caja de ahorros* and deposit them in a special account, separate from any other funds of the promoter, to be used only for the purposes of building the property in question.

4.10   Although this *Law* has been in force for many years, many builders and promoters are reluctant to comply. However, this reluctance may be overcome if the purchaser volunteers to pay all or part of the cost of the guarantee, which, by way of example, may be 0.5 per cent of the amount secured, although the cost will vary according to the arrangement reached with the bank.

Royal Decree of 21 April 1989

4.11 *Article 4* of this Decree states that persons engaged in the property business must make certain information available to the public and to the authorities, including: full details of the vendor, the site and its services, the dwelling to be constructed and any common areas, the materials of construction, the Land Registry details, the total price and form of payment (the text of Article 4 should be consulted for the definitive list of requirements).

4.12 *Article 5* of this Decree sets out certain compulsory terms of the contract of sale which include a provision that the vendor must bear any costs of establishing title and that the purchaser must have the right to choose the Notary.

The contract must make reference to *Articles 1279* and *1280 (1)*, of the *CC*, which set out the formal requirements of executing transfer deeds.

4.13 Despite all the above considerations, the purchaser of a property under construction or *sobre plano* (merely projected) cannot avail himself to such clear-cut protection. Spanish Law only provides the consumer with the right to take out an action for breach of contract, with the consequent economic compensation. Currently, however, Spanish laws do not guarantee the obtention of the real property itself, e.g. in case the works do not reach completion or the flats are sold to someone else.

Spanish doctrine (particularly *De La Cámara*) suggests that the only way to safeguard the purchaser's legitimate expectation to the building, flat or apartment lies in rejecting the equivalence of the purchase of a property *sobre plano* or under construction with a *venta de cosa futura* (sale of a future object) which only produces personal or obligation (not real) effects (real rights (*iura in re*) grant their holder the faculty to pursue, claim and recover the thing whoever may be its possessor, whereas obligational or personal rights (*iura in persona*) only provide their holder with the action to claim economic compensation). Rather, it should be defined as a *venta de objeto en formación* (sale of a developing object) enabling real rights to be obtained by means of the execution of the public deed (*tradición instrumental* ex *Article 1462 (2)* of the *CC*) or, at least, a *ius ad rem* if the deed has not yet been executed.

Furthermore, the resolution of the *Dirección General de los Registros y del Notariado* (Directorate General for the Public Registries and the Notaryship) (the *DGRN*) of 16 May 1996 has recognised that the purchaser of property under construction formalized through *escritura pública* holds a true right to be inscribed in the Land Registry (even before the horizontal division has had access to the Registry).

Planning and the bank guarantee

4.14 Compliance with the building licence issued by the municipal authority is fundamentally important. If a builder departs from the plans and specifications which formed the basis for the building licence, the municipal authority may withhold the occupation licence and habitation certificate or even call for the demolition of those items which do not comply with the building licence.

It is therefore sensible to ensure that the bank guarantee covers such an eventuality (see 4.9(*a*)).

It must also be kept in mind that, pursuant to *Article 22* of the *Law* of 13 April 1998 on the *régimen del suelo y valoraciones*, Notaries and Registrars will not authorise nor register public deeds of *declaración de obra nueva terminada o en construcción* (finished or in the course of construction new building declaration) until the building permit and technical certificate have been provided. If the property has been acquired in the course of construction, an *acta notarial* is necessary to account for its completion. *Articles 45–55* of the *Royal Decree* of 4 July 1997 on the *inscripción de actos de naturaleza urbanística* (complementary of the *Reglamento Hipotecario* with regard to acts of urban nature) set out the conditions necessary to obtain these documents in order to gain access to the Land Registry.

Pre-contract matters

Initial negotiations

4.15   Until a final choice of property has been made, no document should be signed which will commit the prospective buyer to the purchase of the property, or to make payments of money. Once such a document is signed it may be difficult to withdraw from the transaction without losing any deposit made, or, worse, it may be necessary to complete the purchase.

Reservation

4.16   At an early stage the estate agent or vendor may request that an option or reservation form is signed, or even a contract. Pressure may be exerted, but it should be withstood, or alternatively a temporary reservation involving payment of a comparatively minor sum could be agreed if this is felt essential to secure the property.

Preliminary investigations

4.17   Before any document committing the purchaser to proceed with the purchase is signed, the following checklist should be completed.

1.   Information to be provided by the vendor

4.18

(*a*)   Personal details (name, address etc.) of the owner(s) registered at the relevant Property Registry;

(*b*)   A copy of the entry at the Property Registry or alternatively the full reference of the registration (number, volume, folio) to facilitate a Land Registry search to check ownership and to verify whether the property is mortgaged or otherwise encumbered;

(*c*)   Photocopies of the documents required for the construction and occupation of the dwelling, namely building permit, architect's completion certificate, habitation certificate, electricity, gas and *boletines* (water certificates, although in some areas the water companies do not require a certificate);

(*d*)   A list of the overheads on the property with up-to-date receipts for local taxes, community service charge, electricity, water and refuse collection bills: if membership of a community of owners is involved, it is also necessary to obtain the latest set of community accounts together with a certificate from the Secretary confirming that the vendor has paid his bills, and details of any extraordinary expenditure on the building which may be anticipated; and

(*e*)   If a furnished property is to be bought, a full inventory should be prepared, and any items which were in the property when inspected, but which the vendor is excluding from the sale, should be listed.

2.   Inspection of property

4.19   A survey of the property is not a frequent practice in Spain. Obviously, a professional inspection of the drains, septic tank, electrical and plumbing installations, and of the overall structure of the building may alert a potential purchaser to defects. Alternatively, it is possible to insist that the contract makes proper provision in respect of defects. *Article 1490* of the *CC* provides that if the vendor is a private individual, his liability to the purchaser would endure for six months for 'hidden defects'. *Article 1591* of the *CC* recognises builder and architect liability in the case of *ruin* (i.e., serious deterioration) verified within a ten-year period. The *Law* of 5 November 1999 on the *ordenación de la edificación* (building planning) expands *Article 1591* extending its liability to other building agents, namely, the promoter, the works director and the works execution director. Their liability can be claimed within one, three or ten years in accordance with the damage appearing.

However, to avoid actions against third parties with whom a direct contractual relationship exists, it would be preferable for the vendor (whether a developer or a private individual) to state expressly in the contract of sale that the property has no hidden or manifest defect and that, if any should arise, the vendor would be liable for a specified term of, for example, six months.

3.   Land Registry search

4.20   Written application should be made to the Land Registry for a certificate stating the owner of the property itself, and setting out any encumbrances or charges (see 4.18(*b*)).

There is no procedure in Spanish law similar to the 'notice' or 'caution' under English law whereby a prospective purchaser can forestall or block entries in the Land Registry for a short period. The only comparable concept in Spain is the 'preventive annotation' but *Article 42* of the *Ley Hipotecaria* of 30 December 1944 (mortgage law), as amended, does not in any of its paragraphs provide for the purposes which in English law are served by the 'caution' or 'notice' to protect prospective purchasers.

Nevertheless, there is a special procedure established by *Royal Decree* of 29 December 1994 concerning collaboration between Notaries and the Land Registry, that enables sufficient registry information to be supplied to the purchaser and provides a period of priority for the purchaser on the basis that the public deed of transfer is presented to the Land Registry immediately after execution (see 4.28).

Transfer of title

Definition of contract

4.21   Under *Article 1261* of the *CC*, no contract exists unless there is:

(*a*)   consent of the parties;

(*b*)   a definite object; and

(*c*)   a reason for the obligation.

Contracts entered into by correspondence are deemed to be executed and delivered from the date the acceptance is received/sent.

Option to purchase

4.22   An option to purchase may be granted whereby, for a non-refundable sum, the option holder may purchase specified property at an agreed price, within a given period. An option to purchase may be transferred with the consent of the grantor, which may be given at the time the option is granted, or subsequently. The grantor of the option is prohibited, throughout the period of the option, from executing agreements with third parties which are incompatible with the rights of the option holder.

Pursuant to *Article 14* of the *Reglamento Hipotecario* (mortgage regulations), an option to purchase may be registered, provided that both parties have agreed to registration, and the option price, the acquisition price of the property and the duration of the option are specified.

Private contracts and public deeds

4.23   A contract of sale of property may be created by means of a private document or an *escritura pública* (public deed) both of which transfer ownership and possession of the property.

Often a private contract of sale may be signed first, followed by a subsequent 'raising' of the contract to a public deed. This is not an essential condition for the validity of the contract, unless the parties expressly agree. However, in accordance with *Articles 2* and *3* of the *Ley Hipotecaria* (mortgage law), only public deeds relating to immovable property (apart from judicial documents) may be recorded in the Land Registry, thus protecting the purchaser against third party claims against the vendor (for example, by creditors) (judgment of 30 May 1980). A purchaser is therefore best advised to pay as little as possible to the vendor on signing a private contract and to release the balance on signature of the public deed.

Protection of title/registration

The role of the Spanish Notary

4.24   An *escritura pública* (public deed), is a document executed before a Notary. The function of the Notary is of prime importance in Spanish law and in particular in transactions involving real property. It is necessary, therefore, to appreciate the purpose and extent of notarial intervention.

4.25   Notaries are highly qualified legal public servants, selected by competitive examination and appointed by the state. Their intervention is required in a wide range of transactions, including company formations, wills, mortgages and generally any documents which must be recorded in public registries to be fully effective.

4.26   Function in land transactions:

(*a*)   to comply with the obligation of giving information to the purchaser and the Land Registry as stated in 4.28;

(*b*)   to identify the parties and satisfy himself as to their capacity to execute documents: unless the signatory appears in person he will need to authorise a third party to act by means of a power of attorney which in turn must be granted before a Notary – a company should generally appoint an attorney as their authorised representative;

(*c*)   to prepare the document in correct form from instructions or a draft submitted to him, assisting in the interpretation of the wishes of the parties;

(*d*)   to explain the document to the parties present in person or duly represented, giving particular emphasis to the requirement to declare the
true price of the transaction and to pay the applicable taxes within the
statutory period of 30 working days;

(*e*)   to witness the signature of the document, giving it probatory force;
and

(*f*)   to retain the original in his protocol (or records) and issue certified and
plain copies on proper application.

The Notary normally restricts himself to stating in the *escritura* that the
vendor declares under *Article 175* of the *Notarial Regulations* that the
property is free from tenants and charges.

Therefore, it is always advisable for a purchaser to instruct a lawyer to conduct land registry and planning enquiries. The *escritura* should also state that
the property is free of tenants and/or occupants to avoid delay and the
possible cost and worry of legal proceedings.

Foreign Notaries

4.27   In accordance with *Article 36* of the *Ley Hipotecaria*, documents
attested by foreign Notaries and duly legalised with the apostille of the
British Foreign Office under the Hague Convention, are acceptable in Spain.
Such documents include powers of attorney, *escrituras de compraventa*
(purchase/sale deeds), mortgages and wills. They should preferably be
drawn up in Spanish, or in Spanish and English parallel columns and contain the wording usual for such documents in Spain. For the reasons given in
4.28, it may be preferable to execute the *escritura de compraventa* in Spain so
that it may be lodged immediately at the Land Registry.

Registration

4.28   Until the *escritura de compraventa* has actually been accepted for
registration by the local Land Registry, the purchaser will be exposed to
claims against the property brought by the vendor's creditors.

Under *Article 17* of the *Ley Hipotecaria*, if any document transferring title to
the property has been registered or noted in the Registry, no other document
may be registered or noted of the same or an earlier date which conflicts with
or is incompatible with that document.

An *escritura de compraventa* should therefore be presented for registration
immediately after execution. Purchasers are protected from vendors effecting a double sale by *Royal Decree* of 29 December 1994 which grants a
ten-day period of priority for registration, provided that the procedure set
out below is followed.

(1) Before the deed is executed, Notaries should obtain information from the Land Registry about ownership and charges over the property;

(2) The Land Registry should provide Notaries with this information within three days, including details of any other request for information they may have received from other Notaries regarding the same property; and

(3) The *escritura de compraventa* should be executed within ten days from receipt of this information from the Land Registry and confirmed immediately by Notaries to the Land Registry. This communication shall be deemed to constitute presentation of the *escritura de compraventa* for registration, provided that the subsequent presentation is actually made within ten days from the date of execution of the *escritura de compraventa*. According to *Article 418* of the *Reglamento Hipotecario*, the title can also be presented to the Registry:

   (i) personally by the holder during the official time limit; or

   (ii) by mail (*e-mail* and other telematic means are also acceptable pursuant to the resolutions of the *DGRN* of 12 November 1999 and 26 April 2000, and with regard to the *Royal Decree* of 17 September 1999 on the *firma electrónica* (electronic signature)).

   In the above cases, the *asiento de presentación* (presentation entry) will be in force for sixty days.

Once the *escritura de compraventa* has been executed, it should be presented to the tax office within 30 working days for payment of the relevant taxes (see 4.37–4.41) and then lodged at the Land Registry. These procedures may be handled by the Notary, a *Gestor* (a type of agent), the purchaser's lawyer, or the purchaser personally. In no case should the vendor be given the task of registering and taxing the *escritura de compraventa*.

The concept of original 'title deeds' is unfamiliar to Spanish law. Unlike the UK, land registries do not issue Land or Charge Certificates, presentation of which is required to effect changes to the Register. The *escritura de compraventa* is the deed of transfer, rather than the title deed to the property. Mere possession of an official copy of the *escritura de compraventa* of itself conveys no right to the property nor, for that matter, any form of equitable charge over it.

Notaries' and registration fees

4.29   Both the costs of executing a contract of sale or a purchase option before a Spanish Notary and the costs of registration in the Land Registry are fixed in accordance with a scale based on the value of the transferred property.

Exchange control/foreign investment regulations

Introduction

4.30   Spanish legislation governing the movement of capital has been radically modified in recent years. There has been a progressive liberalisation of transactions entered into between residents and non-residents and in some areas there is now virtually complete freedom of action. The speed with which legislation is changing may quickly render these comments out of date. The old administrative clearance procedure has been virtually abolished and is only required in a few cases. Nevertheless, there are some requirements which persist in order to enable the government to monitor the balance of payments and to levy appropriate taxes. These requirements are as follows.

4.31   In principle, following the *Royal Decree* of 20 December 1991 payments between residents and non-residents must be made via the Spanish banking system through a bank legally established in Spain. If the payment exceeds 100,000 pesetas (€601.01) a written declaration is required stating:

(i)   the name and home address of the non-resident;

(ii)   the amount, currency and origin or destination country;

(iii) the reason for payment.

The exports of actual bank notes is still subject to prior declaration for amounts exceeding 1 million pesetas (€6,010.12). Originally, the *Royal Decree* required administrative authorisation for currency exports over 5 million pesetas (€30,050.61), but as far as transactions between EU countries are at concerned the Court of Justice of the European Communities found this incompatible with the EC Treaty in its judgments *C-358* and *416/93* of 23 February 1995, *Ministerio Fiscal v Bordessa & Mellado [1995] ECR I-361, ECJ*.

4.32   Brief details of the transaction must be declared by the resident or non-resident who wishes to transfer money out of Spain, including the individual or company *Número de Identificación Fiscal (NIF)* (Fiscal Identification Number), the amount transferred, the currency and the destination of the transfer and the reason for payment.

Legal requirements

4.33   Foreign investment in property may be defined as the acquisition by non-resident individuals or entities of property in or rights to immovable property located in Spain exceeding 500 million pesetas or its equivalent in euros. Time sharing schemes are included in this definition. In general and following the latest liberalisation (*Royal Decree* of 23 April 1999) prior clearance for such investment property will no longer be required.

When property is acquired in the course of a business, the investment made will be subject to the rules and procedures governing direct investment into Spain.

Registration of the foreign investment

4.34   In pursuance of the *Royal Decree* of 23 April 1999, once the investment has been made, it should be declared to the Foreign Investments Register with its administrative, statistical or economic aims. This is normally done by the non-resident investor by means of a standard form identifying the holder of the investment, the official (usually the Public Notary) who has witnessed the execution of the documentation and giving details of the bank through which the payment has been made. If the investment originates from one of the countries or territories listed in the *Royal Decree* of 5 July 1991 (*paraíso fiscal* or tax heaven) the holder of the investment is required to declare it prior to the investment itself being carried out. The procedural aspects of the declaration are contained in the *Orden Ministerial* of 28 May 2001.

Rights of the foreign investor

4.35   Foreign investors have the right to transfer abroad, without any restriction or limitation, invested capital and any eventual gain obtained legally as a result of the disposal of their investments in Spain. They have also the right to remit abroad any dividends and profits arising from their investments. The disinvestment of such funds from Spain must also be recorded at the Foreign Investments Register (see *Orden Ministerial* of 28 May 2001). They should ensure they comply with the fiscal regulations set out in 4.37–4.60.

Financing the purchase

Loan secured by mortgage

4.36   Mortgage finance is available from English sources including banks and building societies and from Spanish banks based in England and Spain. If a UK resident borrower raises finance outside the UK he may be liable to withholding tax upon his payments of interest under *section 349* of the *Income and Corporation Taxes Act 1988*. Tax should be deducted at the basic rate from the interest payments made to the foreign lender. There is an exemption from withholding tax where the annual interest is payable in respect of a loan made by a bank which is recognised (by the Inland Revenue) as carrying on a bona fide banking business in the UK, which may assist the borrower. Alternatively, the borrower may be able to claim relief under the Anglo–Spanish double tax treaty which would reduce the rate of withholding tax applicable (see 4.68–4.70).

A mortgage deed is executed before a Notary by both lender and borrower and registered at the Land Registry. Tax is payable at 0.5 per cent of the amount secured on creation of the mortgage and on cancellation. Notary's fees and registration fees will be payable.

Spanish tax consequences of acquisition

IVA (Impuesto sobre el Valor Añadido)

4.37   This is the Spanish equivalent of VAT and is generally levied on purchases from a developer of newly constructed property or on land immediately available for construction. It is payable by the purchaser. It is levied at a reduced rate of 7 per cent for dwellings and 16 per cent for land or business premises upon the true value of the property acquired. A *superreduced* rate of 4 per cent is levied on certain transactions (e.g., first delivery of *viviendas de protección oficial*). VAT is governed by the *Law* of 28 December 1992 and regulations contained in the *Royal Decree* of 29 December 1992.

Certain transfers of property, although made by property developers, are exempt from VAT and are taxed instead under the capital transfer tax regulations set out below. For example, second and subsequent deliveries of buildings, including the land on which they are located, are exempt if they take place after construction or renovation is completed. In certain cases the seller can waive the exemption.

4.38   This exemption does not, however, extend to the sale of buildings:

(*a*)   upon the exercise of a purchase option inherent in a lease, by companies normally in the business of carrying out leasing operations;

(*b*)   to be immediately renovated by the acquirer, provided that such renovation exceeds 25 per cent of the sale price.

VAT borne by a company or business person may be recovered in accordance with general VAT rules set out in the legislation referred to above.

Stamp Duty (Impuesto sobre Actos Jurídicos Documentados)

4.39   Property transfers which are subject to VAT shall also be subject to a form of Stamp Duty or Tax on Legal Documents at 0.5 per cent on the declared purchase price, payable by the purchaser according to the *Texto Refundido* of 24 September 1993 and *Royal Decree* of 29 May 1995.

Tax on Capital Transfers (Impuesto sobre Transmisiones Patrimoniales)

4.40   As mentioned in 4.37, property transfers which are exempt from VAT and transfers by individuals for valuable consideration are subject to this tax. It is also regulated by the legislation set out in 4.39.

It is levied at a rate of 6 per cent on the true value of the property whether the property transferred is a building plot, business premises or residential property (*Article 11* of the *Texto Refundido* of 24 September 1993). The true value is reduced by the value of charges registered against the property. Such charges do not include debts, even when secured by mortgages (*Article 10(1)* of the *Texto Refundido*). This tax is payable by the purchaser and is not recoverable. The amount of such tax effectively increases the acquisition cost of the property for the purpose of calculating liability to capital gains tax when the property is sold (see 4.51).

The Spanish Revenue may review and reassess the value declared for the purposes of this tax on a justified basis pursuant to any of the means listed in *Article 52* of the *Ley General Tributaria* of 28 December 1963 (the *LGT*). *Article 14 (7)* of the *Texto Refundido* of 24 September 1993 established that, in the event that the assessed value exceeds the declared value by more than 20 per cent and such excess is greater than two million pesetas, the parties shall be liable to gift tax pursuant to *Law* of 18 December 1987 and *Royal Decree* of 8 November 1991 which govern inheritance and gift tax. However, the *Tribunal Constitucional* (Constitutional Court) in its judgment of 19 July 2000 annulled *Article 14 (7)* as a result of its incompatiblity with the principle of economic capacity set out in *Article 31* of the Spanish Constitution.

Municipal Tax on the Increased Value of Land (Impuesto Municipal sobre el Incremento de Valor de los Terrenos) (Law of 28 December 1988 on the Haciendas Locales)

4.41   This tax is defined in *Article 105* as a tax on the increase in the value of land, as revealed by each transfer of ownership. The tax applies to the increase in value of the land or the share in the land on which the property is built, and not to any buildings thereon. It is not payable on transfers of rural property.

It is a direct tax payable by the vendor (*Articles 105* and *107*) as a consequence of the disposal of land, and is levied on the capital gain arising since the last transfer. Unlike the old *plus valía* tax, which it replaced, if the vendor fails to pay, tax due does not become a charge on the property. It is difficult to generalise as to the calculation of the rate of this tax.

Relevant factors include the number of years the property has been owned, the number of inhabitants in the municipality in which the property is located and its cadastral value (see 4.44).

A return must be made to the competent *ayuntamiento* within 30 working days for *inter vivos* transactions and within six months (which may be extended to one year) in the case of death.

Spanish tax consequences of ownership/annual taxes

Non-resident individuals

Wealth tax (Impuesto sobre el Patrimonio)

4.42   The statutory provisions regulating this tax are contained in *Law* of 6 June 1991:

(*a*)   it is a direct personal tax payable throughout Spanish territory. The Autonomous Communities enjoy limited legislative capacity with regard to this tax by virtue of the *Law 14/1996* on *cesión de tributos a las Comunidades Autónomas*. Liability arises from ownership of any property or title to any rights having a financial or economic content, although some goods are exempt (e.g., household furnishings, goods subject to economic activities or habitual dwellings up to a value of 25 million pesetas (€15,0253.03);

(*b*)   liability is classified as either 'personal' or 'real' as follows:

    (i)   taxpayers liable by 'personal' obligation are private individuals, resident for tax purposes in Spain – their obligation relates to all property and rights attributable to the taxpayer wherever the property is situated or the rights exercisable;

    (ii)   taxpayers liable by 'real' obligation are private individuals not considered resident in Spain for tax purposes who own property or rights in such territory (generally, 'residence' is acquired for tax purposes if a person resides in Spain for more than six months (more than 183 days to be exact) in any calendar year or establishes in Spain the principal base of his interests, whether business, professional or economic);

(*c*)   a declaration must be filed and any tax arising must be paid by the following:

    (i)   private individuals (resident in Spain) whose *base imponible* (taxable base or net worth) is in excess of 18 million pesetas (€10,8182.18) (*Article 28* of *Law* of 6 June 1991);

    (ii)   persons liable by 'real' obligation, i.e., non-residents who are not entitled to the exemption from tax referred to above (wealth tax is payable upon all assets owned in Spain and upon any rights that may be exercised in Spain, regardless of their value);

(*d*)   valuation of residential property – this is the greater of the cadastral value (see 4.44), the acquisition price or the value verified by the Spanish authorities in relation to other taxes;

(*e*)   the total value of all assets after deduction of properly evidenced debts and burdens will constitute the taxable base; and

(*f*)   this tax is applied progressively in accordance with brackets of wealth – the applicable rate for the first 27,808,000 pesetas (€167,129.45) is 0.2 per cent increasing gradually to a maximum of 2.5 per cent.

Property tax (Impuesto sobre Bienes Inmuebles)

(This tax replaced *Contribución Territorial Urbana y Contribución Territorial Rústica* and *Impuesto Municipal sobre Solares*.)

4.43   The *Law* of 28 December 1988, Second Transitory Provision, states that this tax applies from 1 January 1990. It is levied annually on the owner of urban and rural property located within the relevant Municipality or on the beneficial ownership of the property. *Article 61* provides that it is a direct tax, therefore the owner of such rights or property is obliged to pay the tax. The tax falls due on the first day of the tax period (which coincides with the calendar year) and, being of a 'real' nature, the property will remain liable for payment of any outstanding tax where there is a change of ownership. It is important, therefore, to verify that payment of this tax is up-to-date when an existing property is purchased.

4.44   According to *Article 66*, the taxable base for this tax is the *valor catastral* (cadastral value) of the property. This is a term used to describe the official value attributed to the property by the Municipality. The cadastral value is fixed by reference to the market value of the property which it must not exceed. Generally, the tax rate is a very reduced percentage of the cadastral value of the properties.

4.45   *Article 73* provides that the amount payable will be the result of applying to the taxable base a rate of 0.4 per cent in the case of urban property and 0.3 per cent in the case of rural properties. These indices may be increased in any Municipality on the basis of population criteria and other geographic conditions.

Income tax (Impuesto sobre la Renta de las Personas Físicas)

4.46   *Law* of 9 December 1998 and *Royal Decree* of 5 February 1999 contain the provisions which regulate this tax. *Article 1* of *Law* of 9 December 1998 describes it as a direct personal tax.

As in the case of wealth tax, there is a distinction between liability by personal obligation (namely any person residing in Spanish territory) and liability by real obligation (namely any private individual not residing in Spanish territory) in respect of income obtained in Spain. The above legislation should be referred to in the case of individuals with a personal obligation.

The mere ownership of property by non-residents in Spain, even where no income is generated by letting, is subject to *impuesto sobre patrimonio*, following the brackets of wealth set out in *Article 30* of the *Law* of 6 June 1991. The value is calculated in accordance with the criteria used for valuing assets for wealth tax, as indicated in *Article 10* of the *Law*, namely the greater of:

(*a*)   the cadastral value (see above);

(*b*)   the acquisition price; or

(*c*)   the value verified by the authorities.

Local taxes

4.47   The local authorities may also introduce additional local taxes and charges from time to time, to finance local developments and services. These are generally levied on the cadastral value of the property.

Non-resident companies

Special corporation tax

4.48   In pursuance of *Article 32* of the *Law* of 9 December 1998 on the *Impuesto sobre la Renta de No Residentes,* non-resident companies that own or possess in Spain, under any title, property or rights to enjoy and benefit from property, are liable to pay tax at 3 per cent of the cadastral value of such property.

There are various exemptions:

(*a*)   foreign governments, foreign public institutions or international organisations;

(*b*)   companies with the right to benefit from a treaty to avoid the double payment of tax, provided that:

   (i)   the treaty contains a provision with regard to information exchange; and

   (ii)   the individuals who ultimately possess the capital or assets of the entity are resident in Spanish territory or are subject to the application of a treaty to avoid double taxation containing an information exchange provision;

(*c*)   companies which habitually or continuously carry on business activities in Spain other than in relation to the property in question;

(*d*)   companies listed in official secondary markets; and

(*e*)   non-profitmaking institutions recognised under the laws of a State which have arranged with Spain a treaty to avoid double taxation and which contain an information exchange provision, provided that real property (real estate, landed property (assets, buildings, plots, etc.)) owned by the relevant institution is devoted to the pursuance of non-lucrative aims (promoting charity, beneficence, public welfare, etc., on a non-lucrative basis).

Property tax (Impuesto sobre Bienes Inmuebles)

4.49 See 4.43.

Local taxes

4.50 See 4.47.

Spanish tax consequences of sale

Capital gains tax (CGT)

4.51 Generally, the Spanish Revenue will levy CGT on the gain made on a disposition of the property by a non-resident vendor, namely the difference between the acquisition price and the sale price. In order to calculate the capital gain, the purchase price will be increased by the costs and taxes inherent to the purchase paid by the buyer and the sale price will be reduced by the costs and taxes inherent to the sale paid by the vendor.

4.52 It is important to distinguish whether a vendor is a non-resident individual or a non-resident company (see 4.42(*b*)(ii) for definition of 'residence').

Non-resident individuals

4.53 According to *Law 41/1998* of 9 December, tax is levied on an annual basis on any chargeable gain at 35 per cent if the non-resident individual or company operates through *establecimiento permanente* (permanent establishment); otherwise, tax is levied at 25 per cent for every single taxable operation.

Non-resident companies

4.54 Companies are subject to the same regime as described in 4.53 for individuals.

4.55 It is a rule of English law that the courts will not enforce the tax claims of foreign governments. Many English owners have relied on this precept and do not pay Spanish capital gains tax when they sell their Spanish properties to another non-resident. With the ever-growing co-operation between the EU tax authorities, the present apparent immunity to prosecution may be removed.

Withholding tax

4.56 *Law* of 9 December 1998 on the *Impuesto sobre la Renta de No Residentes* provides for a withholding tax whereby a person purchasing property from a non-resident individual or non-operating company through *establecimiento permanente* (permanent establishment) is obliged to withhold 5 per cent of the purchase price. This amount must be paid to the tax authorities on account of any liability of the vendors to capital gains tax. The onus is then on the vendor to argue that no tax is due so that the money may be released.

There is no obligation to withhold part of the purchase price if the property is purchased from an individual who, by 31 December 1996, has owned it for more than ten years, provided that improvements have not been carried out nor contributions to resident companies made (*Article 24 (2) of Law 41/1998* of 9 December).

Spanish law consequences of inheritance

Inheritance tax

4.57　Any individual, whether or not resident in Spain, who acquires assets in Spain by inheritance, is liable to pay Spanish inheritance tax. The basic rules are contained in the *Law* of 18 December 1987 and *Royal Decree* of 8 November 1991.

As for wealth tax (see 4.42), the *Law* of 19 December 1987 distinguishes between residents and non-residents in its tax treatments of Spanish inheritances. Persons resident in Spain are liable by 'personal obligation', irrespective of the location of the property involved. Non-residents are liable by 'real obligation' if they receive assets situate in Spanish territory. The persons liable for payment of the tax are the heirs or beneficiaries.

The tax authorities verify the value of property transferred, by the means listed in *Article 52* of the *LGT*. In principle, penalties are not applied where the value verified by the authorities exceeds the value stated by the beneficiary if such latter value is that calculated by reference to the regulations governing wealth tax.

4.58　The taxable base comprises the net value of the property acquired by each individual beneficiary. Details of allowable deductions may be found in *Articles 31* and *32* of *Royal Decree* of 8 November 1991. The taxable base may be further reduced according to the relationship between deceased and beneficiary, as provided by *Article 20* of *Law* of 19 December 1987. The closer the blood relationship, the greater is the relief. Additional relief is available when property is acquired by persons suffering from a disability. If, over a maximum term of ten years, the same property has been the subject of two or more transfers on death to descendants, then tax paid on earlier transfers may be deducted from the amount levied on second and later transfers.

Rate of tax

4.59 The rate of tax varies depending upon the value of the legacy, the value of the beneficiary's existing assets and his relationship to the testator. The *cuota íntegra*, or tariff, is calculated by reference to the amount of the legacy. The rate is progressive from a minimum of 7.65 per cent on a legacy up to 1,330,000 pesetas (€7,993.46) to a maximum of 34 per cent on a legacy exceeding 132,702,000 pesetas (€797,555.10).

Then, the *cuota tributaria*, or tax payable, is determined by applying to the *cuota íntegra* a multiplier calculated by reference to the existing assets of the beneficiary and the relationship of the beneficiary to the testator.

The 2001 multipliers are as follows:

Existing wealth or net worth	*Groups under Article 22*		
Million of ptas.	*I & II*	*III*	*IV*
0–67	1	1.5882	2
67–334	1.05	1.6676	2.1
334–669	1.1	1.7471	2.2
669 and thereafter	1.2	1.9059	2.4

Existing wealth or net worth	*Groups under Article 22*		
euros	*I & II*	*III*	*IV*
0–402,678.11	1	1.5882	2
402,678.11–2,007,380.43	1.05	1.6676	2.1
2,007,380.43–4,020,770.98	1.1	1.7471	2.2
4,020,770.98 and thereafter	1.2	1.9059	2.4

4.60 A tax return must be filed for the assessment of Spanish inheritance tax within six months of death. The tax authorities have five years in which to review the declared value and raise a supplementary assessment, if appropriate.

The purchase vehicle

Acquisition by a non-resident company

4.61 The widespread practice of acquiring Spanish property through an offshore company has arisen principally because a transfer of ownership of the property can be achieved by a sale of the company (i.e., the transfer of shares) rather than a transfer of the property. This eliminates the need for signature of a Spanish *escritura de compraventa* and the payment of attendant transfer and inheritance taxes, notarial fees, Land Registry charges and other costs. It also eases the entry and departure of syndicate members when a property is held by a group of persons. Companies incorporated for this purpose usually own one sole asset, namely the Spanish property.

4.62   It has not escaped the attention of the Spanish authorities that purchases by companies can and do give rise to loss of tax revenues on a large scale. As a result, the special corporation tax referred to in 4.48 was introduced and the taxation of capital gains obtained as a result of the sale of shares. Fiscal transparency regimes must also be taken into account according to *Articles 75–77* of the *Law* of 27 December 1995 on the *Impuesto de Sociedades* (corporation tax). As a result, although it has generally been tax effective to structure the acquisition of Spanish property via an offshore company unless confidentiality as to the origin of funds and the identity of the shareholders has to be preserved, the fiscal advantages may be restricted to avoidance of municipal tax on the increased value of land and wealth tax. Other factors to bear in mind are set out below.

Also, it should be noted that use of a non-resident company does not bypass UK tax on income derived from the Spanish property owned by such a company. By virtue of *section 739* of the *Income and Corporation Taxes Act 1988*, where the income received by an intermediate non-resident is 'enjoyed' by a resident, such income is imputed to the resident and subject to UK tax.

Choice of jurisdiction for incorporation of the company

4.63   The choice of jurisdiction for incorporation of the company will depend on various factors.

(*a*)   Double tax treaties: a number of countries have entered into treaties with Spain to avoid tax being payable in both jurisdictions. Consideration of the resultant advantages and possible tax reliefs is necessary. The relevant Convention between the UK and Spain is dated 21 October 1975.

(*b*)   Cost of formation and annual taxes: the company may have to pay tax on incorporation together with annual taxes, based either on profits earned or at a flat rate, irrespective of profits or losses. Usually the company will not trade so that no profits will be obtained in which case a profit-based tax jurisdiction is more attractive. In any event, an annual fee is generally charged by the agent responsible for dealing with correspondence and preparing the annual return.

(*c*)   CGT: if disposal of shares is likely to give rise to CGT, then it is advisable to check whether the amount of tax payable will exceed that payable in one's own jurisdiction. In many tax havens there is no CGT on disposals by non-residents, although this does not necessarily avoid CGT in, for example, the UK or in Spain.

Formation of company

4.64   Minimal share capital is often used, which raises the question of how the purchase is to be financed. A loan may cause problems or delay on a subsequent disposal. Borrowing from a bank or institution may require a guarantee or mortgage from an investor. Loans from non-resident banks may be difficult to obtain as enforcement of Spanish mortgages may be perceived as difficult, while Spanish banks are often unwilling to lend to non-Spanish companies. A simple solution is to provide sufficient share capital to finance the acquisition, including the attendant costs and taxes although this will reveal the actual cost of purchase and hence the profit achieved on any subsequent sale.

Ownership

4.65   Spanish taxes levied are set out in 4.48–4.50. A liability to UK income tax may also arise (but see comments on double taxation relief in 4.68–4.71 below). In respect of income tax, care should be taken if property is acquired by a UK resident company for use by employees. The employees in question may be charged to income tax on a substantial portion of the value of the property under the 'benefit in kind' provisions of the *Income and Corporation Taxes Act 1988*.

Disposal of the property

4.66   Liability to withholding tax is discussed in 4.56 above and reference to capital gains tax is made in 4.61–4.62 above.

In addition, there exists the risk that transfer tax should, in fact, be paid on the sale of a property owned by a company whose principal asset is a Spanish property.

It should be noted that the purchaser's legal adviser will normally require the company to provide undertakings regarding the company's financial position, including audited accounts, payment of taxes etc. It is preferable that the company should not have traded.

The fiscal representative

4.67   It should be borne in mind that all non-resident taxpayers (whether individuals or companies) must appoint a representative resident in Spain in respect of their fiscal obligations. This obligation is set out generally in *Article 46* of the *LGT* (referred to in 4.57) and more particularly in *Article 10* of the *Corporate Tax Law* (*Ley del Impuesto sobre Sociedades*), *Article 9* of the *Law* of 9 December 1998 of non-residents income tax (*Ley sobre el Impuesto sobre la Renta de no Residentes*) and *Article 6* of the *Wealth Tax Law* (*Ley del Patrimonio*). Such representative may be an individual or a corporate body resident in Spain. Notification of the appointments duly evidenced e.g., by means of a power of attorney, must be made to the tax authorities by the individual or his representative within two months of the appointment. Failure to comply with these obligations may be penalised by a fine of between 25,000 (€150.25) and two million pesetas (€12,020.24).

Double taxation relief

General United Kingdom tax

4.68   It is likely in some cases that a property owner will be liable to tax on the same sum of money in both Spain and the United Kingdom. Some United Kingdom tax consequences have already been referred to in passing. It is beyond the scope of this work to set out the full UK tax consequences of owning property in Spain. Nevertheless, the following general points may be of some guidance and assistance.

A UK resident may be liable simultaneously to UK income tax on any income arising from the property (Case IV, Schedule D of the *Income and Corporation Taxes Act 1988*: see *section 18*). As to capital gains tax, a UK resident is taxed on his *worldwide* chargeable gains made during a year of assessment (see *Taxation of Chargeable Gains Act 1992, section 2(1)*). For both income tax and capital gains tax a UK resident who is domiciled overseas may avoid UK tax by avoiding the remittance of funds to the UK. Generally, inheritance tax is chargeable on all property, including foreign property, which is beneficially owned by an individual domiciled in the UK (see *section 6(1)* of the *Inheritance Tax Act 1984* where foreign property is only 'excluded' if the beneficial owner is non-UK domiciled). A UK resident company may be liable for UK corporation tax on income and chargeable gains in the same way that an individual is liable for separate income and capital gains taxes (but note there is no liability for inheritance tax).

Fortunately there are double taxation relieving provisions in force.

Income tax, capital gains tax and corporation tax

4.69   Relief in relation to these taxes is governed by the Convention entered into by Spain and the UK on 21 October 1975 which came into force on 1 April 1976.

The Convention establishes that income and capital gains arising from immovable property are fully taxable in both countries according to their national tax laws (i.e. there is no exemption in either country: see *Articles 6* and *13*) but to the extent that the tax payments overlap they are relieved under the provisions of *Article 24*.

Double taxation is eliminated by a system of credit relief. The taxation jurisdiction required to give the credit for the amount of tax already paid in the other country will depend on in which jurisdiction the tax falls to be paid earliest.

Inheritance tax

4.70   The Convention does not apply to this tax. However, the credit provisions described above are reproduced in *section 159* of the *Inheritance Tax Act 1984.*

5 Immigration Controls in the United Kingdom

Caroline Stack LLB
(Reynolds Porter Chamberlain)

Updating material by Matthew Chapman LLB LLM and Kim Vowden BA
(CMS Cameron McKenna)

General principles

Introduction

5.1   The general principles governing immigration controls are set out in the *Immigration Act 1971* ('the *Act*' or '*IA 1971*').

> 'All those who are in this Act expressed to have the right of abode in the United Kingdom shall be free to live in, and to come and go into and from, the United Kingdom without let or hindrance except such as may be required under and in accordance with this Act to enable their right to be established or as may be otherwise lawfully imposed on any person.'
> *[IA 1971, s 1(1)]*.

> 'Those not having that right may live, work and settle in the United Kingdom by permission and subject to such regulation and control of their entry into, stay in and departure from the United Kingdom as is imposed by this Act.'
> *[IA 1971, s 1(2)]*.

The right of abode

5.2   A person has the right of abode in the UK if:

(*a*)   he is a British citizen; or

(*b*)   he is a Commonwealth citizen who immediately before the commencement of the *British Nationality Act 1981* was a Commonwealth citizen, having the right of abode in the UK either by virtue of having a parent who was born in the UK or by virtue of marriage and, in either case, has not ceased to be a Commonwealth citizen in the meanwhile.

[IA 1971, s 2(1)].

5.3   For convenience, the term 'British citizen' is used in the *Act* to include Commonwealth citizens who have the right of abode. *[IA 1971, s 2(2)]*. The term is also so used in this chapter.

Regulation and control

5.4   A person who is not a British citizen may be given leave to enter the UK or to remain in the UK for a limited or for an indefinite period. If he is given limited leave to enter or remain in the UK, it may be given subject to all or any of the following conditions, namely, a condition restricting his employment or occupation in the UK, a condition requiring him to maintain and accommodate himself, and any dependants of his, without recourse to public funds, and a condition requiring him to register with the police. [*IA 1971, s 3(1)(c)*].

The Home Secretary is responsible for establishing rules governing the practice to be followed in the administration of the *Act*. [*IA 1971, s 3(2)*]. The current *Immigration Rules* ('the *Rules*' or '*IR*') came into effect on 1 October 1994 and have been modified since that date.

The *Rules* are not rules of law but of administrative practice. A departure from the *Rules* in any specific case will not therefore be a breach of law and the Home Secretary retains a residual discretion in all cases. In spite of this, the *Rules*, and their proper construction, are of great importance in appeals brought before immigration adjudicators and in applications for judicial review. The *Rules* are expressly referred to in the *Immigration and Asylum Act 1999 (IAA 1999)*, which provides that an adjudicator shall allow an appeal if the decision or action appealed against was not in accordance with any applicable immigration rules. [*IAA 1999, Sch 4, para 21*].

Exemptions

5.5   Exemption from immigration control occurs in the following cases.

Common travel area

5.6   The UK, the Channel Islands, the Isle of Man and Ireland collectively form the common travel area. A person who has been examined for the purpose of immigration control at the point at which he entered the area does not normally require leave to enter any other part of it. [*IA 1971, s 1(3)*].

Diplomatic exemption

5.7   The provisions of the *Act* do not apply to any person who enters the UK as a member of a mission within the meaning of the *Diplomatic Privileges Act 1964*, or a member of his family. [*IA 1971, s 8(3) as amended by IA 1988, s 4*]. A person other than a diplomatic agent shall only count as a member of a mission if he was resident outside the UK when he was offered a post as such a member. [*IA 1971, s 3A*].

Military personnel

5.8   The provisions of the *Act*, other than those relating to deportation, do not apply to members of the home forces, Commonwealth forces undergoing training in the UK or visiting forces. [*IA 1971, s 8(4)*].

Seamen and air crews

5.9   With certain exceptions, a person arriving in the UK as a member of the crew of a ship or aircraft may, without leave, enter the UK and remain until the departure of his ship or aircraft. [*IA 1971, s 8(1)*].

European Economic Area (EEA) nationals

5.10   EEA nationals are nationals of the following states:

Austria, Belgium, Denmark, Finland, France, Germany, Greece, Holland, Iceland, Italy, Liechtenstein, Luxembourg, Norway, Portugal, Ireland, Spain, Sweden.

5.11   An EEA national must be admitted to the UK if he produces, on arrival, a valid national identity card or passport issued by an EEA state [*The Immigration (European Economic Area) Regulations 2000 (IEEA Regulations), reg 12(1)*].

5.12   Once admitted, an EEA national may apply for and, on the production of a valid national identity card or passport issued by an EEA state and proof that he is a 'qualified person', will be issued with a residence permit. [*IEEA Regulations, reg 15(1)*].

A residence permit will usually be valid for at least five years [*IEEA Regulations, reg 18(1)*] and may be renewed on application. [*IEEA Regulations, reg 19(1)*].

5.13   A person is a 'qualified person' if he is a worker, self-employed, a provider or recipient of services, a self-employed person who has ceased economic activity in the UK, a self-sufficient person, a retired person or a student. [*IEEA Regulations, reg 5(1)*].

5.14   EEA nationals who work on short-term contracts, who provide or receive services on a short-term basis, or who return frequently to homes in another EEA state may be refused a residence permit. [*IEEA Regulations, reg 16(1)*].

5.15   A family member of an EEA national who is not himself an EEA national must be admitted to the UK on production of a valid national identity card issued by an EEA state or a valid passport and either, where the family member is a visa national or a person who seeks to be admitted to instal himself with a qualified person, a valid EEA family permit or residence document or, in all other cases (but only where required by an immigration officer) a document proving that he is a family member of a qualified person. [*IEEA Regulations, reg 12(2)*].

5.16   A family member of an EEA national who is a qualified person must, on application, and on the production of a valid identity card issued by an EEA state or a valid passport and proof that he is a family member of the qualified person, be issued with a residence permit. [*IEEA Regulations, reg 15(2)*]. The residence permit shall be of the same duration as the residence permit granted to the qualified person and shall be subject to the same terms as to renewal. [*IEEA Regulations, reg 20*].

5.17   Any person (other than a student) who has been issued with a residence permit or residence document valid for five years and who has remained in the UK in accordance with the *Immigration (European Economic Area) Order 1994* or the *IEEA Regulations* for four years and continues to do so may apply for permission to remain in the UK indefinitely. [*IR, para 255*].

Entry clearance procedure

5.18   A person who is not exempt from immigration control may be required to obtain an 'entry clearance' before travelling to the UK, depending on his nationality and the purpose for which he seeks entry.

An 'entry clearance' is defined as a visa, entry certificate or other document which, in accordance with the *Rules* is to be taken as evidence of a person's eligibility, though not a British citizen, for entry into the UK, but does not include a work permit. [*IA 1971, s 33(1)*].

5.19   Nationals of certain countries listed in Appendix 1 to the *Rules* and who are referred to in the *Rules* as 'visa nationals', are required to obtain a visa before travelling to the UK, regardless of the purpose for which they seek entry. The list contained in Appendix 1 is as follows:

Afghanistan	Gabon	Peru
Albania	Georgia	Philippines
Algeria	Ghana	Qatar
Angola	Guinea	Romania
Armenia	Guinea-Bissau	Russia
Azerbaijan	Guyana	Rwanda
Bahrain	Haiti	Sao Tome e Principe
Bangladesh	India	Saudi Arabia
Belarus	Indonesia	Senegal
Benin	Iran	Sierra Leone
Bhutan	Iraq	Slovak Rebublic

Bosnia-Herzegovina
Bulgaria
Burkina Faso
Burma
Burundi
Cambodia
Cameroon
Cape Verde
Central African Republic
Chad
China
Colombia
Comoros
Congo
Republic of Croatia
Cuba
Democratic Republic of
the Congo (Zaire)
Djibouti
Dominican Republic
Ecuador
Egypt
Equatorial Guinea
Eritrea
Ethiopia
Fiji

Ivory Coast
Jordan
Kazakhstan
Kenya
Kirgizstan
Korea (North)
Laos
Lebanon
Liberia
Libya
Macedonia
Madagascar
Maldives
Mali
Mauritania
Moldova
Mongolia
Morocco
Mozambique
Nepal
Niger
Nigeria
Oman
Pakistan
Papua New Guinea

Somalia
Sri Lanka
Sudan
Surinam
Syria
Taiwan
Tajikistan
Tanzania
Thailand
Togo
Tunisia
Turkey
Turkmenistan
Uganda
Ukraine
United Arab Emirates
Uzbekistan
Vietnam
Yemen
The territories formerly
comprising the Socialist
Federal Republic of
Yugoslavia excluding
Croatia and Slovenia

Additionally, a person who holds a passport or travel document issued by the former Soviet Union or by the former Socialist Federal Republic of Yugoslavia, a stateless person and a person who holds non-national documents will also need a visa.

5.20   Any other person who wishes to ascertain in advance whether he is eligible for admission to the UK may apply for the issue of an entry clearance. [*IR, para 24*].

An applicant for an entry clearance must be outside the UK at the time of the application. [*IR, para 28*].

An applicant should apply in the country where he is living for the issue of an entry clearance. Applications should be made to the nearest British High Commission, Embassy, Consulate or other designated office. [*IR, paras 28–29*]. The officers who handle the applications are referred to as 'Entry Clearance Officers'.

Such an application is a requirement of many immigration categories (e.g. investors, retired persons of independent means) but is optional for non-visa nationals seeking entry as visitors, students and work permit holders.

In most cases an entry clearance has the effect of granting the holder leave to enter. [*Immigration (Leave to Enter and Remain) Order 2000, art 2*]. A person arriving in the UK with leave to enter may be examined by an immigration officer for the purpose of establishing whether there has been a change in the circumstances of the case or another reason why the leave to enter should be cancelled. [*IA 1971, Sch 2, para 2A*].

Visitors

5.21   A person admitted to the UK as a visitor may transact business (which includes attending meetings and negotiating and concluding contracts) during his visit. [*IR, para 40*]. Business transacted must not constitute establishing a business or employment in the UK.

A person seeking entry as a visitor must show that:

(*a*)   he is genuinely seeking entry as a visitor for a limited period, not exceeding six months;

(*b*)   he intends to leave the UK at the end of the visit as stated by him;

(*c*)   he does not intend to study at a maintained school or take employment or produce goods or provide services within the UK;

(*d*)   he will maintain and accommodate himself and any dependants without working or recourse to public funds; and

(*e*)   he can meet the cost of the return or onward journey.

[*IR, para 41*].

A passenger admitted as a visitor may be given leave to enter for up to six months subject to a condition prohibiting employment. [*IR, para 42*].

Students

5.22   A person seeking entry to the UK to study must show that:

(*a*)   he is able and intends to follow a full-time course of study at a publicly funded institution of further or higher education or an independent fee-paying school or bona fide private education institution;

(*b*)   he intends to leave the UK at the end of his studies;

(*c*)   he will not take employment (except approved part-time or vacation work) nor engage in business; and

(*d*)   he will maintain and accommodate himself and any dependants without working or recourse to public funds.

[*IR, para 57*].

A person admitted as a student may be admitted for an appropriate period depending on the length of his course of study and his means, with a condition restricting his freedom to take employment. [*IR, para 58*].

Students are permitted to work in the UK subject to the following rules:

(*a*)   the student should not work for more than 20 hours per week during term time, except where the placement is a necessary part of their studies and is undertaken with the consent of the educational institution;

(*b*)   the student should not engage in business or self-employment or provide services as a professional sports person or entertainer; and

(*c*)   the student should not pursue a career by filling a permanent full-time vacancy.

5.23   The spouse and children under 18 of a person admitted to the UK as a student may be given leave to enter the UK for the period of the student's authorised stay. Leave to enter will be refused unless the Immigration Officer is satisfied that there is adequate accommodation for the person admitted and his dependants and that they can maintain themselves without recourse to public funds. The dependants may be prohibited from taking up employment except where the period of leave being granted is twelve months or more. [*IR, paras 76–80*].

5.24   A prospective student may be granted entry if he can demonstrate a genuine intention of undertaking, within six months of the date of entry, an approved course of study. [*IR, para 82*].

Initially, he may be admitted for a period not exceeding six months with a condition prohibiting employment. [*IR, para 83*].

Au pairs

5.25   A person of either sex may be admitted to the UK to take up an au pair placement if aged 17 to 27 inclusive, unmarried with no dependants and a national of one of the following countries:

Andorra, Bosnia-Herzegovina, Croatia, Cyprus, Czech Republic, The Faeroes, Greenland, Hungary, Macedonia, Malta, Monaco, San Marino, Slovak Republic, Slovenia, Switzerland or Turkey.

He must be coming to the UK to learn English, to live for a time as a member of an English speaking family and to help in their home for a maximum of five hours per day in return for a reasonable allowance and with two free days per week. He must not intend to stay in the UK for more than two years as an au pair and he must be able to maintain and accommodate himself without recourse to public funds. [*IR, paras 88, 89*].

A person may be admitted as an au pair for a period not exceeding two years with a prohibition on employment except as an au pair. [*IR, para 90*].

A person who has previously spent time in the UK as an au pair may be granted an extension of stay for a further period provided that the total length of stay will not exceed two years. [*IR, para 92*].

Working holidaymakers

5.26   A Commonwealth citizen aged 17 to 27 inclusive may be admitted to the UK as a working holidaymaker for up to two years. He must intend to take employment which is incidental to a holiday and not to engage in business, provide services as a professional sportsman or entertainer or pursue a career in the UK. [*IR, para 95*].

UK ancestry

5.27   A Commonwealth citizen aged 17 or over may be granted an entry clearance to the UK to take or seek employment upon proof that one of his grandparents was born in the UK, the Channel Islands or the Isle of Man and that he intends to seek or take employment in the UK and will be able to maintain and accommodate himself and any dependants without recourse to public funds. He will not require a work permit. Leave to enter may be given for a period not exceeding four years. [*IR, paras 186, 187*].

If a person completes four continuous years in the UK in this category he may be eligible to apply for indefinite leave to remain. [*IR, para 192*].

Work permits

5.28   A person seeking to enter the UK for work permit employment must show that:

(*a*)   he holds a valid work permit;

(*b*)   he is not of an age which puts him outside of the limits for employment;

(*c*)   he is capable of undertaking the employment for which the work permit was issued;

(*d*)   he does not intend to take employment other than that permitted by his work permit;

(*e*)   he is able to maintain and accommodate himself and any dependants without recourse to public funds; and

(*f*)   if he holds a work permit valid for twelve months or less, he intends to leave the UK on the expiry of his permit.

[*IR, para 128*].

He will be admitted to the UK for the period specified in the work permit, not exceeding five years. [*IR, para 129*].

5.29   The work permit must be obtained by his employer from Work Permits (UK), which is part of the Home Office, or, in Northern Ireland, the Department of Employment and Learning. Their addresses are as follows:

Work Permits (UK)	Department of Education and Learning
Immigration and	Work Permits Unit
Nationality Directorate	Adelaide House
Home Office	39–49 Adelaide Street
Level 5, Moorfoot	Belfast BT2 8FD
Sheffield S1 4PQ	Phone 028 9025 7505
Phone 0114 259 4074	Fax 028 9025 7545
Fax 0114 259 3776	
www.workpermits.gov.uk	

A work permit will be issued for a specific employee and a specific post.

5.30   Work Permits (UK) gives information on the criteria for work permit applications in guidance notes, which are available on its website. The skills criteria are summarised below.

The job is expected to require the individual to have:

(*a*)   a UK equivalent degree level qualification; or

(*b*)   a Higher National Diploma (HND) level qualification which is relevant to the post on offer; or

(*c*)   a HND level qualification which is not relevant to the post on offer plus one year of relevant work experience; or

(*d*)   three years' experience of using specialist skills acquired through doing the type of job for which the permit is sought. This should be at National/Scottish Vocational Qualification level 3 or above.

Work permits can also be issued for entertainers and sports persons (see the relevant Work Permits (UK) guidance notes for details).

5.31   A simple application procedure exists for employees in the following categories:

(*a*)   intra company transfers (for employees of multinational companies who have at least six months' in-house experience gained overseas and are being transferred to the UK);

(*b*)   board level posts;

(*c*)   inward investment (for posts that are essential to an inward investment project bringing jobs and money to the UK); and (*d*)   shortage occupations (for occupations in which Work Permits (UK) recognises that suitably qualified people are in very short supply).

5.32   In other cases a more rigorous application procedure applies, requiring the employer to show why they cannot fill the post with a 'resident worker'. A 'resident worker' is a person who is an EEA national or has settled status within the meaning of the *IA 1971*.

5.33   If a person completes four continuous years in the UK as a work permit holder he may be eligible to apply for indefinite leave to remain. [*IR, para 134*].

Training and work experience

5.34   The Training and Work Experience Scheme (TWES) is designed to allow individuals to gain skills and experience through work based learning which builds on their previous education and training, and which they intend to use on their return overseas. The person must be additional to the employer's normal staffing requirements.

TWES permits are issued on the understanding that the person intends to leave the UK at the end of the agreed period. A person who has held a TWES permit will not normally be eligible for another work permit until he has completed twelve months outside the UK. If the TWES permit was issued for over twelve months the person will not normally be eligible to return for another work permit until he has completed 24 months outside the UK.

Permit free employment

5.35   A person in any of the following categories, although coming to the UK for employment, will not need a work permit but may be admitted if he holds a valid entry clearance (or, in the case of seasonal workers at agricultural camps, a valid Home Office identity card) and if he meets the other requirements of the *Rules* for the particular category of employment:

(*a*)   seasonal workers at agricultural camps [*IR, paras 104–109*];

(*b*)   teachers and language assistants under approved exchange schemes [*IR, paras 110–115*];

(*c*)   representatives of overseas newspapers, news agencies and broadcasting organisations [*IR, paras 136–141*];

(*d*)   representatives of overseas firms which have no branch, subsidiary or other representative in the UK [*IR, paras 144–149*];

(*e*)   private servants in diplomatic households [*IR, paras 152–157*];

(*f*) employees of an overseas government or approved international organisation [*IR, paras 160–166*];

(*g*) ministers of religion, missionaries and members of religious orders [*IR, paras 169–175*];

(*h*) airport based operational ground staff of overseas owned airlines [*IR, paras 178–183*].

Persons seeking to enter the UK for business

5.36   A person seeking to enter the UK for the purpose of establishing himself in business must hold a valid entry clearance issued for that purpose and must also show that:

(*a*) he has not less than £200,000 of his own money under his control and disposable in the UK which is held in his own name and which he will be investing in the business in the UK;

(*b*) until his business provides him with an income, he will have sufficient additional funds to maintain and accommodate himself and any dependants without recourse to other employment or to public funds;

(*c*) he will be actively involved full time in the running of the business;

(*d*) his level of financial investment will be proportionate to his interest in the business;

(*e*) he will have either a controlling or equal interest in the business;

(*f*) he will be able to bear his share of the liabilities of the business; and

(*g*) there is a genuine need for his investment and services.

[*IR, para 201*].

A business means an enterprise as a sole trader, partnership or company registered in the UK. [*IR, para 200*].

5.37   Where he is taking over or joining as a partner or director an existing business, he must produce evidence that his services and investment will create at least two new full-time jobs for persons already settled in the UK. [*IR, para 202*].

Where he wishes to establish a new business in the UK he must produce evidence that he will be bringing into the country sufficient funds of his own to establish the business and that the business will create full-time paid employment for at least two persons already settled in the UK. [*IR, para 203*].

5.38   Admission may be granted for an initial period not exceeding twelve months with a restriction on taking employment. [*IR, para 204*].

Applications for a three year extension of stay in order to remain in business in the UK will be considered by the Home Office who will require evidence that the respective conditions have been fulfilled. [*IR, para 206*].

If a person completes four continuous years in the UK in this category he may be eligible to apply for indefinite leave to remain. [*IR, para 209*].

Persons intending to establish themselves in business under the provisions of EC association agreements

5.39   Nationals of Bulgaria, the Czech Republic, Estonia, Hungary, Latvia, Lithuania, Poland, Romania, Slovakia and Slovenia may be given leave to enter the UK for the purpose of establishing themselves in business. They must hold a valid entry clearance issued for that purpose and satisfy requirements similar to those to be satisfied by a person seeking leave to enter to establish himself in business. [*IR, para 212*]. However there is no requirement of a minimum investment of £200,000 and no requirement to create two new full-time jobs.

Innovators

5.40   In September 2000 the British Government introduced a new immigration category, the Innovator category, which is designed to attract entrepreneurs to the UK, especially those intending to set up e-commerce businesses.

A person seeking entry as an Innovator must show that:

(*a*)   his proposed business will create at least two full-time jobs for people who are settled in the UK;

(*b*)   he will have, in his own name, at least 5 per cent of the shares in the company, which must be registered in the UK;

(*c*)   he will be able to support and accommodate himself and any dependants without having to do other work or get help from public funds until the business gives him an income; and

(*d*)   he has enough money available (or agreed in principle) to finance the business for the first six months after he arrives in the UK.

The application is considered on a points system divided into three sections – the personal characteristics of the applicant, the viability of the business and the economic benefit to the UK. The application must score a specified number of points in each of the three sections and a specified overall total.

Permission is given for 18 months initially, with the possibility of a 30-month extension.

If a person completes four continuous years in the UK as an Innovator he may be eligible to apply for indefinite leave to remain.

Highly Skilled Migrant Programme

5.41 In January 2002 the British Government introduced a new programme, the Highly Skilled Migrant Programme, which is designed to enable talented individuals with exceptional skills to enter the UK.

Applications are decided on a points systems. Points can be accrued in the following areas: educational qualifications, work experience, past earnings and achievement in the person's chosen field (in addition to a section for people seeking to work as General Practitioners).

Permission is given for twelve months initially, with the possibility of a three-year extension.

If a person completes four continuous years in the UK under the Highly Skilled Migrant Programme he may be eligible to apply for indefinite leave to remain.

Investors

5.42   A person seeking admission to the UK as an investor must hold a valid UK entry clearance issued for that purpose and must also fulfil the following conditions:

(*a*)   he must have money of his own of not less than £1,000,000 which must be under his control and disposable in the UK;

(*b*)   he must intend to invest not less than £750,000 of his capital in UK Government bonds or in share capital or loan capital of active and trading UK registered companies;

(*c*)   he must intend to make the UK his main home and be able to maintain and accommodate himself and any dependants without taking employment (other than self-employment or business) or recourse to public funds.

[*IR, para 224*].

A person admitted as an investor may be admitted for an initial period not exceeding twelve months with a restriction on taking employment. [*IR, para 225*]. He may, however, be self-employed or engage in business. Thereafter, a three-year extension of stay as an investor may be granted provided that the respective conditions continue to be satisfied. [*IR, para 228*].

If a person completes four continuous years in the UK as an Investor he may be eligible to apply for indefinite leave to remain. [*IR, para 230*].

Writers, composers and artists

5.43   A person seeking to enter the UK as a writer or a composer or an artist must hold a valid UK entry clearance. He will also need to show that he has already established himself in his particular field outside of the UK, that he does not intend to work other than in self-employment as a writer, composer or an artist and that he will be able to maintain and accommodate himself and any dependants from his own resources. [*IR, para 232*].

Admission to the UK may be granted for an initial period of 12 months subject to a condition restricting his freedom to take employment. [*IR, para 233*].

A three-year extension of stay may be granted if the respective conditions continue to be satisfied. [*IR, para 236*].

If a person completes four continuous years in the UK in this category he may be eligible to apply for indefinite leave to remain. [*IR, para 238*].

Retired persons of independent means

5.44   A person seeking leave to enter the UK as a retired person of independent means must hold a valid UK entry clearance. He will also need to show that he is at least 60 years old, that he has under his control and disposable in the UK an income of not less than £25,000 per annum. He must be able and willing to maintain and accommodate himself and any dependants indefinitely in the UK from his own resources without working and without assistance from any other person or from public funds. In addition, he must demonstrate a close connection with the UK and must intend to make the UK his main home. [*IR, para 263*].

5.45   A person may be admitted as a retired person of independent means for an initial period of up to four years, subject to a condition prohibiting employment. [*IR, para 264*].

5.46   If a person completes four continuous years in the UK in this category he may be eligible to apply for indefinite leave to remain. [*IR, para 269*].

Dependants

5.47   The spouse and unmarried children under the age of 18 of a person admitted to the UK for any of the purposes described at 5.27–5.44 above (but excluding seasonal workers at agricultural camps) should be given leave to enter for the period of that person's authorised stay if they hold current entry clearances. An entry clearance will be refused unless the Entry Clearance Officer is satisfied that there will be adequate accommodation for them in accommodation which they will own or occupy exclusively and that they will be able to maintain themselves without recourse to public funds. [*IR, paras 122–127, 194–199, 240–245* and *271–276*].

5.48   Leave to enter or remain in the UK for the spouse and children under the age of 18 of a person admitted as a retired person of independent means will be subject to a condition prohibiting employment. [*IR, paras 272–275*].

5.49   A child will not be admitted unless both parents are admitted, or the parent whom the child will be joining has had sole responsibility for the child's upbringing, or there are other compelling considerations which make the child's exclusion from the UK undesirable.

Registration with the Police

5.50   A person aged 16 years or over who is a *relevant foreign national* and has been given a limited leave to enter the UK or who is granted an extension of stay which has the effect of allowing him to stay in the UK for more than six months, calculated from the date of arrival, is normally required to register with the police. [*IR, paras 325–326*].

A 'relevant foreign national' is defined by the *Rules* as a stateless person, a person holding a non-national travel document or a national or citizen of a country listed in Appendix 2 to the *Rules*. [*IR, para 324A*]. The list in Appendix 2 is as follows:

Afghanistan	Iran	Qatar
Algeria	Iraq	Russia
Argentina	Israel	Saudi Arabia
Armenia	Jordan	Sudan
Azerbaijan	Kazakhstan	Syria
Bahrain	Kirgizstan	Tajikistan
Belarus	Kuwait	Tunisia
Bolivia	Lebanon	Turkey
Bhutan	Libya	Turkmenistan
Brazil	Moldova	United Arab Emirates
China	Morocco	Ukraine
Colombia	North Korea	Uzbekistan
Cuba	Oman	Yemen
Egypt	Palestine	
Georgia	Peru	

The requirement of registration with the police is imposed only in respect of certain classes of limited leave to enter the UK. It applies when a relevant foreign national is given limited leave to enter the UK for employment for longer than six months, unless he has been admitted for permit free employment as:

(*a*)   a seasonal worker at an agricultural camp;

(*b*)   a private servant in a diplomatic household;

(*c*)   a minister of religion, missionary or member of a religious order.

[*IR, para 325(1)(i)*].

Relevant foreign nationals given limited leave to enter the UK for longer than six months as students, au pairs, businessmen and self-employed -persons, investors, persons of independent means and creative artists are also under an obligation to register, as is the relevant foreign national spouse or child of a person required to register with the police. [*IR, para 325(1)(ii)–(iii)*].

Variation of leave

5.51   Where limited leave to enter or remain in the UK has been granted, such leave may be varied, whether by extending or restricting or removing the limit on its duration or by adding, varying or revoking conditions. [*IA 1971, s 3(3)(a)*].

Applications relating to employment for which a work permit or training and work experience permit is required are made to Work Permits (UK) at the Home Office. [*IR, para 33*]. Other applications are made to the Home Office in London. Applications must be made before the applicant's current leave to enter or remain in the UK expires. [*IR, para 32*].

Settlement

5.52   A person is 'settled' in the UK when he is:

(*a*)   free from any restriction on the period for which he may remain; and

(*b*)   ordinarily resident in the UK without having entered or remained in breach of the immigration laws.

[*IR, para 6*].

5.53   A person seeking leave to enter the UK as a returning resident may be admitted for settlement provided the immigration officer is satisfied that the person concerned:

(*a*)   had indefinite leave to enter or remain in the UK when he last left;

(*b*)   has not been away from the UK for more than two years;

(*c*)   did not receive assistance from public funds towards the cost of leaving the UK; and

(*d*)   now seeks admission for the purpose of settlement.

Family members coming for settlement

5.54   A person seeking leave to enter the UK as the spouse of a person who is present and settled in the UK or who is at the same time being admitted for settlement must hold a valid UK entry clearance. An entry clearance will be refused unless the Entry Clearance Officer is satisfied that each of the parties intends to live permanently with the other as his and her spouse and that there will be adequate accommodation for the parties and any dependants without recourse to public funds. [*IR, para 281*].

The spouse may be admitted for an initial period not exceeding 12 months. [*IR, para 282*]. Thereafter, provided that the marriage is subsisting, a spouse may be granted indefinite leave to remain in the UK. [*IR, para 287*].

5.55   A person seeking leave to enter the UK as the fiancé(e) of a person present and settled in the UK or who is at the same time being admitted for settlement will require a valid UK entry clearance. The Entry Clearance Officer must be satisfied that it is intended that the parties should live together permanently and that adequate maintenance and accommodation will be available for the person seeking leave to enter both before and after the marriage without recourse to public funds. [*IR, para 290*].

Such person will be admitted for six months with a prohibition on employment [*IR, para 291*]. An extension of stay as a fiancé(e) may be granted for an appropriate period if the applicant can show good cause why the marriage will not take place within the initial period of leave. [*IR, para 294*].

5.56   Unmarried children under 18 will be admitted for settlement if both parents or one parent with the sole responsibility for the children's upbringing are present and settled in the UK. [*IR, para 299*].

In certain circumstances, adopted children, older children and other dependent relatives may be admitted for settlement. [*IR, paras 310, 317*].

5.57   A person seeking leave to enter the UK as the unmarried partner of a person present and settled in the UK or who is at the same time being admitted for settlement will require a valid UK entry clearance. The Entry Clearance Officer must be satisfied that:

(*a*)   any previous marriage (or similar relationship) by either partner has permanently broken down; and

(*b*)   the parties are legally unable to marry under UK law (or than by reason of consanguineous relationships or age); and

(*c*)   the parties have been living together in a relationship akin to marriage which has subsisted for two years or more;

(*d*)   the parties intend to live together permanently.

The Entry Clearance Officer must also be satisfied that adequate maintenance and accommodation (owned or exclusively occupied) will be available
for the parties and any dependants without recourse to public funds.
[*IR, para 295A*].

The applicant partner may be admitted for an initial period not exceeding 24
months. Thereafter, providing the relationship is subsisting, a partner may
be granted indefinite leave to remain in the UK. The *Rules* also contain provision for leave to remain as an unmarried partner to be granted to an
applicant partner with existing limited leave to remain, provided that
requirements of the kind set out above are met. [*IR, para 295D*]. There are
two additional requirements for leave to remain: first, that the applicant
partner has not remained in the UK in breach of the immigration laws; secondly, that the parties' relationship pre-dates any decision or
recommendation to deport the applicant.

Appeals

5.58   A person who is refused leave to enter the UK under the *Act* may
appeal to an adjudicator against the decision that he requires leave or against
the refusal. [*IAA 1999, s 59(1)*].

A person who, on an application duly made, is refused an entry clearance
may appeal to an adjudicator against the refusal. [*IAA 1999, s 59(2)*].

5.59   A person may appeal against a decision to vary, or to refuse to vary,
any limited leave to enter or remain in the UK which he has if, as a result of
that decision, he may be required to leave the UK within 28 days of being
notified of the decision. [*IAA 1999, s 61*]. A variation shall not take effect so
long as an appeal is pending against the variation. An appellant shall not be
required to leave the UK by reason of the expiration of his leave until the
end of the period allowed for appealing the decision. [*IA 1971, s 3C*].

5.60   These rights of appeal are subject to certain exceptions.

For instance, there is no right of appeal against a refusal to vary leave if the
Home Secretary certifies that the appellant's departure from the UK would
be conducive to the public good. [*IAA 1999, s 62(4)*].

No right of appeal to an adjudicator lies against the refusal of Work Permits
(UK) to issue a work permit or to approve a training or work experience
scheme (*Pearson v Immigration Appeal Tribunal [1978] Imm AR 212*) and no
appeal lies against a variation of leave or a refusal to vary it if the application
to vary was made after the expiry of the existing limited leave (*Suthendran v
Immigration Appeal Tribunal [1977] AC 359*). Work Permits (UK) has an
internal appeals procedure for the independent review of its decisions about
the issue of work permits.

5.61   A person in possession of a valid UK entry clearance or named in a current work permit who is refused leave to enter the UK may exercise his right of appeal before removal from the UK. Any other person entitled to appeal against refusal of leave to enter may usually only exercise the right of appeal after he has left the UK. [*IAA 1999, s 60(3)*].

5.62   The time limits for appeals to an adjudicator are set out in the *Immigration and Asylum Appeals (Procedure) Rules 2000* (*IAAPR*).

Appeals against the decision of an adjudicator lie to the Immigration Appeal Tribunal, with leave from the adjudicator or the Tribunal. [*IAAPR*].

A person may appeal to an adjudicator if he alleges that, in taking a decision relating to his entitlement to enter or remain in the UK, the Home Secretary, an immigration officer or an entry clearance officer has racially discrimated against him or breached his human rights. [*IAA 1999, s 65(1)*].

5.63 In its February 2002 White Paper, *Secure Borders, Safe Haven*, the Home Office proposes wide-reaching changes to immigration, nationality and asylum law. Areas under review include unmarried partners (the Home Office intends to remove the requirement that unmarried partners must be legally unable to marry), spouses (the probationary period may be increased to two years) and working holidaymakers (the scheme may be extended to citizens of EU candidate countries and the restrictions on the type of work which working holidaymakers can carry out may be lifted).

6 Income Tax and Capital Gains Tax Planning for Non-Domiciled Individuals

F Michael Mitchell MA (Oxon) MA (Cantab)
(Withers LLP) and

Janette Cattell LLB
(Withers LLP)

Introduction

6.1   The income tax and capital gains tax position of those individuals who are resident in the UK but are domiciled elsewhere will be considered in this chapter. Such individuals are in a privileged position in the UK tax system. Although the Revenue proposed some material restrictions on these privileges in its 1988 consultative document 'Residence in the United Kingdom: The Scope of UK Taxation for Individuals', the amount of opposition to the proposals led to their total withdrawal and an announcement that no new proposals were to be introduced. In 1991 the Revenue published a consultative document 'Trusts' on the income tax and capital gains tax treatment of UK resident trusts. Although this proposed a number of radical changes, the government announced in early 1993 that they did not intend to proceed with the principal changes. Since coming into power in 1997, however, the Labour Government has made the tax position in relation to non-UK resident trusts far less favourable and, in particular, the *Finance Act 1998* restricted considerably the capital gains tax advantages of trusts established by non-UK domiciled individuals.

Principal tax provisions

Capital gains tax

6.2   An individual cannot be liable to capital gains tax unless he is either resident or ordinarily resident in the UK during the year in which the chargeable gain is realised. *FA 1998, s 127* introduced new rules (now contained in *TCGA 1992, s 10A*) to prevent individuals going abroad for a short period in order to realise gains while non-resident. These rules apply only to those who became non-resident on or after 17 March 1998. Subject to this, any person who has been resident in the UK for four out of seven years before leaving the UK and who is not non-resident for at least five full tax years will be caught by the new provisions. The effect of this is that any capital gains realised during the period of non-residence will be treated as realised in the year of a person's return to the UK and he will pay tax on them accordingly. These provisions will also apply in relation to the attribution to beneficiaries of gains realised by non-resident trustees (see 6.6). *Section 10A(6)* provides that the provisions of the section are without prejudice to any right to claim relief in accordance with any double taxation arrangements (see 6.32).

In the case of an individual who is domiciled in the UK, the location of the assets disposed of is immaterial. In the case of an individual who is domiciled outside the UK, his liability will depend on the location of the assets. Gains realised on the disposal of UK situs assets are fully taxable. Gains realised on the disposal of assets with a non-UK situs become taxable only if and when 'amounts in respect of the gain' (i.e., in normal circumstances, the proceeds of the disposal) are remitted to the UK. [*TCGA 1992, s 12*]. The amount of gain remitted will be that proportion of the amount remitted which the gain bore to the total proceeds of sale.

6.3   The rules relating to trusts, like those for individuals, depend on residence. Resident trustees are fully taxable; non-resident trustees are not taxable at all. *TCGA 1992, s 69* determines the residence of trustees. Trustees will be treated as resident in the UK unless at least a majority of trustees are resident outside the UK and the general administration of the trust is carried on outside the UK. There are special rules for UK resident professional trustees who will, in certain circumstances, be treated as non-resident for capital gains purposes, with the general administration of the trust being treated as carried on outside the UK. For this rule to apply, all of the assets in the settlement must have derived from a settlor who was at the time of the settlement domiciled and resident outside the UK.

6.4   Professional trustees are defined as those persons who act as trustees in the course of a business which includes the management of trusts. Trust corporations would normally be professional trustees as would solicitors and accountants who habitually perform a trustee role. It is understood that the Revenue does not regard investment advisers as falling within the definition of professional trustees and there may be some question about solicitors and accountants who do not normally act as trustees in the typical course of their business. Professionals who are employed (as opposed to self-employed) do not fall within the definition since they will not be acting in the course of a business carried on by them.

6.5   There is a range of anti-avoidance provisions dealing with the taxation of offshore trusts that are now contained in the settlement provisions of *TCGA 1992*. The main provisions in this connection are as follows.

Section 87

6.6   The broad effect of *TCGA 1992, s 87* is, subject to a surcharge, to allow the deferment of liability on capital gains realised by non-resident trustees until such time as 'capital payments' are made to beneficiaries resident or ordinarily resident and domiciled in the UK.

In each year a calculation has to be made of the 'amount' on which the trustees would have been chargeable to capital gains tax had they been resident in the UK. As and when a beneficiary receives a capital payment out of the trust, then a corresponding amount of the trust gains are imputed to him. The beneficiary, if he is resident or ordinarily resident and domiciled in the UK, is taxed on the imputed capital gain which is also subject to a 'surcharge'. The surcharge [*TCGA 1992, s 91*] is broadly 10 per cent of the tax payable for each year of deferral, up to a maximum of six years. Since it is an amount by reference to the gains, rather than the gains themselves, which is imputed to the beneficiary under *section 87*, the Revenue relies upon this to deny the beneficiary credit for any foreign tax suffered by the trustees on disposals of assets giving rise to the gains.

The term 'capital payment' is given a wide meaning and includes any payment or other benefit which is not chargeable to income tax on the recipient or, in the case of a non-resident recipient, any payment received otherwise than as income. It includes any form of benefit and not just a payment of money. The Court of Appeal in the case of *Billingham (Insp of Taxes) v Cooper; Edwards (Insp of Taxes) v Fisher [2001] STC 1177* upheld the decision of the High Court that an unsecured loan made to a settlor life tenant, interest free and repayable on demand, gave rise to an annual charge to tax on trust gains in the hands of the life tenant for each year in which the loan was outstanding by reference to the amount of interest which the life tenant would have paid on the loan had it been on commercial terms. The fact that the life tenant was entitled to the income under the settlement made no difference. Lord Justice Walker in the Court of Appeal seems to have had some difficulty with adopting the Revenue's interpretation of the matter, namely that the trustees make a series of day to day decisions to keep the loan outstanding that continually confer a benefit (and that hence there is a series of capital payments); but he concluded that the construction of the legislation adopted by Lloyd J was 'a permissible (although awkward) construction which gives effect to the manifest purpose of the legislation'. Leave to appeal to the House of Lords was refused by both the Court of Appeal and, on petition, by the House of Lords.

There appears to be no material difference between an interest free loan and the rent free occupation of a trust property by a beneficiary. It should, therefore, be assumed that a beneficiary in this position will be assessable to tax each year under *section 87* by reference to the market rent which would otherwise be payable on the property (to the extent that he is not assessable pursuant to *ICTA 1988, s 740* – (see 6.21)).

As a rule, the Revenue does not regard the appointment of an interest in trust assets as a capital payment. However, it is understood that the Revenue may regard an exercise of a power of advancement for the benefit of a particular beneficiary by way of a transfer to another settlement as a capital payment. It is, therefore, sensible for trustees, when transferring funds to another settlement, to exercise a power of appointment for the benefit of beneficiaries generally rather than for the benefit of one specific beneficiary. It may also be better to advance assets rather than cash – this view is based upon the wording of *TCGA, s 97(4)*, which makes it clear that on an advancement of cash the amount advanced is clearly the cash sum, whereas arguably, on an advancement of other assets, the amount of the capital payment is the value of the interest taken by the beneficiaries under the new settlement, which could be negligible where the interest is defeasible. It is not clear how far the Revenue subscribe to either of the above views – certainly the distinction between cash and other assets does not seem to be a logical one. A transfer of assets to another settlement which is not for the benefit of a specific beneficiary and cannot, therefore, be a capital payment falls within the provisions of *TCGA 1992, s 90*. In a case where the transferor settlement has outstanding trust gains within it at the time of the transfer, *section 90* provides that the trust gains of the transferee settlement for the year shall be treated as increased by an amount equal to the outstanding trust gains for the year of the transferor settlement or, where part only of the settled property is transferred, to a proportionate part of those trust gains. (See also 6.40.)

Prior to 6 April 1998, *section 87* only applied when the settlor was either resident (or ordinarily resident) and domiciled in the UK when he made the settlement or subsequently became both domiciled and resident (or ordinarily resident) in the UK in a year in which gains were realised by the trustees. For the settlor who continued to be domiciled outside the UK, therefore, *section 87* had no application and trust gains only 'counted' if the settlor became resident (or ordinarily resident) and domiciled in the UK. *FA 1998, s 130* provided that, with effect from 6 April 1998, any gains realised by trustees and any capital payments made to beneficiaries will be within the *section 87* regime no matter where the settlor is resident or domiciled. This applies to all trusts, whenever established, and even in cases where the trust may have been set up with absolutely no thought of UK tax avoidance.

Section 86

6.7   The *section 87* regime has been supplemented by and, to a large extent, replaced with *TCGA 1992, s 86* which was introduced in 1991.

Section 86 imputes gains realised by certain offshore trusts to their settlors for UK capital gains tax purposes. It only applies if the settlor is resident or ordinarily resident and domiciled in the UK at some time in the year.

When originally introduced, *section 86* applied only where, *inter alia*:

(*a*)   the settlement was created on or after 19 March 1991, or

(*b*)   the settlement was created before 19 March 1991 but was 'tainted' by an event detailed in *TCGA 1992, Sch 5 para 9(3)-(6)*; and (*c*)   any person within the 'defined categories', broadly, the settlor, his spouse or children or their spouses (and any company controlled by them) was capable of benefiting under the settlement.

FA 1998 extended these rules in two ways.

(i)   The rules now apply to all trusts under which the settlor or other persons mentioned in sub-paragraph (*c*) above are capable of benefiting, regardless of when they were created. Certain transitional provisions were introduced which permitted pre-1991 settlements to be re-arranged in order to avoid the *section 86* charge and any settlement which was a 'protected settlement' as at 6 April 1999 falls outside the scope of the charge whilst it remains protected. Broadly speaking, a settlement is protected if the only persons capable of benefit are children of the settlor or his spouse who are under the age of 18 and their respective spouses or other persons who are outside the 'defined categories'. [*TCGA 1992, Sch 5 para 9(10A)*].

(ii)   In relation to any trusts established after 17 March 1998 and any pre-existing trusts which are 'tainted' after 17 March 1998, *section 86* will also apply if the settlor's grandchildren or their spouses (or any companies controlled by them) can benefit under the terms of the settlement.

As mentioned above, *section 86* applies only where the settlor is resident or ordinarily resident and domiciled in the UK. An individual who continues to be domiciled outside the UK can, therefore, avoid an immediate charge to capital gains tax even where the trust disposes of assets situated in the UK and in circumstances where he and his immediate family are beneficiaries of the trust. However, *section 87* will apply to gains realised by the trustees so that the benefit is a deferral rather than an exemption from tax.

6.8   *TCGA 1992, s 13* applies to non-UK companies that would be close companies if they were resident in the UK. Capital gains realised by such companies are attributed to UK resident participators in the company. In its original form, the section attributed gains only to 'shareholders', excluding any who were not domiciled and any who held less than 5 per cent of the equity of the company (calculated by reference to rights on a liquidation). *Finance Act 1996* substantially amended the section so that gains are to be apportioned among participators (as defined for close company purposes in *ICTA 1988, s 417*). It therefore catches loan creditors and guarantors of a guarantee company. The part of the gain attributed to a participator is that proportion which corresponds to the extent of the participator's interest as participator in the company and this must be ascertained on a 'just and reasonable' basis. [*section 13(13)*]. A 5 per cent threshold still applies but, for this purpose, the interest of a participator is aggregated with that of any 'connected persons' within the meaning of *TCGA 1992, s 286*. The exclusion for participators who are non-UK domiciled still applies.

Section 13 gains can be attributed to both resident and non-resident trustees and also to non-resident companies. There is no motive test for *section 13*, although *subsection (5)* provides for various exclusions which have been reduced by the *FA 1996* changes. In particular, the exception for gains which were distributed within two years of their realisation, either by way of dividend or on a liquidation, no longer applies. Instead, *section 13(5A)* provides that where a gain is distributed within two years of having been realised, the capital gains tax paid by a person in respect of that gain is applied to reduce or eliminate any liability to income tax or capital gains tax of that person arising in respect of the distribution. Thus, the *section 13* tax must still be paid at the outset and the relief operates only to reduce or eliminate liability – it does not confer a tax credit in respect of which a repayment claim can be made. The exact operation of *section 13(5A)* is at present unclear but there may be scope for double taxation where there is a mismatch between the person liable to tax under *section 13* and the recipient of the distribution. There is an exception for gains on the disposal of assets used for the purposes of a non-UK business.

Income tax

6.9   Liability to income tax depends on residence, domicile and the source of the income. An individual who is resident and domiciled is liable to income tax on all of his income, regardless of source. An individual who is resident but not domiciled is liable to tax on all of his UK source income on an 'arising' basis and on his non-UK source income on a 'remittance' basis. Unlike the capital gains tax rules for remittances (where the remittance is treated as proportionately capital and capital gain) the income tax rule is that any remittance will be treated as income unless it can be conclusively shown that it is not. The rationale for this is that a person is assumed to live off his income so that he will have remitted his income first and only remitted his capital once he has exhausted his income.

A non-resident is liable to income tax on his UK source income subject to any particular exemptions (e.g., on certain government securities) and any reliefs offered by applicable double tax treaties.

6.10   In the case of earned income, the position is slightly different in that the tax liability will be determined additionally by the place in which the duties of the employment are performed. Schedule E has three cases.

(*a*)   Case I – individuals who are resident and ordinarily resident are taxable on all of their earnings. Non-domiciled residents have the benefit of an exemption (from Case I) for 'foreign emoluments', i.e., earnings from non-UK duties performed for a non-UK resident employer.

(*b*)   Case II – individuals who are either not resident or not ordinarily resident are taxable on earnings from duties performed in the UK.

(*c*)   Case III – individuals who are resident (whether or not ordinarily resident) but not domiciled are taxable under Case III on any earnings remitted to the UK which are not taxable under either Case I or Case II, e.g., because they are foreign emoluments for the purposes of Case I.

Trusts

6.11   The position of trusts is particularly complex in relation to income tax. There is first the question of the residence of the trustees. There was no statutory provision that determined this until 1989 when, following the decision in *Dawson v IRC [1989] STC 473, HL*, such a provision was introduced. [*FA 1989, s 110*]. Under *section 110*, when the trustees are all resident they will be treated as resident; when they are all non-resident they will be treated as non-resident. When they are 'mixed residence' trustees, i.e., not all either resident or non-resident, they will be treated as resident unless the settlor was neither domiciled nor resident nor ordinarily resident in the UK when he made the settlement, in which case they will be treated as non-resident.

6.12   The second issue that determines the income tax treatment of trusts is the nature of the trust. Where there is a life tenant or other beneficiary entitled as of right to the income, the income will be treated as his for tax purposes; it will not be treated as that of the trustees (see *Williams v Singer (1920) 7 TC 387, HL*) except for any income that is retained by the trustees to meet their expenses. It follows from this that the tax treatment of the trust income will be determined by the position of the beneficiary, not that of the trustees. Where there is no beneficiary entitled to the income, most clearly in the case of a discretionary or accumulation and maintenance trust, the residence of the trustees will determine the tax treatment of the trust income.

6.13   The third issue that determines the tax treatment of trust income is, of course, the location of the source of income. This will be of particular importance where the trustees are non-resident. First, it determines whether the trustees have any liability for additional rate tax. Such a liability will arise only in relation to UK source income (see *IRC v Regent Trust Co Ltd (1979) 53 TC 54, ChD*). Secondly, it will determine how the anti-avoidance sections will apply in relation to the trust income since these all provide for a remittance basis of taxation for non-domiciled individuals.

Income tax anti-avoidance provisions

6.14   While all of the income tax anti-avoidance provisions can apply to both resident and non-resident trusts, there are two in particular that apply where the trustees are non-resident, or resident but not domiciled; these are *ICTA 1988, ss 739, 740*. These need to be considered in some detail. For simplicity the following discussion will assume that the sections only relate to trusts; it must, however, be recognised that companies and other entities also fall squarely within the scope of the sections.

ICTA 1988, s 739

6.15   *ICTA 1988, s 739* applies where there has been a transfer of assets as a result of which income arises to a person either resident or domiciled outside the UK. If a person ordinarily resident in the UK has power to enjoy the income and if that person was the original transferor (or in some circumstances otherwise associated with the transfer) then all of the income that arises to the non-resident will be treated as if it was his. *Section 739* also applies where the transferor receives a capital payment from the trust even where he has no power to enjoy the income; such a receipt of capital will cause all of the past income to be treated as his.

The House of Lords (upholding the decision of the Court of Appeal) held in the case of *IRC v Willoughby [1997] STC 995* that *section 739* did not apply where, at the time of the relevant transfer of assets, the transferor was not ordinarily resident in the UK. Legislation to counteract the effect of this decision was introduced in *FA 1997* so that, in relation to income arising on or after 26 November 1996 (irrespective of when the transfer or associated operations took place), *section 739* applies whether or not the individual was ordinarily resident in the UK at the time the transfer was made. The transfer of assets does not have to originate from the UK. A transfer from one foreign jurisdiction to another would almost certainly be within the ambit of *section 739.*

6.16   The meaning of the phrase 'power to enjoy' is set out in *ICTA 1988, s 742(2)*. It covers not only the ability to derive any benefit from the income, directly or indirectly, but also a power to control the application of the income even if the individual cannot himself benefit from it. The phrase was considered in *IRC v Schroder (1983) 57 TC 94, Ch D* which considered the position of the settlor who had power, in certain circumstances, to appoint trustees and who also had power to appoint members of a committee of protectors which had the power to remove and appoint trustees. It was held that the powers of both the settlor and the committee of protectors were fiduciary in nature and, in the absence of evidence to prove that the settlor in fact controlled the committee, it could not be assumed that it would act otherwise than in accordance with its fiduciary obligations with the result that the settlor could not be said to have power to enjoy within the meaning of the section.

6.17   A non-domiciled settlor has (although only since 1981) the benefit of the remittance basis in relation to *ICTA 1988, s 739*. This is to be found in *ICTA 1988, s 743(3)* and provides that the settlor will only be taxed on income treated as his under *section 739* if he would have been taxable on it had it actually been his. The Revenue has confirmed that a non-UK domiciled settlor who is outside the charge to tax under *section 739* by virtue of the remittance rules, will not be assessed under *section 740* (Tax Bulletin Issue 40, April 1999).

6.18   *ICTA 1988, s 741* provides for a total exclusion from *section 739* if it can be shown either that the transfer was made for bona fide commercial reasons or that the purpose of the transfer or any associated operation was not to avoid tax. 'Tax' is not limited to income tax; it includes any UK tax. Where the taxpayer has been able to establish that at least one of the purposes for undertaking the transaction did not entail tax avoidance, the Revenue will explain their reasons to the taxpayer as to why, in its view, tax avoidance may also have been involved. If the transaction does involve tax avoidance, the Revenue seeks to apply an objective test arguing that tax avoidance must be a purpose even if the transferor did not form the subjective intention of avoiding tax. However, in the case of *A Beneficiary v IRC [1999] STC (SCD) 134* the Special Commissioners concluded that a subjective test should be applied and that the settlor in that case (who was Japanese) could not be deemed to have had in contemplation all the fiscal consequences of making the settlement.

The expression 'bona fide commercial' is taken to apply only to the furtherance of a trade or business, and not to the making or managing of investments. The definition of an 'associated operation' is to be found in *ICTA 1988, s 742(1)* and is extremely broad; it includes any operation affecting the assets transferred or the income arising from the assets or any assets representing such assets or income. It also includes the making of a will but, it seems, not a person's death. In practice, it is comparatively rare to find a situation where there is genuinely no UK tax avoidance purpose. If one does have such a situation it is of the greatest importance to ensure that no steps are taken which might constitute an associated operation and which are tainted with a UK tax avoidance purpose since these would taint the whole structure.

The deferment of liability to tax can constitute the avoidance of liability to tax for the purposes of *section 739*, although if the deferment is as a result of a special regime determined by Parliament there is no avoidance merely on the ground that the taxpayer might have chosen a different application which would have subjected him to less favourable tax treatment (see the *Willoughby* case above).

ICTA 1988, s 740

6.19   When *section 739* was first introduced in 1936 it was stated that its application would be limited to those who were responsible for the transfer of the assets. In *Congreve & Congreve v IRC (1948) 30 TC 163, HL* the House of Lords held that the section applied to anyone who had power to enjoy the income resulting from the transfer regardless of whether he had been responsible for the transfer. In 1980, the House of Lords, in *Vesty v IRC (1979) 54 TC 503, HL*, reversed themselves and held that *section 739* was restricted to those who had made the transfer of the assets and, possibly, others closely associated with the transfer.

6.20   In response the Revenue introduced what is now *section 740*. This *section* applies in the same circumstances as *section 739* but it only applies to those who are not liable to tax under *section 739*. As with *section 739*, only individuals who are ordinarily resident in the UK are potentially taxable under *section 740*. The decision in *IRC v Willoughby* (above) is limited in its effect to *section 739* (and the Revenue has confirmed that a transferor of assets who is outside the charge to tax under *section 739* in respect of income arising before 26 November 1996 through being non-ordinarily resident in the UK at the time of the transfer, is not assessed under *section 740*). *Section 740* can, however, apply to other individuals who receive benefits under the terms of the settlement.

The section works in a similar way to *TCGA 1992, s 87* in relation to capital gains tax. A beneficiary has no liability to income tax unless and until he has received a benefit out of the trust which is not taxable as income under normal principles. If he does receive such a benefit, the amount of the benefit will be treated as income in his hands and he will be liable to tax accordingly if and to the extent that the amount of the benefit falls within the amount of relevant income at the time. If the amount of the benefit exceeds the amount of relevant income available at the time, the relevant income of future years will be attributed to the beneficiary until he has been taxed on an amount equal to the value of the benefit received by him. 'Relevant income' is defined in *section 740(3)* to mean income received by the non-resident or non-domiciled person which can be used directly or indirectly for the purpose of providing a benefit to the individual in question. The Revenue accepts that income used in payment of trust expenses properly attributable to income or which is paid to a non-UK resident beneficiary ceases to be relevant income. In the latter case it is necessary to be able to show clearly that what was paid out is actual income or assets representing income. This may in practice be difficult where income has accrued over a number of years and has been invested without keeping it separate from capital.

6.21   *Section 740*, like *section 739*, provides for a remittance basis for non-domiciled beneficiaries, albeit in modified form. A non-domiciled beneficiary will not be taxable on any benefit unless either the income had a UK source or the income was remitted to the UK or the benefit was enjoyed in the UK. In determining the source of the income, it is necessary to look through offshore holding companies to the 'real' source of the income; UK source income cannot be turned into non-UK source income by holding the UK income producing asset through an offshore company.

The Revenue does not consider that the appointment of a beneficial interest in trust assets by itself constitutes a benefit for the purposes of *section 740*. *Subsection (1)(b)* refers to a 'benefit provided of assets' and the Revenue normally construes these words as a requirement either that property must have left the settlement or that the benefit consists of the actual enjoyment of specific property, e.g., an interest-free loan or being allowed to occupy a house owned by the trust.

Tax planning for individuals without using trusts

Income tax and capital gains tax

6.22   The key to income tax and capital gains tax planning for non-domiciled UK residents is the remittance basis. Before considering practical measures that might be taken by a non-domiciled individual, it is necessary to consider what is meant by the term 'remittance' and its companion term 'constructive remittance'.

The meaning of remittance

6.23   At its simplest, a remittance will take the form of a transfer of money to the UK. A constructive remittance is something which is not a simple remittance but which involves either bringing something which is not money into the UK or bringing money into the UK which is not received in the form of income, e.g., a loan.

The classic case on the meaning of constructive remittance is *Harmel v Wright (1973) 49 TC 149, Ch D*. In this case income was used to subscribe for shares in one company which lent the funds to a second company which lent the money to the taxpayer in the UK. The judge remarked on the fact that one could trace 'with fascination, with certainty and with no difficulty at all' the path taken by the money through its series of conduit pipes before it finally ended up in the UK and held that the receipt of the funds in the UK should be construed as a remittance. Whether the same result would follow if the money had become intermingled with other funds or was otherwise impossible to identify at some point in its journey is less clear.

6.24   The question arises as to whether or not the bringing in of something other than money can constitute a remittance. The wording of *ICTA 1988, s 65(5)(a)(b)* which defines the remittance basis for Schedule D, Cases IV and V, refers to 'sums received in the United Kingdom' and it is sometimes argued that anything which is not a sum cannot be taken into account for the purposes of these subsections. It must be doubtful whether such a literal interpretation can be relied upon, since it would create considerable scope for simple avoidance of the *section*. For instance, an individual could use his overseas income to purchase negotiable securities which he would then bring into and sell in the UK. This situation arose in *Scottish Provident Institution v Allen [1903] AC 129* where it was held that the sale of the investments gave rise to a liability to tax. The Revenue Inspectors' Manual, however, makes it clear (para 1564) that a simple remittance of an asset that is something other than a commercially recognisable form of money, which is not followed by a sale of the asset, would not constitute a remittance (*Scottish Widows Fund Life Assurance v Farmer (1909) 5 TC 502*).

6.25   The case of *Timbrell v Lord Aldenham's Executors (1947) 28 TC 293, CA* involved a sum of income owing by an Australian firm to partners in

England. At the request of the latter, the funds were lent to a partnership in Chile which had an outstanding capital debt to the UK partners and which used the loan from the Australian firm to discharge part of its debt. It was held that this did not constitute a remittance of the income. Whether this case would be decided differently following *Harmel v Wright* (see 6.23) cannot be entirely certain.

6.26   Another obvious way to avoid the remittance rules might seem to be to borrow funds abroad, remit them to the UK and then use one's overseas income to repay the borrowing. *ICTA 1988, s 65(6)* covers this expressly and provides that any overseas income which is used to repay a debt incurred in the UK or a debt for money brought into the UK or a debt incurred to satisfy such a debt will be treated as remitted to the UK. Overseas income that is used to pay interest on a debt incurred in the UK will likewise be treated as remitted to the UK, although not overseas income that is used to pay interest on a debt incurred outside the UK (even if the money borrowed has been remitted to the UK). *ICTA 1988, s 65(8)* is designed to cover back-to-back loans. If overseas income is used as security (formal or informal) for the borrowing and the bank can, by set-off or otherwise, avail itself of the money to satisfy or discharge the debt, the income so used will be treated as having been remitted to the UK.

6.27   A non-domiciled resident may wish to bring money into the UK in order to discharge a debt or to benefit some third person. The question in these circumstances is whether a transfer of the overseas income to the third person will constitute a constructive remittance. This was considered in *Carter v Sharon (1936) 20 TC 229, KB* where a woman transferred income to her daughter outside the UK and the daughter subsequently brought the money into the UK. It was held that this did not constitute a constructive remittance by the mother. In *Carter v Sharon* the woman had transferred the money to her daughter's bank account outside the UK so that what the daughter remitted was her own money. Had the woman transferred the money to her daughter's bank account in the UK the money would not have been her daughter's until it had reached her bank account. In these circumstances the remittance would have been made by the mother. The same would apply if overseas income was used to discharge a debt in the UK; if the funds did not belong to the creditor until they reached his bank account in the UK then there would clearly have been a remittance. If the creditor had a bank account outside the UK the position might be different although there would be some concern that a payment to such an account might be treated as a constructive remittance.

Caution should be exercised if the funds are likely in some way to be used to provide a benefit to the donor in the UK. In the case of *Grimm v Newman [2002] STC 84* a non-UK domiciled husband gifted income to his wife offshore who then used the money to purchase a house jointly with her husband in the UK. Mr Grimm's adviser, Mr Newman, had advised that provided the gift was completed abroad and that there was no reciprocity, no tax charge would arise even though Mrs Grimm brought the funds back to the UK. The matter was raised by the Revenue in the course of an investigation into Mr Grimm's tax affairs and the point was conceded by Mr Grimm's advisers. Mr Grimm then brought an action against Mr Newman for negligent advice. Etherton J (stating that his view was not conclusive or binding on the Revenue) indicated that there had been a remittance; although Mr Grimm purchased his 'share' with the aid of a mortgage he still derived some benefit from the off-shore funds because he had a right to occupy the whole property and also a right to the whole if Mrs Grimm predeceased him.

Planning to utilise the remittance basis

6.28   The scope for an individual to use his overseas income to support his living expenses in the UK without actual or constructive remittances is therefore limited. If, however, he has sufficient capital he may be able to structure his affairs so that he can live off his capital and remit little or nothing by way of income or capital gains to the UK. In this way he can live in the UK while restricting his income tax or capital gains tax liability to the amounts of income or gains that he actually remits plus, of course, any UK source income or gains he may have. In order to achieve this, it is essential that he should keep his capital entirely separate from his income and capital gains. There are certain basic principles that determine how this should be done.

(*a*)   The individual must be able to distinguish which of his assets, for UK tax purposes, represent pure capital. This is straightforward for a person who has not previously been resident in the UK since all of his assets will be regarded as capital. A person who has been resident for a number of years without segregating his income, capital and capital gains in the necessary manner will find the task much more difficult.

(*b*)   Separate bank and investment accounts must be kept for income, capital gains and pure capital. All income must be credited to the income account. The proceeds from any disposal of a capital asset which gave rise to a capital gain must be credited to the capital gains account. In this connection, it is important to remember that the UK has no 'deemed acquisition' rule for individuals who become resident in the UK; the acquisition cost of his assets for capital gains tax purposes will be calculated exactly as if the individual had always been resident in the UK.

(*c*)   Income retains its character as income, even if invested. The proceeds from the sale of an investment made out of income must be credited to the income account. Similar rules apply to capital gains.

Remittances from the capital account will be tax free. Remittances from the capital gains account will give rise to a capital gains tax liability based on the relative proportions of capital and capital gain. Remittances from the income account will be fully liable to income tax.

Commencement and cessation rules

6.29 Prior to the *Finance Act 1994*, income tax on Cases III, IV and V income was normally computed on a preceding year basis; i.e., the liability, although it was the liability for the current year, was calculated by reference to the income received in the previous year. *ICTA 1988, s 66* contained special rules for new sources of income which, in normal circumstances, provided for the liability to be calculated on an 'arising' (i.e., an actual year) basis for the first two years and only thereafter on the preceding year basis. *ICTA 1988, s 67* contained special rules that applied when a source of income ceased. These were more complex but, in normal circumstances, provided for the liability in the year in which the source closed to be calculated on an arising basis and for the liability for the previous year likewise to be calculated on an arising basis if this would increase the amount of the taxable income.

ICTA 1988, ss 66, 67 both contained provisions that applied where Case IV or V income was taxable on a remittance basis. In these circumstances, references to income arising were to be read as references to income received in the UK.

FA 1994, with a view to facilitating self-assessment, repealed *sections 66* and *67* and amended *section 65*. The new rules apply, in relation to income from a source arising (or received) on or after 6 April 1994 with effect from the year 1994/1995, and in relation to income from a source arising (or received) before 6 April 1994 with effect from the year 1996/1997. The broad effect of these changes is that income tax on Cases III, IV and V income is computed on a current year basis; i.e., by reference to the income received in that year. The previous principle that required one to read 'arising' as 'received in the UK' where income is taxable on a remittance basis is unchanged.

6.30 The so-called 'source closing' rules relied in part on the provisions of *section 67* and to that extent will no longer apply. However, the source closing rules rely more fundamentally on a basic principle of income tax law that, in the absence of a special provision to the contrary, one cannot be taxable by reference to a particular source of income unless that source exists in the year of assessment (see *National Provident Institution v Brown (1921) 8 TC 57, HL*). Thus, if a source of income has closed and the income from it is received (or, in the case of a non-domiciled individual, remitted to the UK) in a subsequent tax year, all liability to income tax may be avoided. This rule used to apply to Case I and II income also until special 'post-cessation receipts' provisions were introduced (now in *ICTA 1988, s 103*). The rule still applies to the Case IV or V income of a non-domiciled individual. If he remits no income from a particular source to the UK in the year in which the source closes, he has no liability by reference to that source for that year. If he remits the income in a subsequent year, the source of the income no longer exists and he cannot therefore be subjected to any tax liability by reference to it.

6.31   There is some uncertainty about the meaning of the term 'source'. *ICTA 1988, s 67(1)* refers to 'any particular source . . . or any part of such source' which suggests that it is not necessary that the taxpayer ceases to have any Case IV or V income at all; it is enough that he has sold a particular investment or closed a particular bank account. The judgments in the *National Provident* case are consistent with this view. Taken to extremes, a taxpayer would merely need to close his deposit account each 5 April and open a new one and so be able to remit the interest from the closed account in the following tax year. To adopt such a course as routine tax planning might be regarded as unnecessarily provocative. In appropriate circumstances, however, the source closing rules can play a very useful role.

Double tax relief

6.32   In many cases an individual will have a non-UK source of income on which some foreign tax has been paid. In such circumstances he may be able to remit it to the UK with little or no additional tax liability depending on the size of the foreign tax credit attaching to the income or gain remitted.

Some double tax treaties contain special provisions which provide that capital gains realised on movable property are taxable only in the country of residence. It may be possible to rely on such a provision so as prevent a charge to UK tax under *TCGA 1992, s 10A* on chargeable gains realised during a period of non-UK residence which lasts for less than five full tax years (see 6.2).

Similar treaty provisions may also be relied upon by trustees of off-shore settlements seeking to avoid charges under *TCGA 1992, s 86* or *s 87*. With effect from 20 March 2000, however, the trustees of an offshore settlement cannot rely upon the provisions of a double tax treaty in order to avoid the gains of an off-shore holding company being attributed to them under *TCGA 1992, s 13 (TCGA 1992, s 79B* inserted by *FA 2000, s 94*).

Tax planning for individuals using trusts

General

6.33   It is not necessary for a non-domiciled individual to use the mechanism of a trust in order to minimise his UK income tax exposure. If, however, the individual is likely to remain in the UK for a prolonged period, particularly if he is in danger of acquiring a deemed domicile for inheritance tax purposes, he will almost certainly be well advised to use at least one trust in his asset holding structure for inheritance tax purposes. The capital gains tax benefits of a trust are much reduced following *FA 1998* unless both the settlor and the beneficiaries are non-UK domiciled.

A number of factors will need to be considered quite apart from tax. These include the type of property which is to be held in the trust, the location of the property and, not least, the wishes of the individual in relation to his family. These factors will all influence the form of the trust to be established and whether or not it will be necessary or desirable to use a holding company in conjunction with the trust. The following discussion will consider the issues arising in relation to capital gains tax and income tax.

Capital gains tax

6.34   Non-domiciled individuals, as noted at 6.2, are only liable to capital gains tax on gains from the disposal of UK assets and gains from the disposal of non-UK assets which are remitted to the UK. Non-resident trustees are not liable to capital gains tax unless they are carrying on a trade in the UK through a branch or agency and the assets disposed of were used or held for the purpose of such trade. [*TCGA 1992, s 10(1)*].

6.35   From a capital gains tax planning viewpoint, the use of a non-resident trust by a non-domiciled individual offers two particular possibilities. The first is that he can 'step up' the base cost of his non-UK assets by transferring them to trustees. This does not, in the absence of a pre-ordained scheme which might be subject to a *Furniss v Dawson* type attack, give rise to any problems in relation to the remittance rule contained in *TCGA 1992, s 12* where capital is distributed out of the trust to the settlor. *Section 12* applies only to amounts received in the UK in respect of the chargeable gains in question. Since a gift generates no proceeds, it is difficult to see what amount could be remitted to the UK 'in respect of the chargeable gains'. A transfer into trust will, however, set a new period running for the purposes of UK taper relief.

6.36   The second and more significant possibility is that a non-domiciled settlor can, by transferring his assets to non-resident trustees, at least defer any charges to capital gains tax in relation to UK assets (to which the remittance basis would not otherwise apply) for as long as he retains his non-UK domicile. In cases where the settlor and his family retain their non-UK domicile for a prolonged period or at least until they have received substantial distributions from the trusts, these distributions can be received entirely free of capital gains tax notwithstanding the *FA 1998* changes to the operation of *section 87*. Similarly, if the settlor acquires a UK domicile but there are other beneficiaries who remain non-UK resident or domiciled, those beneficiaries can receive benefits from the trust without capital gains tax charges. It is immaterial whether the assets are situated inside or outside the UK; it is only the non-resident status of the trustees that is relevant. Resident 'professional' trustees will be treated as non-resident, but only when the settlor was both non-domiciled and non-resident when he made the settlement – see 6.3 and 6.4.

6.37   Should *sections 86* or *87* come into play, the trustees will need to consider whether, in capital gains tax terms, it is necessarily beneficial for the trust to remain offshore given the fact that gains realised by resident trustees will be taxable at the rate applicable to trusts – (34 per cent (based upon the rates in force for the tax year 2001/2002), whereas liability under *section 86* will probably lead to the settlor paying tax at the higher marginal rate of 40 per cent and gains imputed under *section 87* will carry the surcharges, giving a maximum effective rate of tax of 64 per cent.

6.38   Following *FA 1988* and prior to 6 April 1998, capital gains of interest in possession trusts were taxed at basic rate and the capital gains of other trusts were taxed at the rate applicable to trusts. With effect from 6 April 1998, all UK resident trustees are taxed at the rate applicable to trusts no matter what the form of the trust. If the settlor or his spouse is capable of benefiting under the settlement, the gains of the trustees will be taxed in the settlor's hands under *TCGA 1992, s 77*. These provisions apply only in the case of resident settlements.

6.39   If the trust is to remain offshore, the trustees may wish to review their investment strategy with a view possibly to investing in longer term assets in order to take advantage of the new taper relief rules for capital gains tax introduced by *FA 1998* and/or in order to generate income as opposed to capital growth. The taper relief rules reduce proportionately the chargeable gain on assets disposed of by individuals and trustees on a sliding scale, depending upon the length of time for which the asset has been held. The relief is higher for business assets. Indexation relief was capped as at 17 March 1998. Income distributed to UK resident and domiciled beneficiaries and which is taxed under *section 740* will not be subject to a surcharge. However, a non-UK domiciled beneficiary who receives income benefits in the UK will be taxable under *section 740* by reference to those benefits but would not be taxable under *section 87*. The trustees might also consider pooled investments which constitute offshore funds and where offshore income gains will be taxable under *section 740* as opposed to *section 87*.

A decision as to whether to bring a trust onshore will be dictated not only by tax factors but also, *inter alia*, by the personal position of the beneficiaries, including whether or not a beneficiary is or is likely to become non-UK resident.

6.40   As mentioned at 6.6, *TCGA 1992, s 90* operates to transfer trust gains between settlements where transfers of trust assets are made. This provision formed the basis for the so-called 'flip-flop' scheme used prior to March 2000 to avoid charges under *TCGA 1992, ss 77, 86 and 87*. In an attempt to counter this, *FA 2000* introduced *Schedule 4B* into *TCGA 1992*. This applies where there is a transfer of value by the trustees of a settlement within the scope of *section 77*, *section 86* or *section 87* at a time when there is an outstanding trustee borrowing. A transfer of value includes any loan or giving of security as well as a simple transfer of assets to any person, in each case provided it is for no consideration or at an undervalue. There will be an outstanding trustee borrowing where the trustees have an outstanding loan the proceeds of which have not been applied for normal trust purposes (or previously been taken into account under S*chedule 4B)*. The term, 'applied for trust purposes' is difficult but clearly includes the purchase of trust assets or the payment of trust administration expenses. In circumstances where there is a transfer of assets between settlements to which *Schedule 4B* applies, *section 90* does not apply to the transfer but the trustees of the transferor settlement are deemed to realise the remaining assets (or a proportion of them depending upon the amount of the outstanding trustee borrowing as compared with the value of the assets transferred). Gains arising on this disposal (and indeed on the actual disposal to the transferee settlement) will either be taxed in the hands of the settlor under *section 77* or *section 86* or form part of the total of *section 87* trust gains.

A more detailed consideration of *Schedule 4B* is outside the scope of this chapter but great care should be taken whenever trustees have any outstanding borrowings, as the scope of the provisions is wide and, in some respects uncertain, and they could apply to transfers by trustees which have no tax avoidance motive.

Income tax

6.41   The extent to which trusts can be used by a non-domiciled individual to minimise his income tax liability on an on-going basis will depend on a number of factors of which the most material will be the individual's need to have access to the income in the UK. As was seen at 6.18, unless it is possible to claim the benefit of *ICTA 1988, s 741* on the basis either that the avoidance of tax was not one of the motives for the creation of the settlement or that the settlement was created for bona fide commercial reasons, there is no simple exclusion for non-domiciled but ordinarily resident settlors or beneficiaries from the principal income tax anti-avoidance sections.

Even if these sections do not apply, a settlor with an interest in the settlement may be caught by other anti-avoidance sections. The most notable is *ICTA 1988, s 660A*. This applies to the income of any settlement, no matter where the trustees are resident, under which the settlor or his spouse has an interest and treats that income for all purposes of the UK *Income Tax Acts* as the income of the settlor. Generally, if *section 739* would apply to a settlement in the absence of the *section 741* defence, then *section 660A* will apply. Unlike *section 739*, however, *section 660A* does not apply to the income of a company which is wholly owned by the settlement.

Where income could be assessed under both *section 739* and *section 660A*, the Revenue will not, in practice, seek to tax it under both, although it may raise alternative assessments, for example, if it suspects the taxpayer has not provided full information.

ICTA 1988, ss 660A, 739, 740 offer a remittance or modified remittance basis to non-domiciled individuals. If the settlor or his family do not need the trust income to meet their living expenses in the UK, they will be able to avoid any income tax liability if sufficient care is taken in any dealings with income. If they do need the trust income in the UK, the remittance basis will not offer any real benefit and they will be taxable on all of the income that is brought into the UK.

6.42   As indicated at 6.41, if the settlor falls within the terms of *section 739* or *section 660A* he will be treated as if the income arising to the trustees was his. Since a non-domiciled settlor has the benefit of the remittance basis provided by *ICTA 1988, s 743(3)*, the consequence, assuming that all of the income has a non-UK source, is that he will only be taxable on the income if he brings it into the UK. Even if the trustees pay capital to him which he brings into the UK or they provide some other benefit such as the free use of trust property, the settlor will have no liability to tax provided that the income remains offshore. It is irrelevant, so far as *sections 739* and *660A* are concerned, whether the income is paid out to the settlor (who keeps it offshore in his own account) or retained in the trustees' hands (but see 6.43 and 6.47 regarding *section 740*).

6.43   The beneficiaries' position is governed by *section 740*, which works in a very different way from *section 739*. First, a liability under *section 740* is triggered by the actual receipt of a benefit out of assets in the trustees' hands. Secondly, if a liability is triggered, the consequence is not that the income is treated as that of the beneficiary but that he is treated as being in receipt of income equal in value to the benefit received by him. The quantum of his liability is limited to the amount of relevant income in the hands of the trustees at the time. If this is less than the value of the benefit, future relevant income is attributed to the beneficiary on an annual basis until he has been taxed on an amount equal to the value of the benefit received by him. The remittance basis provided by *section 740(5)* will preclude liability only if the income has a non-UK source and is not remitted to the UK and if the benefit itself is not received in the UK. If the benefit took the form of an interest-free loan or the free use of trust property, the fact that the property was located in the UK or the borrowed money was brought into the UK would, it seem, constitute the 'receipt' of the benefit in the UK.

It has already been noted that a settlor can avoid any liability under *sections 739* and *660A* in relation to non-UK source income by ensuring that none of the income is brought into the UK (see 6.41). It makes no difference whether the income is retained in the settlement or distributed out to him. The position of the beneficiaries under *section 740* is very different. Any income that is retained in the settlement (or any underlying entity) will be relevant income and will be attributable to any beneficiary who receives a benefit out of the trust.

6.44   If the beneficiary is to escape liability under *section 740* it is necessary to ensure that there is no relevant income in the trust. This can only be done by distributing the income out of the trust. Although *section 740* is silent as to the point in the year at which relevant income is to be determined it is understood that the Revenue takes the practical view that it should be determined as at the end of the tax year. Income that has been accumulated and capitalised remains relevant income for the purposes of the *section*. If it is invested and the value of the investment declines, it is the amount initially invested that remains relevant income. The amount of relevant income will be reduced by distributions of income, or of assets which can clearly be shown to represent income, to resident or non-resident beneficiaries and also by the provision of other benefits to them (if such benefits have given rise to tax in the hands of a resident beneficiary under *section 740*).

There is some uncertainty as to whether the conferring of a benefit on a UK resident but non-domiciled beneficiary who does not remit the income has the effect of reducing the pool of relevant income. The 'safe' view is that, unless the payment can clearly be shown to have been made out of income (or assets representing it), the relevant income does not reduce unless and until the beneficiary remits the benefit to the UK and, therefore, becomes taxable by reference to it – see *ICTA 1988, s 744(2)(c)*.

It is understood that the Revenue has indicated that income expenses and other amounts (such as interest) that are properly chargeable against income will normally be allowed as deductions in calculating what is relevant income. In this respect also *section 740* is different from *sections 739* and *660A*. Under *ICTA 1988, s 743(2)* (in relation to *section 739*) and *section 660C(2)* (in relation to *section 660A*) the settlor can deduct from the trustees' gross income only those amounts that could have been deducted had the income actually been received by him. This point was clearly illustrated by *Chetwode v IRC (1977) 51 TC 647, HL*, when the expenses incurred in administering an overseas company were not allowed as a deduction in computing the *section 739* liability.

6.45   In certain circumstances it may be possible to extract the income from a settlement by having it pass to a new settlement for a separate class of beneficiaries. If benefits have been provided to members of a particular generation in a family, it may be attractive in terms of long-term estate planning as well as short-term income tax planning to divert the income to a separate settlement for a younger generation. Provided that all of the settlement income is clearly dealt with in this way, the capital of the first settlement can be kept untainted by income and therefore available for providing non-taxable benefits to UK residents. In order to be entirely sure that all of the income of the original settlement has been distributed this should either be paid out on an annual basis or kept in a separate account or portfolio so that it can easily be identified in the original settlement. It would have to be accepted that the income passing to the new settlement would constitute relevant income, with the result that any benefit provided out of this settlement would be subject to income tax. Benefits provided out of the first settlement to any beneficiary who is also a beneficiary of the new settlement would also be taxed under *section 740* by reference to the income of the new settlement. There might, however, be a significant amount of time before it was intended that any benefits should be provided to the beneficiaries of the new settlement and any liability could accordingly be deferred until such time. A lengthy deferment could produce material benefits.

Great care should be taken when transferring income or capital (or indeed providing some other form of benefit, such as a guarantee for borrowings on less than fully commercial terms) from one settlement to another in circumstances where the first settlement retains some relevant income, since this can be taxable in the hands of beneficiaries who receive benefits out of the transferee settlement and are also beneficiaries of the transferor settlement. This appears to be the case even if the transferee settlement is on-shore and the trustees have paid tax on an income receipt from the off-shore settlement. Once the link between the settlements is made, it is unclear how much of the relevant income in the transferee settlement can be taxed by reference to distributions from the second settlement. Common sense suggests that it should be limited to the value of the assets or benefit received by the transferee settlement from the transferor settlement, but it is not clear whether the Revenue share this view.

6.46   It was noted above that liability to tax under *section 740* is initially calculated by reference to the relevant income available when the benefit was received but that, if the amount of available relevant income is less than the amount of the benefit, future relevant income is attributed to the beneficiary. The trustees may seek to prevent any liability under *section 740* by distributing all of the income to some beneficiary who is not liable to tax in respect of it; indeed they could distribute it to the same beneficiary who has received the capital benefit (assuming that the benefit was not received in the UK) provided that the income has a non-UK source and that the beneficiary is non-domiciled and keeps income outside the UK. If they do seek to do this, it is essential that they continue to distribute all of the income so long as the trust exists unless all beneficiaries who have received a capital benefit have either died or ceased to be ordinarily resident in the UK.

6.47   Where both *sections 739* and *740* could apply, the Revenue has a discretion as to which it will apply, apportioning any liability in a manner it considers just and reasonable. [*ICTA 1988, s 744(1)*]. Liability under *section 740* cannot therefore be avoided on the grounds that the settlor could be liable to tax under *section 739* but only if he has actually been taxed. One consequence of this is that although a non-domiciled settlor would avoid any liability under *section 739* if the income (if it has a non-UK source) is kept offshore, the retention of the income within the settlement would result in the accumulation of an amount of relevant income which could be used to ground a liability under *section 740* for any beneficiary who received a capital benefit from the settlement at some future time.

6.48   If *section 739* or *section 740* applies to a settlement and *TCGA 1992, s 87* also applies, benefits received will be taxed first under *section 739* or *section 740* and, only to the extent that the benefit is not fully taxed in a particular year under one of these sections, will it become taxable under *TCGA 1992, s 87*. If, even after the application of *section 87* (and any gains which are taxable under the capital gains charging regime which applied prior to *section 87* – see *CGTA 1979, s 17*), there remains a balance of untaxed benefit, this balance is carried forward to the next year to be taxed according to the same rules.

It will be apparent from the foregoing discussion that the scope for avoiding liability to income tax by accumulating income in an offshore settlement is, even for non-domiciled beneficiaries, very limited if any benefits are to be provided out of the settlement to beneficiaries in the UK. It is possible to defer any liability until such time as capital benefits are received in the UK but complete avoidance is unlikely to be achieved so long as the beneficiaries remain ordinarily resident in the UK. Deferment of liability can be valuable, particularly if the liability can be deferred for a number of years. How valuable the deferment will be, as in relation to capital gains tax, depends on various factors, particularly the investment performance achieved by the trustees and the difference between the rates of income tax that would have been paid by the beneficiaries had the income been distributed to them on a current basis and the rates payable on actual receipt of the taxable benefit.

6.49   After a period of time, individuals who have been relying on the remittance basis in their tax planning without using trusts find themselves in a position where their capital resources are severely depleted but they have significant amounts of income accumulated offshore. A trust is sometimes considered as a means of converting this income to capital, using the *Carter v Sharon* principle (see 6.27), i.e., that a transfer of income from A to B has the consequence that what was income in A's hands becomes capital in the hands of B. If the settlor is a beneficiary of the settlement it is likely that the Revenue would seek to tax as income any capital received by the settlor out of the settlement either as a constructive remittance (using the type of approach found in *Harmel v Wright* (see 6.23) or on the basis of *Furniss v Dawson*: i.e., that the transfer of the income into the settlement and the payments of capital to the settlor formed part of a preordained series of transactions). If neither the settlor nor his spouse was a beneficiary of the settlement the position would be on all fours with *Carter v Sharon* and the settled income would clearly be capital in relation to the beneficiaries of the settlement.

6.50   Another situation in which a trust can be useful is where an individual wishes to utilise the source closing rules but, for whatever reason, cannot dispose of the assets which comprise his source of income. A transfer of the assets to a life interest settlement would not achieve the desired goal since the life tenant would be treated as remaining entitled to the income from the underlying investments and would therefore, in income tax terms, still have the same sources of income. If the transfer was to a discretionary settlement the position would appear to be somewhat different. It is accepted that, for income tax purposes, a discretionary settlement is a source of income separate and distinct from the assets comprised in the settlement; the rationale for this is that any entitlement to income results from the exercise by the trustees of their discretion over income and it is therefore the exercise of this discretion which is the 'source' of the income, the location of the source being the place of residence of the trustees. On this basis, a transfer by an individual of his assets to a discretionary settlement will constitute the cessation of one source and the opening of another.

The use of companies in offshore tax planning

General

6.51   When planning an appropriate structure for a non-domiciled individual's assets, consideration will always be given to the possible use of a holding company. There can be a number of reasons apart from tax for having a company, particularly the ability to centralise control over assets that might otherwise be split between a number of individuals or entities. The advantages and disadvantages, in tax terms, of using a company vary widely depending on which of the main taxes causes the greatest difficulty in the particular circumstances. The inheritance tax implications are particularly important and are considered at CHAPTER 8: Inheritance Tax Planning for the Non-UK Domiciled Individual.

Capital gains tax

6.52   In relation to capital gains tax, the use by an individual of a company without a trust is limited to holding UK assets the disposal of which would give rise to an immediate capital gains tax charge if they were held directly by the individual. By holding such assets through an offshore company it is possible to avoid any such immediate tax charge. So long as the individual remains non-domiciled the gains of the offshore company cannot be attributed to him under *TCGA 1992, s 13*.

The use of a company with a trust, so far as capital gains tax is concerned, provides little benefit. *TCGA 1992, s 13(10)* attributes gains falling within *TCGA 1992, s 13* to non-resident trustees in the same way as if they were resident and domiciled in the UK. If and so long as the settlor retains his non-domiciled status, *section 86* will not apply to these gains. However, they will be potentially taxable under *section 87*. It should be borne in mind that, unless it has been structured with extensive loan capital or shares that can be redeemed or repurchased or is situated in a jurisdiction the law of which permits it to make gifts, an on-going company will only be able to distribute its capital gains to its trustee shareholders by way of dividend. If dividends are paid, the trustees will have income rather than capital gains in their hands. Whether or not this is beneficial in tax terms will depend upon the tax status of the settlor and beneficiaries. If the settlor is non-UK domiciled and is to receive distributions from the trust in the UK, then converting capital gains to income will be disadvantageous. If, however, either the *section 86* regime applies to the settlement because the settlor is domiciled in the UK or, where *section 86* does not apply, benefits are to be received by UK resident and domiciled beneficiaries, it could well be more advantageous to realise income instead of capital gains in order to avoid the surcharge. If capital gains are within the UK net, then the use of a company could be disadvantageous since not only will the gains realised by the company be attributed to the trustees but also the increase in the value of the company's shares will be within the potential charge to tax on a disposal of the shares or the winding up of the company. There is, therefore, the possibility of material double taxation.

The risks of double taxation are unlikely to be mitigated by the operation of the provisions of *s 13(5A)* even where gains are distributed within two years (see 6.8). Take, for example, the case where shares in an offshore company are held by a discretionary settlement from which the settlor is excluded but under which his children are beneficiaries. Within two years of the company realising a chargeable gain, the profits are distributed from the company to the trustees by way of dividend. The gains apportioned to the trustees under *s 13* will be deemed to be the settlor's pursuant to *s 86*, but the dividend will not be deemed to be his. Accordingly, the credit will not be available to the settlor but the dividend may still form part of the pool relevant income for the purposes of *ICTA 1988, s 740* and so potentially taxable in the future when distributions are made to the children.

The taper relief rules for capital gains tax do not apply to companies and any gains of an offshore company continue to be subject to indexation relief.

Income tax

6.53   There is little benefit, in income tax terms, in an individual holding his assets through an offshore company. As indicated above, a company falls within the scope of *ICTA 1988, ss 739, 740* in exactly the same way as a trust.

6.54   A possible exposure to liability under *ICTA 1988, ss 739, 740* in relation to trust income cannot be avoided by holding trust assets through an underlying company. The definition of 'power to enjoy' in *ICTA 1988, s 742(2)* is broad enough to cover income held in subsidiary entities, regardless of whether or not they are controlled by the trustees. Likewise, the definition of 'relevant income' in *section 740(3)* includes all income which has been received by a non-resident person and which can be used, directly or indirectly, for providing a benefit to the beneficiary or enabling a benefit to be provided for him. Both definitions, strictly construed, could apply to any entity in which the trust is interested, regardless of how remote the interest and regardless of the degree of control exercisable by the trustees. Taken to extremes, they could apply to major public companies in which the trustees have invested as part of a conventional investment portfolio. There is, as yet, no authority on how these provisions would be construed in practice, although it is understood that the Revenue does not normally apply the rules except to companies controlled by the trustees.

6.55   It is also not possible to use a non-UK holding company to hold shares in a UK company so as to convert into non-UK source income what would otherwise be UK-source income in the trustees' hands. A strict interpretation of the definition of relevant income would suggest the opposite conclusion. If one assumes that the UK company has made a distribution to a non-UK holding company which in turn distributes all of its income to the trustees, the only income that is then available for providing any benefits is the income in the hands of the trustees and this income itself has a non-UK source even though it originated in a UK company. It is understood that the Revenue has indicated that, in this situation, they would have regard to the underlying source and would not restrict themselves to looking at the proximate source of the trustees' income.

6.56   A further point that needs to be considered in relation to offshore companies is the availability of tax credits. Prior to 6 April 1999, it was clearly undesirable for shares in UK companies to be held via an offshore company since the trustees, and hence beneficiaries, did not receive the benefit of tax credit for ACT paid by the UK company which an individual or the trustees would have received had they owned the shares directly. Following the changes to the tax credit rules for UK dividends which came into effect on 6 April 1999, beneficiaries of interest in possession trusts will still be at a disadvantage if UK shares are held via an offshore holding company. However, in relation to discretionary and accumulation trusts, the position will be tax neutral whether the shares are held directly or via a holding company. As far as non-UK source income is concerned, foreign tax credits may well be available where income is received directly by the trustees and distributed to a beneficiary (or taxable in the hands of the settlor under *ICTA 1988, s 739* or *s 660A*). These foreign credits may be lost if shares are held via an underlying company. However, the position depends very much upon the nature of the foreign holding and the location of the holding company. If the income was received by an offshore company located in a tax haven, no such credit would be available. In this type of situation a tax haven location may be disadvantageous. The converse may be true in the case of a holding company which is established in a jurisdiction which has a tax treaty with the UK since this could enable the settlor or beneficiaries to receive tax credits that might not have been available had the assets been held directly by the trustees.

7 Inheritance Tax Double Taxation Agreements

Bernard Geoffrey Owen Clutton BALLB BCL ATII
(Partner, Macfarlanes)

Introduction

7.1   The different legal and taxation systems of different countries give rise to the possibility of taxation arising in more than one country on the same person in respect of the same assets. This is particularly true with the greater mobility of individuals and of capital. The rules on inheritance, gifts and taxation can lead to greatly differing liabilities. For example, some countries assess tax by reference to nationality while others assess tax by reference to domicile or even residence, and most countries assess tax on assets situated within their boundaries and which pass on death or (in the case of those countries which tax lifetime gifts) are situated within the country at the date of the gift.

7.2   There are two types of relief which can be given and, in the case of the UK, are given. The first is unilateral relief. The UK will in certain cases give relief against UK inheritance tax on a gift on death for similar foreign tax which arises on that gift or on death, irrespective of the rules of that foreign country and whether the foreign country would give similar relief in a converse situation.

Unilateral relief is given by *IHTA 1984, s 159*.

7.3   The second type of relief is that given by double taxation agreements, which are provided for by *IHTA 1984, s 158*. There was also provision for the negotiation of double taxation agreements from 1945 onwards under the old estate duty regime. Ten agreements were concluded for estate duty between 1945 and 1968 and six agreements have been concluded since the introduction of capital transfer tax. While the existence and applicability of the double taxation agreements on income and capital gains may be more widely known (and many more treaties on income and capital gains have been concluded), the agreements relating to death duties and inheritance tax are no less important and they can be of great relevance in international estate planning situations.

Where the relief given by a double taxation agreement is less beneficial than that afforded by unilateral relief the taxpayer may claim the benefit of unilateral relief in preference to double taxation relief.

Types of treaty

7.4   There are two types of double taxation agreement in existence, as referred to above.

Estate duty treaties

7.5   There were a number of treaties entered into on estate duty between 1945 and 1968. *IHTA 1984, s 158(6)* provides that existing arrangements made for estate duty are to remain in force notwithstanding the repeal of estate duty and that they are to have effect as if any provision made in relation to estate duty extended to capital transfer tax. The estate duty treaties are also extended to inheritance tax by virtue of *FA 1986, s 100*.

7.6   The width of *IHTA 1984, s 158(6)* should be noted. The subsection provides that the estate duty treaties have effect as if the arrangements in relation to estate duty extended to capital transfer tax or inheritance tax. From this, two points follow in particular. Firstly, those treaties are not affected by the deemed domicile provisions of *IHTA 1984, s 267* and references in those agreements to domicile have to be construed accordingly. References to the domicile of an individual do not therefore include deemed domicile (see *IHTA 1984, s 267(2)*). Secondly, they have no application to tax chargeable on lifetime transfers.

7.7   The essence of these treaties was to lay down rules for determining the situs of assets and, in the case of double taxation, to provide that the country in which the asset was not situate should give the tax credit.

The treaties entered into for estate duty (and now continued for capital transfer tax and inheritance tax) are those with France, Italy, India and Pakistan. Only those with France and Italy continue to be of full current relevance as Pakistan abolished death duties with effect from 28 June 1979 and India abolished estate duty in 1985. The treaties with Pakistan and India do (as well as those with France and Italy) nonetheless have the significant effect of restricting the application of the deemed domicile rules for UK inheritance tax in the case of assets passing on death.

OECD treaties

7.8   The second type of treaty consists of those entered into since estate duty was abolished by the *Finance Act 1975*. They are given effect by Order in Council pursuant to *IHTA 1984, s 158* or its predecessor, *FA 1975, Sch 7 para 7*. There are six such agreements.

Country	Date of entry into force	Statutory Instrument Number
Ireland	2 October 1978	SI 1978 No 1107
South Africa	6 May 1979	SI 1979 No 576
USA	11 November 1979	SI 1979 No 1454
Netherlands	16 June 1980	SI 1980 No 706
Sweden	19 June 1981	SI 1981 No 840
Switzerland	7 March 1995	SI 1994 No 3214

7.9   The six new conventions are based in varying degrees on the 1966 draft convention on estates and inheritances prepared by the Organisation for Economic Co-operation and Development (OECD) revised and republished as the 1982 OECD model double taxation convention on estates and inheritances and on gifts. The layout and the concepts behind the OECD model bear many similarities to those of the 1977 OECD model double taxation agreement on income and capital gains. The OECD Commentary on the 1982 model states that 'concepts which are expressed by the same words in both model conventions must be taken to have the same application due regard being had, where appropriate, to the different nature of the forms of taxation in question'.

7.10   The 1966 and 1982 OECD models (which will collectively be referred to as the OECD model) confer primary taxing rights applying to all property (subject to exceptions for immovable property and certain business property in the other country) on the country in which the individual is domiciled for the purposes of the treaty. In certain cases, the other country is given secondary taxing rights, which means it has the right to tax after giving credit for the tax charged in the country with primary taxing rights. In the case of immovable property and business property forming a permanent establishment, the country in which they are situate has the primary taxing rights and the country of domicile (if different) has secondary taxing rights.

7.11   The conventions restrict the scope of UK inheritance tax on settled property. Under UK domestic law the worldwide assets of any settlement are liable to inheritance tax if the settlor was domiciled in the UK for inheritance tax purposes when he made the settlement. If he was not so domiciled, inheritance tax is restricted to UK situs assets. The conventions entered into by the UK restrict the charge to inheritance tax to certain permitted categories of UK situs assets (normally immovable property and permanent establishment business assets) where the settlor was domiciled for treaty purposes in the other country at the date of making the settlement. The UK has reserved secondary taxing rights over property other than the permitted categories in certain circumstances, e.g. where the settlor was a UK national at the date of making the settlement in the case of the convention with the US.

The basic terms of the OECD model taxation convention will be discussed as an introduction to a consideration of the terms of the individual, post-estate duty conventions themselves. The model convention is particularly relevant because the agreements are modelled on it to a greater or lesser extent.

The OECD model convention

The scope of the convention

7.12 *Article 1* refers to the taxes which the convention covers. The five conventions entered into by the UK each provide that the taxes covered are, in the case of the UK, capital transfer tax and inheritance tax. The conventions also extend to any identical or substantially similar taxes imposed by the UK or the other contracting state after the date of the signature of the convention in addition to, or in place of, the existing taxes. Each state is under an obligation to notify the other of any changes which have been made in their respective taxation laws.

General definitions

7.13 The conventions define the geographical area covered by the convention. For example, the convention with the United States of America provides that the term 'the United States' means the United States of America but does not include Puerto Rico, the Virgin Islands or Guam and the term 'UK' means Great Britain and Northern Ireland. The definition section will also define in more detail the taxes covered by the convention and the meaning of 'competent authority' in each state. In the UK the term means 'the Commissioners of the Inland Revenue or their authorised representative'.

Fiscal domicile

7.14 *Article 4* defines the meaning of domicile for the purposes of the treaties. This definition is fundamental to the structure of the OECD model, as it is the state in which the person is domiciled which has the primary taxing rights, although this is subject to a number of exceptions and qualifications. The resolution of the question of domicile is particularly important to the UK because many countries impose tax on worldwide assets on death or a gift on the basis of nationality, ordinary residence or even residence, whereas the UK uses the test of domicile. It is therefore possible for a person from the UK to go to live in another country which after a comparatively short time may acquire taxing rights under its law in relation to that person's worldwide assets. The agreements entered into by the UK (other than the one with Ireland) contain a definition of fiscal domicile designed to redress any imbalance.

7.15 The article begins by defining domicile by reference to tests within each contracting state (*para 1* of *Article 4*) and there then follow 'tie-breaker' rules similar to those in the conventions on income and capital gains. The definitions of domicile are, in some cases, fairly detailed and elaborate in order to protect the UK's position, as referred to above.

7.16 *Paragraph 2* of *Article 4* provides the 'tie-breaker' rules for determining the status of an individual who under *paragraph 1* is domiciled in both states. The rules are as follows:

(*a*)   he is deemed to be domiciled in the state in which he has a 'permanent home' available to him. If he has a permanent home available to him in both states, he is deemed to be domiciled in the state with which his personal and economic relations are closer (centre of vital interests);

(*b*)   if the state in which he has his centre of vital interests cannot be determined, or if he does not have a permanent home available to him in either state, he is deemed to be domiciled in the state in which he has 'an habitual abode';

(*c*)   if he has an habitual abode in both states or in neither of them, he is deemed to be domiciled in the state of which he is a national;

(*d*)   if he is a national of both states or of neither of them, the competent authorities shall settle the question by mutual agreement.

The word 'home' may include a house or apartment belonging to or rented by the individual and would even include a rented furnished room (the OECD Commentary). The word 'permanent' means that the individual has arranged to have the dwelling available to him continuously at all times, and not occasionally for the purpose of a stay which is necessarily of short duration (travel for pleasure, business travel, educational travel, or attending a course at a school).

7.17   In determining an individual's 'centre of vital interests', reference will be made to his family and social relations, his occupations, his political, cultural and other activities, his place of business, the place from which he administers his property, and so on. The circumstances must be examined as a whole. It may be implicit from the OECD Commentary that the place where a person lives with his family and friends is more important than the place where he works.

7.18   There is less guidance in the OECD Commentary on the words 'habitual abode'. An individual's habitual abode would appear to be in the state in which he or she stays more frequently. For this purpose regard must be had to stays not only at the permanent home in the state in question but also at any other place in that state. However, it would be unusual for the professional adviser to have to go so far down the tie-breaker rules to resolve the question of domicile.

7.19   In practice, the application of the tie-breaker rules is likely to involve negotiation between the contracting states involved in order to agree where an individual's permanent home or centre of vital interests or habitual abode may be, as different states may have different views on the meaning of these terms.

Taxing rights

7.20   The structure of the model convention, in its aim to prevent double taxation, limits the right to tax in the following ways:

(*a*)   in the case of property within *Articles 5* and *6* of the convention (immovable property and business property) the state of situs may tax the property;

(*b*)   in the case of all other property, only the state of domicile may tax.

The state of domicile may also tax immovable and business property in the other state, but must give credit against its own tax for the tax paid on that property in the other state.

Immovable property

7.21   Immovable property is widely defined. The model convention provides that it should be defined in accordance with the law of the contracting state in which it is situated. Importantly, the term includes 'property accessory to immovable property, livestock and equipment used in agriculture and forestry, rights to which the provisions of general law respecting landed property apply, usufruct of immovable property and rights to payments as consideration for the working of, or the right to work, mineral deposits, sources and other natural resources . . .' (*Article 6*).

The provisions of the article also apply to immovable property of an enterprise and immovable property used for the performance of independent personal services.

Business property

7.22   *Article 7* provides that movable property of an enterprise which forms part of the estate of, or a gift made by, a person domiciled in a contracting state, which is the business property of a permanent establishment situated in the other state, may be taxed in that other state.

7.23   Permanent establishment is defined by *Article 6(2)* to mean a fixed place of business through which the business is wholly or partly carried on. The article then goes on to elaborate on the meaning of 'permanent establishment'. The term includes a branch, an office, a factory, a workshop, a mine, an oil or gas well, but not a building site or construction or installation project if it does not last for more than twelve months.

7.24   *Paragraph 5* contains a list of what the term 'permanent establishment' does not include. These are, *inter alia*, a place used solely for the purpose of storage, display or delivery of goods belonging to the enterprise, or a place solely for the purpose of purchasing goods or collecting information, or for the maintenance of goods belonging to the enterprise.

Other property

7.25   *Article 7* provides that property, wherever situated, which forms part of the estate of, or of a gift made by, a person domiciled in a contracting state, and which is not immovable property or business property, is taxable only in the state of domicile.

Example

A person domiciled in State A owning stocks and shares in State B dies leaving those stocks and shares to his grandson. Under the tax legislation of both states the stocks and shares would be liable to inheritance tax or death duties. However, only State A may assess tax on the death of the individual.

Deduction of debts

7.26   The model convention lays down rules for the deduction of debts, but this article is not considered further because the conventions entered into by the UK do not adopt the article. This is because *IHTA 1984, s 158* enables arrangements to be entered into with a view to affording 'relief' from capital transfer tax or for determining the place where property is situated for the purposes of the tax. The section does not enable further provisions to be included. As a result the conventions merely state that, in determining the amount on which tax is to be computed, permitted deductions shall be allowed under the law in force in the contracting state in which the tax is imposed.

Elimination of double taxation

7.27   The conventions entered into by the UK eliminate double taxation by the giving of credit for one tax against another. The model convention contains an alternative method in *Article 9A*, exempting property in one state from tax in another, but this is not adopted in any of the UK conventions apart from the new treaty with Switzerland. The new treaty partly adopts this Article by providing that Switzerland may not tax UK immovable property, business property or ships and aircraft managed from the UK even if the deceased is domiciled in Switzerland.

7.28   The model convention, as usually adopted by the UK in its conventions, provides that the state of domicile shall allow as a deduction from the tax calculated according to its law an amount equal to the tax paid in the other state on any property which, in relation to the same events and in accordance with the convention, may be taxed in that other state (*Article 9B*).

Example

> Mr X is domiciled for the purposes of the treaty concerned in State A but he owns land in State B. The tax in State A in relation to the property is £10,000 and in State B is £2,000. Both States A and B may tax the property but State A must give credit to Mr X for £2,000 of tax assessed in State B and State A may therefore only assess £8,000.

The article goes on to provide that the state of domicile must allow an amount equal to the tax paid in the other state on a previous gift, to the extent that the deduction was not allowed at the date of the gift.

Example

> Mr Y is domiciled in State A and he gives his business in State B to his son. He dies two years later leaving other property. At the time of the gift State A taxes the gift at 30 per cent and State B taxes it at 50 per cent. At the time of the death no tax is payable in State B. State A, however, taxes the estate including the previous gift. State A gives credit for its own previous tax and also the additional tax due in State B on the gift itself.

7.29   *Paragraph 3* of *Article 9B* provides that the deduction is not to exceed that part of the tax of the state of domicile which is attributable to the property in respect of which credit is allowed. In other words, if the state in which the property is situate has a higher rate of tax than the state of domicile, credit is given in the state of domicile only against its tax attributable to the property and not against its tax attributable to other assets of the deceased or donor.

It should be noted that this article in particular has been altered and amended in the different conventions.

Non-discrimination

7.30   This article prevents discrimination against the nationals of the other state and against stateless persons.

Mutual agreement procedure

7.31   The model convention also provides for consultation between the two states in order to resolve difficulties or doubts by mutual agreement. In particular, the states may need to agree the domicile of an individual under the tie-breaker rules (see 7.16–7.19 above).

Exchange of information

7.32   The model convention allows the exchange of information, and this is not restricted to the prevention of fraud or fiscal evasion. Special provision is made for this in *IHTA 1984, s 158(1A)*.

Diplomatic agents and consular officials

7.33   *Article 13* of the model convention provides that the convention does not affect the fiscal privileges of diplomatic agents or consular officials under the general rules of international law or under special agreements.

Territorial extension

7.34   *Article 14* provides that the convention may be extended to any part of the territory of either state which is excluded specifically from the application of the convention or to any state or territory for whose international relations a contracting state is responsible and which imposes taxes substantially similar in character to those to which the convention applies.

Particular double taxation agreements

Convention with Ireland

7.35   This agreement (*SI 1978 No 1107*) came into force on 2 October 1978 and applies with effect from the introduction of capital transfer tax in the UK and with effect from the introduction of gift tax and inheritance tax in Ireland.

Although based on the OECD model, this convention, the first to be entered into after the introduction of capital transfer tax and the first to be based on the OECD model, differs substantially from the model and from the other conventions entered into by the UK based on the OECD model.

7.36   The essence of the convention is to define fiscal domicile and to provide that each party to the convention may tax according to its own laws. There is no special treatment of immovable property and business assets. The convention eliminates double taxation by requiring one state to give credit against its tax for the liability arising in the other state.

Taxes covered

7.37   *Article 2* provides that the taxes which are the subject of this convention are:

(*a*)   in Ireland:

    (i)   the gift tax,

    (ii)   the inheritance tax,

(*b*)   in the UK the capital transfer tax (which includes inheritance tax).

The convention goes on to provide that it shall also apply to any identical or substantially similar taxes which are imposed by either contracting state after the date of signature of the convention in addition to, or in place of, the existing taxes.

Fiscal domicile

7.38   *Article 4(1)* provides that the question whether a person is, or was at any material time, domiciled in a contracting state is determined by whether he is, or was at that time, domiciled in that contracting state in accordance with its law, or is or was treated as so domiciled for the purposes of a tax which is the subject of the convention. Two points should be noted. Firstly, domicile may be determined not only at the date of a gift or a death but also at any other 'material time', which could include the date of the establishment of a settlement. This is relevant in *Article 5* which confers taxing rights on the contracting states. Secondly, the definition of domicile includes the deemed domicile rules for the purposes of inheritance tax in the UK under *IHTA 1984, s 267.*

Article 4(2) provides tie-breaker rules based on the provisions of the OECD model, where under *Article 4(1)* a person is domiciled in both contracting states.

An amendment to the convention may be required to take into account the change from domicile to residence as the connecting factor for capital acquisitions tax from 1 December 1999, introduced by the *Irish Finance Act 2000.*

Taxing rights

7.39   *Article 5(1)* provides that each state retains the right to tax which it would have under its own law apart from the convention. As mentioned above, this departs fundamentally from the OECD model and leads to the increased likelihood of both states taxing assets passing on a gift or death. *Article 5* (taxing rights) therefore goes on to define the contracting state with subsidiary taxing rights; this is the state which under *Article 8* has to give credit against its own tax for the tax levied in the other contracting state. In this way, the convention affords double tax relief.

7.40   *Article 5(2)* provides that, in relation to property not comprised in a settlement, where a person's domicile has been determined under the tie-breaker rules in *Article 4(2)*, the contracting state with subsidiary taxing rights is the state in which the person is treated under that article as not being domiciled. *Article 5* also contains detailed provisions for determining the contracting state with subsidiary taxing rights in relation to settled property. The domicile of the settlor at the time the settlement was made and the proper law of the settlement are primary considerations.

Situs of assets

7.41   In line with the other conventions entered into by the UK based on the OECD model, the convention provides that the situs of any property shall be determined by each contracting state under its own law. There is, however, an exception to this. *Article 6(1)* provides that where part of the value by reference to which tax is imposed in the UK is represented by a liability to tax which is satisfied out of property situated outside the UK, then that part of the value is deemed to be attributable to that property (i.e. the property situated outside the UK). The point here is that, for UK inheritance tax, where a disposition of UK property is liable to inheritance tax and the donor pays it out of property outside the UK which is excluded property, the gift will have to be grossed up even though the tax is being paid out of excluded property. *Article 6(1)* will prevent grossing up in these circumstances.

7.42   *Article 6(2)* contains rules to resolve a conflict between the rules of the UK and Ireland on the situs of property. Where a conflict between the rules of the two states arises and this affects the credit to be allowed under *Article 8*, then the question shall be determined by the law of the contracting state which has subsidiary taxing rights. If there is no such contracting state it shall be determined by mutual agreement.

Example

MacDonald, born in Scotland, has settled in Ireland although he has retained links with Scotland and has permanent homes available both in Scotland and in Ireland. However, his centre of vital interests is in Ireland and for the purposes of the convention he is treated as domiciled in Ireland under *Article 4(2)* even though under UK law he is still domiciled in the UK. He sold assets to a purchaser in Scotland who resides in Scotland but the debt is under seal and the deed is kept in Ireland. The property is, therefore, situated in Ireland under Irish law and in Scotland by Scots law. The UK has subsidiary taxing rights under *Article 5(2)* (see 7.40 above). The situs of the debt affects the credit to be allowed under *Article 8* (see 7.43–7.45 below) and the debt is therefore treated as situated in the UK. As will be seen below, it will therefore follow that the UK may tax the debt but not give credit for Irish tax.

Elimination of double taxation

7.43   *Article 8(1)* provides that where the UK or Ireland imposes tax on property situated in one of those contracting states but not in the other, the state in which the property is not situated shall allow credit against so much of its tax as is attributable to that property (but not exceeding the amount of its own tax).

7.44   *Article 8(2)* provides that where both contracting states impose tax on property which is not situated in either contracting state but is situated in a third country, the contracting state which has subsidiary taxing rights shall allow a tax credit against its tax for the tax imposed in the other contracting state on the same event.

7.45   As referred to above, both the UK and Ireland retain taxing rights under their domestic law and this leads to the possibility of unilateral relief being granted by the UK under *IHTA 1984, s 159*. This will arise if property is situated neither in the UK nor in Ireland, and where neither state has subsidiary taxing rights (e.g. if the question of a double domicile cannot be resolved under *Article 4*) or where Ireland gives credit for UK tax but some tax is still payable in Ireland. Unilateral relief will be available under *IHTA 1984, s 159(3)* because tax will be payable in such circumstances under the laws of Ireland on property in a third country and the UK would not otherwise give any credit for the Irish tax actually payable. It should be noted that the unilateral relief given by the UK in those circumstances will only be for a proportion of the Irish tax, the so-called 'split credit'. There is less scope for the application of unilateral relief in the case of the other OECD-based conventions because the UK, where it has taxing rights over property outside the UK, will either have sole taxing rights (for example, property situated in a third country) or it will have subsidiary taxing rights (for example, immovable property situated in the other contracting state) in which case credit for the other state's tax must be given under the convention.

Other articles

7.46   The treaty contains non-discrimination, mutual agreement procedure, exchange of information and other supplementary articles based on the OECD model.

Convention with the Republic of South Africa

7.47   This convention (*SI 1979 No 576*) came into force on 6 May 1979 with effect from 1 January 1978.

The convention adopts a definition of fiscal domicile by reference to ordinary residence in South Africa and domicile in the UK, subject to certain qualifications and the usual tie-breaker rules. The convention grants specific taxing rights for certain categories of property, i.e. immovable property, business property, ships and aircraft, and shares, debentures and unit trust holdings. It then requires one state, in cases where both states would otherwise tax the transfer, to give credit for the other state's tax.

Taxes covered

7.48   The taxes covered by the convention are, in the UK, capital transfer tax and inheritance tax, and, in South Africa, estate duty and donations tax. The convention also applies to identical or substantially similar taxes imposed by either contracting state after the signature of the convention.

Fiscal domicile

7.49   For the purposes of the convention, an individual is domiciled in the UK if he is domiciled in the UK in accordance with its law or is treated as so domiciled for the purposes of a tax which is the subject of the convention. An individual is domiciled in South Africa if he is ordinarily resident in South Africa.

7.50   There are three qualifications to this definition, as well as the normal tie-breaker rules.

The first qualification (*Article 4(2)*) is that (subject to *Article 4(4)*, discussed at 7.52 below), where an individual is treated under *Article 4(1)* as domiciled in both contracting states and

(*a*)   he was a national of the UK but not of South Africa, and

(*b*)   he had not been resident or ordinarily resident in South Africa in seven or more of the ten income tax years of assessment immediately before that time,

then he is deemed to be domiciled at that time in the UK and not in South Africa.

7.51   The second qualification (*Article 4(3)*) deals with the converse situation, where an individual was domiciled in both contracting states, and

(*a*)   he was a national of South Africa but not of the UK, and

(*b*)   he had not been resident or ordinarily resident in the UK in seven or more of the ten income tax years of assessment ending with the year of assessment in which that time falls,

he is deemed to be domiciled at that time in South Africa. The question of whether an individual was resident or ordinarily resident in the UK is determined in accordance with income tax principles but without regard to any available accommodation. It should be noted that available accommodation is no longer a test of residence in the UK since 6 April 1993 by virtue of *section 208* of the *Finance Act 1993*.

7.52   The third qualification is provided in *Article 4(4)*. An individual is not, as a result of *Article 4(2)* or *(3)*, to be deemed to be domiciled in a contracting state if under the law of that contracting state, other than its law relating to a tax which is the subject to the convention, he had ceased to be domiciled in that contracting state more than three years before that time. It will be noted that *IHTA 1984, s 267* provides for a deemed domicile (after the loss of actual domicile in the UK for a period of up to three years). *Paragraph (4)* would prevent the statutory extension of that from affecting the application of *Article 4(2)* or *(3)*.

Article 4(5) contains tie-breaker rules in the normal form.

General taxing rights

7.53   *Article 5* contains the rules on general taxing rights, although this is, more than with any of the other OECD based conventions, subject to exceptions related to the type of property concerned.

7.54   *Article 5(1)* states that if the deceased or the transferor was domiciled in one of the contracting states at the time of the death or transfer, property shall not be taxable in the other contracting state unless he had been domiciled in that other contracting state within ten years immediately preceding the death or transfer. That other contracting state, unless it has the right to charge tax under *Articles 6, 7, 8* or *9*, has subsidiary taxing rights to those of the state where the person is domiciled. It therefore has to give credit for the tax paid in that state of domicile.

7.55   *Article 5* contains specific provisions regulating the charging of tax by the UK on property comprised in a settlement and also on the taxing rights where tax is not paid in one particular state otherwise than as a result of a specific exemption, deduction, credit or allowance.

Immovable property

7.56   Immovable property may be taxed in the contracting state in which such property is situated (*Article 6(1)*). Immovable property is defined using the words of the OECD model but with the additional provision that debts secured by mortgage or otherwise are not to be regarded as immovable property.

Article 6(3) provides that *paras (1)* and *(2)* are also to apply to immovable property of an enterprise and to immovable property used for the performance of independent personal services. The result is that it is taxed in the state where situated rather than the state in which the enterprise is carried on.

Business property

7.57   *Article 7(1)* provides that, except for assets referred to in *Articles 6, 8* and *9* (immovable property, ships, aircraft, shares, debentures and unit trusts), assets forming part of the business property of a permanent establishment of an enterprise may be taxed in the contracting state in which the permanent establishment is situated.

A permanent establishment is defined using the OECD model but incorporating further provisions taken from the OECD 1977 model convention on income and capital gains.

7.58   *Article 7(3)* provides that assets (other than immovable property) pertaining to a fixed base used for the performance of independent personal services may be taxed in the contracting state in which the fixed base is situated.

Ships and aircraft

7.59   Ships and aircraft operated in international traffic and movable property pertaining to the operation of such ships and aircraft may be taxed in the contracting state in which the place of effective management of the enterprise is situated (*Article 8*).

Shares, debentures and unit trust holdings

7.60   Shares, stock, debentures and debenture stock issued by companies incorporated in one of the contracting states (including any such property falling within *Article 7*) and the rights of unit holders in any unit trust scheme where the register of unit holders is kept in one of the contracting states, may be taxed by that contracting state.

Conflict as to the nature of property

7.61   *Article 10* provides that if the deceased or the transferor was domiciled in one of the contracting states at the time of the death or transfer and by the law of that state any right or interest is not regarded as property falling within *Articles 6, 7, 8* or *9* (immovable property, business property, ships and aircraft or shares, debentures or unit trusts), but by the law of the other contracting state that right is regarded as falling within those articles (thereby giving that contracting state taxing rights), then the article of the convention under which the property falls shall be determined by the law of the other contracting state (i.e. by the contracting state of non-domicile). That contracting state will thereby have the primary taxing rights.

Credit provisions

7.62   It will be noted that the treaty prevents double taxation in two ways. Firstly, in certain cases, *Article 5* will prevent one state from taxing property passing on a death or gift. Where, however, both states under the convention can impose tax *Article 12* allows credit. The credit provisions operate as follows.

(*a*)   Where a contracting state imposes tax by reference to any property which the other contracting state may tax in accordance with *Articles 6, 7, 8* or *9*, the former contracting state must give credit against its tax for the tax imposed by the other contracting state.

(*b*)   Subject to (*c*) below, where a contracting state imposes tax by reference to property not within *Articles 6, 7, 8* or *9* and the deceased or transferor was domiciled in the other contracting state at the time of death or transfer, the former shall allow credit for the tax imposed by the latter (the state of domicile).

Example

Smith has a fiscal domicile in the UK under the treaty but had been domiciled in South Africa within the ten years before his death in 1988. He owns valuable chattels in South Africa (not within *Articles 6, 7, 8* or *9*) in respect of which South Africa imposes estate duty. Under *Article 12(2)*, South Africa must give credit for UK inheritance tax on those chattels.

(*c*)   Where the UK imposes tax on property not within *Articles 6, 7, 8* or *9*, in relation to settled property where an individual domiciled in South Africa was entitled to an interest in possession in settled property, the UK gives credit.

7.63   In each case above, the state giving the credit gives a credit of an amount not exceeding its own tax attributable to the property and for so much of the other state's tax as is attributable to the property.

Article 12(4) contains three specific rules.

(*a*)   The tax attributable to any property in a contracting state is tax in that state as reduced by any double tax credit granted by that state.

(*b*)   Tax is imposed in a contracting state if it is chargeable by that state and paid to it. In other words, credit will not be given for tax due but not paid in that state.

(*c*)   Where tax is imposed on the death of a transferor by reason of a transfer within three years before his death, that tax shall be treated as if it were imposed in connection with that transfer. Relief is therefore available even though charges to tax arise at different times in the UK and South Africa on a transfer within three years of death.

Any claim for a credit or repayment of tax under the convention shall be made within six years from the date of the event giving rise to a liability to tax, or, where later, within one year from the last date on which tax for credit is given is due. This time the limit can be extended.

Other provisions

7.64   The convention contains provisions on non-discrimination, mutual agreement procedure, exchange of information, and diplomatic and consular privileges.

Convention with the United States of America

7.65   This convention (*SI 1979 No 1454*) came into force on 11 November 1979. The convention contains a definition of fiscal domicile, with the country of domicile having the primary taxing rights except in the case of immovable property and business property which may be taxed where they are situated. Certain taxing rights are also reserved to the state of nationality.

Taxes covered

7.66   The convention applies to the following taxes. In the United States, federal gift tax and federal estate tax, including 'generation skipping' tax and in the UK, capital transfer tax and inheritance tax. The convention also applies to any identical or substantially similar taxes which are imposed by a contracting state after the date of signature of the convention in addition to, or in place of, the existing taxes.

Fiscal domicile

7.67   *Article 4(1)* provides that for the purposes of the convention an individual is domiciled:

(*a*)   in the United States if he was a resident (domiciliary) there, or if he was a US national and he had been a resident (domiciliary) there at any time during the preceding three years; and

(*b*)   in the UK if he was domiciled in the UK in accordance with the law of the UK or is treated as so domiciled for the purposes of a tax which is the subject of the convention.

The reference in *Article 4(1)* to a US resident (domiciliary) is a reference to domicile under the law of the US rather than a reference to residence.

Article 4 contains two specific tie-breaker rules before applying the normal OECD tie-breaker rules.

7.68   *Article 4(2)* provides that where under *para (1)* an individual was domiciled in both contracting states and

(*a*)   was a national of the UK but not of the United States, and

(*b*)   has not been resident in the United States for federal income tax purposes in seven or more of the ten taxable years ending with the year in
which that time falls,

he shall be deemed to be domiciled in the UK at that time.

7.69   *Article 4(3)* provides a corresponding provision in the converse
case, where an individual is a national of the United States but not of the
UK. Residence in the UK is ascertained without regard to any available
accommodation in the UK. It should be noted that available accommodation
is no longer a test of residence in the UK since 6 April 1993 by virtue of
section 208 of the *Finance Act 1993*.

7.70   Subject to these provisions, *Article 4(4)* provides that where an
individual is domiciled in both contracting states, additional tie-breaker
rules (based on the OECD model) apply. There is one variation in that where
an individual does not have a permanent home in either country he is
deemed to be domiciled in the country in which he has his centre of vital
interests rather than in the country where he has an habitual abode.

Taxing rights

7.71   *Article 5(1)* provides that subject to the provisions of *Articles 6*
(immovable property) and *7* (business property) and the following provisions of the article, if the deceased or transferor was domiciled in one of the
contracting states at the time of death or transfer, property shall not be taxable in the other contracting state. *Article 5(1)(b)*, however, provides that
this does not apply if the deceased or transferor was a national of the other
contracting state, in which case that contracting state retains its domestic
taxing rights. This provision is included because the US imposes tax by reference to citizenship and is similar to the 'Saving Clause' in the UK/US
Treaty on income and capital gains.

The question whether the Saving Clause enables the US to tax former US
nationals who have expatriated (i.e. renounced US citizenship) within the prior
ten years under certain US anti-avoidance provisions is unresolved. It would
appear from the wording in *Article 5(1)(b)* which refers to a 'national' of the
State (but unlike certain other US Treaties does not also refer to former nationals) that the US would be precluded from taxing a former citizen where the
convention would otherwise apply. This view is given support by the decision
of the US Tax Court in *Crow v Commissioner 85 TC 376 (1985)*. It is understood, however, that this view is not shared by the US Internal Revenue Service.

7.72   *Article 5(2)* provides that, subject to the provisions of *Articles 6* and
7, if at the time of the death or transfer the individual was domiciled in
neither contracting state and was a national of one but not both states,
property which is taxable in the state of which he was a national shall not be
taxable in the other contracting state.

7.73   The article goes on to provide specific provisions on transfers in United States 'generation skipping' trusts and UK settled property. The rule is that (subject to *Articles 6* and *7*) the UK may only tax settled property if the settlor was a national of or domiciled in the UK when the trust was made, and the United States may only tax a transfer in a generation skipping trust if the person making the transfer was a national of or domiciled in the United States. On the treatment of settled property generally see further paragraph 7.120 below.

7.74   *Article 5(5)*, however, allows one contracting state to tax property otherwise taxable only in the other state if the tax, though chargeable, is not paid (otherwise than as the result of a specific exemption deduction credit or allowance) in that other state.

Immovable property

7.75   Immovable property may be taxed in the contracting state in which the property is situated. A definition of immovable property follows the OECD model with similar provision on debts to that contained in the South African convention (see 7.56 above).

Business property

7.76   *Article 7* provides that assets forming part of the business property of a permanent establishment of an enterprise may be taxed in the contracting state in which the permanent establishment is situated. The definition of permanent establishment is similar to that in the South African convention (see 7.57 above).

Deductions, exemptions etc.

7.77   *Article 8* of the convention deals with these in some detail. *Paragraph 1* states that in determining the amount on which tax is to be computed, permitted deductions shall be allowed in accordance with the law in force in the contracting state in which tax is imposed.

The exemptions covered by the article mainly deal with those applying between spouses, and the loss of the inter-spouse exemption both in the United States and the UK which may result by reason of one of the spouses not being domiciled or a national of one of the countries.

Of particular importance is *Article 8(4)* which provides a relief from inheritance tax for 50 per cent of the value of property passing on the death of a UK domiciled spouse to a non-UK domiciled spouse if:

(*a*)   the property becomes comprised in a settlement on the death of the UK domiciled spouse, e.g. under the will of the spouse;

(*b*)   the personal representatives and the trustees of any settlement in which the deceased had an interest in possession immediately before his death so elect;

(*c*)   the spouse of the deceased is entitled to an immediate interest in possession;

(*d*)   the spouse of the deceased was domiciled in or a national of the US;

(*e*)   the transfer would have been wholly exempt had the surviving spouse been UK domiciled;

(*f*)   greater exemption would not be given under UK law apart from the convention, e.g. the exemption will only be relevant for an estate worth more than double the restricted spouse exemption of £55,000 under *section 18(2)* of the *IHTA 1984.*

The full tax becomes payable if the surviving spouse becomes absolutely entitled to the property at any time after the deceased spouse's death, e.g. on capital being advanced to the spouse. Tax would also be payable under the normal settled property rules on the death of the surviving spouse when the interest in possession comes to an end. This will be the case even though the surviving spouse is not UK domiciled because the settled property would not be excluded property as the settlor was UK domiciled. The tax may be avoided, however, if the will or other settlement contains an overriding power which can be exercised to defeat the surviving spouse's life interest with property remaining in trust after the life interest has been defeated. As long as discretionary trusts were not appointed this would qualify as a potential exempt transfer not giving rise to any charge to inheritance tax if the spouse survived seven years.

7.78   Further, *para 5* provides that where property may be taxed in the United States on the death of a UK national who was neither domiciled in nor a national of the United States and a claim is made, the tax imposed in the United States shall be limited to the amount of tax which would have been imposed had the deceased been domiciled in the United States immediately before his death. The effect of this is to make available potentially higher exemptions applying to US residents but at the price of including the deceased's worldwide property.

Credits

7.79   *Article 9* provides for credit to be given where double taxation would otherwise arise. The principles embodied in *Article 9* are, in cases where property is not settled, as follows.

(*a*)   Where a country is entitled to tax in accordance with *Article 6* (immovable property) or *Article 7* (business property), it does not give credit, but the other state has to give credit. This is the case whether the other state taxes on the basis of domicile or nationality.

(*b*)   In the case of property other than immovable property and business property, the state which imposes tax on the basis of domicile does not give credit, but the other state must give credit. For example, where a person is domiciled in the UK under the treaty but the United States taxes property on the basis of United States citizenship, the United States must give credit and not the UK.

7.80   *Article 9(3)* provides for credits in the case of settled property.

7.81   *Article 9(4)* contains further provisions on the granting of the tax credit, including the normal provision that no credit shall be given in excess of the tax paid in the country giving the credit that is attributable to the property concerned and that credit is only to be given for tax actually paid in the other state.

Remaining articles

7.82   The convention contains articles on non-discrimination, mutual agreement, exchange of information, and the effect on diplomatic and consular privileges.

Convention with the Netherlands

7.83   This convention (*SI 1980 No 706*) came into force on 16 June 1980. A Protocol amending the convention was published in September 1995 and it came into force on 3 June 1996. It makes certain amendments to the convention to be effective in relation to charges to tax arising after 17 March 1986. The convention defines fiscal domicile for the purposes of the convention and, subject to specific provisions in the case of immovable property, business property and ships, aircraft and boats, confers the primary taxing rights on the state of domicile.

The Protocol updates the definition of UK national contained in *Article 2(1)(e)* of the convention.

Taxes covered

7.84   The taxes which are the subject of the convention are capital transfer tax in the case of the UK and succession duty, gift duty and the transfer duty in the case of the Netherlands. The convention also applies to any identical or substantially similar taxes which are imposed after the date of the signature of the convention. The Protocol referred to above provides that the convention covers inheritance tax as well as capital transfer tax although this change was not strictly necessary because it would have been covered in the reference to a substantially similar tax imposed after the date of the convention.

Fiscal domicile

7.85   For the purposes of the convention a person is domiciled in the UK if he was domiciled here in accordance with the law of the UK or is treated as so domiciled for the purposes of a tax which is the subject of the convention. A person is treated as domiciled in the Netherlands if he was a resident of, or was treated as a resident of, the Netherlands for the purposes of a tax which is the subject of the convention, provided that a person shall not be deemed to be domiciled in one of the states if, on death or gift, that state imposes tax only by reference to property situated in that state.

7.86   *Article 4(2)* contains tie-breaker rules and *Article 4(3)* qualifies *Article 4(2)* by providing that if under *para (1)* an individual was domiciled in both states, and

(*a*)   was at that time a national of one of the states but not of the other, and

(*b*)   was resident in that other state but had been so resident for less than seven out of the preceding ten years, and

(*c*)   did not intend to remain indefinitely in that other state,

he shall be deemed to be domiciled at that time in the state of which he was a national.

Immovable property

7.87   *Article 5* provides that immovable property may be taxed in the state in which the property is situated.

Business property

7.88   *Article 6* provides that, except for immovable property and ships and aircraft, assets forming part of the business property of a permanent establishment of an enterprise may be taxed in the state in which the permanent establishment is situated.

Ships and aircraft

7.89   *Article 7* provides that ships and aircraft operated in international traffic and boats engaged in inland waterways transport, and movable property pertaining to the operation of such ships, aircraft and boats may be taxed in the state in which the place of effective management of the enterprise is situated.

Primary taxing rights

7.90   Property, other than immovable property, business property of a permanent establishment, and ships and aircraft, is taxable only in the state in which the deceased or the donor was domiciled at the date of the death or gift.

Subsidiary taxing rights

7.91   *Article 11* grants subsidiary taxing rights in the following cases. If the deceased or donor was domiciled in one of the contracting states and was at that time a national of the other state and had been domiciled in the other state within ten years immediately preceding the death or gift, the other state may impose tax according to its law. It has, however, to give credit (see *Article 13* at 7.93 below) for tax in the first state against its own tax. *Article 11(2)* provides that the UK may impose tax on settled property unless when the settlement was made the settlor was domiciled in the Netherlands and was not a UK national nor domiciled in the UK within the preceding ten years. Further subsidiary taxing rights are given to the UK in respect of property other than immovable property, business property, ships and aircraft where certain UK nationals have not paid tax in the Netherlands.

Exemptions

7.92   *Article 12* grants certain exemptions on property passing between spouses.

Credit provisions

7.93   These are contained in *Article 13*.

(*a*)   Where a contracting state imposes tax by reference to any property which the other state may tax in accordance with *Articles 5, 6* or *7*, the former contracting state must give credit.

(*b*)   Where a contracting state imposes tax by reference to property not being within *Articles 5, 6* or *7*, the state which imposes tax by virtue of subsidiary taxing rights allows a credit for the other state's tax.

(*c*)   Where by virtue of *Article 11(2)* the UK imposes tax on settled property, the UK must give credit for Netherlands tax attributable to that property.

Article 13(4) contains further subsidiary provisions on the granting of the credit.

Other provisions

7.94   The convention contains provisions on non-discrimination, mutual agreement procedure, exchange of information and diplomatic and consular privileges.

Convention with Sweden

7.95   This convention (*SI 1981 No 840*) came into force on 19 June 1981, although it was amended by Protocol (*SI 1989 No 986*) with effect from 17 March 1986.

The convention covers capital transfer tax and inheritance tax in the UK and inheritance tax and gift tax in Sweden.

7.96   Domicile is defined in accordance with the OECD model and, by virtue of *Article 5*, the state of domicile is given the primary taxing rights. The treaty provides that property is not taxable in the other state except in the following cases.

(*a*)   If it is immovable property, business property of a permanent establishment, or a ship or aircraft situate in the other state.

(*b*)   If the deceased or transferor was a national of the other state at the time of the death or transfer and had been domiciled in the other state within the preceding ten years.

Article 5 also contains further exceptions to the rule.

Credit provisions

7.97   *Article 12* contains credit provisions between the two states.

Convention with Switzerland

SI 1957 No 426

7.98   The convention of 1957 (*SI 1957 No 426*) applies to estate duty and inheritance tax in the UK and to Swiss cantonal and communal tax. It has now been revoked by the new treaty with Switzerland outlined at paragraph 7.100 and following below in relation to tax and deaths occurring after 6 March 1995.

The convention was restricted to provisions regulating the locality of property for duty purposes and there was no provision for credit to be given for tax paid in one country against tax paid in the other.

Domicile

7.99   *Article III(2)* provided that, for the purposes of the convention, the question whether a person was domiciled in any part of the territory of one of the contracting parties shall be determined in accordance with the law in that territory.

The convention went on to define the situs of various assets and *Article V* provided that in determining the amount on which tax was to be computed permitted deductions were to be allowed in accordance with the law in force in the territory in which the tax was imposed.

SI 1994 No 3214

7.100   This convention (*SI 1994 No 3214*) came into force on 6 March 1995 and applies to tax charges arising and deaths occurring on or after that date. The 1956 Estate Duty Convention (referred to below) will continue to have effect but only in relation to charges or deaths arising before 6 March 1995. The old convention is briefly discussed at para 7.98 above.

The convention differs in a number of respects from the OECD model and from the other five conventions entered into since the introduction of capital transfer tax.

7.101   Taxes covered:

Article 2(1) provides that the taxes covered by the convention are, for the UK, inheritance tax, insofar as it applies to the estate of a deceased person and, for Switzerland, the cantonal and communal taxes imposed on estates and inheritances. The convention also applies to identical and substantially similar taxes which are imposed in future by either contracting state.

The convention does not cover inheritance tax on lifetime gifts although it may apply to gifts with reservation which are treated as part of the estate of a deceased person. The convention applies

(*a*)   to estates and inheritances where the deceased was domiciled at the date of death, in one or both of the contracting states; and

(*b*)   to property comprised in a settlement made by a person who was domiciled, at the time the settlement was made, in one or both of the contracting states.

Fiscal domicile

7.102   Under *Article 4(1)(a)* of the convention an individual is domiciled in the UK if he is domiciled in the UK in accordance with its law or is treated as so domiciled for the purposes of a tax which is the subject of the convention.

Article 4(1)(b) states that a deceased person is domiciled in Switzerland if:

(*a*)   he is domiciled or resident there in accordance with the law of Switzerland; or

(*b*)   he is a Swiss national and Swiss civil law requires his succession to be ruled in Switzerland.

Article 4(2) goes on to provide the usual tie-breaker rules where a deceased person is domiciled in both contracting states.

It should, however, be noted that in a Protocol to the convention it is provided that:

(*a*)   an individual who was a national of one contracting state without being a national of the other contracting state and is domiciled in the state of which he was a national immediately before coming to the other state shall not be domiciled in the other state for the purposes of the convention if:

   (i)   he is temporarily present in that other state by reason only of his employment, or was a spouse or other dependant of a person temporarily in that other state for such purpose;

   (ii)   that individual had retained the domicile of the state of which he was a national; and

   (iii)   that individual had no intention of becoming a permanent resident of the other contracting state.

It is likely that this provision will benefit UK nationals but is unlikely to benefit Swiss nationals because a Swiss national (unless deemed domiciled) would be unlikely to acquire a domicile of choice in the UK in the circumstances specified in the Protocol.

General taxing rights

7.103   While the convention follows the approach of the model convention in defining fiscal domicile, subject to the provisions of the Protocol, the convention does not adopt the usual approach to taxing rights. The model convention awards taxing rights (subject to exceptions relating to immovable property and business property) to the state where the individual is domiciled. The Swiss convention, however, adopts this principle only in relation to property situated in a third country. Where the deceased was domiciled in both the UK under UK law and in Switzerland under Swiss law each state has generally the sole right to tax property situated within its territory.

Immovable property

7.104   *Article 5* of the convention provides that immovable property which forms part of the estate of a person domiciled in a contracting state and which is situated in the other contracting state may be taxed in that other state. The term specifically includes an interest in the proceeds of sale of land which is held on trust for sale but excludes debts secured by mortgage or otherwise.

Business property

7.105   Movable property of an enterprise which forms part of the estate of the person domiciled in one contracting state which is business property of a permanent establishment situated in the other contracting state may be taxed in that other state.

Article 6(7) applies the article to an interest in a partnership.

Ships and aircraft

7.106   Under *Article 7* ships and aircraft and other movable property forming part of an enterprise operating in international traffic owned by a person domiciled in a contracting state, may be taxed in the other contracting state if the place of effective management of the enterprise is situated there. The terms 'international traffic' and 'place of effective management' are defined in the convention.

Other property

7.107   *Article 8* of the convention sets out the rules dealing with taxing rights over property other than immovable property, business property and ships and aircraft.

(*a*)   Where the deceased was domiciled solely in the UK or solely in Switzerland his other property is taxable only in the state of domicile (*Article 8(1)(a)(i)*). There is an exception to this rule that shares in a company incorporated in the UK may also be taxed in the UK.

(*b*)   *Article 8(1)(a)(ii)* goes on to deal with cases of persons domiciled in both the UK and in Switzerland. In such cases other property situated in the UK or in Switzerland is taxable only in the state where it is situated.

(*c*)   Other property which is not situated in either state is taxable only in the state where the deceased was domiciled under the tie-breaker rules in *Article 4(2)*.

Article 8 goes on to give the UK secondary taxing rights in relation to property in Switzerland if the deceased was domiciled in the UK under the tie-breaker rules. It is also given secondary taxing rights in relation to property in Switzerland or a third country if the deceased was a national of the UK but not of Switzerland and had been domiciled in the UK within the five years preceding his death.

Elimination of double taxation

7.108   *Article 9(1)* of the convention provides that where the UK can impose tax on an event by reference to property:

(*a*)   which may be taxed in Switzerland under *Articles 5, 6* or *7* (i.e immovable property, business property or ships and aircraft managed in Switzerland); or

(*b*)   which may be taxed in the UK under *Article 8(2), (3)* or *(4)*;

the UK shall allow against so much of its tax as is attributable to such property a credit (not exceeding the tax so attributable) equal to so much of any tax imposed in Switzerland.

Paragraph 2 of *Article 9* provides that where the deceased was domiciled in Switzerland at the date of his death, Switzerland is to exempt from tax any property which with *Articles 5, 6* or *7*, may be taxed in the United Kingdom under *Articles 5, 6* or *7*. In other words, UK land, businesses and ships and aircraft are to be exempt from Swiss tax even though owned by a Swiss domiciliary. This is subject, however, to *Article 9(3)* which provides that where any property is exempted from tax by any provision of the convention it may nevertheless be taken into account in computing the tax on other property or in determining the rate of such tax.

Article 9 concludes by providing that tax is imposed in a contracting state if it is chargeable under the law of that state and duly paid.

Miscellaneous

7.109   *Article 10* contains two important rules. The first deals with differing rules in each state on the nature of any property. Under *Article 10(1)* where the state of domicile regards any right or interest as not falling within *Articles 5, 6* or *7* but the other state does regard it as falling within those articles then the nature of the right or interest is to be determined by the law of the other state (i.e. the law of the state where the property is situate).

Article 10(2) deals with the spouse exemption. It provides that property which passes to the spouse from a deceased person who is domiciled in or a national of Switzerland and which may be taxed in the UK shall be exempt as to one-half of the value passing where:

(*a*)   the recipient spouse was not domiciled in the UK but a transfer would have been wholly exempt had the spouse been UK domiciled; and

(*b*)   a greater exemption for transfers between spouses would not have been given under the law of the UK apart from the convention (i.e. the value passing is more than double the restricted spouse exemption of £55,000).

This provision would, for example, assist a Swiss national who was deemed domiciled in the UK leaving assets to a spouse not UK domiciled or deemed domiciled.

It should be noted that there is no similar provision for Switzerland to give these spouse exemptions.

Further provisions

7.110   The convention contains provisions dealing with non-discrimination, mutual agreement, exchange of information and diplomatic agents and consulate officials.

Convention with France

7.111   This convention (*SI 1963 No 1319*) applies to estate duty in Great Britain but not Northern Ireland (and now to capital transfer tax and inheritance tax applying on transfers on death but not extending to Northern Ireland) and in France to French succession duty.

Domicile

7.112   Under *Article II(3)(a)*, a question whether a deceased person was domiciled at the time of his death in any part of the territory of one of the contracting parties shall be determined in accordance with the law in force in that territory. *Article II(3)(b)* then contains tie-breaker rules.

Primary taxing rights

7.113   *Article V* provides that where a person at the time of his death was domiciled in France, duties shall not be imposed in Great Britain on any property which is neither situated in Great Britain nor passes under a disposition or devolution regulated by the law of some part of Great Britain; and in determining the amount or rate of duty payable in Great Britain such property shall be disregarded. It follows that property in Northern Ireland is also disregarded. *Article V(2)* provides that where the deceased was domiciled in Great Britain, the French succession duty shall not be imposed on property situated outside France.

Situs rules

7.114   *Article IV* contains a code deeming certain assets to be situated where the deceased was domiciled. These assets include debts, debentures, bills of exchange, patents, trademarks, and judgment debts.

Credits

7.115   *Article VI* provides that where one contracting party imposes duty on the death of a person domiciled in its territory on property situated in the territory of the other contracting party, the state of domicile shall allow a tax credit equal to the duty imposed by the other party.

Convention with Italy

7.116   This convention (*SI 1968 No 304*) applies to estate duty in the UK and in Italy to succession duty and estate duty.

Domicile

7.117   Under *Article II* each party determines domicile in accordance with its own law (although the deemed domicile rules in the UK do not apply). If the person is domiciled in both countries under their domestic law the question is resolved by a tie-breaker provision (*Article II(2)(b)*).

Article V contains the taxing rights and *Articles VI* and *VII* contain credit provisions in the treaty.

Convention with India

7.118   This convention (*SI 1956 No 998*) remains in force despite the abolition of Indian estate duty in 1985. Its relevance now is that it restricts the application of the UK deemed domicile rules for inheritance tax purposes on death. The UK cannot tax the worldwide assets of a person who dies domiciled in India (under its local law) and who is at the same time deemed to be domiciled in the UK for inheritance tax purposes (but not actually domiciled here under the general law).

Convention with Pakistan

7.119   This convention remains in force despite the abolition of Pakistan death duties with effect from 28 June 1978. It should be noted that the convention does not extend to Bangladesh. The relevance of the convention is limited in the same way as that with India.

Favourable effect of the treaties on settled property

7.120   Under UK domestic law settled property will be excluded property outside the scope of inheritance tax only if the settlor was domiciled outside the UK when the settlement was made and to the extent the property is situated outside the UK. This is provided in *section 48(3)* of the *IHTA 1984*. It is therefore important that trusts made by non-UK domiciled settlors should ensure that they do not invest in or acquire UK situated assets.

7.121   This position is, however, substantially modified by a number of double taxation treaties entered into since 1974.

7.122   The treaty with the United States of America (*Article 5(4)*) supplants the general taxing provisions in *Article 5(1)* and *(2)* and provides that tax shall not be imposed in the UK on settled property if at the time the settlement was made the settlor was treaty domiciled in the United States and was not a national of the United Kingdom. This is, however, subject to the provisions of *Articles 6* (immovable property) and *7* (business property). The effect is that a trust made by a settlor domiciled in the United States under the Treaty who was not a UK national can invest in assets in the UK with protection from inheritance tax as long as immovable property and business assets are avoided. The trustees of such settlements could therefore invest in stocks and shares on the UK stock market without an exposure to inheritance tax.

7.123   The treaty with Sweden *Article 5(4)* also supplants the general taxing provisions of *Article 5(1)* and *(3)* of that treaty and provides that settled property is not subject to tax in the UK if at the time the settlement was made the settlor was domiciled in Sweden unless the settlor was a national of the United Kingdom at the time of making the settlement and had been domiciled for the purposes of the treaty in the United Kingdom within the immediately preceding ten years. This is subject to *Article 6* (immovable property), *Article 7* (business property) and *Article 8* (ships and aircraft) which retain the UK's taxing rights over these categories of property situate in the UK.

7.124   The treaty with the Republic of South Africa under *Article 5(2)* also provides that settled property is not taxable in the UK if at the time the settlement was made the settlor was domiciled in South Africa and had not been domiciled under the treaty in the United Kingdom within the preceding ten years. This treaty protection does not apply to immovable property, business property, ships and aircraft and shares, debentures and unit trust holdings situated in the UK.

7.125   In contrast, the treaty with the Netherlands is rather different. *Article 11(2)* dealing with subsidiary taxing rights provides that the UK may impose tax by reference to property comprised in a settlement unless when the settlement was made the settlor was treaty domiciled in the Netherlands, and was not a national of the UK who had been domiciled in the UK within the prior ten years. This does not expressly exclude the UK's taxing rights under the treaty with the result that it may be possible for the UK to tax settled property situated in the UK on a chargeable transfer by the life tenant.

7.126   The treaty with Ireland in *Article 5(2)* contains detailed provisions dealing with the taxation of settled property in rather different terms.

7.127   It will therefore be apparent that the treaties substantially improve the inheritance tax position of settlements with non-UK treaty domiciled settlors in some cases.

General estate planning and treaty shopping

7.128   It is open to individuals in planning their tax affairs to rely on the provisions of any appropriate double taxation convention between the UK and any other country. In appropriate cases the fiscal domicile rules may be relied on to override the deemed domicile provisions of *IHTA 1984, s 267*, although it should be borne in mind that immovable property and business property of a permanent establishment situated in the UK will not be saved by provisions concerning fiscal domicile. To some extent the situs of assets can be changed by their transfer to a 'shield company' incorporated in some other jurisdiction. The individual will then own shares in the company rather than its underlying assets. It will often be the case, however, that a country with which the UK has a double tax convention will have relatively high rates of tax although it may have more generous exemptions and exempt bands (e.g. the United States).

7.129   Unlike some of the conventions on income and capital gains there are no specific 'treaty shopping' clauses preventing the use of a particular convention by a person from a third country. The OECD Commentary has this to say on the topic:

> 'the Committee on Fiscal Affairs has examined the question of the improper use of double taxation conventions but, in view of the complexity of the problem, it has limited itself, in preparing this model convention, to enlarging the Commentary on *Article 12* enabling states to exchange information to combat improper use of conventions, tax avoidance and evasion. The Committee is engaged, however, in an in-depth study of problems of abuse or improper use of tax conventions and of ways of dealing with them.'

It remains to be seen how the conventions in the future will be adapted in the light of this study. Possible areas of change may be further elaboration of the definition of fiscal domicile and also detailed situs rules to counteract the use of shield companies.

8   Inheritance Tax Planning for Non-UK Domiciled Individuals

Caroline Kirby
(Partner, Farrer & Co.)

Introduction

8.1   The single most valuable attribute which an individual can possess for UK estate planning purposes is a domicile outside the UK. Any gift made by a person domiciled in the UK is liable to inheritance tax (IHT) if the donor does not survive the gift for seven years, no matter where the asset which is given is situated; but if the donor has a foreign domicile, assets which are (in legal terms) situated outside the UK should qualify as 'excluded property' and escape liability or potential liability to the tax. Domicile, rather than residence, is the key factor in determining liability to IHT. From the UK perspective, the two main objectives of IHT planning for an individual with international connections are:

(*a*)   for the individual to acquire, maintain or secure a domicile outside the UK, and

(*b*)   to ensure, ideally, that all assets are situated outside the UK.

Excluded property

8.2   IHT is charged by reference to the reduction in value of assets to which the donor is beneficially entitled (whether outright or in trust) which results from a gift or other transfer. The advantage of excluded property in IHT planning is that any reduction in value of the donor's estate caused by making lifetime gifts, or by dying, or by any other occasion which is a 'transfer of value' for the purposes of IHT, will not be subject to the tax. [*IHTA 1984, ss 3(2), 5(1)*].

Property (in the legal sense, i.e., all assets rights and interests including, but not limited to, freehold and leasehold property [*IHTA 1984, s 272*]) which is situated outside the UK is excluded property in two situations which are relevant here:

(*a*)   if the person beneficially entitled to it is domiciled outside the UK, regardless of his residence [*IHTA 1984, s 6(1)*], or

(*b*)   if it is comprised in a settlement (which broadly means the same as a trust) and the settlor was not domiciled (or deemed domiciled: see 8.7) in the UK at the time when it was made [*IHTA 1984, s 48(3)*].

Domicile

8.3   In English law, domicile means, essentially, the country or state which is considered to be an individual's 'home country' where he or she has settled permanently or indefinitely. It can affect the application of rules on marriage, legitimacy and inheritance as well as liability to taxes. Domicile is not defined in the *Taxes Acts*, except for the statutory extension of its meaning for IHT [*IHTA 1984, s 267*] (see 8.7); it is a common law concept developed by decisions of the courts over many years and its principles derive from the days of coach and horse and sailing ship travel far removed from modern international mobility of business and domestic interests where it is not at all unusual for a person to have connections with more than one country.

Whenever an individual has personal or family connections with a country outside the UK, it is worth investigating the possibility of a foreign domicile very carefully in view of the advantages which it can bring. It should not be forgotten, though, that the law of the domicile country will normally regulate succession on death and the permitted terms of a will (among other matters), and the frying-pan of UK taxes should not be inadvertently exchanged for a fiercer foreign fire. Professional advice will normally be required in the domicile country as well as in the UK.

The treatment of domicile in English law (and in jurisdictions which are based on English law) is quite different from its treatment elsewhere, particularly in continental Europe, where domicile is usually equivalent to habitual residence. Particular care needs to be taken in explaining the concept to clients or advisers abroad.

Domicile is not the same as nationality, citizenship or residence, though some or all may coincide. Everyone must be domiciled in one (but not more than one) territory at any particular time throughout his or her life, and positive action is needed to change a domicile. In a federal country such as Canada, Australia, Switzerland or the US, a domicile in one particular state or province or canton must be shown. 'UK domicile' is convenient shorthand for a status which does not legally exist: domicile can be in England and Wales, or in Scotland, or in Northern Ireland, since the three territories have different legal systems. By contrast, the arm of the Inland Revenue extends across the UK, so usually the objective for tax purposes is to prove whether or not the taxpayer lacked the relevant connection with any part of the UK. The Channel Islands and the Isle of Man are not part of the UK, nor are the other Commonwealth countries, British colonies or dependent or protected territories. (Scots law is not dealt with here and will need separate consideration if a Scottish domicile or real property in Scotland is involved.)

At any one time an individual may have a domicile of origin, a domicile of choice or (less commonly) a domicile of dependence.

8.4   A 'domicile of origin' is the domicile which every individual acquires at birth. A child born legitimate and during the father's lifetime acquires the father's domicile. A child who is illegitimate or born after the death of the father takes the mother's domicile.

The domicile of origin has a special status in that it is difficult to dislodge (*Udny v Udny (1869) 1 Sc & Div 441*) and in that, even if it is later displaced by a domicile of choice, it can revive automatically at a later date, sometimes with unexpected consequences (see 8.5). (For a recent case, within the UK but illustrating the impact of forced heirship rules, see *Anderson (Anderson's Executor) v IRC [1998] STC (SCD) 43.*) However, with careful planning, it is possible for an individual to be a long-term resident of the UK and to own assets and conduct business here without being domiciled in any part of the UK. If a foreign domicile of origin can be shown, it is usually very difficult for the Revenue to prove that it has been lost.

8.5 A 'domicile of choice' is acquired, in place of an existing domicile, by an individual who moves to another country with the intention of settling there permanently (in the sense of intending to continue to reside in the adopted country indefinitely: *Re Fuld's Goods (No 3) [1968] P 675*), and who severs ties with the original country. The standard of proof is often high: it is 'a serious matter not to be lightly inferred from slight indications or casual words'. Moving abroad to work will not bring about a change of domicile unless the person intends to make the new country his permanent home not only during the work assignment but when it has expired.

The strength of the domicile of origin means that unexpected results can happen when a person migrates for a second time. In *Udny v Udny*, Colonel Udny had been living in London for 32 years before having to flee to France to avoid his racing creditors: he was held to have abandoned his domicile of choice in England without a fixed intention of remaining in France, so that his Scottish domicile of origin revived. In modern times this principle may work against an international executive or other career expatriate.

Example

Peregrine, a UK domiciliary, leaves Brussels, where he has spent most of his working life, and goes to Spain to see if he wants to retire there, but dies before settling permanently. Either his domicile of origin in the UK will never have been lost, or, if it has been replaced by a domicile of choice in Belgium, it will revive if he leaves Belgium for good without a fixed intention of moving permanently to Spain.

The intention must be formed voluntarily and independently of external pressures (*Udny v Udny; Re Fuld*) so that refugees may, at least initially, retain their domiciles of origin (*Steiner v IRC (1973) 49 TC 13*); see also *Mrs F v IRC [2000] STC (SCD) 1*, where the deceased never lost his Iranian domicile of origin despite having acquired a UK passport and UK nationality). The motive for moving abroad may be to avoid taxes, but there must be a genuine intention to abandon the home country (*Re Clore (No 2) [1984] STC 609*) and an actual presence in the new country (*Bell v Kennedy*

(1868) LR 1 Sc & Div 307). (This contrasts with the domicile of origin, which need never have been the country of actual residence.) If connections with the old country are retained, the new country must be the chief residence (*Plummer v IRC [1987] STC 698*).

8.6   Before 1 January 1974 a 'domicile of dependence' could be acquired by a child, a mentally disordered person or a married woman. There is now no domicile of dependence for married women, so that one spouse can be domiciled in the UK while the other spouse is domiciled elsewhere. This can produce planning opportunities, though the restrictions on gifts to non-domiciled spouses must be remembered (see 8.20). The domicile of dependence of a wife where the marriage took place before 1 January 1974 was effectively then converted into a domicile of choice, though in practice the IHT deemed domicile rules will now usually take precedence in these circumstances (see 8.7).

The domicile of a child under 16 usually follows that of the father, if the child is legitimate, or the mother, if it is not, but the law is convoluted and complications can arise if the parents are divorced or separated and the child is not living exclusively with only one of them.

Deemed domicile

8.7   Inheritance tax is at present the only UK tax which imposes a secondary test of domicile that has the effect of making it harder to shed, or avoid acquiring, UK domicile for inheritance tax purposes. An individual is treated as domiciled in the UK at a given time by *IHTA 1984, s 267(1)* if:

(*a*)   he was domiciled in the UK at any time within the previous three *calendar* years, or

(*b*)   he was resident in the UK for income tax purposes in at least 17 of the last 20 *tax* years (taking year 20 as the year in which the given time falls).

There is no question of being able to shed domicile before the three calendar year period has expired: this can come as an unpleasant surprise to those who intend (for example) to retire and then emigrate and who expect subsequent lifetime gifts, or their estates on death, to be exempt from inheritance tax even if they die a short time after leaving the UK. The three-year period begins to run from the date when domicile under the common law rules is lost: this may be later than the date of leaving the UK, for example, if a world cruise separates leaving the UK from arrival and settlement in the new country. Therefore, the creation of a large discretionary offshore trust shortly after emigration from the UK would be fully subject to an immediate inheritance tax charge; emigrants may need to consider temporary investment in exempt gilts (see 8.16). Since 1983 the rules for acquiring a Channel Islands or Isle of Man IHT domicile have been no more favourable than the rules applying to any other territory.

Deemed domicile under head (*b*) – the so-called '17-year rule' – can of course arise before the 17th anniversary of arrival in the UK, because residence for any part of a tax year will potentially bring a person within the rule: so a person who became UK resident on 1 January 1986 and stayed resident would become deemed domiciled on 6 April 2001.

Non-domiciliaries who are resident in the UK over a period of time need to review their position carefully after about twelve years, if not before, in order to ensure that they are able to plan ahead for a period of non-residence for themselves (and their families) if necessary.

Residence for deemed domicile purposes is to be determined under the usual income tax rules (for the Revenue interpretation, see the booklet IR20 'Residents and Non-Residents', revised to October 1999) but without regard to the 'available accommodation rule' which previously applied. Under legislation which applied before 1993/94, a person was automatically deemed resident for income tax purposes if he had a dwelling house available in the UK for his use at any time in the year (whether or not owned by him) and if he set foot in the UK even for one day during that year. However, if a person has and uses a UK base, that will remain a fact which may carry weight in a domicile ruling. Additionally, owning or leasing accommodation may cause an incoming 'longer term visitor' to the UK to be treated as immediately resident, which will be relevant to the calculation of the 17-year period (see IR20, paragraph 3.7ff.): though mere availability of accommodation does not bring about that treatment.

Possible changes to domicile law

8.8 In November 1991 the then Conservative Government announced that it had accepted the proposals of the joint Report in 1987 by the Law Commission and the Scottish Law Commission (Law Com. no. 158, Scot. Law Com. no. 107) for reform of the law of domicile. The Report did not dwell on the tax implications of reform and it was stated not to be driven by tax considerations but rather by the need to reform international matrimonial law and other areas. The proposals were shelved in 1993, after strong representations from the expatriate community (among others) that the attraction of London, and the rest of the UK, as a base for individuals in international business would be impaired if residence for a number of years was equated with domicile.

At the time of writing, the tax reforms introduced or proposed by the Labour Government since its election in 1997 and election for a second term in 2001 have still not included any significant changes to IHT (and in particular not to its application to non-UK domiciliaries) nor to the law of domicile itself. Changes are widely expected but, at the time of writing, the scope of any such changes remains speculative. As the previous proposals might be resurrected, it is worth briefly considering them here.

8.9   The Law Commissions' Report did not revive a previous proposal that domicile should be presumed for tax purposes after a fixed period of residence, probably seven years. It recommended the following.

• The domicile of origin should be abolished. In its place a child should at birth be domiciled in the country or state with which he is most closely connected. The child should be able to replace that initial domicile with a domicile of choice at age 16.

• Special status should no longer attach to the domicile acquired at birth, which should be no more difficult to change than a subsequent domicile of choice. The domicile of origin should not revive in the course of any decision to change domicile: instead, the existing domicile should always continue until the decision has been made.

• It should be easier to prove a change of domicile. The test should be the balance of probabilities.

• The two requirements for proof of an adult's new domicile in another country should be:

(*a*)   presence there; and

(*b*)   intention to 'settle' there 'for an indefinite period'.

An indefinite period could be inferred if there is no 'sufficiently substantial possibility of return' to the previous country, especially if that intention is not linked to any particular future event. An intention to return on winning the National Lottery jackpot might be insubstantial, but an intention to return on retirement (even though the date of retirement is not yet known) might be substantial. Some concern was expressed that the new test, when combined with the weakening of the domicile of origin presumption, would have the effect in practice of making a non-UK domicile more difficult to sustain.

Existing law can allow an intention to return to the country of origin at a fairly vague time in the future to preserve the domicile of origin. In *IRC v Bullock [1976] STC 409* a Canadian, who intended to return to Nova Scotia if his wife agreed (which was unlikely) or if she predeceased him, succeeded in maintaining his non-UK domicile despite many years' residence in the UK; though by contrast the long-term UK resident taxpayer in *Furse v IRC [1980] STC 596* was held to have been 'deeply settled' in the UK without any substantial aspiration to return to the US, and accordingly domiciled in the UK. If the law changed, it seems likely that both these circumstances would lead to a UK domicile ruling.

It is an open question how far any new law would be retrospective; but because domicile is assessed over a period of years, current actions and assumptions would inevitably be affected by a change.

If the Law Commission's proposals, or something similar to them, became law, the individual moving abroad would find it easier to satisfy the Revenue that he had acquired a new foreign domicile. The UK expatriate who moves from one country to another would be less likely to retain, or suddenly re-acquire, a UK domicile of choice. It might become easier to acquire a new domicile and still retain UK interests or assets. However, the position would become more difficult for some UK resident foreign nationals who can at present legitimately avoid UK tax on foreign income and gains that are not received in the UK and enjoy immunity from IHT, and it might become particularly difficult for older people who have been resident here for some time. The possibility of new rules should be taken into account when planning and it will be sensible to focus at suitable intervals on whether there is an intention to remain indefinitely in the UK or a definite and credible intention to return home. Another sensible precaution for a person who is not yet deemed domiciled under the '17-year rule' may be to act now to establish an excluded property trust, if the circumstances are right, in case the length of the period before domicile is deemed to have been acquired is reduced in future (though see further 8.26).

Maintaining a non-UK domicile

8.10   A person who is resident in the UK will be treated as also domiciled in the UK unless he proves otherwise to the satisfaction of the Inland Revenue. The Revenue will usually decline to give a ruling on domicile unless there is some tax at stake, so that it may be necessary to take some action to 'test' the Revenue (and if necessary risk acceleration of payment of some tax) so that a domicile ruling is obtained to establish certainty on which future planning can be based. Self-assessment tax returns require a taxpayer to declare each year if he considers himself to be domiciled outside the UK.

If income and/or gains arise outside the UK and are not remitted directly or indirectly to the UK, then it should be possible to obtain a ruling (provided that the sums are large enough to be worth the Revenue assessing and collecting the tax due) because only remitted gains or income are taxable in the UK in the hands of a non-domiciliary. If this is not possible (e.g., if all the person's assets are in the UK) and if a ruling is required, it will be necessary to take some action which would precipitate an immediate IHT charge if the individual were domiciled in the UK. The individual could transfer cash of an amount which well exceeded the IHT 'nil rate band' (£242,000 from 6 April 2001) to an offshore account and then settle it on a discretionary trust (of which he could be a beneficiary). He would then report the transaction to the Revenue and ask for confirmation that no IHT is payable. If he were UK domiciled at the time, immediate IHT would be due since the transfer was not a potentially exempt transfer, and would be chargeable whether or not he survived for seven years; but if the Revenue accepted that he was not UK domiciled, then the transfer into the trust would be of non-UK excluded property and would be outside the scope of IHT.

If non-UK domicile is claimed, and tax rests upon the claim, the Revenue Centre for Non-Residents (CNR) may require the taxpayer to complete

Form DOM1 giving details of life history and current intentions on which the domicile claim will be assessed by the Revenue. If a discretionary trust is established, a return to the Capital Taxes Office may need to be made. Similar questions are contained in Form P86 when an individual arrives in the UK. Although the forms are not couched in obviously technical terms it is very important that the taxpayer takes professional advice before completing them, particularly with regard to the questions about permanent residence and future intentions. Form DOM1 and Form P86 are available on the Inland Revenue website: www.inlandrevenue.gov.uk.

Preserving non-domiciled status

8.11   Once UK non-domiciled status is granted, it will be reviewed regularly by the Revenue, probably at five-yearly intervals. Clearly, the longer a person remains living in the UK, the weaker his case for maintaining foreign domicile becomes (quite apart from the '17-year rule'), even if he is arguing from the strength of a foreign domicile of origin. To evidence a continuing foreign domicile, a person should consider the following:

- keeping, or acquiring, a property in the foreign country, and visiting it regularly, or taking an active part in existing activities of friends or relatives there;

- maintaining cultural, social, business and language ties with the domicile country;

- keeping UK assets to a sensible minimum and investing other assets outside the UK, or through a non-UK channel, if there is a choice;

- making a will under the domicile country's law (to deal at least with assets in that country);

- making plans to retire to that country or permanently move or return there at a definite future date (or on the occurrence of a definite future event).

Acquiring a non-UK domicile

8.12   This could be more difficult as it may involve losing a UK domicile of origin. Certainly a property, or other permanent accommodation, will have to be acquired in the new country. It will not be enough to live in the new country for a period of time: the UK must also be abandoned as a domicile. To give substance to a claim for changed status:

- the UK residence should be disposed of;

- UK house contents, furniture, personal possessions etc. should be disposed of or taken to the new country;

- memberships of UK clubs (except overseas memberships) and UK directorships should be resigned;

- UK investments may need to be scaled down (in any case UK direct investments should be avoided for tax reasons);

- a will should be made under the law and formalities of the new country – this may bring into play the compulsory succession or 'forced heirship' rules which operate in some countries to reserve a fixed minimum proportion of the estate for family members (predominantly the children, sometimes at the expense of a surviving spouse);

- acquiring foreign citizenship or nationality in place of British status should be considered;

- the individual and his family should involve themselves in the local community in the new country, learn the language, play their part in village or town life, attend local places of worship (and indeed plan to be buried there rather than back in the UK) – in general, put down roots in the new country.

It used to be part of such advice that voting rights should be exercised in the new country and not in the UK; but with effect from 6 April 1996 neither registration as an overseas elector nor voting as such will be taken into account when assessing domicile. [*FA 1996, s 200*]. An overseas voter who wishes to retain UK domicile can, however, require the Revenue to have regard to the fact that he is exercising his UK vote. Apart from the deemed domicile provisions, this is the only indicator of domicile which is part of statute law. It should be treated as an exception to the general principle that ties with the mother country must be broken in favour of the adopted country if domicile is to be changed.

Location of assets

8.13   The second strand of the fundamental tax planning to achieve excluded property status for assets is, in nearly all cases, that the assets are outside the UK. The location of an asset is determined according to the law of the relevant part of the UK. Under English law:

- real property or any other interest in land is situated where the land itself is situated;

- chattels and tangible property (except for ships and aircraft) are situated wherever they actually are at the relevant time;

- registered shares and securities are situated where they are registered – so shares in a UK company operating abroad are situated in the UK, though companies incorporated abroad with twin registers can cause problems;

- bearer shares are situated where the share certificate actually is;

- ordinary debts are normally situated where the debtor resides;

- bank debts (e.g., money owed by a bank in respect of an account credit balance) are normally situated at the bank branch where the account is held;

- a specialty debt (a debt due under a document executed under seal) is situated where the document is kept – so a life policy issued by a UK life office under seal and deposited in Jersey is situated there.

Offshore holding companies

8.14   Normally, the most effective way to avoid UK situs is to hold UK assets via a company which is resident outside the UK (and therefore incorporated outside the UK; since 15 March 1988 a company incorporated in the UK is conclusively presumed to be UK resident). The asset is transferred into the ownership of the company in return for an issue of shares in the company to the individual or trustees. The relevant assets are thus the shares in the company, which will be situated for tax purposes in whichever location outside the UK they are registered (see 8.13). The underlying principle is that a limited liability company on the UK model has, unlike a trust or partnership, a separate legal corporate entity. Any asset which a company is capable of holding – including UK land or premises, shares, and interests in businesses or chattels – can be held in this way. Classically, an offshore holding company has been the central feature of IHT planning where UK assets are involved. It remains suitable for holding assets where there is no element of enjoyment in kind for the UK resident beneficiary (e.g., investment property leased to third parties). However, following the decision of the House of Lords in *R v Allen [2001] STC 1537*, it can be a high-risk structure for holding a house used as a residence by a beneficiary, or chattels situated in such a house. See further 8.28.

The offshore company must own the legal and beneficial title to the assets: it will not be effective for IHT planning purposes if the offshore company simply holds the UK assets as nominee for the ultimate owner, nor probably as bare trustee (*IRC v Stype Investments (Jersey) Ltd [1982] 3 WLR 228*). The company should be subject to the law of a country which has legislation similar to UK company law, and 'hybrid' organisations such as *stiftungs* and *anstalts*, which might be treated as having features of both companies and trusts, need to be approached with care; in some cases, the degree of control which may be given to the individual may provoke the argument that control in fact rests with the individual in the UK. It will usually be necessary to have a dedicated company, to hold only the UK assets, and the cost of incorporation and administration, by reputable professional offshore administrators, needs to be taken into account. The main costs of running the company are likely to be the statutory fees charged by the country of incorporation and the basic cost of providing directors, secretary and registered office, plus further corporate fees if the company performs active management or other functions.

Special rules for some UK assets

8.15   Favourable IHT status extends to a few categories of asset which would normally be treated as situated in the UK. Planning possibilities are fairly limited but could be useful for particular circumstances.

Exempt gilts

8.16   Some UK Government securities (known as FOTRA securities, standing for 'free of tax to residents abroad') are issued on terms that they are free of IHT (and other UK taxes) if the beneficial owner is not ordinarily resident in the UK. [*IHTA 1984, s 6(2)*]. FOTRA securities owned by a trust qualify if, in the case of an interest in possession trust, the person currently entitled to the interest in possession is not ordinarily resident in the UK or if, in the case of a discretionary trust, all known persons who are potential beneficiaries are ordinarily resident outside the UK. [*IHTA 1984, s 48(4)*]. For FOTRA securities first issued before 30 April 1996 domicile was also relevant. It is possible, therefore, to use exempt gilts in planning for the emigrant who will not lose UK deemed domicile for three years (see 8.7) because the deemed domicile rules do not apply to exempt gilts, whether held personally or through a trust. [*IHTA 1984, s 267(2)*]. So a UK emigrant can shelter his estate from IHT during the first three years abroad by investing in exempt gilts (raising cash for the purchase on the security of his other assets if necessary) or by establishing a (temporary) life interest trust for his benefit where the trustees make a similar investment. Exempt gilts can also be used in cases which fall short of emigration, where ordinary residence ceases but domicile (under the general law) may not.

Foreign currency bank accounts

8.17   A non-UK domiciliary is best advised to keep as little cash in UK banks as possible. UK sterling bank accounts will be UK assets and subject to IHT and probate requirements on death. However, no IHT is charged on a 'qualifying foreign currency account' i.e., a non-sterling account with specified banks which is held at death by a person who is not domiciled, resident or ordinarily resident in the UK, or by non-UK trustees for him. [*IHTA 1984, s 157*]. The relief is limited – it does not apply to accounts held by or for resident non-domiciliaries, and it applies only to transfers on death – and in most cases it will be better for deposits to be made (whether in sterling or in foreign currency) outside the UK and for the resident non-domiciliary to make use of the remittance rules to bring cash into the UK, or discharge UK debts from the foreign account, as and when necessary.

Works of art

8.18   By concession, no IHT will be charged on a work of art which is in the UK solely for public exhibition, restoration or cleaning, if it is normally kept abroad and would in that case be exempt from IHT (IR Extra-Statutory Concession F7) – though if the work of art is held through an offshore company it will not be necessary to rely on the concession.

Making gifts abroad

8.19   A non-domiciled individual can give away non-UK assets outside the UK without any transfer of value (and potential IHT liability) occurring. In other cases (e.g., if cash or chattels, such as works of art or jewellery or furniture, are given in the UK) the gift will be:

(*a*)   a potentially exempt transfer if it is made to an individual or to (broadly) a non-discretionary trust, causing a potential liability to IHT if the donor dies within seven years; or

(*b*)   if the recipients are the trustees of a discretionary trust – whether or not UK resident or domiciled – a gift which will attract an immediate charge to IHT if no exemptions or reliefs are available and if the amount of the gift, aggregated with any relevant previous gifts, exceeds £242,000 (for gifts made on or after 6 April 2001).

Care needs to be taken that the gift is completed offshore. Gifts by cheque can fall foul of the rule that payment is not completed until the cheque is cleared: so if payment is made by the donor from his foreign bank account to the recipient's UK bank account there will be a gift of UK situated property (because the right of the recipient to payment will be in the UK bank account at the moment when the gift is perfected) and this will not escape potential liability to IHT. The gift should be made by handing over cash to the recipient outside the UK, or by cheque credit or transfer to a foreign branch of the recipient's bank which is then transferred to his UK branch, or by a gift of the foreign bank account itself. (The problem does not usually arise with other assets as some assets – for example, chattels – pass by physical handing over and others – for example, non-bearer shares – pass by registration. It may be necessary, though, for a gift of trans-portable chattels such as jewellery to be made by physical delivery outside the UK.) The remittance rules for income and capital gains tax also need to be considered if the non-domiciled donor is resident, or ordinarily resident, in the UK.

Care must also be taken that the gift does not constitute a remittance for income tax and CGT purposes under *ICTA 1988, s 132(5)* or *TCGA 1992, s 12* if there can be said to be some benefit in the UK to the donor: see the wide interpretation of a remittance as including an artificial 'conduit pipe' in *Harmel v Wright [1974] 1 WLR 325* and the need for extreme caution by professional advisers following the High Court decision in *Grimm v Newman [2002] STC 84*, where tax advice on this point was found to have been negligent.

Gifts to spouses

8.20   If both husband and wife are domiciled in the UK, gifts by either of them to the other are exempt from IHT. The same applies where neither is domiciled in the UK. Since 1 January 1974 it has been possible for husband and wife to have different domiciles (see 8.6), and this is quite a common occurrence. The situation contains a potential trap: a gift by a UK domiciled (or deemed domiciled) person to a spouse who is neither domiciled nor deemed domiciled is only exempt up to the limit of £55,000. [*IHTA 1984, s 18(2)*]. There is no seven-year cut-off period and the limit has not been increased since 1982. Above the £55,000 limit the gift will be potentially chargeable in the usual way. By contrast, there is no limit on the value of assets (whether or not in the UK) which a non-domiciled spouse can give to a domiciled spouse. The opportunity should be taken to accrue assets in the hands of the non-domiciled spouse where possible, by cumulative use of the usual exemptions and reliefs, particularly business or agricultural property at present attracting 100 per cent relief, or by transferring low-value assets with growth potential to that spouse or in trust for him or her. Gifts could also be made to a non-domiciled spouse by post-mortem deeds of variation from the estate of a relative (see 8.21). The non-domiciled spouse might then be in a position to make an excluded property settlement before becoming deemed domiciled (see 8.23).

IHT planning with deceased estates

8.21   The provisions of a will (or the rules which apply on an intestate death) can be rewritten within two years after the death by agreement between the beneficiaries of the estate in such a way that, for IHT purposes, the variation is treated as having been made by the deceased person and not by the beneficiaries. [*IHTA 1984, s 142*]. If a trust is created by the variation, it is treated for IHT purposes as if the settlor were the deceased person and not the beneficiary who has given up or amended his original entitlement by the variation. This is not so for CGT (see *Marshall v Kerr [1994] STC 638, HL*), but the Revenue has confirmed that that decision has no application to the IHT treatment of variations and that variations which meet all the statutory conditions will continue to be treated for IHT purposes as having been made by the deceased (IR Interpretation RI101, February 1995).

The variation principle is not confined to the estates of UK domiciliaries and can extend to a variation of the estate of a non-domiciliary that consists entirely of non-UK assets. A variation may, therefore, provide a route to achieving excluded property status where the terms of the deceased's will would, if unvaried, cause an IHT liability on the subsequent death of a UK domiciled beneficiary.

Example

Granny died domiciled in Switzerland owning a London flat and Swiss investments; her will left everything to her three adult grandchildren, all of whom are domiciled and resident in the UK. All or any of the grandchildren can vary their shares in the Swiss investments so as to write them on trust for themselves for life and then to their respective children, or on discretionary trusts. Although the grandchildren will be considered as the settlors for CGT purposes, the variation trusts will have excluded property status for IHT for as long as they exist, provided that the investments and any replacement trust assets are situated outside the UK at the relevant times. The relevant time for an interest in possession trust would be the death of the life tenant (or the date at which he gives up all or part of his life interest during his lifetime) or, for a discretionary trust, the ten-year anniversaries of Granny's death and any times afterwards when capital is paid out from the trust.

If an excluded property trust is established by variation, there will be no IHT charge on the trust or its beneficiaries, regardless of their domicile, throughout the life of the trust. The reservation of benefit rules (see 8.26) will not apply, so that the original beneficiary can continue to benefit under the revised terms. The trust should be drafted flexibly: the trustees can always accelerate the time when a beneficiary becomes entitled but they cannot prolong it beyond the time specified in the trust document. (See also 8.35.) The variation will not have the desired IHT effect unless an election is made to the Revenue within six months after the variation. [*IHTA 1984, s 142(2)*].

Although it is not necessary for the assets of the trust to be excluded property at all times, it is clearly better that they are kept out of the UK wherever possible, in order to remove the risk of an IHT charge through the unexpected death of a life tenant or failure to remember a ten-year anniversary.

It is crucial that the assets are excluded property at the date of death, whether it is the will, or succession to assets under the law of the deceased's domicile, or a variation which is to be relied on. Assets which are physically situated in the UK may be rescued by being treated as situated abroad under the provisions of a double taxation treaty, but the point needs to be checked and kept under review very carefully and in cases of doubt an offshore holding company should be interposed if appropriate. In the above example, the London flat would not be excluded property if it had been held directly by Granny at her death, unless a double taxation treaty made it so: and it seems that a subsequent transfer to an offshore holding company would not convert the flat into excluded property.

8.22   If the Revenue treatment of excluded property settlements changes (see 8.26), a post-death variation of the will of a non-domiciled individual to convert an absolute interest into an interest in possession trust should still provide protection for the original beneficiary who is non-domiciled but likely to become deemed domiciled in the UK in future; the settlor of the trust for IHT will be deemed to be the deceased so that no reservation of benefit will arise. The settlor must take great care not to pay any expenses etc., which might lead to his being treated as a settlor. Although the original beneficiary will be the settlor for CGT purposes, he and the trust will benefit from *TCGA 1992, s 87* treatment in any case if he is non-UK domiciled.

Despite the attractions of a variation, the best tax planning for the elderly non-domiciled individual with relatives or heirs in the UK may (at least for the present) be for that individual to establish an excluded property trust in his lifetime, rather than relying on (*a*) the variation legislation still being in force at the unknown future date of death, and (*b*) all the beneficiaries concerned having the legal capacity to make the variation, and (*c*) agreeing between themselves to do so.

Pre-immigration planning

8.23   At present, an excluded property trust should achieve substantial IHT benefits for two types of individual in particular:

(*a*)   people who are domiciled outside the UK under the general law but who will shortly be deemed domiciled in the UK for IHT purposes if they continue to be resident; and

(*b*)   non-domiciled people with no previous connection with the UK who are contemplating immigration and establishing residence in the UK.

The type (*a*) individual should consider establishing an excluded property trust before he becomes deemed domiciled, and the type (*b*) individual should consider making an excluded property trust before he becomes UK resident (which will normally be on the day when he first sets foot in the UK with the intention of becoming resident).

At the time of writing, there are two particular beneficial features of the way in which IHT operates in relation to an excluded property trust.

8.24   The first is that the IHT treatment is tied to the settlor's domicile. The important factor is the domicile of the settlor at the time when the trust was established and, if later, the time when assets were transferred to it. [*IHTA 1984, s 48(3)*]. The domiciles of the beneficiaries are not relevant, nor in essence is the subsequent domicile of the settlor. Therefore, the subsequent domiciles of the beneficiaries will not affect the excluded property status of the trust assets provided that the assets are situated outside the UK. A beneficiary who subsequently becomes domiciled in the UK (or who has been domiciled there in the first place) can make a gift of his interest without IHT liability and, in particular, the death of a UK domiciled life tenant will not bring about the charge which is usually imposed by the combination of *IHTA 1984, ss 4* and *49(1)*.

However, any addition made to the trust by the settlor after he becomes domiciled or deemed domiciled will not be excluded property (see Inland Revenue Interpretation RI166 (February 1997)).

8.25   The second advantage of an excluded property trust is that, currently, benefits can be preserved for the settlor personally while preserving the IHT shelter. Normally, a gift where the settlor reserves a benefit (i.e., where the asset is not in future enjoyed entirely, or virtually entirely, to the donor's exclusion) will not escape IHT on the donor's death. [*FA 1986, s 102* and *Sch 20*]. However, the settlor may be a beneficiary of his own excluded property trust (whether having an interest in possession or as a discretionary beneficiary) and it seems that the reservation of benefit rules will not apply to the trust even if the settlor becomes UK domiciled at a later date while remaining a beneficiary, provided that he retains the beneficial interest until his death. For some years the Revenue's published view has been that the excluded property rules [*IHTA 1984, s 48(3)*] prevail over the gift with reservation rules in these circumstances (see correspondence published in the *Law Society Gazette*, 10 December 1986).

The reservation of benefit and excluded property laws do not sit easily together. For example, a non-domiciled settlor should avoid giving up his interest during his lifetime by his surrendering or assigning it himself, or by the trustees appointing his interest to another beneficiary or excluding him from the class of discretionary beneficiaries. The reason is that it appears, by the operation of *FA 1986, s 102(4)*, that a settlor who during his lifetime releases a reserved benefit in excluded property in a settlement makes a potentially exempt transfer even if he is non-domiciled at the time. Also, if a settlor adds assets to the trust when he is UK domiciled, or deemed domiciled, then the added assets will not be excluded property and will be within the normal IHT charging rules.

Sections 80 and *82* of *IHTA 1984* contain a large pitfall. Where a settlement confers an initial interest in possession on the settlor or his spouse and subsequently a discretionary trust arises, the settlement is treated as having been made at the date when the discretionary trust arises rather than at the date of its actual creation; if the settlor or spouse who had the last life interest was domiciled or deemed domiciled in the UK at his or her death, the settlement will be treated for IHT as having been made by that spouse, with the result that there may be a charge on the value of the trust fund which passes on the survivor's death on discretionary trusts and also a vulnerability to the usual ten-year and exit charges which apply to UK discretionary trusts. As a general rule, therefore, settlements should either be fully discretionary or comprise a succession of interests in possession for (say) settlor, spouse and children in turn.

A reversionary interest in a trust – the right to receive income or capital from the trust fund on the death of the current life tenant – will usually be excluded property regardless of where it is situated or who is the beneficial owner, but where a non-UK element is involved care must be taken to ensure that a proposed gift of a reversionary interest does qualify as excluded property.

Possible changes to excluded property rules

8.26   The Revenue appear to be reconsidering their interpretation of the effect of a settlor becoming domiciled (or deemed domiciled) in the UK after making an excluded property trust. If the Revenue view does change, and if it is confirmed by legislation or upheld in the courts, then clearly the attraction of the UK as a non-OECD blacklisted low tax area for long-term residents who retain a foreign connection may wane.

The previous published example (at paragraph D8 of the Revenue's Advanced Instruction Manual), confirming that the gifts with reservation rules did not apply where a settlor subsequently became UK domiciled, read as follows.

> 'The donor, who is domiciled in Australia, puts foreign property into a discretionary trust under which he is a potential beneficiary. He dies five years later domiciled in England and without having released the reservation. The property is property subject to a reservation and is therefore deemed to be part of the donor's death estate.'

The original paragraph continued:

> 'However, as he was domiciled outside the UK at the time the Settlement was made, the property will be excluded property, under *IHTA 1984, s 48(3)*, if still situated outside the UK at the date of death.'

This sentence was replaced in late 2001 by an instruction that 'any cases where this is the situation must be referred to the litigation team'.

At the time of writing it is not known how the Revenue are intending to proceed. In published correspondence with the Chartered Institute of Taxation the Revenue have stated that

> 'there can be no question of the Revenue seeking tax, if in fact the previous view is indeed considered to have been incorrect, where taxpayers have acted in reliance on that previous view. Any change in interpretation would be widely publicised, and no doubt discussed. There is certainly no question of taxpayers being entrapped by the Revenue for steps taken prior to such publication.'

It seems from these comments that existing excluded property trusts, and those completely set up before the 'publication' referred to above (whenever that is considered to be), should continue to qualify for the existing favourable treatment in the future; though whether a person who has simply established a trust of a type that would not to date have incurred any IHT liability for settlor or trustees, whether or not it was excluded property (and who has arguably not 'acted in reliance' on the existing practice), may remain to be seen. It seems clear, though, that

- any excluded property trusts which are in the course of being established should be completed (and the trust assets validly transferred to the trustees) as soon as possible;

- the trust should ideally remain in its original form (which will usually be discretionary);

- additions to the trust fund should only be made after careful consideration;

- if it is possible to identify assets which are surplus to the settlor's requirements, a trust for other family members (i.e., to the exclusion of the settlor, so that no reservation of benefit occurs) could be considered.

Ownership of the UK home

8.27 The operation of the domicile rules, particularly as they apply to tax income and capital gains only on a remittance basis and to a large extent make those taxes voluntary, means that the UK is a very popular place for non-domiciled people to establish residence, possibly on a long-term basis. A question which follows hard on the heels of a decision to establish UK residence is how the UK house or flat in which the family is to reside should be owned. In the past, the usual advice was that the property should be owned by an offshore company which might (but need not) itself be owned by an offshore trust: this provided a shelter from IHT and from capital gains tax. However, there are two areas of difficulty, of which one is serious, though the other appears not to be a practical problem.

Shadow directors

8.28 The House of Lords has decided in *R v Allen (No 2) [2001] STC 1537* that a Schedule E benefit in kind income tax charge under *ICTA 1988, ss 145* and *146* arises on living accommodation provided to a person (i.e., the resident but non-domiciled individual) if his conduct makes him a 'shadow director'; that is, if the individual, although not formally a director of the offshore company, is a person in accordance with whose directions or instructions the (actual) directors of the company are accustomed to act. [*ICTA 1988, s 168(8)*]. Furthermore, a shadow director (in a similar but non-tax context) has been held by the Court of Appeal to include a person who made his wishes known to the directors and whose wishes 'had the potency of directions' and whose suggestions when given, were adopted, but whose conduct fell short of telling the directors what to do: *Secretary of State for Trade and Industry v Deverell [2001] Ch 340*.

If *sections 145* and *146* apply, then assuming that the property is worth over £75,000 (which is virtually certain to be the case), there will be an ongoing annual income tax charge on the individual on the value of the benefits of rent-free occupation of the property, calculated by reference to the official rate of interest. The annual tax is substantial: at the 2000/01 rate of 6.25 per cent it was £62,500 on a property worth £1 million. The existence of a discretionary trust, actively managed by professional offshore trustees and controlling the holding company, should diminish the force of a Revenue argument that it is the individual in the UK who controls the situation in reality, but this factual situation is not always easy to achieve in practice and the Revenue's view is that the existence of a trust is immaterial.

Transfer pricing

8.29   The transfer pricing rules introduced into *ICTA 1988, Sch 28AA* appear to have had an effect (which may have been unintentional) on the situation where an offshore company owns a UK property which is used as a residence. The transfer pricing rules previously applied only in a commercial context but it seems could (from 6 April 1999) apply to impose a tax charge where transactions between a UK resident and a non-UK resident associated company (which can include a non-UK company controlled by a UK resident) are not at arm's length. The rules might, therefore, now apply to impose an income tax charge on notional income received by an offshore company owning a UK property which is occupied by the UK beneficiary.

The rules have, on the face of them, the potential to disrupt the many arrangements which have been made for UK properties to be held through companies. However, the Revenue have confirmed in correspondence that they will not in practice apply the rules so as to impute rental income to an overseas resident company which is 'controlled' (within the meaning of the transfer pricing rules) by a UK resident where that company owns a house in the UK which is occupied rent-free by that resident. That treatment may extend to occupation by beneficiaries of trusts. In any case, the debate has been overtaken by the shadow director developments.

Structures for the home

8.30   There are several approaches to the question of how the UK home should be held: none of them provides the ideal solution to all cases and which is best will depend on the particular situation (and to some extent the psychology) of the individual(s) concerned.

8.31   *An existing company or company-plus-trust structure is left as it is.* This is best for IHT but now very problematic for income tax (see 8.28). Failure to disclose shadow director benefits (which is of course the taxpayer's responsibility under the self-assessment regime) resulted, in *R v Allen*, in conviction and imprisonment of the individual for the offence of cheating the public revenue. As a result of the *Allen* decision some house-plus-company structures are being unravelled. If it is nonetheless decided to use, or keep, this structure then the greatest care needs to be taken not to cut corners. The directors/trustees must control, and be seen to control, decisions about the property, e.g., sale or expenditure on improvements. They might be able to grant non-exclusive licences to various family members to occupy the property on a non-permanent basis. Alternatively, a commercial rent could be paid to the company for the period of occupation.

Various ways of dismantling the structure to take it out of the ambit of *ICTA 1988, ss 145* and *146* have been suggested. For example, it may be possible to convert the legal status of the asset owned by the offshore trust into a specialty debt (for which see 8.13). That would probably involve passing the ownership through the individual who would then create the specialty debt and settle that into a new trust, so (for example) it would be unsuitable if he had become IHT deemed domiciled in the UK.

8.32   *The individual purchases the property in his/her own name.* The CGT main residence exemption may be available. However, the property will be subject to IHT on the individual's death; as real property is taxed principally in the country where it is situated, it should be assumed that any relevant double taxation treaty will only operate to stop the property being taxed in the country of domicile at a higher rate than the rate which applies in the UK. The potential tax can be mitigated, or avoided, in several ways.

- The property can be purchased with a loan so that the outstanding amount of the loan at the individual's death will reduce the value of the property for IHT. The loan should be secured on the property so that it is deducted from the value of the property and not from non-UK assets. [*IHTA 1984, s 162(4)*]. The loan could be serviced in the UK by UK income or remitted foreign capital, or abroad by a back-to-back deposit or direct borrowing. Of course the capital which would otherwise have been used for the purchase is unlocked for investment outside the UK. Care must be taken to avoid income remittances, and the mechanics of making interest payments abroad may bring cash flow disadvantages. One limitation is that any increase in value of the property over the original purchase price is unprotected from IHT.

- If the individual's widow/widower is given the subsequent right to occupy the property, whether outright or via an interest in possession trust, the IHT spouse exemption will apply on the individual's death if the spouse is then UK domiciled for IHT (see 8.20). (Clearly this would postpone the IHT charge but would not eliminate it.) If the trust is established in the individual's lifetime (rather than by will) the need for UK probate may be avoided (see below).

- Ownership could be split between several family members: for example, a London flat worth £1 million owned equally by husband, wife and three children gives each a UK estate of only £200,000 – well below the IHT taxable threshold if the flat is the family's only UK foothold. The legal ownership need not mirror the beneficial ownership, so beneficial interests of minor or young adult children could be accommodated, the property being registered in the parents' names with an accompanying declaration of trust. The owners should each purchase with cash rather than being given a share of the property which was already owned by one of them, which would cause a reservation of benefit to the original owner.

- The IHT liability could be insured against by a policy on the individual's life, written on trust at the outset for the intended heirs so as to be outside his estate for IHT purposes at his death. The drawback is that, although term assurance is usually relatively cheap, whole of life insurance (which is the most appropriate here) may not be.

The disadvantages of direct ownership may be more practical than tax-based, though CGT will be payable on disposal of the property during the lifetime of a resident or ordinarily resident individual if it is not his main residence.

- The entries on the property title at the Land Registry are now open to public inspection, which may not be consistent with a wish for privacy. If this is a problem, an offshore company could hold as nominee; that is not considered to cause a shadow director difficulty.

- If the property is in sole legal ownership, probate in the UK will have to be obtained on the owner's death in order for the legal title to devolve so that the property can be sold. This will involve convincing the Capital Taxes Office of the non-UK domicile, as well as going through the usual probate formalities. (A UK will dealing with the property is also desirable because the law of the part of the UK where the property is situated will govern how it passes on the owner's death. A will is open to public inspection once it has been proved after death.) Again, joint or nominee legal ownership will avoid the need for probate, though it will not avoid the duty of the personal representatives to satisfy themselves that no IHT is payable, and to submit a financial account of the deceased's assets and liabilities to the Revenue where appropriate. This contrasts with the case where the property is owned by an offshore company: on death no UK probate will be required for the company to make title to sell, although probate in the offshore country (where typically there is no death duty) may be needed in order to pass the shares in the company to the heirs.

8.33   *The individual purchases the property in his/her own name and then gives it to an offshore company.* This route is designed to avoid the requirement for benefit to be provided by the company to a person who may be a shadow director: if the property is transferred subject to an occupation right there is arguably no 'cost' to the company in allowing the right to continue.

8.34   *The property is held by an offshore trust (without an intervening company).* This will not protect from IHT, though it will from CGT. No 'shadow director' problem will arise because no company is concerned. It may be possible to reduce the value of the property by trustee borrowing offshore. Where the property is likely to be sold within ten years, a discretionary trust is particularly worth considering, because the ten-yearly and subsequent IHT charges will be avoided if the proceeds of sale are reinvested offshore.

If the trust confers an interest in possession (fixed income interest), there may be an IHT charge on the individual's death (or the subsequent death of his/her spouse) which needs to be provided for, by insurance or otherwise. If the trust is discretionary, the individual may need to be given a licence to occupy which is terminable at will by the trustees, to stop an interest in possession being deemed to exist (IR Statement of Practice 10/79), and ten-year and exit IHT charges need to be addressed. The trust will govern what happens to the property after the individual's death, which may save the need for a UK will and probate.

8.35   Should the trust be revocable? Often it is, whether from a general wish to allow a cautious settlor to back out of the entire arrangement unilaterally if circumstances change, or whether because in some jurisdictions it is standard planning to create revocable settlor trusts (e.g., in the USA). *Melville v IRC [2001] STC 1271* was a victory for the UK taxpayer, because the court held that a general power of appointment reserved to the settlor was 'property' for IHT purposes and thus confirmed the effectiveness of his IHT planning. However, the other face of the decision is that a trust which allows the settlor to redirect benefit for himself by use of a general power of appointment may form part of his taxable estate at his death, if the trust and the power are then still in existence; if he is by then deemed domiciled in the UK for IHT, that value may, it seems, be taxable on his death if the Revenue interpretation of the excluded property rules changes (see 8.26). It is thought that the *Meville* decision applies equally to trusts with a power of revocation.

Double taxation

8.36   Finally, statutory relief may be available if it has not been possible to avoid IHT altogether.

The low tax jurisdictions, of course, characteristically do not impose capital taxes on inheritances or gifts for non-residents. However, if the individual is attached to a country which does impose such taxes, an asset may be liable to tax in more than one country: for example, if country A taxes on the basis of physical location of assets and country B taxes on the basis of owner's domicile. This most frequently happens with real property. A double taxation treaty between the two countries may operate to modify location and/or domicile rules so as to tax the asset only in one of the countries. In these cases *IHTA 1984, s 158* will allow relief in the terms of the relevant treaty (but note that the result will not necessarily be that the lower of the two taxes is applied). It may be useful that the deemed domicile rules (see 8.7), which were introduced with capital transfer tax in 1974, do not apply to the (dwindling) number of treaties that were signed during the previous estate duty regime.

If relief under a treaty is not available (or if it will produce a more favourable result for the taxpayer) *section 159* provides for unilateral relief in the form of a credit against UK tax against equivalent foreign tax which has been paid. The relief may not be of any use if (for example) the foreign law taxes transfers which would be exempt in the UK, such as inter-spouse transfers.

Features of the offshore trust

8.37

- The trustees will normally be non-resident, in order to take advantage of the CGT and income tax treatment of offshore trusts established by non-domiciliaries, although looking at IHT in isolation there is no requirement for this.

- The settlor (or a protector) could retain the power to appoint new trustees and to consent to alterations in the class of potential discretionary beneficiaries, though the powers should be essentially restraining, and not powers that would enable the settlor/protector to direct the trustees what to do: otherwise the trust might be considered to be run from the UK, or ultimately to be a 'sham' that could be looked through (cf. *Rahman v Chase Bank (CI) Ltd [1991] JLR 103 (Royal Court of Jersey)*).

- The question is sometimes asked whether a non-domiciled friend or relative can perform the settlor role if (for example) the individual's own domicile is uncertain. If this is done, the friend or relative who is the settlor must genuinely provide the cash and any other assets to be put into the trust, by way of gift, with no arrangement or informal understanding that recompense will be made; the settlor's own domicile must be indubitably outside the UK; and the settlor needs to receive advice on the impact of the tax laws of his own country on the gift. If the apparent settlor is only a 'phantom' then the person who is really behind the arrangement will be treated as the settlor under *IHTA 1984, s 44* as the person who has indirectly provided funds for the settlement or has made a reciprocal arrangement with another person for him to make the settlement.

- The trust will be outside the offshore trust settlor CGT regime [*TCGA 1992, ss 86, 87* and related provisions] if the settlor is not domiciled in the UK (under the general law definition) at all times during the UK tax year when a gain arises to the offshore trustees, or if he has died during the year.

- If the settlor is ordinarily resident in the UK and can benefit he will be subject to tax on the income of the trust, under *ICTA 1988, s 739*, but if he is non-domiciled (again under the general law) the remittance basis will apply to shelter income which arises offshore and is not remitted to the UK.

- Any professional person concerned with the making of the trust who knows or has reason to believe that the settlor is domiciled in the UK and that the trustees are not or will not be resident in the UK must report the matter to the Capital Taxes Office under the statutory duty imposed by *IHTA 1984, s 218*.

- There is no requirement for the trust to be written under a particular law or to be run from a particular location, and much will depend on individual choice.

- The trust should be drafted so as to endure for the longest possible time allowed by law. If it is a discretionary trust there may be advantages in using the law of a territory where the accumulation period extends beyond the normal 21-year English law period to enable the trustees to roll up income within the trust (though proposals to extend the English accumulation period have been made by the Law Commission). As a general rule the vesting of any outright interest in capital in a beneficiary should be postponed for as long as possible and beneficiaries should be given life interests (interests in possession) entitling them to income, but not to capital unless and until the trustees so decide. At present (though see 8.26), on the death of a UK domiciled life tenant of an excluded property trust, no IHT charge will arise no matter who is the next beneficiary entitled under the terms of the trust, but the death of a UK domiciled person who is entitled outright to assets means that there is no continuing trust and IHT will be payable in full on his estate (subject to spouse or other exemptions) regardless of where the assets are situated.

9 Money Laundering – A Supervisor's Perspective: Guernsey

Steve Butterworth
(Director of Insurance, Guernsey Financial Services Commission and Chairman of the Insurance Fraud Subcommittee of the International Association of Insurance Supervisors)

General background

9.1   The possibility that businesses within the jurisdiction of an Insurance Supervisor might knowingly or unwittingly become involved in money laundering – the processing of criminal proceeds in order to disguise their true origin – is a constant concern. However, it affects not only insurance supervisors worldwide but also all financial services regulators, especially as, since 11 September 2001, 'find the money launderers' has become a key feature of the international war against terrorism.

9.2   It is a constant concern because money launderers are using ever more sophisticated techniques in their efforts to outwit legitimate businesses, regulators and law enforcement agencies as well to circumvent the increasingly voluminous anti-money laundering measures introduced by international bodies and more and more governments. It is a nightmare, too, because money laundering has been around a long time; long enough, for example, for a well-hidden and illicit 'parallel' international banking system to have been evolved and established by experienced and skilled money laundering experts. Often, a money laundering process comprises a lengthy chain of dozens of corporate entities, scattered between numerous host territories, some onshore and some offshore, across the globe and through which the 'dirty' money passes to emerge 'clean' at the end of the chain. It is estimated that money launderers handle some US$1 trillion per year globally and that they exploit perceived anti-money laundering weaknesses in over 50 different countries. It is a major cross-frontier activity fuelled not only by terrorists dependent for their armaments on well-hidden financial resources but also by the needs of drug traffickers and, increasingly, by white collar fraudsters and 'tax-dodgers'.

9.3   Among the reasons why money laundering poses complex problems is that it involves three stages, which mainly occur in sequence but can also overlap. These stages are called placement, layering and integration.

Placement is the physical disposal of criminal proceedings by placing cash in the financial system. It can be achieved in a wide variety of ways depending on the opportunities for exploiting weaknesses in the system and on the ingenuity of the criminal and his advisers and their network.

Layering is the separation of criminal proceeds from their source by the creation of layers of transactions designed to disguise the audit trail and give a semblance of legitimacy. Again, activities involved in this stage can vary according to the skills of the money launderers and their associates.

Integration is the stage at which criminal proceeds, cloaked by apparent legitimacy, are returned to the economy as bona fide funds or assets.

9.4   However, the most worrying and frustrating feature of money laundering, from a supervisor's viewpoint, is that each supervisor is only the third line of defence. The second line, and a key interface with money laundering, comprises the work of international agencies in orchestrating international co-operation in respect of anti-money laundering measures and cross-frontier co-operation. The first line of defence consists of the willingness of supervised businesses in regulated territories to 'blow the whistle' on suspected money laundering transactions. This means that a supervisor is out on a limb if businesses within his jurisdiction fail to observe basic 'know your customer' (KYC) requirements and, even worse, fail to report 'suspicious transactions' to the appropriate investigatory and law enforcement authorities.

9.5   The latter is something which, according to some reports, lawyers and accountants, in particular, are reluctant to do because such disclosure strikes deep into the traditional heart of a client relationship, even when, as in Guernsey's case, the legislation absolves 'whistle-blowers' from breach of confidentiality litigation. (The *Prevention of Terrorism (Bailiwick of Guernsey) Law 1990*, the *Criminal Justice (Proceeds of Crime) (Bailiwick of Guernsey) Law 1999*, the *Drug Trafficking (Bailiwick of Guernsey) Law 2000*, the *Disclosure of Information (Guernsey) Law 1995*, the *Disclosure of Information (Alderney) Law 1998* and the *Disclosure of Information (Sark) Law 2000*.)

9.6   However, money laundering is a vast and complex 'industry' driven to constantly seek new ways and means to outwit by refining tried and tested methods as well as by being extremely creative and innovative. There is nothing more attractive to a money launderer than a territory with an international reputation for integrity and whose businesses and professionals provide a patina of probity. Such features can create a sense of false security.

9.7   Sometimes the sheer scale of attempted duplicity is breathtaking. Take, for example, the practice whereby certain individuals in South America would pay a large single premium of, say, in excess of US $500,000 for a life insurance policy, only to turn around a short time later and surrender the policy, obviously at a loss, so as to receive the surrender value in 'clean' money. A further example would be launderers buying a gold refinement unit in North America, which they then heavily insured. Later, the gold refinement unit was taken out of business by an all-consuming fire and compensatory payments claimed!

Within the insurance system, money launderers may structure transactions, coerce employees to co-operate and not to file proper reports, or establish apparently legitimate 'front' insurance entities and reinsurance companies to launder money.

Smuggling currency out of a country, especially into countries with rigid standards of secrecy, and then wire transferring the funds to financial institutions in the country of origin is a common method used.

But, the most common method, is that of proposals to enter into a single premium contract or policy, the most attractive to money launderers being unit-linked single premium contracts; the purchase of annuities; lump-sum top-ups to existing life insurance contracts and lump-sum contributions to personal pension contracts. Such investments in themselves may merely be one part of a sophisticated web of complex transactions and will often have their origins in non-insurance segments of the financial system.

9.8 Suspicious activities on the non-life insurance side include attempts to return monies, either by way of returned premiums, claims, profit commissions or in some cases dividends, to a different person or corporation to that which originally paid the premiums. Whilst this is quite easy to detect, it is common practice in many areas of non-life insurance and directors should spend some time in training staff to identify which areas are suspicious and which are not.

An example is through bogus claims made through arson or other means, whereby a legitimate business, bought by money launders, tries to recover part of its original investment through a claim against its insurer. It is common to find that such types of non-life insurance money laundering involve re-insurers who have links with money launderers through influence or through affiliation.

9.9 Examples like this owe much to the origins of large-scale money laundering, which took root in organised crime in the USA, particularly during the prohibition years. Money laundering has since blossomed to embrace the huge volumes of illicit proceeds generated internationally by illegal gambling, prostitution, extortion, bank robberies and drug trafficking. The latter is especially relevant in respect of the South American drug trade and the 'Golden Triangle' in Asia. Money laundering related to terrorism is perceived to be a relatively recent addition, although in some cases, notably those of Northern Ireland and Sri Lanka, goes back some two decades.

The domestic dimension

9.10 The jurisdiction of Bailiwick of Guernsey, like many others, first introduced tougher measures to deter the criminal use of local institutions in the late 1960s when the territory was just beginning to emerge as an excellent location for the provision of international financial services. The progress in Guernsey is typical of that in many jurisdictions and it is useful to detail here as it indicates developments occurring elsewhere. These developments are particularly notable in the fields of international co-operation, development of legislation and the total supervision of the insurance and re-insurance sectors, including intermediaries. The first move came with the introduction of the *Protection of Depositors, Companies and Prevention of Fraud (Bailiwick of Guernsey) Law 1969*. Importantly, this provided the Island government with control over the use of the words 'bank' and 'banker' and 'insurance' and 'insurer', or any 'cognate expression thereof', in the names of locally incorporated companies.

9.11   Initially, controls over banking and insurance activities were in the hands of a small department of the government. However, as the Island began to expand rapidly as an international finance centre during the 1970s and 1980s, it was recognised that a politically independent, self-financing, regulatory authority was required and that this should be managed by experienced supervisors. Hence, the establishment of the Guernsey Financial Services Commission in February 1988.

9.12   The establishment of the Commission also heralded a need for new legislation setting out its duties, responsibilities and powers, enabling it to control the identities of financial services businesses qualified to operate in its Bailiwick jurisdiction and to ensure that these businesses would be subject to on-going, adequate supervision. The legislation is entitled *The Financial Services Commission (Bailiwick of Guernsey) Law 1987*. In brief, the law sets out both general and statutory functions for the Commission.

9.13   The general functions include:

> 'The taking of such steps as the Commission considers necessary or expedient for the development of effective supervision of finance business in the Bailiwick.'
>
> [*Section 2(2)(a)*].

They also state that, in exercising these functions: 'The Commission shall, in particular, have regard to:

(*a*)   the protection of the public against financial loss due to dishonesty, incompetence or malpractice by persons carrying on finance business; and

(*b*)   the protection and enhancement of the reputation of the Bailiwick as a financial centre.' [*Section 2(4)*].

9.14   Its statutory functions are set out in the various laws pertaining to its *modus operandi* but its day-to-day working policy, is to have a 'firm and practical' regulatory approach to all those licensed, or seeking to be licensed, to operate in the Bailiwick. The basic principles followed are:

(i)   is the applicant business high quality;

(ii) has it a good track record; and

(iii) are the beneficial owners, managers and directors 'fit and proper' persons?

9.15   One advantage for regulators in Guernsey is that the Island is a compact financial services centre, described by some as 'a one-stop-shop'. The Commission is at the heart of the local financial services industry and not only works towards mutually beneficial goals but is prepared to assist with and encourage innovation as long as new business is of the highest standard. This close working relationship with the providers of financial services is, clearly, an important feature of regulation and, in itself, an anti-money laundering measure. There are also dangers in that it is possible for the regulator to be too close to the financial services sector. It is vital for these dangers to be recognised and together with any conflicts, be eliminated or properly dealt with. On balance, it is considered that a controlled close working relationship with providers is more effective than one that does not exist.

9.16   From 1988 to the present, the Commission has been instrumental in the introduction of legislation designed to penalise those who might try to involve the Island in economic crime and, in particular, to confiscate any profits from drug trafficking, terrorism and other criminal activities. The legislation also includes a *Protection of Investors Law 1987* and legislation for the regulation of fiduciary and corporate administration businesses, the *Regulation of Fiduciaries, Administration Businesses and Company Directors, etc. (Bailiwick of Guernsey) Law 2000*. These are all designed to foster investor confidence and to keep the Bailiwick of Guernsey in the 'top echelon' of international finance centres.

9.17   One simple step, taken by the Guernsey authorities quite early in the Commission's existence, was to insist that the promoters of new local companies should reveal (in confidence), both to the Commission and the Island's Attorney General, in Guernsey known as HM Procureur, the identities of the proposed beneficial owners. Similarly, a voluntary code of practice was established to advise both authorities of any proposed changes in a company's beneficial ownership. This has resulted in the rejection of an estimated 50 new companies per year because of the involvement of questionable individuals and institutions with disreputable backgrounds.

9.18   With its long-standing powers to control the identities of those who might operate banking, insurance and investment fund businesses in the Bailiwick, the Commission has been able to guarantee that only 'blue chip' institutions and 'fit and proper' persons conduct international financial services business from within its jurisdiction. These powers have recently been strengthened to include regulation and enforcement of fiduciary and corporate administration businesses.

9.19   Quite early in its existence the Commission set up its own internal investigatory department which works closely with the Island's Financial

Intelligence Service (FIS) (originally the Financial Investigation Unit), an independent body jointly run and staffed by the Guernsey Police Force and Guernsey Customs.

9.20   The Commission has done much, including issuing a series of printed anti-money laundering guidelines and a CD-Rom version, to encourage 'know-your-client' best practices within the financial institutions it supervises. It has also encouraged the establishment of a Training Agency whose courses include teaching students the importance of client 'vetting' or due diligence.

9.21   It is worth noting that, in spite of a popular myth, Guernsey's financial legislation does not include a 'bank secrecy' law, of the kind which exists in some other territories. However, all end-users of the Island's financial services are afforded the identical levels of confidentiality as are the clients of banks and other financial institutions in the United Kingdom and in other developed jurisdictions. There are 'gateways' in the legislation that deal with exchange of information with other regulators in cases of fraud investigations.

9.22   In summary, Guernsey's anti-money laundering defences can be divided into three areas – the Government's policies, the regulation of the finance sector and the enforcement of economic crime legislation.

The international dimension

9.23   Being fortified domestically against economic crime is only one part of the story. International finance centres, whether onshore or offshore, must be prepared to co-operate with other jurisdictions in the battle against crime. Such co-operation, of course, is mutually beneficial. What is required are authorities within a jurisdiction empowered to receive and deal with legitimate enquiries from recognised authorities elsewhere, including, for example, the Serious Fraud Office in the UK, or the Federal Bureau of Investigation in the USA.

9.24   Guernsey's Attorney-General and Solicitor-General ('Law Officers') and the Island's courts have a wide range of statutory powers which enable them to require the production of documents and the provision of information when investigating alleged or suspected criminal activity.

9.25   The most important legislation in respect of fraud investigations and prosecutions, for instance, is the *Criminal Justice (Fraud Investigation) (Bailiwick of Guernsey) Law 1991*. It is the most used piece of local legislation in the fight against economic crime. Under it the Law Officers can issue production orders and do so many times a year. The law enables the Law Officers to require a suspect to answer questions and produce documents considered relevant to the investigation. Legal sanctions are available in the event of non-compliance or when steps have been taken to falsify, conceal or destroy documents.

9.26 In addition, warrants can be issued authorising police officers to enter and search premises and to seize documents believed to be relevant. There is provision for the local police to be joined by authorised investigators from other jurisdictions.

9.27 Legal professional privilege in Guernsey is identical to that which exists under equivalent legislation in England and Wales.

9.28 In practice, over the past decade, information gathered from such investigations in Guernsey has been passed on to foreign law enforcement agencies, and particularly strong relationships have developed between the Island's law enforcers and those in the USA and Europe. In turn, the Commission also co-operates with other regulatory authorities around the world, especially in relation to investigations into suspected fraud.

9.29 Needless to say, all the law enforcement authorities in Guernsey are in regular and close contact with each other and with their counterparts in the UK, Jersey and the Isle of Man. But, if anything, co-operation between Guernsey and foreign jurisdictions is even greater in respect of suspected money laundering investigations. This is partly due to a significant piece of local legislation – *The Money Laundering (Disclosure of Information) (Guernsey) Law 1995.* This facilitates disclosure, by any person, to the Law Officers, the Police, Customs or the Financial Services Commission of any reasonable suspicions they have that money or other assets entering the Island are derived from, or represent the, proceeds of crime. Those disclosing such suspicions have the assurance in law that they would not be breaking any professional confidences, and that the law will protect them.

The 1995 legislation was extended to cover 'all crimes' as from 1 January 2000.

Disclosures of suspicious transactions are actively encouraged in Guernsey and 605 were reported in 2001.

9.30 While international co-operation between regulatory and law-enforcement authorities in pursuit of criminals is obviously a necessity, there is another important level of international co-operation, represented by membership of a wide variety of organisations.

9.31 Guernsey's Financial Services Commission, for example, is a member of the International Organisation of Securities Commissions, the Enlarged Contact Group on the Supervision of Collective Investment Funds, the Offshore Group of Banking Supervisors, and the International Association of Insurance Fraud Agencies.

9.32 Additionally, we are a founder member of the International Association of Insurance Supervisors (IAIS) which has its origins in a 1983 meeting in San Diego of five professional insurance regulators – two from the USA, the others from the UK, the Cayman Islands and Bermuda. Their aim, at the time, was to prevent insurance fraud by encouraging other insurance regulators to attend meetings of the USA's National Association of Insurance Commissioners (NAIC). Today the IAIS has offices within the Bank of International Settlements, Basel, Switzerland with its own permanent secretariat and is the world's leading body responsible for setting the standard for international insurance supervision.

9.33   The IAIS has produced the industry's first international supervisory training manual (which includes The Core Principles of Insurance Supervision) and in 1999 widened its membership by allowing non-regulators to join the association as observer members. This enabled insurance companies and insurance brokers along with other professionals, such as accountants and lawyers involved in insurance, to be part of the organisation. Their observer status entitles them to take part in consultation procedures for association standards and textbooks, and to attend its conferences and seminars.

9.34   Today the Executive Committee of the IAIS includes participants from the USA, Australia, Canada, Chile, Guernsey, Japan, Mexico (Chair), Poland, Portugal, Singapore, South Africa and the UK. There are two main committees reporting to the Executive Committee, The Technical Committee and the Emerging Markets Committee. The Insurance Fraud Sub-Committee (IFS) reports to the Technical Committee and is responsible for producing a set of principles entitled 'Fit and Proper Principles and Their Application'. These are effectively guidelines for standardising the checking of the bona fides of the promoters of insurance entities.

9.35   The IAIS, with financial support from Guernsey's Financial Services Commission, has also prepared and published a training manual for use by prospective professional insurance supervisors around the world. The IFS has now produced a guidance paper entitled 'Anti-Money Laundering Guidance Notes for Insurance Supervisors and Insurance Entities'. This paper was adopted at the IAIS General Meeting in January 2002 held in Tokyo.

9.36   The IAIS, however, is not the only international insurance organization involved in efforts to improve insurance 'best practice' around the world and to help prevent insurance-linked crime. Nine years ago the Offshore Group of Insurance Supervisors (OGIS) was established, prior to the establishment of the IAIS. Territories are only admitted as members if their domestic insurance legislation is regarded as adequate and they have effective enforcement, sufficient resources, a commitment to exchange information with insurance supervisors in other jurisdictions and are committed to implementing anti-money laundering legislation. The group has established a series of recommendations and guidelines covering a wide range of insurance requirements. Its members are: Bahamas, Barbados, BVI, Cayman, Gibraltar, Guernsey, Isle of Man, Jersey, Labuan, Mauritius, Macau, N Antilles, Samoa, Turks and Caicos with the following as observer members: Anguilla, Aruba, Bahrain, Belize and Vanuatu.

9.37 It should be noted that OGIS not only has the support of the IAIS but also of the United Nations Conference on Trade and Development (UNCTAD) and the International Insurance Foundation of Washington, DC.

9.38 While the work of such bodies is of great importance and value in the fight against economic crime and, in particular, money laundering, there are other major contenders in the ring. These take the shape of the Organisation for Economic Co-operation and Development; the Financial Action Task Force (FATF), set up in 1989; the G7-inspired Financial Stability Forum (FSF) and the Egmont Group of Financial Intelligence Units which has well over 50 members. These are multi-governmental organisations. For example, 31 countries are members of FATF and another five are associated organisations, which combine forces with the IMF and the World Bank to enhance global defences against money laundering. Between them they have branded 19 jurisdictions as Non-Co-operative Countries and Territories (NCCTs) because their anti-money laundering defences are deemed to fall below the standards expected by FATF member countries. This list is dynamic as jurisdictions strive to meet best standards of anti-money laundering.

9.39 The Egmont Group has an interesting background. During the past decade, a number of countries have created specialised government agencies as part of their systems for dealing with the problem of money laundering. These entities are commonly referred to as 'financial intelligence units' or 'FIUs'. These units increasingly serve as the focal point for national anti-money laundering programmes because they provide the possibility of rapidly exchanging information (between financial institutions and law enforcement/prosecutorial authorities, as well as between jurisdictions), while protecting the interests of the innocent individuals contained in their data.

9.40 The establishment of the first FIUs in the early 1990s was seen as a series of isolated events related to the specific needs of those jurisdictions that created them. Since 1995, however, a number of the FIUs began working together in an informal organisation known as the Egmont Group (named for the location of the first meeting in the Egmont-Arenberg Palace in Brussels). The goal of the group is to provide a forum for FIUs to improve support to their respective national anti-money laundering programmes. This support includes expanding and systematising the exchange of financial intelligence, improving the expertise and capabilities of the personnel of such organisations, and fostering better communication among FIUs through the application of new technologies.

9.41 Guernsey has been recognised by both the FSF and FATF as meeting the required standards, including the all-important 40 FATF Recommendations whose elements include statutory and/or treaty provisions that:

- make money laundering a crime and provide appropriate sanctions;

- provide for the reporting, collection and analysis of suspicious or unusual financial transactions (including those that do not involve regulated financial institutions);

- allow the freezing and seizing of assets reasonably suspected to be the proceeds of crime;

- allow the sharing of such information with other jurisdictions; and

- allow cross-border legal assistance in prosecuting money laundering crimes, including collecting evidence and extraditing criminals.

9.42   The IMF and World Bank, which have produced their own methodology for assessing financial supervisory principles in further efforts to enhance global supervisory standards and the effort against money laundering, consider that any assessment of a territory's anti-money laundering measures should include, within an appropriate legal framework, an adequate system of criminal justice embracing effective and fair investigative, prosecutorial and judicial services.

9.43   The IMF reasons that without an adequate criminal justice system a territory is unlikely to have effective anti-money laundering laws and that without a fair system of criminal justice, anti-money laundering laws will be misused, resulting in violations of rights to privacy, property or personal freedom.

9.44   It is generally agreed that banks provide the main channels for criminals to launder the proceeds of their crimes both directly, by deposit placement, and indirectly, through processes known as layering and integration. It is considered that anti-money laundering policies in respect of the insurance sector should be subject to enhanced assessment criteria.

9.45   In the first instance this will require insurance entities to have comprehensive and adequate practices and procedures, especially strict KYC rules, to prevent them being used by money launderers. It is anticipated that the new criteria will embrace five main areas:

(*a*)   underwriting standards;

(*b*)   verification of an insurance entity's identity;

(*c*)   the recognition and reporting by an entity's compliance officer of suspicious customers/transactions;

(*d*)   the keeping of records for at least five to six years; and

(*e*)   adequate anti-money laundering training for new and existing staff.

It can be seen, therefore, that although the practice and techniques of money laundering continue to evolve, the efforts to keep pace with and, perhaps, to eventually overtake this growth, also do so.

9.46 The international bodies and the supervisors are beginning to look more closely at the role of the intermediary in the money laundering process and various intermediary bodies such as the WFII (World Federation of Insurance Intermediaries) are assisting them. They are evolving across four main fronts: within individual businesses, within individual territories, through international professional organisations and through multi-governmental institutions and their orchestrated activities.

9.47 At the end of the day, however, the downfall of almost any money laundering scheme, indeed of most economic crime, depends on the ability of the employees, managers, directors and customers of the world's financial systems to spot and report to competent investigatory authorities anyone or anything which arouses suspicion.

In particular, insurance entities have shown a very low disclosure record. Onsite visits in various jurisdictions have pointed to the lack of anti-money laundering procedures within insurance entities and a lack of realisation of the dangers posed to them and the reputation of their jurisdiction.

The latest press release on this subject will impose new anti-money laundering standards on insurance entities in the Channel Islands and the Isle of Man and, hopefully, to all insurance entities internationally – see Appendix 9:1 below.

Appendix 9:1

Guernsey Financial Services Commission – Press Release: 22 February 2002

Crown dependencies tighten anti-money laundering defences

Joint action by Guernsey, the Isle of Man and Jersey

Strong new measures to tighten the Crown Dependencies' anti-money laundering regimes were announced today by the three financial services regulatory Commissions. The Commissions are taking action in concert and will be moving to implement the required changes to laws and guidance to reflect these measures.

All three Islands have tough anti-money laundering measures currently in place – described by an international evaluation team (including representatives from the US, France and the UK) as already being 'close to complete adherence' to the Forty Recommendations of the Financial Action Task Force. The new measures announced today include three main features:

- In addition to being required to know their own customers, banks and other institutions will be required to look beyond their customers (for example, when they are trusts or companies) to establish the principals behind them.

- The new measures tighten up the requirements on banks and other institutions to ensure that due diligence is done properly – even where the customer is referred to them by another institution which claims to have carried out the background checks already.

- All institutions will be required to embark upon a progressive risk prioritised programme to bring the records of existing accounts up to current standards (where there are deficiencies in information and documentation held) if the nature of the client or transaction meets certain criteria.

A number of other measures, designed to clarify and remove ambiguities and differences in standards between the Islands are also included.

The new measures, which follow consultation in 2000 and 2001 with their respective financial services industries, are in response to previous suggestions made by the international evaluation team in 1999, and in 2000 by the Financial Action Task Force. The measures also reflect a commitment to remove opportunities for arbitrage between the Crown Dependencies in areas related to financial crime, money laundering and terrorist funding.

In a joint statement the Directors General – Peter Neville for Guernsey, John Aspden for the Isle of Man and Richard Pratt for Jersey, said:

> 'We are determined to ensure that the success of our finance centres in attracting honest money does not open up opportunities to criminals, terrorists or corrupt leaders and their associates. This document is an important milestone in our joint commitment to achieve this aim. By establishing a common platform between our three jurisdictions, we demonstrate our determination to ensure that our finance industries continue to meet international standards. The finance industries in the three Islands are being asked to invest in their own future by putting in place a regime which any clear-thinking and honest client will understand and welcome.'

Appendix 9:2

FATF The Forty Recommendations

General framework of the recommendations

Recommendation 1 – Each country should take immediate steps to ratify and to implement fully, the 1988 United Nations Convention against Illicit Traffic in Narcotic Drugs and Psychotropic Substances (the Vienna Convention).

Recommendation 2 – Financial institution secrecy laws should be conceived so as not to inhibit implementation of these recommendations.

Recommendation 3 – An effective money laundering enforcement program should include increased multilateral co-operation and mutual legal assistance in money laundering investigations and prosecutions and extradition in money laundering cases, where possible.

Role of national legal systems in combating money laundering

Scope of the criminal offence of money laundering

Recommendation 4 – Each country should take such measures as may be necessary, including legislative ones, to enable it to criminalise money laundering as set forth in the Vienna Convention. Each country should extend the offence of drug money laundering to one based on serious offences. Each country would determine which serious crimes would be designated as money laundering predicate offences. (See Interpretative Note.) [Not reproduced.]

Recommendation 5 – As provided in the Vienna Convention, the offence of money laundering should apply at least to knowing money laundering activity, including the concept that knowledge may be inferred from objective factual circumstances.

Recommendation 6 – Where possible, corporations themselves – not only their employees – should be subject to criminal liability.

Provisional measures and confiscation

Recommendation 7 – Countries should adopt measures similar to those set forth in the Vienna Convention, as may be necessary, including legislative ones, to enable their competent authorities to confiscate property laundered, proceeds from, instrumentalities used in or intended for use in the commission of any money laundering offence, or property of corresponding value, without prejudicing the rights of bona fide third parties.

Such measures should include the authority to: (1) identify, trace and evaluate property which is subject to confiscation; (2) carry out provisional measures, such as freezing and seizing, to prevent any dealing, transfer or disposal of such property; and (3) take any appropriate investigative measures.

In addition to confiscation and criminal sanctions, countries also should consider monetary and civil penalties, and/or proceedings including civil proceedings, to void contracts entered into by parties, where parties knew or should have known that as a result of the contract, the State would be prejudiced in its ability to recover financial claims, e.g. through confiscation or collection of fines and penalties.

Role of the financial system in combating money laundering

Recommendation 8 – Recommendations 10 to 29 should apply not only to banks, but also to non-bank financial institutions. Even for those non-bank financial institutions which are not subject to a formal prudential supervisory regime in all countries, for example bureaux de change, governments should ensure that these institutions are subject to the same anti-money laundering laws or regulations as all other financial institutions and that these laws or regulations are implemented effectively. (See Interpretative Notes: Recommendation 8 and Recommendations 8 & 9.) [Not reproduced.]

Recommendation 9 – The appropriate national authorities should consider applying Recommendations 10 to 21 and 23 to the conduct of financial activities as a commercial undertaking by businesses or professions which are not financial institutions, where such conduct is allowed or not prohibited. Financial activities include, but are not limited to, those listed in the attached annex. It is left to each country to decide whether special situations should be defined where the application of anti-money laundering measures is not necessary, for example, when a financial activity is carried out on an occasional or limited basis. (See Interpretative Note) [Not reproduced]

Customer identification and record-keeping rules

Recommendation 10 – Financial Institutions should not keep anonymous accounts or accounts in obviously fictitious names: they should be required (by law, by regulations, by agreements between supervisory authorities and financial institutions or by self-regulatory agreements among financial institutions) to identify, on the basis of an official or other reliable identifying document, and record the identity of their clients, either occasional or usual, when establishing business relations or conducting transactions (in particular opening of accounts or passbooks, entering into fiduciary transactions, renting of safe deposit boxes, performing large cash transactions).

In order to fulfil identification requirements concerning legal entities, financial institutions should, when necessary, take measures:

(i)   to verify the legal existence and structure of the customer by obtaining either from a public register or from the customer or both, proof of incorporation, including information concerning the customer's name, legal form, address, directors and provisions regulating the power to bind the entity.

(ii)   to verify that any person purporting to act on behalf of the customer is so authorised and identify that person.

Recommendation 11 – Financial institutions should take reasonable measures to obtain information about the true identity of the persons on whose behalf an account is opened or a transaction conducted if there are any doubts as to whether these clients or customers are acting on their own behalf, for example, in the case of domicilary companies (i.e. institutions, corporations, foundations, trusts, etc. that do not conduct any commercial or manufacturing business or any other form of commercial operation in the country where their registered office is located). (See Interpretative Notes: Recommendation 11 and Recommendations 11 & 15 through 18.) [Not reproduced.]

Recommendation 12 – Financial institutions should maintain, for at least five years, all necessary records on transactions, both domestic or international, to enable them to comply swiftly with information requests from the competent authorities. Such records must be sufficient to permit reconstruction of individual transactions (including the amounts of types of currency involved if any) so as to provide, if necessary, evidence for prosecution of criminal behaviour.

Financial institutions should keep records on customer identification (e.g. copies or records of official identification documents like passports, identity cards, driving licenses or similar documents), account files and business correspondence for at least five years after the account is closed.

These documents should be available to domestic competent authorities in the context of relevant criminal prosecutions and investigations.

Recommendation 13 – Countries should pay special attention to money laundering threats inherent in new or developing technologies that might favour anonymity, and take measures, if needed, to prevent their use in money laundering schemes.

Increased diligence of financial institutions

Recommendation 14 – Financial institutions should pay special attention to all complex, unusual large transactions, and all unusual patterns of transactions, which have no apparent economic or visible lawful purpose. The background and purpose of such transactions should, as far as possible, be examined, the findings established in writing, and be available to help supervisors, auditors and law enforcement agencies. (See Interpretative Note.) [Not reproduced.]

Recommendation 15 – If financial institutions suspect that funds stem from a criminal activity, they should be required to report promptly their suspicions to the competent authorities. (See Interpretative Notes: Recommendation 15 and Recommendations 11 & 15 through 18.) [Not reproduced.]

Recommendation 16 – Financial institutions, their directors, officers and employees should be protected by legal provisions from criminal or civil liability for breach of any restriction on disclosure of information imposed by contract or by any legislative, regulatory or administrative provision, if they report their suspicions in good faith to the competent authorities, even if they did not know precisely what the underlying criminal activity was, and regardless of whether illegal activity actually occurred. (See Interpretative Note.) [Not reproduced.]

Recommendation 17 – Financial institutions, their directors, officers and employees, should not, or, where appropriate, should not be allowed to, warn their customers when information relating to them is being reported to the competent authorities. (See Interpretative Note.) [Not reproduced.]

Recommendation 18 – Financial institutions reporting their suspicions should comply with instructions from the competent authorities. (See Interpretative Note.) [Not reproduced.]

Recommendation 19 – Financial institutions should develop programs against money laundering. These programs should include, as a minimum:

(i)   the development of internal policies, procedures and controls, including the designation of compliance officers at management level, and adequate screening procedures to ensure high standards when hiring employees;

(ii)   an ongoing employee training programme;

(iii)   an audit function to test the system.

Measures to cope with the problem of countries with no or insufficient anti-money laundering measures

Recommendation 20 – Financial institutions should ensure that the principles mentioned above are also applied to branches and majority owned subsidiaries located abroad, especially in countries which do not or insufficiently apply these Recommendations, to the extent that local applicable laws and regulations permit. When local applicable laws and regulations prohibit this implementation, competent authorities in the country of the mother institution should be informed by the financial institutions that they cannot apply these Recommendations.

Recommendation 21 – Financial institutions should give special attention to business relations and transactions with persons, including companies and financial institutions, from countries which do not or insufficiently apply these Recommendations. Whenever these transactions have no apparent economic or visible lawful purpose, their background and purpose should, as far as possible, be examined, the findings established in writing, and be available to help supervisors, auditors and law enforcement agencies.

Other measures to avoid money laundering

Recommendation 22 – Countries should consider implementing feasible measures to detect or monitor the physical cross-border transportation of cash and bearer negotiable instruments, subject to strict safeguards to ensure proper use of information and without impeding in any way the freedom of capital movements. (See Interpretative Note.) [Not reproduced.]

Recommendation 23 –Countries should consider the feasibility and utility of a system where banks and other financial institutions and intermediaries would report all domestic and international currency transactions above a fixed amount, to a national central agency with a computerised data base, available to competent authorities for use in money laundering cases, subject to strict safeguards to ensure proper use of the information.

Recommendation 24 – Countries should further encourage in general the development of modern and secure techniques of money management, including increased use of checks, payment cards, direct deposit of salary checks, and book entry recording of securities, as a means to encourage the replacement of cash transfers.

Recommendation 25 – Countries should take notice of the potential for abuse of shell corporations by money launderers and should consider whether additional measures are required to prevent unlawful use of such entities.

Implementation and role of regulatory and other administrative authorities

Recommendation 26 – The competent authorities supervising banks or other financial institutions or intermediaries, or other competent authorities, should ensure that the supervised institutions have adequate programs to guard against money laundering. These authorities should co-operate and lend expertise spontaneously or on request with other domestic judicial or law enforcement authorities in money laundering investigations and prosecutions. (See Interpretative Note.) [Not reproduced.]

Recommendation 27 – Competent authorities should be designated to ensure an effective implementation of all these Recommendations, through administrative supervision and regulation, in other professions dealing with cash as defined by each country.

Recommendation 28 – The competent authorities should establish guidelines which will assist financial institutions in detecting suspicious patterns of behaviour by their customers. It is understood that such guidelines must develop over time, and will never by exhaustive. It is further understood that such guidelines will primarily serve as an educational tool for financial institutions' personnel.

Recommendation 29 – The competent authorities regulating or supervising financial institutions should take the necessary legal or regulatory measures to guard against control or acquisition of a significant participation in financial institutions by criminals or their confederates. (See Interpretative Note.) [Not reproduced.]

Strengthening of international co-operation

Administrative co-operation

Exchange of general information

Recommendation 30 – National administrations should consider recording, at least in the aggregate, international flows of cash in whatever currency, so that estimates can be made of cash flows and reflows from various sources abroad, when this is combined with central bank information. Such information should be made available to the International Monetary Fund and the Bank for International Settlements to facilitate international studies.

Recommendation 31 – International competent authorities, perhaps Interpol and the World Customs Organisation, should be given responsibility for gathering and disseminating information to competent authorities about the latest developments in money laundering and money laundering techniques. Central banks and bank regulators could do the same on their network. National authorities in various spheres, in consultation with trade associations, could then disseminate this to financial institutions in individual countries.

Exchange of information relating to suspicious transactions

Recommendation 32 – Each country should make efforts to improve a spontaneous or 'upon request' international information exchange relating to suspicious transactions, persons and corporations involved in those transactions between competent authorities. Strict safeguards should be established to ensure that this exchange of information is consistent with national and international provisions on privacy and data protection.

Other forms of co-operation

Basis and means for co-operation in confiscation, mutual assistance and extradition

Recommendation 33 – Countries should try to ensure, on a bilateral or multilateral basis, that different knowledge standards in national definitions – i.e. different standards concerning the international element of the infraction – do not affect the ability or willingness of countries to provide each other with mutual legal assistance. (See Interpretative Note.) [Not reproduced.]

Recommendation 34 – International co-operation should be supported by a network of bilateral and multilateral agreements and arrangements based on generally shared legal concepts with the aim of providing practical measures to affect the widest possible range of mutual assistance.

Recommendation 35 – Countries should be encouraged to ratify and implement relevant international conventions on money laundering such as the 1990 Council of Europe Convention on Laundering, Search, Seizure and Confiscation of the Proceeds from Crime.

Focus of improved mutual assistance on money laundering issues

Recommendation 36 – Co-operative investigations among countries' appropriate competent authorities should be encouraged. One valid and effective investigative technique in this respect is controlled delivery related to assets known or suspected to be the proceeds of crime. Countries are encouraged to support this technique, where possible. (See Interpretative Note.) [Not reproduced.]

Recommendation 37 – There should be procedures for mutual assistance in criminal matters regarding the use of compulsory measures including the production of records by financial institutions and other persons, the search of persons and premises, seizure and obtaining of evidence for use in money laundering investigations and prosecutions and in related actions in foreign jurisdictions.

Recommendation 38 – There should be authority to take expeditious action in response to requests by foreign countries to identify, freeze, seize and confiscate proceeds or other property of corresponding value to such proceeds, based on money laundering or the crimes underlying the laundering activity. There should also be arrangements for co-ordinating seizure and confiscation proceedings which may include the sharing of confiscated assets. (See Interpretative Note.) [Not reproduced.]

Recommendation 39 – To avoid conflicts of jurisdiction, consideration should be given to devising and applying mechanisms for determining the best venue for prosecution of defendants in the interests of justice in cases that are subject to prosecution in more than one country. Similarly, there should be arrangements for co-ordinating seizure and confiscation proceedings which may include the sharing of confiscated assets.

Recommendation 40 – Countries should have procedures in place to extradite, where possible, individuals charged with a money laundering offence or related offences. With respect to its national legal system, each country should recognise money laundering as an extraditable offence. Subject to their legal frameworks, countries may consider simplifying extradition by allowing direct transmission of extradition requests between appropriate ministries, extraditing persons based only on warrants of arrests or judgements, extraditing their nationals, and/or introducing a simplified extradition of consenting persons who waive formal extradition proceedings.

Appendix 9:3

FATF Special Recommendations on Terrorist Financing

Recognising the vital importance of taking action to combat the financing of terrorism, the FATF has agreed these Recommendations, which, when combined with the FATF Forty Recommendations on money laundering, set out the basic framework to detect, prevent and suppress the financing of terrorism and terrorist acts.

I.   Ratification and implementation of UN instruments

Each country should take immediate steps to ratify and to implement fully the 1999 United Nations International Convention for the Suppression of the Financing of Terrorism.

Countries should also immediately implement the United Nations resolutions relating to the prevention and suppression of the financing of terrorist acts, particularly United Nations Security Council Resolution 1373.

II.   Criminalising the financing of terrorism and associated money laundering

Each country should criminalise the financing of terrorism, terrorist acts and terrorist organisations. Countries should ensure that such offences are designated as money laundering predicate offences.

III.   Freezing and confiscating terrorist assets

Each country should implement measures to freeze without delay funds or other assets of terrorists, those who finance terrorism and terrorist organisations in accordance with the United Nations resolutions relating to the prevention and suppression of the financing of terrorist acts.

Each country should also adopt and implement measures, including legislative ones, which would enable the competent authorities to seize and confiscate property that is the proceeds of, or used in, or intended or allocated for use in, the financing of terrorism, terrorist acts or terrorist organisations.

IV.   Reporting suspicious transactions related to terrorism

If financial institutions, or other businesses or entities subject to anti-money laundering obligations, suspect or have reasonable grounds to suspect that funds are linked or related to, or are to be used for terrorism, terrorist acts or by terrorist organisations, they should be required to report promptly their suspicions to the competent authorities.

V.   International co-operation

Each country should afford another country, on the basis of a treaty, arrangement or other mechanism for mutual legal assistance or information exchange, the greatest possible measure of assistance in connection with criminal, civil enforcement, and administrative investigations, inquiries and proceedings relating to the financing of terrorism, terrorist acts and terrorist organisations.

Countries should also take all possible measures to ensure that they do not provide safe havens for individuals charged with the financing of terrorism, terrorist acts or terrorist organisations, and should have procedures in place to extradite, where possible, such individuals.

VI.   Alternative remittance

Each country should take measures to ensure that persons or legal entities, including agents, that provide a service for the transmission of money or value, including transmission through an informal money or value transfer system or network, should be licensed or registered and subject to all the FATF Recommendations that apply to banks and non-bank financial institutions. Each country should ensure that persons or legal entities that carry out this service illegally are subject to administrative, civil or criminal sanctions.

VII.   Wire transfers

Countries should take measures to require financial institutions, including money remitters, to include accurate and meaningful originator information (name, address and account number) on funds transfers and related messages that are sent, and the information should remain with the transfer or related message through the payment chain.

Countries should take measures to ensure that financial institutions, including money remitters, conduct enhanced scrutiny of and monitor for suspicious activity funds transfers which do not contain complete originator information (name, address and account number).

VIII. Non-profit organisations

Countries should review the adequacy of laws and regulations that relate to entities that can be abused for the financing of terrorism. Non-profit organisations are particularly vulnerable, and countries should ensure that they cannot be misused:

(i)   by terrorist organisations posing as legitimate entities;

(ii)   to exploit legitimate entities as conduits for terrorist financing, including for the purpose of escaping asset freezing measures; and

(iii) to conceal or obscure the clandestine diversion of funds intended for legitimate purposes to terrorist organisations.

Appendix 9:4

International Association of Insurance Supervisors – anti-money laundering guidance notes for insurance supervisors & insurance entities

Examples of suspicious transactions

Claims

It is recognised that a claim is one of the principal methods of laundering money through insurance. Outlined below are three examples of where claims have resulted in reports of suspected money laundering.

- A claim was notified by the assured, a solicitor, who was being sued by one of his clients. The solicitor was being sued for breach of confidentiality, which led to the clients' creditors discovering funds that had allegedly been smuggled overseas. Documents produced by the insured attorneys indicated that the solicitor's client might be involved in tax evasion, currency smuggling and money laundering.

- A claim was notified relating to the loss of high value goods whilst in transit. The assured admitted to investigators that the person was fronting for individuals who wanted to invest 'dirt money' for a profit. It is believed that either the goods, which were allegedly purchased with cash, did not exist, or that the removal of the goods was organised by the purchasers to ensure a claim occurred and that they received 'clean' money as a claims settlement.

- Insurers who have discovered instances where premiums have been paid in one currency and requests for claims to be paid in another as a method of laundering money.

- During an onsite visit, an insurance supervisor was referred to a professional indemnity claim that the insurer did not believe was connected with money laundering. The insurer was considering whether to decline the claim on the basis that it had failed to comply with various conditions under the cover. The insurance supervisor reviewed the insurers papers, which identified one of the bank's clients as being linked to a major fraud and money laundering investigation being carried out by international law enforcement agencies.

- After a successful High Court action for fraud, adjusters and lawyers working for an insurer involved in the litigation became aware that the guilty fraudster was linked to other potential frauds, including money laundering.

Return premiums

There are several cases where the early cancellation of policies with return of premium has been used to launder money. This has occurred where there have been:

- a number of policies entered into by the same insurer/intermediary for small amounts and then cancelled at the same time;
- return premium being credited to an account different from the original account;
- requests for return premiums in currencies different to the original premium; and
- regular purchase and cancellation of policies.

Overpayment of premium

The overpayment of premium is more likely to be relevant to an insurance broker rather than an insurer. However, the overpayment of premium, has in the past, been used as a method of money laundering. Underwriters should be especially vigilant where:

- the overpayment is over a certain size (say US$10,000 or equivalent);
- the request to refund the excess premium was to a third party;
- the assured is in a jurisdiction associated with money laundering; and
- where the size or regularity of overpayments is suspicious.

Life business

An attempt was made to purchase life policies for a number of foreign nationals. The underwriter was requested to provide life coverage with an indemnity value the same as the premium. There were also indications that in the event that the policies were to be cancelled, [a] return premium was to be paid into a bank account in a different jurisdiction to the assured.

High brokerage / third party payments / strange premium routes

High brokerage can be used to pay off third parties unrelated to the insurance contract. This often coincides with example[s] of unusual premium routes.

10 Money Laundering, Tax Evasion and Professional Liability

Michael Brindle QC

10.1   Professionals, especially accountants and solicitors, practising in trusts, estates and tax planning, do not need to be told that they must not assist their client either in breaking the criminal law or in committing frauds on third parties. There may, however, be some perception that such professionals need not be concerned, at least so far as the English courts are concerned, so long as their clients' activities remain 'offshore'. If there is any such conception, it is a dangerous one both as to UK criminal law and as to civil liability in constructive trust. I set out below the particular dangers arising in the criminal sphere, and then make certain observations as to risks of professionals becoming liable as constructive trustees.

The Criminal Justice Act 1993

10.2   The *Drug Trafficking Offences Act 1986* introduced stringent laws affecting any persons involved, whether directly or indirectly in drug trafficking. Stringent though these laws were, however, they did relate solely to drug trafficking, and had no major relevance to the trust or tax practitioner. *Sections 29–31* of the *Criminal Justice Act 1993* introduced three new offences under the heading 'money laundering and other offences'. The three offences now take their place as *sections 93A, 93B and 93C* of the *Criminal Justice Act 1988*, within *Part VI* of that *Act*, a part dealing with compensation orders covering all indictable offences (other than drug trafficking offences). The Proceeds of Crime Bill currently before Parliament will amend and extend the provisions of the criminal law relating to money laundering, but is not yet in force and is not considered here.

10.3   The offences introduced in 1993 do not just deal with money laundering as it would generally be understood, but are wider in application. The provisions create offences of assisting others in the retention of the benefit of criminal conduct, acquiring, possessing or using the proceeds of criminal conduct and concealing or transferring the proceeds of criminal conduct. The key to all this is the definition of 'criminal conduct'. Because these offences are positioned in *Part VI* of the *1988 Act*, 'criminal conduct' has the meaning which it generally has in that part, i.e., any indictable offences (other than drug trafficking offences). This means that the three new offences have a wider ambit than may ever have been intended. It is worth noting that the legislation derives from the *EC Money Laundering Directive* (*Council Directive 91/308/EEC*) which is concerned with what one would generally describe as money laundering. The UK legislation goes well beyond money laundering, but it cannot be argued that the legislation can be read as impliedly restricted by reference to the scope of the *Directive*. Not only is there no general principle that an *Act of Parliament* should not be construed wider than necessary to give effect to *Directives* on which they are based, but *Article 15* of the relevant *Directive* specifically permits Member States to adopt stricter provisions than the *Directive* itself demands. A new Directive from Europe is expected in the near future, but that will certainly do nothing to restrict the scope of UK money laundering legislation.

10.4   Therefore, the offences cover a wide ambit. Particularly dangerous is *section 93A*, which provides as follows.

'(1)   Subject to *subsection (3)* below, if a person enters into or is otherwise concerned in an arrangement whereby

(*a*)   the retention or control by or on behalf of another ("A") of A's proceeds of criminal conduct is facilitated (whether by concealment, removal from the jurisdiction, transfer to nominees or otherwise); or

(*b*)   A's proceeds of criminal conduct

(i)   are used to secure that funds are placed at A's disposal; or

(ii)   are used for A's benefit to acquire property by way of investment, knowing or suspecting that A is a person who is or has been engaged in criminal conduct or has benefited from criminal conduct, he is guilty of an offence.

(2)   In this section, references to any person's proceeds of criminal conduct include a reference to any property which in whole or in part directly or indirectly represents in his hands his proceeds of criminal conduct.

(3)   Where a person discloses to a Constable a suspicion or belief that any funds or investments are derived from or used in connection with criminal conduct or discloses to a Constable any matter on which such a suspicion or belief is based

(*a*)   the disclosure shall not be treated as a breach of any restriction upon the disclosure of information imposed by statute or otherwise; and

(*b*)   if he does any act in contravention of *subsection (1)* above and the disclosure relates to the arrangement concerned, he does not commit an offence under this section if

(i)   the disclosure is made before he does the act concerned and the act is done with the consent of the Constable; or

(ii)   the disclosure is made after he does the act, but is made on his initiative and as soon as it is reasonable for him to make it.

(4)   In proceedings against the person for an offence under this section, it is a defence to prove

(*a*)   that he did not know or suspect that the arrangement related to any person's proceeds of criminal conduct;

(*b*) that he did not know or suspect that by the arrangement the retention or control by or on behalf of A of any property was facilitated or, as the case may be, that by the arrangement any property was used, as mentioned in *subsection (1)* above; or

(*c*) that

(i) he intended to disclose to a Constable such a suspicion, belief or matter as is mentioned in *subsection (3)* above in relation to the arrangement; but

(ii) there is reasonable excuse for his failure to make disclosure in accordance with *subsection (3)(b)* above.'

10.5 The effect of this is that any professional who knows or suspects that his client is engaged in or has benefited from anything constituting an indictable offence and is in any way concerned with assisting in the making of arrangements to retain or dispose of any proceeds of such activity is guilty of a criminal offence unless he can establish the defences at *subsections (3) and/or (4)*. This must include fiscal offences, although it is dubious whether the legislature intended that fiscal offences should be covered. Thus, any professional who knows or suspects that his client is involved in tax evasion may be criminally liable if he in any way assists, including by the giving of advice, the success of any such evasion. This provision goes a long way towards undermining the principle of English law which has existed since the abolition of the offence of misprision of felony, that there is no obligation to report a crime. That may still be the case, but if a person plays any part whatsoever in the chain of events which leads to the crime being accomplished, he may fall within the ambit of the new offence.

10.6 Some relief might be sought by reference to the concept of 'proceeds of criminal conduct'. It might be argued that this concept does not extend to monies retained (for instance) as a result of non-disclosure to or fraud of tax authorities. It is true that as a matter of ordinary language 'proceeds' does connote something obtained rather than something retained, but this avenue of argument is closed off by *section 29(2)* of the *1993 Act*, which provides as follows: ' "Proceeds of criminal conduct", in relation to any person who has benefited from criminal conduct, means that benefit'. This must be read with *section 71(4)* and *71(5)* of the *1988 Act*, which define 'benefit' for the purposes of *Part VI* of that *Act*. Whilst *section 71(4)* does echo the concept of obtaining property, *subsection (5)* clearly extends the concept of 'benefit' to any pecuniary advantage obtained from or in connection with criminal conduct. This is a very wide definition and it seems to me to be inconsistent with any limitation of the definition of 'proceeds' to sums of money obtained as a result in criminal activity. If a taxpayer gets away with the retention of monies which he ought to pay in tax, he has clearly obtained a pecuniary advantage as a result of his crime, or in connection with it, and the wording of the statute is clearly satisfied.

10.7 It might even then be argued that 'pecuniary advantage' might be given a narrow meaning in line with that attributed to the similar phrase in *section 16* of the *Theft Act 1968*. In that *Act*, 'pecuniary advantage' is specifically defined as including and including only certain specified situations. Escaping or deferring a liability is included, but it is well established that this does not include a future liability. However, there is no trace of any of this in *section 71* of the *1988 Act*. Neither the *Theft Act 1968* nor the later *Theft Act 1978* are mentioned, and no attempt is made to give any limited meaning to 'pecuniary advantage'. In ordinary parlance, a taxpayer who gets away with the retention of money which he ought not to be allowed to retain has obtained a pecuniary advantage from his crime. This is supported by the decision of the Court of Appeal in *R v Allen [2000] 2 All ER 142*, a case on confiscation orders, where the same statutory definition applies as also applies to money laundering.

10.8   There may yet be scope for some limitation of the apparent scope of this liability. Even on the wide definition of 'proceeds of criminal conduct' it must be possible to say in relation to a particular sum of money that it does derive from the criminal conduct in question. If one takes an example of a bank account, it may be wholly unclear to a bank whether certain monies of its customer represent the pecuniary advantage obtained from a tax fraud or not. In general, a taxpayer is not obliged to pay his tax from any particular fund, provided that he pays it. Thus, a professional who is involved in the flow of money belonging to his client may be able to argue that certain monies cannot be identified as the 'proceeds of criminal conduct' even if that professional suspects that his client is engaged in criminal conduct. Whilst there is force of this argument, it cannot be taken too far. One must remember that Parliament has chosen to treat the concept of 'proceeds of criminal conduct' as the same as the concept which applies for the purposes of confiscatory or compensatory orders, in respect of which no question of tracing or the like arises. If it is clear, in any given case, that money standing to the credit of a particular bank account is money which represents the pecuniary advantage which the account holder had derived by reason of a fiscal offence, then it seems that the requirements of the statute are satisfied. See on this topic generally the article by Peter Alldridge in the *Journal of Money Laundering Control* Volume 4 No 4 (Spring 2001).

10.9   It may help to take an example. A professional man advising an individual may know that the individual's employer is paying money in contravention of PAYE regulations, which is neither being declared for tax nor being deducted at source from the employee's remuneration. On this assumption, the professional knows that the employee is being paid money which ought to be declared and paid to the Inland Revenue, but is not being declared or paid. In order to complete the picture, let it be assumed that the professional knows that all the sums paid to the employee as remuneration are paid away, as soon as received, to offshore accounts in the Cayman Islands. Here the position presented to the professional is as clear as can be. He knows full well that an employer and employee are engaged in a fraud on the Revenue, and that monies passing through his hands include sums which ought to have been deducted and paid to the Revenue and are in every possible sense the benefit of or a pecuniary advantage flowing from the tax fraud in question. In such a case, all the requirements of *section 93A* of the *1988 Act* are satisfied. The adviser would be under a duty to report the criminal conduct and he would have no defence under *section 93A(4)*. It does not seem to me to be possible to contend in such a situation that the sums flowing through the professional's hands were not 'proceeds of criminal conduct'. Where there might be some room for genuine argument is as to the meaning of the requirement of 'suspicion' contained in *section 93A*, as to which I say more below (see 10.26).

Offshore activities

10.10   As if this is not all bad enough, *section 93A(7)* of the *1988 Act* then proceeds to extend the definition of 'criminal conduct' so as to include not only conduct which constitutes an offence under *Part VI* of the *1988 Act*, but also 'would constitute such an offence if it had occurred in England and Wales or (as the case may be) Scotland'. Thus, the professional adviser, agent or banker is not concerned simply with UK activities, but is at risk in relation to offshore activities as well. It is the effect of this provision that causes particular difficulties to those who give advice spanning more than one jurisdiction. The immediate question is whether this means that the professional needs concern himself with the substantive criminal law of foreign jurisdictions. Is the UK legislature passing enactments to assist foreign governments in policing breaches of their own criminal law, including tax and exchange control?

10.11   It seems that the statute does not go that far. It does not define criminal conduct so as to include, or even make relevant, any foreign criminal legal code at all. Rather, *section 93A(7)* of the *Act* is concerned with the place where the conduct takes place, not the law by reference to which it takes place, which remains at all times English (or where relevant Scottish) law. Therefore, if a professional becomes involved in his client's activities, where the only possible criminal law to be infringed is the substantive criminal law of a foreign country, and that activity would not be criminal in England if committed in England, then the professional need have no fear, at least in respect of English criminal law. There is no need for all solicitors and accountants specialising in trust or tax work to take a crash course in international and comparative tax laws.

10.12   Reassuring though that message may be, *section 93A(7)* still has a very significant effect. It requires professionals to ignore the place where conduct occurs and to treat everything (for relevant purposes) as if it had actually taken place in England. The purpose of this provision is to overcome the jurisdictional difficulties which English law has often faced in relation to activities, typically conspiracies, which take place abroad, but which have some effect within England. In order to eliminate any such argument, *section 93A(7)* asserts jurisdiction over criminal activity for the purposes of *section 93(A)* wherever that activity actually occurs.

10.13   But the effect of the provision is much wider than that. It includes activities which may have nothing to do with England or the United Kingdom at all. A conspiracy between A and B, hatched in Paris to rob a German bank, ought to have nothing to do with English criminal law. However, if C, an accountant practising in London, who acts as A's adviser, has any suspicion of a conspiracy and plays any role whatsoever in facilitating the obtaining by A of the proceeds of the conspiracy, he risks being guilty of a criminal offence under *section 93A*. Even this may be thought acceptable in the international context in which the *Directive* was introduced, especially where the focus is on money laundering and international fraud. The position is much more uncomfortable when one applies it to fiscal offences. Where the professional, C, knows or suspects that his client, A, is engaged in a course of conduct which involves infringement of French revenue law, then (as stated above) he is not concerned with breaches of French law as such. However, frequently the conduct in question would, if it had all taken place in England, have infringed parallel provisions of English revenue law. In such a case, *section 93(A)* will apply, or at least would seem *prima facie* to apply. At this point, however, it seems to me that the position becomes more complex.

10.14   In a case where A is evading French revenue law, the mere translation of the geographical location of his activities to England will not create an offence under English revenue law. *Section 29(2)* only translates to England the physical place where the conduct occurs. It does not seem to me that it is easy to analyse evasion of revenue law in this way. More is involved here than the locality in which the evasive conduct takes place. Even if that conduct is notionally moved to England, *section 29(2)* does not provide that the victim of the criminal conduct, viz. the French revenue authorities, should notionally be replaced by the English revenue authorities. At this stage, it seems to me that the principle in the decision in *Government of India v Taylor [1955] AC 491* comes into effect. That decision is a clear statement of a well established principle of English law, namely that the English courts will not enforce foreign revenue laws. It is true that in extradition law the courts have not applied this principle (see *R v Chief Metropolitan Stipendiary Magistrate, ex p Home Secretary [1989] 1 All ER 151*), but extradition is quite different, since the whole point is that the English courts are assisting foreign courts to facilitate proceedings abroad. Judges are generally vigilant to prevent foreign revenue laws from being enforced through the English courts and the principle was recently reaffirmed in strong terms by the Court of Appeal in *QRS 1 APS v. Flemming Frandsen [1999] STC 616*. This rule is generally encountered in the context of civil proceedings, but there is no reason why it should not also apply in the hitherto unusual situation where an English court seeks to apply criminal penalties to foreign tax evasion.

10.15   There is no doubt that the current view of the UK Government is that the legislation does extend to cover the proceeds of foreign tax evasion, as was made clear in evidence to the Treasury Select Committee on 28 February 2000. However, this is not necessarily the view which will be adopted by the Courts when the matter arises in a specific case. An English judge would come to the construction of *section 93A(7)* with the Government of India principle in mind. There would be a natural aversion to the indirect enforcement of French revenue law by reference to the geographical deeming provision in *subsection (7)*. Conduct which is directed towards the defrauding of a foreign revenue authority cannot be treated as if it was directed towards defrauding the UK revenue authorities, irrespective of the place where criminal conduct may or may not have actually occurred. The conclusion stated above, namely that a professional need not be concerned for the purposes of English criminal law with breaches of foreign revenue statutes is not undermined by the definition of 'criminal conduct' in *section 93(A)(7)* of the *1988 Act*.

10.16   The real problem is not that of a deemed breach of UK revenue laws but rather the breach of general English criminal law as a result of the notional translation of the occurrence of criminal conduct provided by *section 93A(7)* of the *1988 Act*. In many cases of foreign tax evasion, the conduct in question is deceptive and fraudulent in the broad sense. Treating such conduct, if in fact taking place abroad, as notionally taking place in England, then even if one does not replace the French revenue authorities with the English revenue authorities, one may well have the elements of an offence under English law, quite irrespective of English tax law as such. In particular, there may well be a case disclosed of false accounting, the obtaining of money by deception, or a conspiracy to defraud, which does not depend on the commission of a substantive offence other than the fraudulent conspiracy (i.e., agreement) itself.

10.17   How does the *Government of India* principle apply here? It seems that it may well still apply insofar as, for example, in the case of conspiracy to defraud, the defrauded party is the foreign revenue authority. The refusal to enforce French revenue law seems also to extend, as a matter of principle, to a case where the foreign revenue authority might dress up its complaint as a conspiracy to defraud it, i.e., the revenue authority itself. But foreign tax evasion may often involve not just the taxpayer and the foreign revenue authority themselves.

10.18   Where offshore activity designed to defraud a foreign revenue authority is something more than simply a denial of revenue to that authority, then *section 93A* of the *1988 Act* may well apply. False accounting may be the easiest case. Tax evasion, as opposed to tax avoidance, frequently involves false accounting. If such activity occurs in France, albeit as part of an attempt to deprive the French authorities of revenue, then *section 93A(7)* treats such activity as if it had physically taken place in England. If it had physically taken place in England, then irrespective of any tax offences, the offence of false accounting would have been disclosed. It is hard see any way round this.

10.19   Conspiracy to defraud is more complicated but is dangerous from the point of view of the professional. If the dishonest conduct has the effect not only of defrauding the foreign revenue authority but also some other party, for instance the taxpayer's wife or business partner, then there is nothing in the *Government of India* principle which would prevent *section 93A(7)* from making such activity criminal, even if all relevant acts took place abroad. Had they taken place in England, they would have constituted the common law offence of conspiracy to defraud. Provided that this is not a back door way of enforcing foreign revenue laws, there is no reason why the wording in the *1993 Act* should not be given full force. Tax fraud is sometimes accompanied by other frauds and, as pointed out below in the discussion on constructive trust, a professional who is forced to admit that he knew that his client was engaged in tax fraud is in a difficult position if it turns out that the fraud was not only on the tax authorities but on others.

10.20   An interesting counter-example is exchange control. Professionals often find themselves advising clients who are seeking to circumvent, and sometimes to evade foreign exchange control regulations. It might be thought that such activity would come within *section 93A* of the *1988 Act*, but that is clearly not the case. Since 1980 exchange control has not existed in the United Kingdom, and it has therefore not been possible for acts, wherever they might physically be conducted, to constitute criminal conduct in England by virtue of the circumvention or evasion of exchange control regulations. Thus, however blatant the activity may be, if all that the professional's client is seeking to do is to evade foreign exchange control, and there is no other element to his activity, the professional cannot become liable under the criminal law by virtue of the provisions of the *1993 Act*.

10.21   Two other situations might be dealt with briefly. In some foreign jurisdictions, there are rules providing for community of property or other similar property regimes between husband and wife. These rules may be infringed by arrangements in which professionals are asked to assist. However, since there are no such rules in the UK, it seems to me that the answer in this respect must be similar to that which obtains in the case of exchange control. In England, dispositions may be set aside if they have the effect of adversely affecting the rights of wife against her former husband, but such activity would not be criminal. The same is probably true, and indeed more clearly true, in relation to foreign forced heirship rules such as are frequently found in foreign jurisdictions. A professional may be asked to assist an individual to evade mandatory provisions of a foreign law whereby certain fixed proportions of the individual's estate must pass to particular relatives. This sort of activity, however, could not be criminal in England and Wales (although Scotland may here be somewhat different) since the only similar provision of English law is the *Inheritance (Provision for Family and Dependants) Act 1975* which enables a court to order financial provision from an estate where reasonable financial provision has not been made for a particular relative or dependant. Again, however, this is nothing to do with criminal law. Attempts by an individual during his lifetime to prefer certain prospective beneficiaries to close family members is not criminal conduct.

10.22   The most likely practical situation in which a professional might find himself embroiled in *section 93A* as a result of advising or assisting in relation to purely offshore activities relates to the offence of false accounting. Many of the activities discussed above, including attempts to evade foreign revenue legislation, will involve activity which, if it took place physically in England, would amount to false accounting as defined in the *Theft Act 1968*. A professional who assists his client in such activity, even if he thinks that the activity has got nothing whatsoever to do with England or indeed the United Kingdom, could find himself ensnared by *section 93A*. This may be beyond anything which the legislature intended to enact when it brought in provisions to deal with money laundering and similar matters. Nonetheless, it is clear that the provisions under consideration do have an effect much wider than money laundering, and that offshore activity of the sort discussed above does come within the ambit of the *1993 Act* and the *1988 Act* into which the relevant provisions have been inserted.

10.23   It might be helpful to end this part of the discussion with an example, perhaps in part to reassure professional practitioners, but also to illustrate the scope of false accounting under English law. Suppose that a manufacturing company in a high tax jurisdiction manufactures plastic containers which it sells to a company in a low tax jurisdiction such as the Cayman Islands at an undervalue. The company in Cayman then sells the items on to a third party at their full market value. As a consequence, the profit will have largely been derived by the company in the low tax jurisdiction. The accounts of each company will reflect the price actually received or paid for the merchandise. It seems to me that in such a case, although there has been a sale at 'an undervalue' there has not been any relevant criminal conduct. The relevance of an 'undervalue' primarily arises in the event of insolvency (as to which see in particular *section 238* of the *Insolvency Act 1986*). The mere sale at an undervalue does not involve criminal conduct. There is no false accounting, because the accounts of each company truly reflect the transaction which has occurred. If the manufacturing company becomes insolvent, there may well be claims against the Cayman company arising out of the sale at an undervalue, but if the two companies are in the same group it may be said that the overall transaction was beneficial to the group and does not constitute impropriety. The crucial point is whether or not there is a dishonest or false statement in the records of the companies or individuals involved in such transactions. In many cases of tax fraud there will be dishonest documentation. The presence or absence of such false documentation will often be critical as to whether *section 93A* of the *1988 Act* applies or not.

'Knowing or suspecting'

10.24   Insofar as the new legislation applies to persons who actually know the relevant facts, it may be thought that despite the stringency and wide ambit of the new offences, they are only fair and reasonable. A professional adviser who actually knows that his client is involved in dishonest activity, even if that is conducted offshore as part of an attempt to evade foreign income tax, may be thought by many to be legitimately at risk of being implicated in that dishonest activity, perhaps even by the commission of a criminal offence. But what of 'suspecting'? *Section 93A* talks of 'knowing or suspecting that A is a person who is or has been engaged in criminal conduct or has benefited from criminal conduct'. This is potentially very worrying for professionals involved in trust estate or tax planning work. Such professionals frequently suspect or have cause to suspect that transactions on which they are asked to advise are not 100 per cent above board. The client will not usually tell the adviser more than he needs to know, and the adviser who deliberately sets about effecting a dishonest purpose does not deserve much sympathy. What, however, of the ordinary practitioner who puts into effect arrangements which are not on their face illegal or even dishonest, but where there is suspicion that the client is involved either in attempts to evade tax, or possibly to defeat the interests of other persons in the property?

10.25   Much will depend here on how strict the courts are in interpreting the concept of 'suspecting' in this context. It does not seem to me that the courts are likely to regard this phrase as including simply the worldly cynicism of the experienced tax adviser. In order for somebody to suspect something he must have solid grounds for that suspicion. Something more than a bad smell is required and the client is entitled to the benefit of the assumption that he is not involved in criminal conduct unless there is reason to believe that he is so involved.

10.26   A further point is available to be made by the professional adviser in this context. *Section 93A* makes it clear that it is a defence for a person to prove that he did not know or suspect that the arrangement in question related to any person's proceeds of criminal conduct. In other words, even if there was a suspicion that A was involved in criminal conduct, the professional will not be liable if he did not suspect that the arrangement of which the professional was involved related to the 'proceeds of criminal conduct'. To return to the example of the client who receives offshore the emoluments from an employment where there has been no deduction of tax at source in accordance with PAYE regulations. Assume that a professional suspects that such activity has occurred. His client maintains considerable funds offshore, only some of which come from his UK employer. If the professional becomes involved in making arrangements for the investment or disposal of such monies, how is he to know what part if any of those funds represents the proceeds of criminal conduct? In the first place the money is mixed, but more importantly it does not follow from the fact that the client may have been involved in tax evasion that the sums accruing offshore, even if deriving directly from the UK employment, necessarily constitute the 'proceeds' of UK tax evasion. In other words, although the 'proceeds of criminal conduct' can include sums retained as a result of fraud on tax authorities and is not limited to monies obtained from a fraud, the fact that the obligation to pay tax is not in general fund-specific does have a relevance as to the extent to which the professional can contend that he did not have reasonable cause to suspect that particular monies passing through his hands represented the proceeds of criminal conduct. They may in fact do so, but from the point of view of the professional he will often have no idea whether or not the client is accounting for the tax due out of other funds (whether or not the PAYE regulations have been infringed).

10.27   The courts will be vigilant to require that if the professional is to be found guilty under *section 93A*, he must not only suspect criminal activity, but have solid grounds for suspecting that particular funds with which he is dealing represent monies deriving from the client's criminal conduct. In a case where a professional is privy only to a small part of an individual's financial affairs, this point seems to me to be of importance. Conversely, if the professional is fully versed in all aspects of the client's financial affairs, it will be difficult for him to maintain a defence under *section 93A(4)* where he knows or suspects that monies he is being asked to invest or dispose of represent monies which the client has in his hand as the benefit of criminal conduct which he has perpetrated or is in the course of perpetrating.

10.28   Much here will depend on the meaning which the courts give to the word 'suspecting'. If analogy with the law of constructive trusts is legitimate (which may be debatable) then there is likely to be some reluctance on the parts of the courts to hold professionals liable, especially in the criminal context, on the basis of facts which in a sense they ought to know or of which they are 'on notice': see the case law as now summarised by the Privy Council in *Royal Brunei Airlines v Tan [1995] 3 WLR 64*. Whilst suspicion obviously falls short of knowledge, any criminal case must be proved beyond reasonable doubt, and no one is likely to be convicted unless it can be clearly shown that objective facts existed giving rise to a situation where an honest man would have concrete grounds for his suspicion. It may be that the courts would bear in mind in seeking to judge a professional man both (*a*) the probability that Parliament did not really intend to focus on fiscal offences and related matters at all, and (*b*) the general recognition that a man's tax affairs are broadly a matter between him and the Revenue and are quite different from activities such as money laundering.

Civil liability

10.29   Leaving aside cases where a professional man incurs liability to his client in contract or to third parties with whom he has a proximate relationship, such as to give rise to a duty of care in negligence, the likely means by which he may become involved in accessory liability in relation to frauds on third parties is by the law of constructive trust.

10.30   There is a well established distinction between knowing receipt and knowing assistance. Knowing receipt liability, as to which it may well be that the requirements for liability are less stringent (especially in relation to knowledge), only arises where the person sought to be held liable receives money for his own benefit: see *Agip (Africa) Ltd v Jackson [1990] Ch 265*, especially at *291B–292E*. What we are concerned with here is knowing assistance, i.e., becoming involved in a fraud on a third party without the beneficial receipt of trust property. For more than 25 years there has been serious doubt as to what is required to render an accessory liable for knowing assistance, but it is profoundly hoped that the law has now been clarified by the *Royal Brunei Airlines* case referred to above, although an analysis of recent Court of Appeal authority reveals real differences between a harsher view of the requirements which a claimant must satisfy, exemplified by *Heinl v Jyske Bank [1999] Lloyd's Rep Bank 511* and *Grupo Torras v Al Sabah [2001] Lloyd's Rep Bank 36*, and a more objective approach, as seen in *Twinsectra v Yardley [2000] Lloyd's Rep PN 239* and *Walker v Stones [2001] QB 902*. The *Twinsectra* case is under appeal to the House of Lords.

10.31   The Privy Council has now clearly affirmed that liability under this head requires dishonesty on the part of the accessory. Thus, insofar as professionals such as trust or estate practitioners or tax planning advisers find themselves enmeshed in transactions which are frauds on third parties, they do not incur liability to that third party unless they have acted dishonestly, or, as is sometimes said with 'want of probity'. Negligence does not suffice, nor does suspicion. Sighs of relief will no doubt be uttered at this point, but there are still dangers. Dishonesty includes not only obvious and direct dishonesty, but also the deliberate or reckless shutting of eyes to the obvious, which is sometimes referred to as 'Nelsonian knowledge'. If a professional chooses not to ask questions because he would rather not receive the obvious answers, he is in the same position as if he had discovered the truth. If he allows himself to become involved in a transaction which he strongly suspects to be dishonest, but forbears from questioning it and simply keeps his head down, he is at risk of being found liable. There is a huge difference between failing to acquire knowledge which one ought with reasonable care to acquire (which does not attract liability) and putting the means of knowledge deliberately beyond one's reach (which may very well attract liability).

10.32   In this connection, the *Agip* case referred to above is instructive. There a firm of accountants was involved in arrangements whereby it received (not beneficially but for another) funds which were later held to represent the proceeds of a fraud on the plaintiff. In considering whether or not the accountants were guilty of knowing assistance in the fraud or the plaintiff, attention focused on the state of knowledge of the accountants and the degree of their honesty or dishonesty. They gave no evidence to the Court, and it was held by Millett J (as he then was) at first instance *[1990] Ch 265* and also by the Court of Appeal *[1991] Ch 547* that the accountants were liable. They were certainly on notice that the sums received were the proceeds of a fraud, and they put no material before the Court to rebut the inference that they must have known the truth. This was nothing to do with tax fraud, but rather a straightforward case of money laundering. The Courts concluded that the accountants must have known they were laundering money and were consequently helping their clients to make arrangements to conceal dispositions of money which had such a degree of impropriety that neither they nor their clients could afford to have them disclosed.

10.33 This case neatly illustrates where the borderline lies as far as the professional accountant or solicitor is concerned between liability and non-liability. Some think the case is hard on the accountants, but it must be remembered that the courts were effectively saying that they were dishonest and that their silence was eloquent to that effect. Usually, a professional who gives evidence and explains how he did not realise that he was involved in a fraudulent transaction will stand an excellent chance of being believed and escaping liability. Once he puts forward such a case in court, it is incumbent on the plaintiff to show that the professional acted dishonestly or with a reckless disregard for the truth. This is a much higher hurdle than the requirement of showing suspicion of criminal conduct in *section 93A* of the *Criminal Justice Act 1988*.

10.34 In the *Agip* case Millett J considered the merits of an argument put forward on behalf of the accountants that they did not act dishonestly because what they suspected was 'only' a breach of exchange control or 'only' in a case of tax evasion. This approach received a dusty answer from the judge. He said this at page 294H:

> 'What did Mr Jackson and Mr Griffin think was going on? There is some evidence of this in the minutes of the first meeting of the Directors of Keelward Limited of 22 March 1984 and it will be wrong of me to ignore it. This suggests that they thought that their clerk was engaged in evading Tunisian Exchange Control, possibly with the connivance of the Plaintiffs and on their behalf – though the minutes do not say so. In my judgment, however, it is no answer for a man charged with having knowingly assisted in a fraudulent and dishonest scheme to say that he thought that it was "only" a breach of exchange control or "only" a case of tax evasion. It is not necessary that he should have been aware of the precise nature of the fraud or even of the identity of its victim. A man who consciously assists others by making arrangements which he knows are calculated to conceal what is happening from the third party, takes the risk that they are part of a fraud practised on that party'.

10.35 This is salutary advice. Once a professional sinks to a position of knowing that his client is involved in fraudulent activity, he will find it very difficult to argue that he was not sufficiently on notice of a fraud on a particular party. While the courts are very reluctant to enforce, directly or indirectly, foreign revenue law, they do not look kindly on professionals who get involved in what they know to be dishonest activity, even if the professional believes that that is 'only' a fraud on a foreign tax or exchange control authority. A narrower view was taken by Rimer J in *Brinks Ltd v Abu-Saleh (No 3) (Times, 23 October 1995)* and the Court of Appeal in *Grupo Torras v Al Sabah [2001] Lloyd's Rep Bank 36* cautiously approved his approach. This was, however, obiter and the trial judge, Mance J, stated the test to be whether dishonesty could be shown 'towards the plaintiff in relation to property held or potentially held on trust or constructive trust'. The practical advice to professionals must be to guard against the position that the view of Millett J is correct. If the professional is acting honestly in general, he will not be liable for knowing assistance, and he will have the Court's sympathy if faced with a charge under *section 93A* of the *1988 Act*. Conversely, if he is acting dishonestly or closing his eyes to the obvious, he is very exposed in both situations, whatever technical arguments may be available to him.

10.36   A final point to make in connection with knowing assistance is that a professional can take no refuge, where he gets involved in laundering the proceeds of a fraud, by pointing to the fact that the monies have passed through a series of foreign jurisdictions before they reached him. In *El Ajou v Dollar Land Holdings Plc [1994] 2 All ER 685* the Court of Appeal affirmed the views of Millett J (as he then was) at *[1993] 3 AER 717* to the effect that money can be traced pursuant to English laws of tracing even though they pass through a series of foreign jurisdictions which do not have any such rules, or indeed any rules of tracing at all. In that case a fraud was perpetrated which caused money to move from Geneva to Gibraltar to Panama and back to Geneva before arriving in London. An argument was rejected to the effect that the monies could not be traced to London unless the rules of each jurisdiction through which the money passed permitted the continued identity of the plaintiff's funds to be recognised. Since the money ended up in England and it was the English court which was deciding the liability of the recipients in London according to English law, the laws of the intervening jurisdictions were held to be irrelevant.

10.37   Thus, if a professional practising in England receives money from his client which he has reason to believe derives from a fraud, he can be liable as constructive trustee (providing all the necessary requirements are met) without being able to argue in his favour that monies cease to belong to the plaintiff because they passed through jurisdictions which would not have recognised the plaintiff's continuing proprietary interest in those monies. This is a simple and beneficial rule and (although the Court of Appeal differed from Millett J on other aspects of the case), this point attracted little attention on appeal, and cannot be regarded as controversial as a matter of English law. Thus, the matter comes down even more clearly to a question of whether or not the professional has behaved dishonestly, assuming that the plaintiff can trace the money into his hands at least as a matter of the English legal principles of tracing.

Conclusion

10.38   The rules on civil liability discussed above should not worry the honest and diligent practitioner. It is tempting to seek to apply the principles of civil law by analogy to the provisions of the criminal law contained in *section 93A* (and to a lesser extent *93B* and *93C*) of the *Criminal Justice Act 1988*. It is tempting to argue that professionals should not be condemned for criminal misconduct where they would not be liable at all in a civil suit, but there is a limit to the extent to how far this can be pressed. The provisions of the statute are very different, and they were clearly intended to be enforced as part of the international war against money laundering. It is perhaps unfortunate that the UK legislature has strayed beyond the confines of the

EC Directive so as to include all forms of indictable criminal conduct under the criminal umbrella. Unfortunate or not, there are clear danger signs for professionals practising in trusts, estates and tax planning. Whilst they need not make themselves experts on foreign law, they need to look very hard at transactions in which they become involved, even if apparently offshore, to see whether the facts known to them would, if they all took place in the United Kingdom, constitute a criminal offence. This requires a certain knowledge of English criminal law, particularly the provisions of the *Theft Acts* and the law of conspiracy, at least in outline.

10.39   Where a professional knows facts which lead him to conclude that a criminal offence would have been conducted if the facts had all occurred in England, he has an uncertain basis for escape if the best he can do is to argue that he did not know what would constitute criminal conduct in England. He also has the problem that the phrasing of *section 93A* throws the burden of proof on to the defendant, once he suspects that his client has been involved in criminal conduct. These legislative innovations require professionals to tighten their working practices and adopt a stricter approach than hitherto to the extent to which they can turn a blind eye to the true commercial purpose behind transactions in which they are instructed to advise and participate. This may impose a burden on the professionals, but it is arguable that this may be justified in the interests of worldwide efforts to reduce crime. Further legislative innovations are imminent, and one can be certain that these will do nothing to reduce the burden of protection against what is now, especially in the current climate of anti-terrorist activity, regarded as a serious social evil. It is only a few years ago that the phrase 'money laundering' was coined. It is now a settled term in the vocabulary of anyone who has any concern in the flow of money.

11 Non-Resident Entertainers

Richard Citron MA (Cantab) FCA FTII TEP
(BDO Stoy Hayward)

Introduction

11.1   Non-resident entertainers and sportsmen have always presented a problem to national revenue authorities. Governments have thought it proper to try and extract tax from entertainers who perform in their countries, but for those who operate a residence-based system of taxation, such as the UK, the difficulty has been that the entertainer's presence is seldom long enough for him or her to become resident. Non-residents are, of course, chargeable to UK tax on their profits arising here, but, unless there was a person in this country to whom liability could be attached, the Revenue was often unable even to gather sufficient information to raise an assessment before the entertainer had left the country. As the sums of money involved became ever greater, this problem intensified. Accordingly, in his 1986 Budget speech, the then Chancellor of the Exchequer, Nigel Lawson, expressed concern at what he called the 'pay as you please' system of taxation that operated for non-resident entertainers and sportsmen. He claimed that the UK was losing some £75 million annually through failure to collect tax due from entertainers for their appearances in this country. To remedy this situation, he proposed to introduce a withholding tax on all direct or indirect earnings, leaving the true liability to be settled in due course. The necessary legislation was enacted in fairly skeletal form in *FA 1986, Sch 11 paras 1–11* (now *ICTA 1988, ss 555–558*). Flesh was put on this legislation by the *Income Tax (Entertainers and Sportsmen) Regulations 1987 (SI 1987 No 530)*. It is interesting to note that the amount actually collected in 1998/99 was £26.5 million, although it should be pointed out that original tax projections included proposed withholding tax on record royalties; this was not, subsequently, included in the legislation as enacted.

11.2   The existence of the regulations adds a third layer to the UK adviser's task in dealing with the tax affairs of a non-resident entertainer or sportsman (referred to hereon as an 'entertainer'). Once the withholding tax has or has not been applied, the entertainer's actual UK tax liability has to be negotiated and agreed. Moreover, in considering both these aspects, the adviser will have to weigh up the interaction between UK domestic law, including the regulations, and any relevant double tax treaties, most of which have special provisions dealing with entertainers.

Inland Revenue administration

11.3   When the regulations were introduced, the Revenue reorganised its internal structure for dealing with overseas entertainers. The special foreign artistes section of Covent Garden district, which had been the office previously dealing with overseas entertainers, was disbanded and a new Foreign Entertainers Unit (FEU) was set up in Birmingham. FEU is now under the aegis of the Special Compliance Office and deals with all aspects of the tax affairs of overseas entertainers other than cases where PAYE operates, e.g., a foreign rugby league player would normally have PAYE deducted by his club. The PAYE aspect is usually dealt with at local district level. FEU is, thus, the office that administers and enforces the withholding tax levied under the regulations themselves and is responsible for determining the entertainer's eventual liability to UK tax, including nearly all investigations work. The address of FEU is:

Inland Revenue
Special Compliance Office
Foreign Entertainers Unit
Royal House
Prince's Gate
2–6 Homer Road
SOLIHULL
West Midlands B91 3WG
Tel: (0121) 712 8600 Fax: (0121) 712 8662
E-mail: sco.ir.birm@gtnet.gov.uk

Taxation of non-UK residents

11.4   A person who is not resident in the UK is normally taxable only on income arising in the UK, although this liability may be restricted further by the terms of a double tax treaty.

This general rule applies to income from a trade, profession or vocation carried on in the UK [*ICTA 1988, s 18(1)(a)(iii)*], taxable under Schedule D, Case I or II, and to emoluments of an employment, taxable under Schedule E, Case II [*ICTA 1988, s 19(1)*] to the extent that the duties are performed in the UK. Therefore, an entertainer working in the UK will *prima facie* be liable to UK tax on his or her earnings.

The withholding tax

11.5   The withholding requirement on account of the entertainer's final liability is central to the regime *of ICTA 1988, ss 555–558* .

Scope of the regulations

11.6   The withholding tax applies where an 'entertainer or sportsman of a prescribed description performs an activity of a prescribed description' in the UK in a year of assessment in which he or she is non-resident. [*ICTA*

1988, s 555(1)]. These activities are called 'relevant activities'. In such circumstances, the payer of a payment (or the transferor of a 'transfer') having a 'connection of a prescribed kind with the relevant activity' and made to whatever person (whether or not resident in the UK) must account to the Revenue for a 'sum representing income tax'. In the case of a payment, that sum must be deducted from the payment. [*ICTA 1988, s 555(2)(3)*].

An entertainer or sportsman of a prescribed description is:

'any description of individuals (and whether performing alone or with others) who give performances in their character as entertainers or sportsmen in any kind of entertainment or sport; and "entertainment or sport" in this definition includes any activity of a physical kind, performed by such an individual, which is or may be made available to the public or any section of the public and whether for payment or not'.

[*SI 1987 No 530, reg 2(1)*].

11.7 A 'relevant activity' is, briefly, either an activity performed in the UK by an entertainer in his or her character as entertainer on a commercial occasion or event or an activity performed in the UK by an entertainer in his or her character as such in connection with a commercial occasion or event. [*SI 1987 No 530, reg 6(2)*].

11.8 A payment or transfer has a 'connection of a prescribed kind' with a relevant activity where it is made for, or in respect, of the performance of that relevant activity or it derives in any way directly or indirectly from such a performance [*SI 1987 No 530, reg 3(2)*] or, as paragraph A1 of the Inland Revenue Booklet FEU 50 'Payer's Guide: Foreign Entertainers' puts it a good deal more succinctly:

'Any payer who makes a payment, to any person, which in any way arises directly or indirectly from a UK appearance by a non-resident entertainer must deduct tax at the basic rate.'

This statement must be tempered by the knowledge that it is possible, with the prior agreement of FEU, to withhold at a lower rate (see 11.24–11.28 below).

The above specialised terms and definitions require clarification.

Entertainer or sportsman

11.9 In many cases, it is obvious whether an individual is or is not an entertainer. Unfortunately, the definition in the regulations (see 11.6 above) is not helpful in cases of doubt. The definition does limit itself to individuals giving a performance, so it must exclude related professions such as football managers, cricket umpires and referees generally, as well as producers, directors, playwrights, screenwriters, stage and film technicians, road managers etc. Booklet FEU 50 cites the following (non-exclusive) occupations: athletes, golfers, cricketers, footballers, tennis players, boxers, snooker players, darts players, motor-racing drivers, jockeys, ice skaters, contestants in chess tournaments, pop stars, musicians, conductors, dancers, actors, TV and radio personalities and variety artistes (paragraph A6). Only chess players, and, possibly, conductors, might not have immediately fallen within a common sense definition of entertainer or sportsman.

However, if the test of an entertainer is put in another context, the concept might become easier to understand. An entertainer is someone who is paid and has his or her performance eventually watched by the public. Therefore, the professional chess player and conductor are entertainers. However, those who are out of the public eye, for example, directors and producers behind the camera, and stagehands who are off-stage, are not entertainers.

The Inland Revenue list of 'back stage' occupations for the quite independent purpose of determining whether PAYE should be applied is a useful general guide as to whether or not the individual is an entertainer. This list is given in Appendix 11:1 at the end of this chapter.

Relevant activity

11.10   We have already seen that a relevant activity is one performed by the entertainer (in his or her character as such) on, or in connection with, a commercial event or occasion. Specifically included are:

(*a*)   an appearance by the entertainer in the promotion of a commercial event or occasion;

(*b*)   an appearance by the entertainer in connection with the promotion of a commercial event or occasion;

(*c*)   participation in a sound recording, film or video, or in a live or recorded radio, television or other similar transmission.

[*SI 1987 No 530, reg 6(2)*].

Thus, if a singer agrees to give an interview on a TV programme in order to promote a forthcoming concert, he or she may not be appearing in his or her character as a singer, but the appearance is nevertheless a relevant activity.

11.11   A 'commercial occasion or event' is not itself defined, but the regulations again give specific examples. Accordingly, any occasion or event

(*a*)   for which any person might receive or become entitled to receive cash or any other form of property by virtue of the entertainer's performance of the relevant activity, or

(*b*)   which is designed to promote commercial sales or activity by advertising, the endorsement of goods or services, sponsorship or other promotional means

is a commercial occasion or event. [*SI 1987 No 530, reg 6(3)*].

The sort of activities falling within head (*b*) above would include an appearance by a famous actor at the opening of a supermarket in order to attract custom, or by a tennis player in a TV advertisement for a particular type of soft drink. It does not matter that the entertainer himself or herself might not receive any payment: it is enough that some other person receives or becomes entitled to a payment, in cash or kind, as a result of the entertainer's appearance.

Performance in the UK

11.12   It is clear that the relevant activity need not be carried out in front of an immediate audience, since participation in a sound or TV recording etc. is explicitly included. [*SI 1987 No 530, reg 6(2)(b)*]. However, FEU will not regard an appearance by an entertainer in a video recording made abroad but broadcast or replayed in the UK as constituting a relevant activity.

Where part of the entertainer's performance will take place in the UK and part elsewhere (e.g., a singer may undertake a European tour, with some dates in the UK and some in continental Europe or a film being shot largely in the UK may involve some shooting in overseas locations), withholding will only be required from the payments for UK work. Normally, an apportionment can be made on an appropriate basis (e.g., a time basis would be appropriate for the film example cited above, or a concerts basis might be more appropriate for the singer example). Separate contracts can be drawn up, one for UK work and one for overseas work, with an appropriate split of fees between them. FEU will always look 'behind the paperwork' to the actual facts to check that the contracts truly represent the position. Also, separate contracts can be drawn up where the entertainer has another 'behind the camera' or 'off-stage' role, e.g., an actor-producer. Even separate contracts for overseas rehearsals are possible. FEU will usually closely review all such arrangements to ensure they correspond more or less with commercial reality.

Payment or transfer

11.13   We have seen that, in principle, any payment or transfer directly or indirectly connected with the performance of a relevant activity falls within the scope of the rules.

A 'payment' specifically includes a loan of money. [*ICTA 1988, s 555(5)(a)*]. A transfer is not defined but obviously refers to a payment or loan in kind, such as the award of a car as a tournament prize, or, commonly, the provision of airline tickets for the entertainer and his family or staff. A transfer is not a transfer of money but can be a temporary transfer (where, for example, an entertainer is given the use of a car while in the UK) or the transfer of a right (e.g., to receive money). [*ICTA 1988, s 555(5)(b)*].

Booklet FEU 50 gives examples of the payments the Revenue considers as subject to the rules: appearance fees, achievement bonuses, exhibition income, box-office percentages, TV rights, broadcasting and media fees, tournament winnings, prize money, advertising income, merchandising income, endorsement fees, film fees and tour income. They will also include daily (*per diem*) and other expense allowances. Most of these are, again, fairly obvious, but not all of them would seem to fall within the legislation in every circumstance. For instance, a performance must include a physical activity of some description. [*SI 1987 No 530, reg 2(1)*]. Where, for example, an entertainer allows use of existing still photographs of himself or herself to be used in promotional brochures, no physical activity is taking place and the payment is not subject to withholding tax. In the case of film, an entertainer may be able to sell his or her rights to prevent distribution of the film in various territories for up to 263 per cent of his fee by virtue of the PACT:Equity agreement. Withholding should probably also be applied to these payments.

11.14   However, it should be noted that participation in a 'film' is a relevant activity. [*SI 1987 No 530, reg 6(2)(b)*]. The meaning of 'film' is extended by *SI 1987 No 530, reg 6(4)* to include a sequence of visual images capable of being used as a moving or still picture. Hence, if the entertainer is filmed or photographed especially for the purpose of using a series of photographs for a promotional brochure, payments for making the film are caught. Payments to the photographer in such circumstances are not normally regarded by the FEU as falling within the regulations.

11.15   To fall within the rules, payments or transfers have to be made in connection with the *performance* of a relevant activity. Where there is no performance, there ought, therefore, to be no withholding tax liability. So a cancellation fee paid by the promoter compensating an entertainer for cancellation of his or her performance or insurance recovery, will not be within the scope of the rules. It is understood, however, that in such situations FEU will still want to exclude any expenses associated with the cancelled performance(s) (including the costs of cancellation insurance) from any overall consideration of UK income and expenditure. FEU has reached this position after taking legal advice; until recently, it was reluctant to accept that cancellation fees or insurance recoveries fell outside the scheme at all.

11.16   Four types of payment are exempted by the regulations.

(*a*)   Payments from which tax has already to be deducted under some other provision of the *Taxes Acts*, such as remuneration subject to PAYE.

(*b*)   Payments *to an entertainer* for record royalties, that is, payments calculated by reference to the proceeds of sale of records produced from a sound recording made by the entertainer (or payments on account of those payments, e.g., an advance). The Revenue interprets this exemption to include a non-recoupable advance (Booklet FEU 50, paragraph A8), although it is, strictly speaking, not a payment on account.

'Record' is nowhere defined, in either the legislation or the regulations; the normal dictionary definition would appear to include a compact disc, but not a tape cassette. Nevertheless, the exemption is in practice applied to all the conventional means of reproduction: black vinyl, pre-recorded cassettes and compact discs (see FEU 50, paragraph A8), and now, presumably, also DVDs. With respect to videos, in some cases there is no withholding tax and in some cases there is. Music videos may not be subject to withholding but royalties on videos of concerts will always require withholding tax. The prior agreement of FEU should be obtained to establish the correct procedure.

(*c*)   Payments to persons resident and ordinarily resident in the UK for services ancillary to the performance of the relevant activity. The payments must not exceed arm's length values and the persons must neither be connected with, nor be associates of, the entertainer. The usual meanings of 'connected person' [*ICTA 1988, s 839*] and 'associate' [*ICTA 1988, s 417(3)*] are used.

(*d*)   Payments that, taken together with other connected payments and the value of connected transfers in the tax year, do not exceed £1,000 (see also 11.18 below).

[*SI 1987 No 530, reg 3(3)*].

Ancillary services

11.17   This exemption is meant to cover expenses such as the hire of a hall or other venue, payment for security, stage hands, equipment hire, advertising, ticket printing, hire of chairs, barriers or marquees, lighting, PA equipment etc. Clearly, in order to come within this exemption, all ancillary services should be purchased from UK-resident suppliers, who need to be independent of the entertainer or his or her associates. If the stage hands or roadies are employed by a company with which the entertainer is in partnership, for example, the payments are not exempt. Where possible, it is also better to hire rather than purchase equipment etc. outright. This is because the exemption applies to services but not to goods. Whatever the original intention of the legislation, therefore, payments for costumes and equipment (rather than costume or equipment hire), even where made to a UK company, seem, in principle, to be subject to the withholding rules. In practice, however, FEU does not as a rule seek to impose withholding tax on such payments when made to independent third parties.

Where a lump-sum payment is made (e.g., for recording a concert by a non-resident entertainer), part of which covers the entertainer's fees and part of which is intended to provide payment for exempt ancillary services, an apportionment has to be made and withholding tax applied to the part not specifically exempt. Generally speaking, where any payment or transfer is partly in respect of a relevant activity and partly not, it has to be apportioned in a manner that is 'just and reasonable'. [*SI 1987 No 530, reg 16(2)*].

De minimis exemption

Theory

11.18   No tax need be deducted (strictly speaking, the regulations refer to the making of a nil payment to the Revenue) where the total of 'connected payments' and 'connected transfers' in the tax year made to the entertainer, an associate or connected party is £1,000 or less. 'Connected' payments and transfers made by any other person connected with the payer are taken into account. [*SI 1987 No 530, reg 4(3)(b)*]. A 'connected' payment or transfer is any payment or transfer with the prescribed connection, i.e., one to which the regulations apply. [*SI 1987 No 530, reg 3(2)*].

Although the regulations do not specifically limit the scope in this way, Booklet FEU 50 treats the £1,000 limit as applying to any one payer at a time. So, according to paragraph A8 of Booklet FEU 50, a payer need only take into account payments made by himself and his connected parties and associates in deciding whether the limit applies; not all payments made or to be made in that year of assessment by all persons to the entertainer or his or her associates. A note of caution is in order, however. The wider meaning, however unreasonable, is what the regulations themselves appear to suggest.

A payer ought not to avail himself of the *de minimis* exemption unless it is reasonably clear in advance that the payments (including payments for expenses) will not exceed £1,000. If the payer knows he will be making, say, three payments of £400 in the same tax year, tax should be deducted from each of the payments in turn. Where it is not certain that payments will remain below £1,000 the payer would be well advised to deduct tax, retain it and come to an arrangement with the entertainer about repayment and ultimate liability for interest on overdue tax.

Practice

11.19   FEU may not accept that entertainers paid below the *de minimis* limit will not return to the UK before the end of the tax year, and hence merely because their payment for this particular trip to the UK is less than £1,000 that does not mean they will not earn more than £1,000 over the whole year to 5 April.

However, FEU cannot disregard the *de minimis* limit. It is up to the payer as to whether or not to withhold if he or she is making a payment beneath the *de minimis* limit, but the payer would be advised to err on the side of caution. Since, in general, the entertainer will be liable to tax in his or her home country on a calendar-year basis, he or she will be able to credit the UK tax, and hence, it may not be worth arguing with FEU about the withholding.

With respect to the US$15,000 *de minimis* limit in the UK–US Treaty, this will only ever be applicable towards, or after, the end of the tax year, see

11.43–11.47 below. From 1 January to 5 April (towards the end of the tax year) FEU is more likely than in earlier months to agree that the entertainer will not return before the end of the tax year and hence, will agree to waive the withholding. It also becomes more important for the entertainer not to suffer tax in this last quarter of the UK tax year as, generally, the tax year of the foreign entertainer will be to 31 December, and, therefore, double tax relief will be deferred one year as compared to payments of UK tax prior to 31 December.

Calculating the deduction

11.20   Where a payment or loan is made, the calculation of the tax deduction is simple. Assuming that no application for reduced tax payment (RTP) has been made (see 11.24–11.28 below), the amount to be deducted is 22 per cent (the basic rate of income tax) of the payment or loan. [*SI 1987 No 530, reg 4(2)*].

Where a transfer is made, the actual value of what is transferred is taken as a net amount after deduction of tax at the basic rate. The net value must, therefore, be grossed up to arrive at the amount treated as paid to the entertainer or some other person. The actual value of the asset transferred is measured not by reference to its market value, as might be expected, but by the cost of providing it, less any amount reimbursed *by the entertainer*. The cost of providing the asset includes any cost incurred in providing it to the transferor. [*SI 1987 No 530, reg 17*].

Example

Fielding, an international grandmaster chess player, resident in Ireland, is awarded £3,000 and a Citroën Saxo, which cost the organisers £7,800, for winning a UK chess tournament. The amount the organisers *must account for* (in the absence of an RTP claim) is:

Amount of payment	£3,000
Gross value of asset transferred	
£7,800 × 100/78 =	£10,000
Total treated as paid	£13,000
Tax to be *accounted for* at 22%	£2,860

If the Saxo is worth £7,800 on the open market but cost the organisers only £6,000 (in return for advertising opportunities, say) the gross value to be taken into account in calculating Fielding's withholding tax would have been £7,692 (i.e. £6,000 grossed up at 22 per cent). Since the legislation cannot oblige the payer to deduct tax at a greater rate than the basic rate from any payment, the organisers in the above example would not be expected to deduct the full £2,860 tax owing from the £3,000 cash payment. The Inland Revenue would expect the organisers to deduct £660 from the payment and account for the remaining £2,200 separately under the quarterly accounting procedure.

11.21   Clearly, if the cost of providing the asset is less than its market value, the entertainer will derive a substantial benefit.

What is not clear is the position where the entertainer is offered free use of an asset already in the transferor's possession. The loan of an asset constitutes a transfer on which withholding tax is due. [*ICTA 1988, s 555(5)(b)*].

Suppose an entertainer is given free use while he or she is in the UK of the promoter's private light aircraft, which cost the promoter £1,000,000. The cost of lending the aircraft may be nil, but on a strict interpretation of the regulations, withholding tax of £282,051 might appear to be payable. However, FEU takes a sensible approach and regards the sum transferred as an additional cost borne by the promoter as a result of the loan (e.g., fuel, airport fees etc.) incurred by the entertainer and met by the promoter. Negotiation of a compromise figure with FEU along these lines would thus be in order, although it is probably best, if at all possible, to avoid such transfers.

A chain of payments

11.22   Quite often payments in respect of an entertainer's appearance will pass along a chain before they reach the entertainer or pass outside the scope of UK tax. In theory, withholding tax has to be deducted at each stage. The regulations contain rules to avoid excessive deductions.

Where a payer has to make a payment but has himself or herself received, in connection with the same entertainer, a payment that was subject to withholding tax, he may treat the previous withholding tax as a payment on account of the tax he or she has to deduct and pay over. [*SI 1987 No 530, reg 4(7)*]. As in most cases the second and subsequent payments will be less than the first, there will usually be no more tax to pay after the first amount of the withholding.

> *Example – strict treatment*
>
> A concert promoter arranges with Shandy Ltd, a UK based management company, for Sterne, a US resident rock singer, to play two dates in the UK on his forthcoming tour of Europe. The promoter pays Shandy Ltd £300,000 less tax. Shandy deducts commission and expenses of £30,000 and pays the balance to Sterne.
>
> The promoter must deduct tax from the payment to Shandy Ltd, as it is connected with Sterne's appearance in the UK and does not fall within any of the exemptions. In turn, Shandy is obliged to deduct tax from its payment to Sterne.
>
> Tax deducted by promoter: £300,000 × 22% = £66,000
>
> Sums received by Shandy Ltd: £234,000
>
> Gross sum payable to Sterne: £204,000
>
> Tax due from Shandy Ltd: £204,000 × 22% = £44,880
>
> As the promoter's £66,000 exceeds the £44,880 due from Shandy, Shandy can treat its withholding tax as paid.

Example – FEU booklet treatment

Shandy still pays the net amount (£155,120) to Sterne but need not pay anything over to the Revenue. The balance of tax suffered by Shandy (£66,000 – £44,880) = £21,120) is available for set-off or repayment. Sterne is treated as having paid £44,880 towards his ultimate liability.

Tax deducted by promoter: £300,000 × 22% − £66,000

Sums received by Shandy Ltd: £234,000

Paid to Sterne: £204,000 – £44,880 = £159,120

Shandy Ltd subject to corporation tax on: £234,000 – £159,120 = £74,880

Corporation tax thereon at 30% = £22,464

Withholding tax suffered = £66,000

No corporation tax to pay.

Tax refundable: £66,000 – £44,880 = £21,120

Payment chains and 'middleman' applications

11.23   Where payments are made in a chain, say, from venue to promoter to entertainer, tax would normally have to be withheld at each stage, subject to the franking rules described in 11.41. In order to avoid the possibility of multiple withholding, payers may apply to FEU for an arrangement allowing the point of withholding further down the chain. If such an application (known as a 'middleman application') is successful, payments between specified payers can be made gross. In the above example, the promoter could apply to receive payments gross from the venue.

The rules for making such an application are identical to those for an RTP application. The Inland Revenue will normally require supporting documentation such as copies of contracts, appearance dates and a copy of the budget for the appearance.

There is no need to make specific applications for every event if the promoter or other middleman is eligible for, and joins, the simplified middleman scheme operated by FEU by way of concession. Originally, the scheme was limited to the field of classical music, but was extended to cover all forms of music in April 2001. Performances outside the field of music are apparently not covered by the simplified scheme.

Under the scheme, any UK promoter or merchandiser is eligible, provided he or she is given the nod by FEU. FEU may withhold or withdraw approval if the applicant has, or develops, a poor record of compliance with the legislation. Applicants are required to sign a simple statement (reproduced in Appendix 11:2). Once approved, they are included on a list posted on the Inland Revenue website and are eligible to receive payments gross from venues or concessionaires without the need for a separate application. By referring to the web page, venues or concessionaires can check whether tax needs to be deducted from the payments to the promoter/merchandiser or not. If the promoter's/merchandiser's name does not appear there, and no separate notification of nil payment (a 'nil FEU 4 clearance') has been received, tax should be withheld.

Participating middlemen receive a certificate from FEU as proof of their membership of the scheme. This certificate is of finite duration, but is renewable at FEU's discretion. Membership of the scheme does not relieve the middleman from his duty to withhold tax from payments to, or on behalf, of the entertainer.

Reduced tax payments

11.24   The entertainer's eventual liability will, in many cases, be less than the full rate of withholding tax suffered on payments attributed to him or her. In order to avoid frequent instances of repayment claims, the regulations provide for agreement of a lower rate of withholding with the Revenue.

Making and negotiating an RTP application is an important part of the professional adviser's role in dealing with an entertainer's affairs. Applications may, in fact, be accepted from the entertainer (or via the adviser as agent), the person who receives the payment, if this is not the entertainer, or the payer. [*SI 1987 No 530, reg 4(4)*]. FEU may bypass the entertainer's professional advisers in favour of the production accountant or other persons responsible for these matters in the payer's organisation, especially in film cases when FEU does not know who is advising the entertainer. FEU may even approach film companies in advance to ask whether they intend using foreign entertainers. Obviously, where the entertainer has appointed an adviser, the latter, having knowledge of the entertainer's complete UK (and, where appropriate, overseas) affairs, is in a far better position to handle all dealings, including the RTP application, with the Revenue.

It is the Revenue's duty in considering an RTP application, to aim at receiving a tax payment as near as possible equal to the entertainer's (or other person's) ultimate liability on the payment. [*SI 1987 No 530, reg 4(6)(a)*]. An application must, therefore, be in the form of a computation of the entertainer's liability to UK tax on the income represented by the payment less deductible expenses. An application may be made on a form FEU 8, prepared in this format by the Revenue, or by letter accompanied by a projection of the entertainer's UK source income and expenditure.

11.25   Where the entertainer is not likely to incur many expenses, his or her liability may well be near or even in excess of 22 per cent. Although the Regulations only envisage the making of applications where the ultimate liability is less than 22 per cent of gross payments, FEU will always consider an application where the overall tax rate is in excess of the basic rate. Apart from any other consideration, it is in the interests of fairness to ensure that all non-resident entertainers have an equal opportunity to seek early finality on their UK tax liability — regardless of their level of income. Frequently, however, the entertainer will be expected to bear a considerable amount of expenditure out of his or her fee, and in such circumstances an RTP application is essential. Similarly, where a single payment is made for duties within the UK and overseas, an RTP application must be made.

11.26 What expenses are deductible is, of course, a matter of general law, but the Revenue gives in Booklet FEU 50 (paragraph B7) some examples of the expenses likely to be acceptable. They are general subsistence expenses, manager's and agent's fees and commissions, travel within the UK between performances and international airfares into the UK to the extent they are incurred for the entertainer's notional UK trade (see 11.52 below). FEU 50 implies that return fares are allowable only where an entertainer flies directly back to his or her home country. However, an entertainer who flies to the UK and then on to the continent for a tour, before flying back home, will in, practice, be allowed a proportion of the return fare. The Revenue requires certain specific documents and information to be submitted with an application. These are as follows:

Reduced Tax Payment Applications Standard Requirements

1. Details of all anticipated UK source income from or connected with the relevant activity. This should include not only any guaranteed performance fees but also any income from secondary or ancillary sources such as venue merchandising, income from TV/video/radio rights, sponsorship income and any support or contribution received to supplement income or subsidise expenditure.

2. Verification for each source of income in the form of a copy of the contract or agreement under which each source arises.

3. A schedule setting out the dates covered by the UK activity, indicating the venues and the anticipated chain of payments.

    Where the UK activity represents part of a larger activity, e.g., a concert tour covering various countries or a film involving work in different territories, the nature and extent of activities in each country or territory should be clarified.

4. An itemised schedule of all expenses being claimed as appropriate to the UK activity. Each category of expenditure should indicate the basis on which the figures have been arrived at, with particular reference to the following factors:

    (*a*) where professional commissions [manager, agent etc.] are charged on a percentage basis, the name of the individual/organisation should be shown together with confirmation of the base to which the percentage commission is applied;

    (*b*) where payments are being made to accompanying entertainers, business companions, crew etc., a full schedule of those individuals and their business functions as well as of the payments being made in connection with the UK activity will be required;

(*c*)   evidence should be provided in support of major items of expenditure [for example, in a concert tour the major production costs including – sound, lights, bus/truck hire, equipment rental etc.];

(*d*)   where expenditure is common to the UK and other territories, the basis of any apportionment to the UK should be explained;

(*e*)   where a group of entertainers is involved, the names of the individuals should be supplied, together with an indication of the manner in which the net UK income should be apportioned between them;

(*f*)   a computation of the anticipated UK liability should be provided [to include the liability of any accompanying non-resident entertainers].

(FEU Newsletter no. 7).

11.27   The Revenue is under no obligation to agree to an application and there is no right of appeal against an outright refusal or a decision to require a rate of deduction different to that applied for. The entertainer does, however, have the option of revisiting the whole issue by completing a UK self-assessment return after the end of the year.

The application must be made in writing and at least 30 days before the payment or transfer needs to be made. [*SI 1987 No 530, reg 5(1)*]. The Revenue's agreement, if forthcoming, is communicated on form FEU 4, which will specify how much is to be deducted and, until it has been received, the payer is obliged to deduct tax at the full 22 per cent rate. [*SI 1987 No 530, reg 5(2)*]. The Revenue can authorise deduction either at a lower percentage or of a fixed sum. [*SI 1987 No 530, reg 4(5)*].

11.28   In certain circumstances, the Revenue will instruct the payer to make no deduction at all (i.e., authorise payment gross). This will tend to be the case where the Revenue is satisfied that there is no ultimate liability on the payments in question, or where an amount has been paid on account at least equal to the estimated tax liability from the UK appearances (*SI 1987 No 530, reg 4(6)(b)* and Booklet FEU 50, paragraph B7).

In view of the 30 days' advance notice required, it is sensible to make the RTP application well in advance of the entertainer's arrival, as soon as the details the Revenue needs are reasonably definitive and ascertainable.

Example

Sophia Weston, an American actress, is engaged to appear in a film being shot entirely in the UK. She is to be paid a fee of US$100,000 plus daily allowances estimated at $8,000 in total. She is also given return airline tickets costing

£3,000 for herself and her partner. Her work in the UK is expected to last from 30 June to 5 September 2001 and she does not intend to return to the UK on business again during 2001/02. An RTP application for her film work would look like this:

	£	£
Fees:		
$100,000 @ $1.42 = £1		70,423
'Per diems' ($8,000)		5,634
Airline tickets £3,000 × 100/78		3,846
		79,903
Expenses:		
Agent's commission £70,423 @ 25%	17,606	
Equity fee £70,423 @ 2%	1,408	
Air fares £3,846 × 1/2	1,923	
Accommodation	3,500	
Subsistence	2,700	
UK travel	300	
Accountancy	500	
		27,937
Taxable profits		£51,966
Tax due:		
£1,880 @ 10%		188.00
£27,520 @ 22%		6,054.40
£22,566 @ 40%		9,026.40
		£15,268.80

Effective rate of withholding tax: 19.1%

Notes:

1. Payments in foreign currency have to be translated at the rate applicable at the time of payment.

2. The cost of the airline ticket is grossed up (at 22 per cent) to find the value of the transfer.

3. A fee is usually paid to Equity for its agreement to a foreign artiste's working in the UK.

4. The deductible cost of air fares is limited to Sophia's own fare to the UK and return.

5. The accommodation and subsistence expenses are necessarily estimates, as is the amount of *per diem* allowances, which will be finally known only after Sophia has left the UK.

6. The adviser might consider a claim for medical and other insurance, but unless this is incurred specifically for the film, it is unlikely to be allowed under the duality of purpose rule.

7. Without the RTP, the film production company would have to pay over £79,903 × 22% = £17,579. The difference is not inconsiderable even in this instance, and could be very significant where, for example, the

11–15

entertainer is liable at the basic rate only. If shooting had taken place over the nine weeks between 1 March and 5 May 2001, say, Sophia Weston's presence here would have straddled two tax years. The income and expenses would be apportioned between 2000/01 and 2001/02, but, roughly speaking, she would have had taxable profits of $5/9 \times £51,966 = £28,870$, say, in 2000/01 and $4/9 \times £51,966$, i.e. £23,096, say, in 2001/02. The resulting tax due, and hence withholding tax payable, would have been approximately £11,109, representing an effective withholding rate of 13.9 per cent.

In practice, this straddling of the year end is one of the most important techniques in reducing the final liability of the entertainer, and if necessary the rate of withholding tax as well through an RTP application. An entertainer present over two years is entitled to two 10 per cent and two basic-rate bands, and two personal allowances, where such allowances are given under the relevant double tax treaty (not in the case of the US, as above). See also 11.48ff.

11.29 There has been a tendency for RTP applications to be made late. In 1999, FEU announced (in its Newsletter No 7) that, although it made every reasonable effort to process late applications timeously, there were occasions when such an expectation was unrealistic. It warned that in some circumstances, late applications, particularly those supported by insufficient information, would have to be rejected.

Despite this warning, the situation apparently continued to worsen. In reaction to the growing number of RTP applications (4,500 in 1999/2000) and what was felt the deteriorating quality of those submitted, FEU announced in its Newsletter No 9, November 2000 a new system of monitoring applications on the day of receipt, or as shortly thereafter as possible, to check whether they met certain essential criteria.

According to FEU's data, only 25 per cent of applications in the period under review had been submitted on time. Approximately 10 per cent were submitted less than seven days before the date of the payment, thus leaving almost no time for clarification of any difficult issues. Even worse, from FEU's point of view, another 25 per cent were actually received after the relevant performance had taken place. Many were lacking essential details or supporting documents.

Under the new system, if any of the essential criteria are seen to be lacking, FEU immediately issues a standard letter indicating the missing information. The letter warns the applicant that, if he or she wishes to proceed with the application, they must submit the missing information within seven days of receipt. Failure to do so will result in FEU considering the application to have lapsed.

Submission of the requested information does not, of itself, mean that further enquiries will not be made.

FEU has also warned that it considers so-called advance applications (by which advisers give advance notice of the fact that they intend to make a detailed application at some subsequent stage) as serving no useful purpose, and will not act on them. In particular, the submission of an advance application will not, by itself, satisfy the 30-day time limit.

Becoming UK resident

11.30   It can immediately be seen that one way of avoiding the legislation is for the entertainer to become UK resident. However, taking that course of action may itself create a number of problems. Firstly, *prima facie* UK residents are liable to UK income tax at rates of up to 40 per cent on their worldwide income and gains. Even if a UK-resident entertainer is non-domiciled, all of his or her earnings as a self-employed entertainer may be brought into the UK tax net on the grounds that the entertainer's profession as such was carried on partly inside and partly outside the UK. Under those circumstances, the remittance basis will not be available. It is notoriously difficult (although, in the experience of the author, not impossible) to argue that a non-domiciled UK resident is carrying on separate and distinct self-employments, one in the UK and one outside. Therefore, this technique is only available where the entertainer is an employee with separate UK and non-UK employments. Fortunately, this is often the case, especially with American entertainers.

Techniques for becoming resident include staying more than 183 days in one UK tax year or spending more than three months on average over each of four years. The 183-day test is most useful where the project will last a considerable length of time, and the entertainer will simply remain in the UK slightly longer.

It is, of course, essential that the entertainer remain non-domiciled if he or she is contemplating becoming resident.

Becoming resident may require the entertainer to register for VAT, but that may be only an administrative burden.

PAYE

11.31   As previously mentioned, there is no withholding requirement when payments are made to a foreign entertainer under PAYE.

The territorial extent of PAYE is very broad. Any payment of, or on account of, income assessable under Schedule E by an employer or intermediary is to be made subject to PAYE. [*ICTA 1988, s 203(1)*]. There is no explicit exclusion of non-resident employers or indeed of any category of employer. Clearly, however, the Revenue would face almost insuperable difficulties in attempting to enforce and collect PAYE deductions from employers with no presence in the UK and no intermediate employer or agent to whom liability could be attached.

The extent to which the duty to operate PAYE extended was tested in the courts in *Clark v Oceanic Contractors Inc [1983] STC 35, HL*. In that case, a non-resident company had a UK branch, which operated PAYE in respect of mainland UK employees. However, the company also had employees working in the North Sea within the UK areas of the Continental Shelf. These workers were paid in US dollars, without application of PAYE, from the company's administrative centre in Belgium. By virtue of what is now *ICTA 1988, s 830(5)*, their earnings were assessable under Schedule E as earnings in respect of duties performed in the UK. The Revenue's claim that PAYE had to be applied to those earnings was upheld, on the grounds that the employer had a 'tax presence' in the UK through its branch. Although the employees concerned were not under the general control and management (see 11.32 below) of the branch, the presence of the branch in the UK was sufficient to make the collection of PAYE effective, since the branch was assessable to UK corporation tax, and thus a mechanism existed to ensure that any PAYE deducted could effectively be recovered by the Revenue.

11.32   This concept of a tax presence in the UK has been expanded by *sections 203B* to *203E* of *ICTA 1998*, which apply to impose PAYE obligations in various circumstances where the employee is non-resident or is employed by a non-resident employer, or is engaged on contract work in circumstances where correct PAYE deductions may not be made.

It is the general duty of employers (under *SI 1993 No 744, reg 6*) to operate PAYE on the payment of emoluments. An employer is, for this purpose, any person who pays emoluments. [*SI 1993 No 744, reg 2(1)*]. Accordingly, if an individual in receipt of emoluments stemming from an employment with a non-resident employer is in fact paid by arrangement with a UK-resident employer, the UK-resident employer (the person making the payments) must operate PAYE.

Under *ICTA 1988, s 203B*, payments channelled through an intermediary, wherever resident or present, are treated as if they were payments directly by the employer, who has to account for PAYE. This provision is aimed at the situation where the intermediary has no tax presence in the UK (so that the decision in *Clark v Oceanic Contractors* does not apply), but is not limited to such a situation. An intermediary is any person making payments on behalf of and at the expense of the employer or a person connected with him, or a trustee holding property for a person or class of persons including the employer. The provision does not apply if the intermediary deducts and accounts for PAYE whether required to do so or not.

Section 203B is ineffective where the employer has no tax presence in the UK, and *section 203C* is intended to deal with this loophole. It applies to employees who during any period (i) work for a person who is not their employer but (ii) are paid by the employer or an intermediary of the employer and (iii) the employer or as the case may be, the intermediary, is not subject to PAYE regulations. In such a case, where no deductions of income tax are made under PAYE, the person for whom the employee is working is made responsible for operating PAYE. Thus where a foreign entertainer employed by, say, a foreign 'Rent a Star' corporation performs services in the UK for a UK-resident subsidiary of that corporation, but is paid by the foreign corporation, the UK subsidiary will be held responsible for paying over to the Revenue the PAYE deductions due from the entertainer's salary. Any UK payments to the foreign corporation may also, of course, have to be made subject to the withholding tax.

Another approach is taken by *section 203D*, which tackles the situation where a non-resident or not ordinarily resident employee works partly in the UK and partly abroad, or is likely to work partly abroad – which could easily apply to an entertainer. In such circumstances, where part of the employee's income will be assessable to UK tax under Schedule E, Case II (emoluments for work in the UK) but an as yet unascertainable part not, then all payments of or on account of remuneration to the employee will be treated as subject to PAYE. The employer or a person designated by him, can mitigate this by applying to the Revenue for a direction that a specific proportion only of payments be subject to PAYE. The Revenue has the right to withdraw a determination by giving 30 days' notice. This provision is without prejudice to an assessment on the employee concerned.

It will be seen from these rules that avoiding the liability to PAYE would now require that neither the payer of the remuneration, nor the ultimate employer nor an intermediary should have any trading or other presence in the UK liable to UK tax. In the absence of a liability to PAYE, withholding tax applies, but that is generally considered to be the lesser of the two evils.

Accounting for withholding tax

Accounting to the Inland Revenue

11.33 Payers have to account for withholding tax quarterly. They must complete a form FEU 1 at the end of every quarter (30 June, 30 September, 31 December and 5 April for this purpose) and send it, together with a cheque, where appropriate, to the Inland Revenue Accounts Office at Shipley in West Yorkshire, no later than 14 days after the end of each quarter. [*ICTA 1988, s 555(7)(b); SI 1987 No 530, reg 9(1)–(3)*]. Subsequently, a form FEU 1 must be completed every quarter, even if there is nothing further to return. [*SI 1987 No 530, reg 9(1)*]. Where a payer makes a large number of payments regularly, he or she may find it more convenient to submit their own list of payments (e.g., in the form of a computer print-out) rather than re-itemise them on a form FEU 1. This is acceptable to the Revenue provided prior permission has been obtained and all the information asked for on the form FEU 1 is supplied (Booklet FEU 50, paragraph B4).

11.34   The usual special return penalties under *TMA 1970, s 98* (a maximum of £300 plus £60 daily default fine thereafter) apply to failure to furnish returns and interest is charged under *TMA 1970, s 87* on overdue tax. Tax becomes due at the time the return is made and it is payable by the person who made the relevant payment or transfer. [*SI 1987 No 530, reg 10*].

The Revenue has the power to issue an assessment where tax has not been paid by the due date. The assessment may be in respect of a whole year of assessment or any one or more periods and will be raised on the payer or transferor. The normal rights of appeal apply to these assessments. Tax charged by the assessment becomes due and payable on the earlier of the normal due date and 14 days after the issue of the assessment [*SI 1987 No 530, reg 11*], so no advantage is gained by delaying payment until the issue of an assessment.

Accounting to the payee

11.35   The payer is under an obligation to give the payee a certificate showing the gross amount of the payment or transfer, the tax deducted or deemed to be deducted and the amount actually paid (or value transferred). [*SI 1987 No 530, reg 12(5)*].

In practice this is done by means of a three-part form, FEU 2. The first part must be sent to the Revenue together with the form FEU 1 (so that the Revenue can reconcile payments made with income declared by entertainers). The second part is intended for retention by the payer and the third part is given to the payee. The Revenue is adamant that no duplicate forms FEU 2 are to be issued. Where the payee loses his copy, he must apply to FEU. No form FEU 2 need be issued if no tax is deducted, either because the payment falls within the *de minimis* exemption or the Revenue has authorised a nil deduction. However, the amount that has not suffered tax must still be entered on the FEU 1. The *de minimis* limit is, of course, an exemption from withholding, not from UK tax as a whole.

Receipts attributed to the entertainer

11.36   We have seen how the regulations require withholding tax to be accounted for whenever a 'connected payment' is made in respect of a 'relevant activity', subject to the specific exceptions discussed above.

The payment does not have to be made directly to the entertainer, nor does the payee have to be non-resident. The statute and the regulations provide that payments made to certain persons are deemed to be made to the entertainer. Accordingly, withholding tax should be applied to the payment, and the payment will be brought into the entertainer's Schedule D, Case II computation.

11.37   Under *ICTA 1988, s 566(2)*, a 'connected payment' or 'connected transfer' (*SI 1987 No 530, reg 3*, see 11.8 and 11.13 above) made not to the entertainer but to a person fulfilling a 'prescribed description' is treated as made to the entertainer for the purposes of the *Taxes Acts* and as made to him in the course of a trade, profession or vocation carried on by the entertainer within the UK (the entertainer's UK trade, see 11.53).

11.38   Persons fulfilling a 'prescribed description' are defined in *SI 1987 No 530, reg 7(2)*. Essentially they are:

(*a*)   persons (e.g., loan-out companies) under the control of the entertainer;

(*b*)   persons not liable to UK tax and taxable in a territory where the tax charged on their profits or income is no more than 25 per cent;

(*c*)   persons directly or indirectly in receipt of a payment or transfer that is, or is treated as being, income of a settlement of which the entertainer is a settlor;

(*d*)   any person not included in (*a*) to (*c*), but who directly or indirectly receives a payment or transfer whilst there is an arrangement or contract in force between him and the entertainer, under the terms of which it can reasonably be supposed that the entertainer, an associate of the entertainer or a person connected with the entertainer will receive, or become entitled to receive, amounts 'not substantially less' than the 'appropriate amount' of profits or gains arising from the connected person or transfer.

The reference to a rate of 25 per cent (not so far amended to 22 per cent) or less in head (*b*) is probably a reference to nominal rather than effective rates as the payer cannot be expected to know the payee's true tax liability.

11.39   References to 'settlement' and 'settlor' are as defined in *ICTA 1988, s 660G*, and 'income arising under a settlement' is as defined in that section also. It should be noted that these definitions are very wide and encompass virtually any non-commercial arrangement with an element of bounty.

The sort of arrangement aimed at in head (*d*) is where payments are made to an intermediate management company etc., which deducts a fee and passes on the balance of the payment to the entertainer or connected parties.

Treatment of third-party payees

11.40   Where a payment or transfer subject to the regulations is made to a third party (i.e., not the entertainer) but is attributed to the entertainer under *SI 1987 No 530, reg 7(2)*, then it is treated as income of the entertainer and the withholding tax is creditable by the entertainer. It does not constitute taxable income of the third party, and neither is the withholding tax creditable by nor repayable to the third party (Booklet FEU 50, paragraph B10).

11.41   Where, on the other hand, a payment is not attributed to the entertainer, *SI 1987 No 530, reg 4(7)* will not apply, and the third party must include the gross amount of the payment or transfer in its taxable profits. The withholding tax can be used to set off its income tax or corporation tax liability, and is repayable where appropriate.

Example – strict treatment

Parrot Productions engages the services of Emma Bovary, a French actress, through the medium of Gustave F Ltd, a UK resident company, to appear in a West End play. Parrot pays Gustave F £60,000. Mlle Bovary receives a fee from Gustave F of £40,000. Gustave F's expenses amount to £2,000. The payments by Parrot to Gustave F and from Gustave F to Mlle Bovary are both subject to withholding tax. Mlle Bovary's fee is not regarded as 'not substantially less' [*SI 1987 No 530, reg 7(2)(d)(ii)*] than Gustave F's profits from the deal (£58,000), so the payment by Parrot is not attributed to her.

Gustave F's corporation tax computation will include the following:

Receipts:	£60,000
Payments:	£40,000

Withholding tax on payment received:
£60,000 × 22% = £13,200

Withholding tax on payment made:
£40,000 × 22% = £8,800

Example – FEU booklet treatment

As in the example at 11.22, Gustave F does not have to pay the £8,800 to the Revenue, as this amount is considered fully franked by the £13,200 deducted from the payment it received from Parrot Productions.

Parrot Productions deducts: £60,000 × 22% = £13,200

Gustave F Ltd receives: £60,000 – £13,200 = £46,800

Gustave F Ltd pays to Bovary: £40,000 – 22% = £31,200

Gustave F Ltd suffers 30% corporation tax on £60,000 – £40,000 = £6,000

Franked by £13,200 suffered on £60,000 received

Can claim refund of £13,200 – £8,800 = £4,400

Mlle Bovary treated as paying tax of £8,800

The excess withholding tax of £4,400 can be set against Gustave F's income tax liability under *ICTA 1988, Sch 16 para 5*.

Revenue information powers

11.42   Whether or not a form FEU 1 has been filed, the Revenue has the power (under *SI 1987 No 530, reg 9(4)*) to require payers to provide it with further particulars including, but not limited to:

(*a*) the dates and amounts of payments and transfers, the business and private names and addresses of the payees and transferees;

(*b*) a sufficient description of the subject matter of the transfer;

(*c*) the name and address of the relevant entertainer; and

(*d*) full details of the entertainer's appearances in the UK.

The demand must be in writing and specify the time within which the information must be supplied, but no minimum time (e.g., 30 days) is mentioned in the regulations.

Double tax treaties

Entertainers articles

11.43 In dealing with the tax affairs of a non-resident, an adviser must, of course, always bear in mind the terms of any double tax treaty between the UK and the non-resident's country of residence. Before going on to discuss the interaction of treaty provisions with the withholding regulations and UK domestic law generally, it would be useful to analyse the UK's treaties according to how they treat the income of entertainers and sportspersons.

First, it is important to appreciate how the profits and earnings of non-residents generally are treated. Although the wording of treaties differs, they essentially all provide that:

(*a*) the profits of a business carried on in the UK by a non-resident are not taxable here unless carried on by or through a permanent establishment in the UK;

(*b*) the income from 'independent personal services', that is to say, self-employment of a professional or similar nature, are not taxable in the UK unless the person concerned has a fixed base in the UK regularly available to him for that purpose; and

(*c*) the income from 'dependent personal services' (i.e., employment) is not taxable in the UK unless the non-resident is employed by a UK resident company, or the remuneration is borne by a permanent UK establishment.

11.44 However, entertainers have long been recognised as deserving exception to these rules, so as to bring their earnings within the charge to tax in the country where they perform their activities. Most of the UK's treaties have a separate article specifically addressed to this class of taxpayer, in line with the OECD Model Treaty, *Article 17.*

> '1.   Notwithstanding the provisions of articles 14 [independent personal services] and 15 [dependent personal services], income derived by a resident of a contracting state as an entertainer, such as a theatre,

motion picture, radio or television artiste, or as a musician, or as a sportsman, from his personal activities as such exercised in the other contracting state, may be taxed in that other state.

2.   Where income in respect of personal activities exercised by an entertainer or a sportsman in his capacity as such accrues not to the entertainer or sportsman himself but to another person, that income may, notwithstanding the provisions of articles 7 [business profits], 14 and 15, be taxed in the contracting state in which the activities of the entertainer or sportsman are exercised.'

The Model article would allow the UK to tax both payments made directly to the entertainer for his UK activities *as such* and payments to third parties, such as loan-out companies, although it is silent as to the person who is to be assessed on the third party's income. In practice, however, just over half of the UK's treaties contain both arms of the Model article. Many others incorporate a form of words corresponding to paragraph 1 of the Model (limiting tax rights to payments to the entertainer himself or herself), while still others (mostly the older variety) have no special entertainers article at all, although they all (bar one) except entertainers from the scope of the personal services articles (the equivalent of Model *Articles 14* and *15*), thus effectively leaving payments to entertainers alone within the UK taxing jurisdiction; it is also FEU's firm opinion that payments in respect of UK duties made by loan-out companies resident in category B and C (see below) countries are taxable by the UK.

The former USSR treaty stands in a category of its own, in that it effectively reserves taxing rights to the country of residence. Since that treaty is still in force, for example, between the UK and some members of the Commonwealth of Independent States, entertainers from those countries are effectively exempt from UK tax on their UK earnings as entertainers. The countries affected are shown in the category D column in the following table. For the history of the USSR treaty following the dissolution of the USSR in 1991, see Inland Revenue SP3/92 and SP4/01.

11.45   The treaties break down among four categories as follows:

● category A = those with Model *Article 17* or equivalent;

● category B = those with paragraph 1 of the Model article or equivalent only;

● category C = those excepting entertainers from personal services articles;

● category D = the former USSR treaty.

Category A	Category B	Category C	Category D
Argentina	Australia	Antigua	Armenia (until 6.4.02)
Austria	Barbados	Belize	Belarus
Azerbaijan	Botswana	Brunei	Georgia (until 6.4.02)
Bangladesh	Cyprus	Greece	Kyrgyzstan (until 6.4.02)
Bolivia	Fiji	Grenada	Lithuania (until 6.4.02)
Canada	Finland	Guernsey	Moldova (until 6.4.02)

China
Croatia
Czech Republic
Denmark
Egypt
Estonia
Falkland Islands
Ghana
Guyana
Iceland
India
Indonesia
Ireland
Italy
Ivory Coast
Korea
Kuwait
Latvia
Lesotho
Macedonia
Malaysia
Malta
Mauritius
Mexico
Mongolia
Morocco
Netherlands
New Zealand
Nigeria
Norway
Oman
Pakistan
Papua New Guinea
Philippines
Poland
Russia
Singapore
Slovakia
Slovenia
Spain
Sri Lanka
Sweden
Switzerland
Thailand
Trinidad and Tobago
Tunisia
Turkey
Uganda
Ukraine
USA*
Uzbekistan
Venezuela
Vietnam
Zimbabwe

France
Germany
Hungary
Israel
Jamaica
Japan
Kazakhstan
Kenya
Luxembourg
Namibia
Portugal
Romania
South Africa
Sudan
Swaziland
Tajikistan
Turkmenistan
Zambia

Isle of Man
Jersey
Kiribati
Malawi
Montserrat
Myanmar (Burma)
St Kitts
Sierra Leone
Solomon Islands
Tuvalu

*Except where earnings do not exceed US$15,000 in the tax year (the new US treaty, concluded on 24 July 2001 but not yet in force, increases this *de minimis* limit to US$20,000).

The treaty with Gambia seems unique in making no reference at all to entertainers. Gambian-resident entertainers would, therefore, seem to escape UK tax if the conditions specified in *Article 16* (Employments and professional services) are satisfied.

11.46   As noted earlier, the standard personal services article(s) provide(s) that the income derived from personal services is taxed in the state in which the services are carried on only if the person concerned has become resident there or has a permanent establishment in that state. Since most entertainers would not come into the scope of these conditions, the 'category C override' has the effect of granting tax rights to the state in which the entertainer renders his or her services.

All the overrides, without exception, refer to income derived by the entertainer in person, so it is arguable that they do not catch fees paid to third parties. Consequently, only category A treaties do so unambiguously. The Revenue view, however, is that *paragraph 8* of the commentary to *Article 17* in the OECD Model Treaty does make it clear that category B treaties do entitle tax regimes with domestic 'look-through' provisions (e.g., the UK) to tax fees payable to certain connected third parties. The Revenue also considers that category C treaties, by effectively removing treaty protection for non-resident entertainers, enable the UK's domestic 'look-through' provisions to take effect.

It should also be noted that even many of the category A and B treaties do not allow the UK to tax the earnings of entertainers whose appearance here is arranged or funded by an overseas government or state authority, e.g., as part of a state-sponsored cultural exchange.

Treaties and the withholding regulations

11.47   It will be seen that the withholding regulations are potentially wider in scope than the taxing rights granted to the UK with respect to residents of certain treaty countries.

As far as the Revenue is concerned, it is clear that the regulations take precedence. According to Booklet FEU 50, paragraph A8:

> 'Even if the payments you withhold tax from may not ultimately be assessed on the recipient (e.g. because they are protected by a Double Taxation Agreement) you must not exclude these payments from the scheme'.

The regulations make no presumption as to the final liability to tax or otherwise of the payments but merely provide a mechanism whereby a sum is withheld on account of a potential liability. The opportunity to agree a reduced (or nil) rate of withholding tax should allow for most situations to be accommodated. On no account should demands or correspondence from FEU be overlooked!

Personal allowances

11.48   Non-residents are not, in general, entitled to personal allowances. However, there are three main exceptions to this rule. The first concerns primarily Commonwealth citizens and residents of the Isle of Man or Channel Islands. Individuals in this category are entitled to full personal allowances to set against their UK taxable income. [*ICTA 1988, s 278(2)*].

11.49   The second exception extends to residents of those territories having tax treaties with the UK that specifically provide for the granting of personal allowances. These treaties tend to be the UK's older treaties, negotiated for the most part before 1970; treaties negotiated after that date do not, on the whole, contain such an article. As the older treaties come up for renegotiation, the personal allowances article is likely to be dropped. At present the treaties granting personal allowances are the following: Austria, Fiji, France, Germany, Greece, Ireland, Kenya, Luxembourg, Mauritius, Myanmar (Burma), Namibia, Netherlands, Portugal, South Africa, Swaziland, Switzerland, Zambia. The German treaty also entitles German nationals whether or not they are resident in Germany for treaty purposes to allowances.

11.50   The third exception has effect from 1996/97. It makes personal allowances available to all nationals of countries in the European Economic Area (the European Union plus Iceland, Liechtenstein and Norway) as of right, whether or not the existing treaty with that country (see 11.49) extends allowances to residents of that country.

If the entertainer's presence in the UK straddles a UK tax year-end (5 April), the entertainer will be entitled to two years' worth of allowances.

To minimise year-end adjustments, FEU will include personal allowances in calculating the correct amount of withholding tax in an RTP application, whether or not a claim for allowances has been made, if the available information suggests that they are due.

Attributable income

11.51   As noted earlier, the legislation deems income received by third parties to be income of the entertainer in prescribed circumstances. [*ICTA 1988, s 556(2)*]. However, it is at least arguable that this is not sufficient to bring third-party income into the charge to UK tax where a category B or C treaty applies, as the right to tax under the treaty goes with the income, not the recipient. The Revenue's view, as we have seen, is contrary. This difference of view has not yet been tested in the courts.

The entertainer's ultimate liability

Schedule D treatment

11.52   We have seen how general UK domestic and treaty law affects the tax position of non-resident entertainers, but it is important to realise that the 1986 legislation and regulations, in addition to charging withholding tax, also provide a new regime for non-resident entertainers, taxing them under Schedule D, Case II.

Before the introduction of *ICTA 1988, ss 555–558* and the regulations, entertainers who were carrying on a trade or profession, being charged under Schedule D, Case I or II, were, strictly speaking, assessable on the preceding-year basis. An appearance in the UK in the tax year 1986/87 would consequently have given rise to a tax charge on a fraction of the profits of the accounting year ending in 1985/86, irrespective of whether any of those profits were earned in the UK. In practice, to avoid those complications, entertainers were assessed on a current-year basis.

The opportunity was taken in *ICTA 1988, ss 556, 557* to put this practice on a statutory footing and indeed to extend the Schedule D treatment to certain employed entertainers. First, where a payment to which the regulations apply is made in respect of an activity, whether to the entertainer or to a third party, the activity is treated for all tax purposes as performed (by the entertainer) in the course of a trade, profession or vocation exercised in the UK. This rule does not apply where the entertainer is an employee. [*ICTA 1988, s 556(1)*]. However, even where the entertainer is employed, when payments made to third parties are attributed to the entertainer under the regulations for withholding tax purposes (e.g., when they are made to a company controlled by the entertainer, see 11.39), they are also deemed to be made to him or her for all other tax purposes and in the course of a trade, profession or vocation exercised by the entertainer in the UK. [*ICTA 1988, s 556(2)*]. This will be so whether or not the entertainer is actually employed, so that Schedule E treatment is overruled in this instance.

The current-year basis is now, of course, of universal application.

11.53   Where payments are attributed to the entertainer in this way, the entertainer is deemed to be carrying on a single trade etc. in the UK separately from any other trade he or she may carry on. Assessment of this 'UK trade' is on a current-year basis on the full profits arising [*ICTA 1988, s 557(1)*] and this is unaffected by self-assessment and the current-year basis. In calculating those profits or gains, any expenses incurred by third parties can be deducted to the extent that they are just and reasonable. [*ICTA 1988, s 556(3)(a); SI 1987 No 530, reg 8(2)*]. Clearly, if the whole of a payment to a third party is deemed to be the entertainer's, allowance ought to be made for expenses incurred by the third party in connection with the payment.

11.54   Where an amount included in the entertainer's income under these rules would otherwise be chargeable under some other provision, the charge under Schedule D takes precedence [*ICTA 1988, s 556(3)(b)*; *SI 1987 No 530, reg 12*], but amounts which have already been charged under Schedule E may be deducted as expenses of the UK trade. [*SI 1987 No 530, reg 12(3)*].

Example

Lovelace, a Canadian actor, is employed by Clarissa Productions, a Canadian company he controls. He comes to the UK to shoot a film during 2001/02. Under the terms of his contract with the company, he is paid a basic salary of £60,000 a year and he is entitled to a contingent salary of 90 per cent of the company's net profits from the hire of his services. For the UK film, the net profits realised by Clarissa Productions are £350,000 (payments received £420,000; expenses £70,000). He spends 90 days in the UK in 2001/02.

(i)   Under *ICTA 1988, ss 556(2), 557(1)* and *SI 1987 No 530, reg 7(2)*, he is assessable in 2001/02 on the following amounts:

UK element of salary	£60,000 × 90/365 = £14,794 (Schedule E)
Share of profits	100% × (£420,000 – £70,000) = £350,000 (Schedule D, Case II)
Less allowable corporate overheads	10% × (£420,000 – £70,000) = £35,000

This treatment applies only to the deemed 'UK trade', not to any trade etc. the entertainer may already be carrying on. It also remains possible for employed entertainers to remain under Schedule E, provided they do not control their employing companies and only in respect of payments that are not attributed to them for any other reason under *SI 1987 No 530, reg 7* (see 11.39). Now that the foreign emoluments deduction for Schedule E has been withdrawn, there is probably no benefit in the Schedule E treatment, especially given the more generous expense and NIC treatment available under Schedule D.

11.55   It is not automatically the case that FEU will approach the entertainer to 'tidy up' the entertainer's UK tax position for a particular year. First, if tax has been withheld at too high a rate generally, the entertainer will have to wait until after 5 April before FEU will accept that a repayment should be made and the entertainer would be advised to make the first move. It should be noted that a self-assessment tax return may well be sent to the entertainer after the end of the tax year. It is now FEU's practice to issue full self-assessment returns rather than repayment-claim forms (R43), even where it is known that repayments will be made.

11.56   Alternatively, FEU has very limited enforcement powers if the entertainer owes more tax than has been withheld. However, assuming that the entertainer may return to the UK at some point in the future, he or she would again be well advised to settle affairs on a timely basis, especially as interest on tax paid late will generally not be creditable as foreign tax in the entertainer's home country. Early settlement also avoids the possibility of exceeding any tax-credit time limit in the entertainer's country of residence if the UK tax is not settled until much later.

The lack of enforcement powers puts the entertainer in a strong position to argue the best possible deal firstly with FEU and, secondly, with the promoter. It is quite common for entertainers returning to the UK to stipulate that the promoter must settle their past tax liability as part of the contract. The settlement should be made in a different tax year to that in which the performance took place.

Treatment of withholding tax

11.57   Withholding tax deducted and/or paid is treated as a payment on account of the entertainer's liability (unless the payment is not attributed to the entertainer, in which case it counts towards the recipient's liability). [*SI 1987 No 530, reg 12(1)*]. Where the entertainer is also liable to tax in respect of the payment under some other provision of the *Taxes Acts*, the Revenue can apportion the withholding tax between the various liabilities as it deems fit. [*SI 1987 No 530, reg 12(2)*].

Should the entertainer's liability be less than the amount deducted, the excess is repayable by the Revenue. [*ICTA 1988, s 555(9)*]. However, any interest on overdue tax that was charged on any of the withholding tax payments is not repayable. [*ICTA 1988, s 555(11)*]. Prior to the introduction of self-assessment, repayment supplement was not available, unless due in respect of years of assessment in which the taxpayer was resident in an EU Member State. [*ICTA 1988, s 824(1)(a)* and concession A82]. Since 1996/97 this restriction has been lifted and repayment supplement is now due to all non-resident entertainers.

Treatment of losses

11.58   A loss arising in the deemed UK trade can be carried forward under *ICTA 1988, s 385* and set against future profits both in the deemed UK trade and in the entertainer's actual trade (if any), since the two trades are treated as one for this purpose. [*SI 1987 No 530, reg 15(2)*]. Terminal loss relief under *ICTA 1988, s 388* is not available on the cessation of the deemed UK trade unless the actual trade (referred to as the worldwide trade) is permanently discontinued in the same year of assessment, in which case it may be used to relieve profits of either trade in the three immediately prior years. [*SI 1987 No 530, reg 15(3)*].

11.59   The carry-back of relief for losses from new trades [*ICTA 1988, s 381*] is available on a restricted basis in the case of the deemed UK trade.

Losses in the early years of the deemed trade, measured from the year of first taxable appearance in the UK (of which 1987/88 is the earliest possible year) may only be carried back to a year no earlier than the commencement of the worldwide trade. [*SI 1987 No 530, reg 15(4)*].

There is no reference in the regulations to relief under *ICTA 1988, s 380* (set-off against general income of that or the preceding year). It is understood that the Revenue will not recognise an *ICTA 1988, s 380* claim in respect of a loss arising from the deemed UK trade.

Foreign emoluments

11.60   Where the entertainer is employed, special rules applied to 'foreign emoluments' in the past.

'Foreign emoluments' are the emoluments of a person who is not *domiciled* in the UK from an employment with a *non-UK resident* employer. [*ICTA 1988, s 192(1)*]. Thus, both UK residents and non-residents can be in receipt of foreign emoluments. 'Emoluments' include not only basic salary, but also allowances, such as cost of living allowance, educational expenses etc. An individual in receipt of foreign emoluments who pays certain expenses out of those earnings is entitled to claim a deduction in assessing his income liable to tax. The expenses must be analogous to those for which a UK resident would have been entitled to a deduction. Examples include contributions to a pension fund, mortgage interest on a sole or main residence in the home country and maintenance payments to a separated or divorced spouse. [*ICTA 1988, s 192(3)*].

11.61   A further relief attaching to foreign emoluments was the 50 per cent/25 per cent deduction. Although the deduction is no longer available (the last year in which it could have applied was 1988/89), it may still be relevant where a number of years' back tax is demanded by the Revenue in a case involving fraud or negligence.

Sale of earnings for a lump sum

11.62   The anti-avoidance legislation of *ICTA 1988, s 775* aimed at capital sums derived from the sale of earning capacity applies also to non-residents carrying on a trade partly in the UK. [*ICTA 1988, s 775(9)*].

Sale of copyrights etc.

11.63   An entertainer who receives a capital sum as a result of a transaction that is not entered into in the normal course of his business will not be chargeable to income tax in respect of the sum. An example of such a transaction might be the sale of UK copyright in a film by an actor (as in *Shiner v*

Lindblom (1960) 39 TC 367, Ch D). The capital sum is chargeable to capital gains tax but disposals made in a year of assessment in which a taxpayer is neither resident nor ordinarily resident are exempt from CGT.

National insurance contributions

11.64   Entertainers who are employees of a company having its original place of business outside the UK and whose employment is carried out mainly outside the UK will not normally be liable to pay employee's (primary) Class 1 national insurance contributions until they have been present in the UK for a minimum of 52 consecutive contribution weeks. [*Social Security (Contributions) Regulations 2001, (SI 2001 No 1004), reg 145(2)*]. If the employer has no UK tax presence and the employee is not under the general control and management of some other person with a UK tax presence, then no employer's (secondary) Class 1 NIC will be due, even after 52 weeks.

11.65   Self-employed entertainers (the deeming provisions of *ICTA 1988, s 556* and the regulations have no effect here) who are not ordinarily resident have no liability to pay Class 2 (flat rate) national insurance contributions until they have been resident in the UK for at least 26 out of the preceding 52 contribution weeks. [*SI 2001 No 1004, reg 145(1)(d)*]. They are *entitled* to pay Class 2 contributions, should they wish to do so, for any contribution week in which they are 'present' in the UK. [*SI 2001 No 1004, reg 145(1)(c)*]. The term 'present' is not defined, but simply means physically present. Non-residents are not liable to pay Class 4 contributions. [*SI 2001 No 1004, reg 91(b)*].

Value added tax

11.66   A supply of services made in the UK in the course of a business is a taxable supply. Services are treated as supplied in the UK where the person supplying them 'belongs' in the UK. Belonging is determined by the location of the supplier's business establishment or main business establishment; failing which, by his usual place of residence.

A non-resident entertainer will, therefore, not generally be required to register for VAT if he or she has no business establishment in the UK. However, if the entertainer has business establishments both in the UK and abroad, there will be a VAT liability (provided always the turnover threshold is reached) if the UK establishment is the one most directly concerned with the supply. Customs and Excise has made it clear that it regards a theatre to be a business establishment. Thus, a non-resident entertainer may well come within the VAT net if he or she hires a theatre in the UK in which to give a performance (VAT leaflet No 700/4/87 (now withdrawn), paragraph 3). If it is desired to avoid registration for VAT, it is, therefore, best for UK-resident and VAT-registered companies to hire venues etc. On the other hand, if the inconvenience of registration and accounting for VAT is acceptable, registration will enable the entertainer to recoup the VAT suffered on business expenditure.

It should be noted that a branch or agency through which a person carries on a trade in the UK is regarded as a business establishment. A UK-based theatrical agent, who arranges an entertainer's UK appearances almost certainly constitutes a branch or agency, so a liability to VAT may well arise by this means. There is some doubt as to whether the UK legislation on this point is entirely consistent with the *Sixth VAT Directive* and decisions of the European Court.

Royalties

11.67   It is important to distinguish between genuine royalties and payments for services, as the term tends to be loosely used in the industry.

Royalties are payments for the use of copyright and an entertainer will receive royalties only where he or she at some time owns the copyright in the finished product of a performance (e.g., a compact disc released after a studio recording or live performance). It follows that where the copyright stipulates that the copyright belongs not to the entertainer but to a third party (e.g., the record company or, in the case of a film, the film company), payments received by the entertainer, albeit based on sales or box-office takings, are a payment for services and not royalties.

The distinction is important because where copyright royalties are payable to a person whose 'usual place of abode' is outside the UK, there has always been a requirement to deduct basic-rate tax. [*ICTA 1988, s 536*]. Copyright royalties for this purpose do not extend to rights in a cinematograph film or video recording or to the accompanying sound track, as long as it is not separately exploited. Nor is deduction of tax required where the work has been exported from the UK for distribution abroad. [*ICTA 1988, s 536(2)*].

It will be recalled that payments already subject to deduction of tax are exempt from the special withholding tax [*SI 1987 No 530, reg 3(3)(a)*] as, specifically, are payments made in respect of sales of records deriving from the entertainer's performance in the UK. [*SI 1987 No 530, reg 3(3)(c)*]. Normally, in the music industry, copyright in the recording does not at any time vest in the artiste, so, strictly speaking, deduction of tax under *ICTA 1988, s 536* is not appropriate and payments, unless falling within the specific exemption in *SI 1987 No 530, reg 3(3)(c)*, would be subject to the withholding tax. However, it is also normal practice in the industry to deduct tax under *ICTA 1988, s 536* regardless, and where tax has thus effectively been voluntarily deducted at source, the Revenue has not been disposed to argue.

The new rules on the corporation tax treatment of intellectual property, due to be introduced from 1 April 2002, do not (at the time of writing) contain any change to the withholding tax position on copyright royalties.

Allowable expenses

11.68   What expenses the entertainer is allowed to set against taxable income is a matter of general law, and will depend, in the first place, on whether the entertainer is, or is deemed to be, carrying on a trade, profession or vocation (assessable under Schedule D, Cases I or II) or (more rarely) performing the duties of an employment (assessable under Schedule E). Readers are reminded that, following the introduction of *ICTA 1988, ss 555–558* and the regulations, the number of instances in which a non-resident entertainer will be assessed under Schedule E are significantly reduced. As far as expenses are concerned, this is all to the good, of course.

11.69   Although expenses under Schedule D need to be wholly and exclusively incurred, the Revenue does in practice allow a proportion of certain expenditure having a dual purpose. Among the types of expense for which deductions are normally recognised are:

(*a*)   accountancy expenses;

(*b*)   agents' and managers' commission;

(*c*)   books, records, cinema and theatre etc. visits where directly relevant;

(*d*)   coaching;

(*e*)   cosmetics and make-up;

(*f*)   insurance (e.g., public indemnity, equipment etc.);

(*g*)   laundry of costumes and other professional clothing;

(*h*)   medical expenses where specifically incurred (e.g., resulting from injuries connected with the performance). Medical insurance is not normally deductible unless specifically required for the particular engagement; it is not generally possible, for example, for US performers to claim a proportion of their annual medical insurance premiums;

(*i*)   press and publicity costs;

(*j*)   professional subscriptions (where they relate to the UK);

(*k*)   research assistance and material, where relevant;

(*l*)   secretarial, postage and stationery;

(*m*)   supporting artists, stage hands (including tips);

(*n*)   telecommunications (excluding personal use);

(*o*)   travel to the UK, travel between locations in the UK and subsistence expenses;

(*p*)   TV hire; and

(*q*)   wardrobe, prop and equipment repair.

11.70   The expenses must, of course, be borne by the entertainer; where payments made to third parties are deemed under *ICTA 1988, s 556(2)* and *SI 1987 No 530, reg 7(2)* to be the entertainer's income, however, a just and reasonable proportion of the third party's expenses may be deducted by the entertainer (*ICTA 1988, s 556(3)(a)* and *SI 1987 No 530, reg 8(2)*; see further at 11.53).

11.71   The Schedule E expenses rule [*ICTA 1988, s 198*], that expenses must be necessarily, as well as wholly and exclusively incurred, is not reiterated here; however, its effect can be substantially mitigated in that the employing company will usually bear the burden of most of the expenditure and the entertainer's remuneration will reflect this (as a percentage of net profits, say).

Investigations

11.72   An investigation into earlier years may be triggered by an application for reduced tax payment under the regulations, where it comes to the Revenue's attention that the entertainer's tax position for previous years has not been settled. Many entertainers will be employees of captive companies and, in those rare instances where liabilities for years before 1987/88 are yet to be determined, the possible availability of the 50 per cent foreign emoluments deduction (see 11.60) should not be forgotten.

Investigations will normally be carried out by FEU.

Investigations into entertainers' affairs are essentially no different to other investigations and the same tactics are and ought to be followed by both sides. Clearly, the co-operation of production accountants, agents and the entertainer's worldwide advisers is crucial, as is the timely provision of necessary and sufficient accounting information. FEU is aware that difficulties can be encountered in obtaining prior-year information from the entertainer and his or her staff, foreign advisers etc. but excessive delays will not be conducive to arriving at a favourable settlement.

There was a tendency for FEU to take a tough stance, especially in the early years, but recently there is evidence of a more pragmatic approach.

Contracts

11.73   Although it is beyond the scope of this section to deal in any detail with an entertainer's contractual arrangements, it is clear that the contract plays a fundamental part in ultimately determining the entertainer's liability. The use of multiple contracts to isolate what is being paid to an individual for his or her duties as an entertainer in the UK has already been discussed. Contracts should be reviewed in draft stage by the entertainer's professional advisers to ensure maximum tax efficiency within the general terms of the assignment.

The contract should be explicit about the following items:

(*a*)   its duration and how it may be terminated;

(*b*)   the exact services to be rendered and where those services are to be performed;

(*c*)   where any products associated with those services (goods, sound and video recordings, etc.) are to be sold and by whom;

(*d*)   to whom any copyright arising from performances belongs;

(*e*)   the exact nature and amount of the entertainer's remuneration: salary, royalties, profit shares, expense allowances, additional remuneration for overruns etc.;

(*f*)   what advances are to be made and to what extent they may or may not be recoupable;

(*g*)   which party is to bear which expenses (e.g., supporting artists, venue hire, stage and technical staff, costs of promotion, travel to and from the UK and between venues); and

(*h*)   what commission is to be payable and to whom.

General planning points summary

11.74   The following points should be considered when reviewing the affairs of an entertainer for the first time.

1.   Is the individual an entertainer for these purposes? (See 11.6)

2.   Is the individual an entertainer for all aspects of their UK activities, or are they a 'hyphenate', e.g., actors-director? (See 11.12)

3.   Should he or she become UK-resident? (See 11.30)

4.   Is withholding appropriate? (See 11.31–11.35)

5.   Negotiate a reduced rate of withholding tax with FEU. (See 11.24–11.28)

6.   Does the entertainer's presence in the UK straddle a UK tax year-end? (See 11.28)

7.   Can the entertainer take advantage of a double tax treaty? (See 11.43–11.47)

8.   What allowable expenses can be claimed? (See 11.68–11.71)

9.   Are the contracts tax-efficient?

10.   Has the entertainer a past UK tax liability which will be triggered by the forced disclosure imposed by the regime? (See 11.72)

If in doubt contact FEU.

Conclusion

11.75   The UK tax adviser of a non-resident entertainer or sportsperson will have to deal with the UK Revenue in two distinct stages. First, the appropriate rate of withholding tax has to be agreed: tax will be deducted at the basic rate from a wide range of payments to the entertainer and connected and other parties unless a reduced rate, based on a reasonable projection of the entertainer's ultimate liability from his UK appearances, is negotiated. Second, the ultimate liability must be agreed, taking into account both UK domestic legislation and the UK's double tax treaty network. In settling that ultimate liability, it should be remembered that the withholding tax regime also altered the underlying treatment of entertainers by significantly reducing the instances in which they are taxed under Schedule E, especially when they are employed by controlled companies. Familiarity with the *modus operandi* of and good relations with FEU are important. In order to achieve the optimum efficiency in planning, the UK tax adviser must liaise closely with the entertainer, the entertainer's staff, the accounting staff of the UK promoter, production company etc. responsible for paying for the entertainer's services and other professional advisers, particularly lawyers. Since the entertainer's contract is fundamental in determining liability, the UK tax adviser should ideally be involved at as early a stage as possible.

Appendix 11:1

List of grades where PAYE need not be applied on payments to casual and freelance staff.

— Animation director

— Animation production co-ordinator

— Animator – where providing own facilities and equipment

— Animatronics model designer

— Art director

— Associate producer

— First assistant director

— Camera operator – where the contract includes provision of substantial equipment, e.g., dollies, cameras etc.

— Casting director

— Chief make-up artist – if engaged for specialised skills

— Choreographer

— Composer

— Continuity girl

— Co-producer

— Costume designer

— Designer – where providing own facilities and equipment

— Director

— Driver – where providing own vehicle

— Editors – all types (but not assistants)

— Executive producer

— Film/photographic stylist

— Lighting cameraman

— Location manager

— Model cameraman

— Model designer – where providing own facilities and equipment

— Modeller

— Musical associate

— Musical director

— Producer

— Production accountant

— Production designer/head of art department

— Production manager

— Production supervisor

— Property master

— Publicist

— Script supervisor

— Sculptor

— Senior special effects technician

— Set decorator

— Set dresser

— Sound maintenance engineer

— Sound recordist/mixer

— Special effects supervisor – where contract includes provision of equipment

— Specialised researcher

— Stills photographer – where contract includes provision of cameras and developing facilities

— Story editor

— Supervising animation director

— Transport manager – where providing own vehicle

— Writer

PAYE need not be applied to payments made to the following when the work is done on premises other than those provided by the company.

— Assistant art director

— Background artist

— Dressmaker

— Hairdresser in charge of production

— Lettering artist

— Lettering designer

— Musical arranger/copyist

— Production buyer

— Scenic artist

— Storyboard artist

— Tracer/painter

Appendix 11:2

Merchandiser application (sample)

NAME OF MERCHANDISER . . . .
('the Merchandiser')

REFERENCE NUMBER . . . .

I am prepared to enter into a Middleman Agreement along the following lines:

1. When a UK performance involves a non-resident entertainer the Merchandiser may receive merchandising income gross from UK venues/concessionaires.

2. The Merchandiser will be responsible for Withholding Tax deductions in accordance with Part XIII Chapter III Income & *Corporation Taxes Act 1988* in respect of: all venue merchandising payments made to or for the artiste

3. Under the terms of this Agreement, the Merchandiser is obliged to deduct tax at Basic Rate tax unless notified otherwise by the Foreign Entertainers Unit.

4.   I understand and acknowledge that this agreement may be withdrawn without notice if I fail to comply correctly with the Withholding Tax Regulations.

5.   Should any change occur in the circumstances in which specified payments etc. are made, then the Merchandiser is requested to notify me immediately.

6.   This Agreement comes into force now and shall be operative until 5 April 2002, unless revoked at an earlier date.

MRS J ASHMORE, HMIT . . . .

MERCHANDISER'S . . . .

AUTHORISED SIGNATORY

Promoter's application (sample)

NAME OF PROMOTER . . . .
('the Promoter')

REFERENCE NUMBER . . . .

I am prepared to enter into a Middleman Agreement along the following lines:

1.   When a UK performance involves a non-resident entertainer the Promoter may receive box office monies and appearance fees gross from UK venues.

2.   The Promoter will be responsible for Withholding Tax deductions in accordance with Part XIII Chapter III income & *Corporation Taxes Act 1988* in respect of: all payments made to or for the artiste, including expenses paid on the artiste's behalf

3.   Under the terms of this Agreement, the Promoter is obliged to deduct at Basic Rate unless notified otherwise by the Foreign Entertainers Unit.

4.   I understand that membership of this scheme is a privilege which may be withdrawn if my Returns/tax payment history becomes less than satisfactory.

5.   Should any change occur in the circumstances in which specified payments etc. are made, then the Promoter is requested to notify me immediately.

6.   This Agreement comes into force now and shall be operative until 5 April 2002, unless revoked at an earlier date.

MRS J ASHMORE, HMIT . . . .

PROMOTER'S AUTHORISED . . . .

SIGNATORY

12 Secondments in and out of the UK

Robert Maas
(Blackstone Franks)

Introduction

12.1 A secondment of an employee normally involves a short-term move from a business in one country to a business in another. The tax position will depend to a large extent on the length of the secondment. If it is very short the employee may well remain taxable in his home country and, subject to double taxation relief, be taxable also in the host country (i.e. the one in which he is working). A number of other factors can also affect the tax position, such as will he be employed overseas by the home country business or a host country one, will he become resident in the host country and who will pay for his living accommodation in the host country?

Secondments into the UK

12.2 The term 'secondments' implies an intention to return at some stage to the seconding business, therefore a secondee will almost certainly be non-UK domiciled while he is working in the UK (see Chapter 8). This is so even if he was born in the UK and has acquired a domicile of choice outside the UK. Returning temporarily to the UK will not bring about an abandonment of the overseas domicile provided that there is a genuine intention to return to the country in which the person is currently living.

12.3 A person who is resident but not domiciled in the UK is not taxable in the UK on overseas income and gains except to the extent that they are brought into the UK. If the secondee's UK income will be sufficient to meet his living expenses here the obvious strategy with non-UK income is simply not to remit it to the UK. If there is a possibility that overseas monies will be needed in the UK there may be a need to plan for this before he comes to the UK.

12.4 A person who is UK domiciled and resident but not ordinarily resident in the UK is also taxable in the UK on a remittance basis in relation to overseas earnings [*ICTA 1988, s 19*] and also, if he is a Commonwealth or Irish citizen, in relation to overseas investment income [*ICTA 1988, s 65(4)*]. Such a person is, however, still liable to UK capital gains on overseas assets. Ordinary residence is considered in Chapter 1. Broadly speaking, a secondee who comes to the UK with the intention of living here for less than three years will initially not be regarded as being ordinarily resident in the UK (booklet IR20, 'Residents and non-residents liability to tax in the UK', para 3.1). The three years refers to actual years, i.e. periods of 365 days, not tax years. If there is no such intention but the employee subsequently decides to stay for more than three years he is regarded as becoming ordinarily resident from the beginning of the tax year in which he changes his intention (or from the date he originally came to the UK if the change of intention occurs during the tax year in which he comes to the UK) (IR20, para 3.10).

12.5   The Revenue will also regard a secondee as ordinarily resident in the UK from the date of his arrival if:

(*a*)   he already owns accommodation here;

(*b*)   he buys accommodation during the tax year in which he comes to the UK; or

(*c*)   he acquires accommodation on a lease of three years or more during the year in which he comes to the UK.

If such accommodation is acquired in a later year that will of course trigger ordinary residence from the start of that year (IR20, para 3.11). If the accommodation is disposed of within the first three years the Revenue say that 'you may be treated as not ordinarily resident for the duration of your stay if this is to your advantage' (IR20, para 3.12). It is not clear if the word 'may' implies a right to the taxpayer to claim non-ordinary residence or a discretion to the Revenue to apply such a status.

12.6   It should be emphasised that booklet IR20 has no statutory force. The courts will not allow the Revenue to act contrary to their published views on an application for judicial review, but that is a fairly expensive procedure. Furthermore, the booklet itself states that the views expressed in it will not necessarily be applied where tax avoidance is suspected. Accordingly, although the booklet refers to accommodation owned or leased by the employee, it is probably not possible to avoid ordinary residence merely by putting the ownership of the property in the hands of a third party, such as an offshore company.

12.7   A short term visitor to the UK is treated as UK resident from the day of his arrival in the UK if he comes to the UK for a purpose that will require him to remain here for at least two years (IR20, para 3.7). If he does not he will be regarded as UK resident in any tax year in which he spends more than 182 days in the UK. If he spends less than 183 but more than 90 days in the UK on a regular basis he will be treated as resident in the UK from the beginning of the fifth tax year in which he spends over 90 days in the UK, unless it was clear initially (or from some intermediate date) that he would average 90 days in the UK, in which case he will be treated as resident from 6 April in the first tax year in which he spends 90 days in the UK or forms the intention to do so (IR20, para 3.3). The rules in 12.5 above in relation to accommodation apply to residence also, i.e. owning a house in the UK will automatically make a person resident in the UK from the day of his arrival if he spends more than 90 days on average in this country from that time (IR20, para 3.7).

12.8   The rules have been outlined in some depth because the length of the secondment and the employee's accommodation in the UK can of themselves affect his tax status. For example, if a person is seconded to the UK for a year and the secondment is renewed for a further year and then a further year he may never become either resident or ordinarily resident in the UK if he spends less than six months in this country in any one tax year. If the employee is given a three year secondment he will be resident here from the time he arrives if he spends over 90 days here in that tax year or over 182 days in the next. Renting a house for four years when he arrives would make the employee resident and ordinarily resident here from day one (if he meets the 90 day test), whereas if the rental agreement is for two years that would make him resident but not ordinarily resident here.

12.9   It will be apparent that ordinary residence is an important concept for the secondee, particularly if he is a Commonwealth citizen entitled to the protection of *section 65(4)*. It should also be borne in mind that a non-Commonwealth citizen may be entitled to this protection under the non-discrimination clause of a double tax agreement. This prevents the UK taxing its own citizens (who are of course Commonwealth citizens) less heavily than a citizen of the other Contracting State.

Taxation of earnings

12.10   The basic rule is that the UK is entitled to tax the worldwide earnings of its residents and also the UK earnings of non-UK residents [*ICTA 1988, s 19*]. This is, however, modified in a number of situations.

(*a*)   An employee who is not resident in the UK is taxable here only on earnings in respect of duties performed in the UK [*ICTA 1988, s 19(1), Case II*].

(*b*)   An employee who is resident but not ordinarily resident in the UK is taxable here on:

    (i)   earnings in respect of duties performed in the UK [*ICTA 1988, s 19(1), Case II*]; and

    (ii)   earnings in respect of non-UK duties which are brought into (or remitted to) the UK [*ICTA 1988, s 19(2), Case III*].

(*c*)   An employee who is resident but not domiciled in the UK is taxable here on:

    (i)   the whole of his earnings in respect of an employment that is carried on wholly or partly in the UK [*ICTA 1988, s 19(1), Case I and s 192*];

    (ii)   the whole of his earnings in respect of an employment carried on wholly outside the UK where the employee is UK ordinarily resident [*ICTA 1988, s 19(1), Case I*]; and

    (iii)   earnings in respect of an employment under a person who is not a resident of the UK where the duties are performed wholly outside the UK, to the extent that such earnings are brought into the UK (called 'foreign emoluments') [*ICTA 1988, s 19(1), Case III*].

(*d*)   Where the employee is a resident of a non–UK company the UK may be prevented under the terms of a double tax agreement from imposing UK tax even on UK earnings and even if the employee is also a UK resident under UK tax rules.

12.11   Clearly no UK tax planning is required if a double tax agreement prevents the UK from taxing the income. The OECD Model Tax Convention provides that remuneration derived by a resident of one Contracting State can be taxed in the other only if:

(*a*)   the employee is present in the other State (i.e. the UK in this instance) for a period or periods not exceeding in the aggregate 183 days in any twelve month period commencing or ending in the fiscal year concerned (a year to 5 April in the case of the UK);

(*b*)   the remuneration is paid by, or on behalf of, an employer who is not a resident of the other State (i.e. who is non–UK resident or deemed to be non–UK resident for the purpose of the double tax agreement); and

(*c*)   the remuneration is not borne by a permanent establishment or a fixed base which the employer has in the other State (i.e. for a secondee to the UK, is not an expense of a UK branch of the employee's foreign employer).

Most of the UK's double tax agreements adopt this provision. The wording of some of the older agreements differs though.

12.12   It should particularly be noted that the secondee needs to remain an employee of his foreign employer. The exemption does not apply if he becomes an employee of a UK company [*para (b)*]. The Revenue view is that *para (b)* is not satisfied if the remuneration is paid by, for example, the UK subsidiary company to whom the employee has been seconded (Double Tax Relief (DTR) Manual, para 1922). It is doubtful if this conforms with the treaty if the UK company merely pays the remuneration for convenience, as agent of the overseas company. Nevertheless it is safer not to risk an argument and a possible appearance before the Commissioners. The OECD commentary to the Model Agreement indicates that the term employer should be interpreted in the context of the provision of the agreement and that substance should prevail over form. Where there is an intermediate employment company the employer for the purpose of the agreement is likely to be the person having rights over the work produced and bearing the relevant responsibility and risks. This could well be the end user, not the intermediary.

12.13   In calculating the 183 day test part days are taken into account as part days (DTR Manual, para 1921); they are not ignored as happens for the purpose of determining whether a person is resident in the UK (but this treatment is a little more generous than the OECD suggests in its commentary to the Model Agreement, namely that a part day should be treated as a whole day).

12.14   The OECD commentary gives no guidance as to the meaning of (*c*) in 12.11. However, the Revenue interpret it in a broad manner. They regard the 'remuneration' as having been borne by a UK branch if it is an element in the calculation of a management charge to that branch. Where the employee is seconded to work for a UK company they similarly contend that the exemption does not apply if the UK company

> 'for all potential purposes functions as his employer during the UK assignment and the UK company bears the cost of the employee's remuneration either by a direct recharge or as part of a management charge made by the non-resident employer.'
>
> (DTR Manual, para 1922)

They do, however, say that in the case of very short-term secondees (under 60 days in a tax year) it is unlikely that a secondee would be sufficiently integrated within the business of the UK company for it to be regarded as his employer. The safest approach is to ensure that the seconded employee is given some specific responsibilities to his foreign employer such as liaison, reporting and dealing with UK suppliers of customers of the employer (if there are any). Provided that these are genuine responsibilities they are a strong indication that the 'employer' is not the UK company.

12.15   There is an obligation to operate PAYE even where the double taxation agreement applies, as it is for the employee to prove that he is entitled to the benefit of the agreement. However, there is a procedure under which the Revenue will agree not to operate the formal procedure and to take such cases out of the scope of PAYE, provided that the employer agrees that, if the DTR claim proves to be unjustified, it will accept responsibility (on a grossed up basis) for the PAYE that should have been deducted. The employer must also agree to provide certain information to the Revenue (Employment Procedures Manual, paras 8127–8).

12.16   Where a double tax agreement does not exempt the income from UK tax it is next necessary to consider whether the employment will be carried out wholly in the UK or partly in the UK and partly overseas. If it is wholly in the UK PAYE needs to be applied in the normal way. If the employee is being sent not to work for a UK branch or entity, but, say, to research the feasibility of setting up a UK operation, and there is no one in the UK to operate PAYE, the Revenue will collect the tax on the remuneration direct from the employee. However, they will normally do this only if they accept that the employer has no presence in the UK. If the employee is sent to set up a UK branch they consider that the branch needs to apply PAYE once the company has established a presence here, i.e. set up the branch.

12.17   Where the employment will be performed partly in the UK and partly overseas two factors need to be considered. Is the employee ordinarily resident in the UK? If not, only part of the salary is taxable here. If he is, should he have a separate employment for non-UK work? This is not always feasible though. It depends on the nature of the work.

12.18   If the employee is not ordinarily resident in the UK (or indeed, not resident here), and is thus taxable only on earnings from UK work, and he has a single global employment contract the Revenue have power to agree that PAYE need be charged on only the appropriate part of his salary [*ICTA 1988, s 203D*]. In most cases the taxable proportion cannot be ascertained in advance as it will not be known precisely how much time the individual will spend on UK duties. Accordingly an estimate has to be agreed with the Revenue. If the estimate proves too low the Revenue have power to recover the underpayment from the employee (not the employer) [*ICTA 1988, s 203D(9)*].

12.19   There is normally little point in having separate contracts for UK and overseas work when only the UK element is taxable, unless the employee is UK resident and there is a possibility that he will want to bring overseas earnings into the UK. The Revenue have power to aggregate and re-apportion the remuneration where the two contracts are with connected employers, as will normally be the case [*ICTA 1988, Sch 12 para 2*]. They are likely to seek to do this if the two salaries do not approximate to the time spent on the respective employments – which is how they approach the apportionment under *section 203D*.

12.20   The Revenue tend to scrutinise dual employment situations fairly closely. If they can show that any part, however minor, of the duties of the non-UK employment are performed in the UK the strategy will not work because the duties of that employment must be performed wholly outside the UK [*ICTA 1988, s 192(2)*]. Accordingly, the UK and overseas duties must be such that they could have been performed by different people. If the employee visits a customer overseas and comes back to the UK to write and confirm the order from memory, the Revenue are likely to contend that the agreements are a sham if the employee contends that he has written the confirmation under his UK contract. On the other hand, if he writes a note of the order while he is overseas and confirms the order in the UK from that note the Revenue would find it difficult to attack the arrangement, as someone else could then have written the confirmatory letter. Where in practice it is not practical to create a split in this way for some of the overseas work, but it is for other parts of it, it is generally safest to limit the work under the overseas employment agreement to the 'safe' operations. There is no problem in the UK agreement also including some overseas duties; the key thing is that the overseas agreement must not include any UK duties. In such a case the duties obviously need to be fairly fully defined in the two agreements so it is clear what activities are in pursuance of which agreement. It is a good idea to do this in any event. It forces the parties to consider precisely what duties need to be performed and whether some of such duties are incapable of being split between the UK and overseas. It also makes clear to the employee what work he needs to do under each contract.

12.21   The other problem with dual employment (sometimes called Double Schedule E) arrangements is that the employee must be capable of ensuring that the work under the two contracts is separated in practice, not merely in theory. This includes not only remembering to write letters, orders, etc. on the right notepaper but also such things as charging expenses to the right company. If a dual employment arrangement is used it is of course important to ensure that the salary is paid into a non-UK bank account of the employee. If it is paid into a UK account it will have been remitted to the UK and thus be taxable here.

12.22   What is a remittance? The legislation provides that for the purposes of *Case III of Schedule E* (under which the remittance of overseas earnings is taxed) earnings are to be treated as received in the UK if they are:

(*a*)   paid in the UK;

(*b*)   used in the UK;

(*c*)   enjoyed in the UK; or

(*d*)   in any manner or form transmitted or brought to the UK.

[*ICTA 1988, s 132(5)*].

12.23   For this purpose income arising outside the UK which is applied outside the UK in (or towards) settlement of:

(*a*)   a debt for money lent in the UK (or interest on such a debt);

(*b*)   a debt for money lent outside the UK and brought into the UK (N.B. interest on such a debt is a non-UK liability and the payment of that interest will not trigger a remittance provided that it is paid outside the UK); or

(*c*)   a replacement debt for one falling within (*a*) or (*b*),

must be regarded as having been transmitted to the UK. [*ICTA 1988, ss 132(5), 65(6)*].

12.24   If money is borrowed outside the UK, the loan is repaid out of overseas earnings and then the money is brought into the UK this is still a remittance. In such a case the date of the remittance is obviously the date the money is brought into the UK not the date the loan is repaid [*ICTA 1988, ss 132(5), 65(7)*]. If, instead of using income to repay a loan, the money is deposited with the lender in circumstances that it is available to the lender to satisfy the debt (by set-off or otherwise) the income is treated as having been used to satisfy the debt [*ICTA 1988, ss 13(5), 65(8)*]. If an employee borrows money before coming to the UK and remits it to the UK it is accordingly important that he does not deposit his income overseas with the same bank if there is a right of set-off, as is likely to be the case. Similarly, he should not pledge his overseas income account as security to the lender.

12.25   If an asset is purchased out of the income overseas and brought into the UK the Revenue do not regard that as a remittance of the earnings to the UK, albeit that the use of that asset will be enjoyed in the UK. However, if the asset is sold here they regard the sale proceeds as a remittance (Inspector's Manual, para 1569). It should, however, be noted that whilst most people would not regard using a credit card to pay bills overseas as a remittance where the credit card bill is paid overseas, the Revenue consider the payment to be a remittance if the credit card company is a UK company (Inspector's Manual, para 1569). It is highly questionable whether this is a correct analysis.

12.26   Where an employee is taxable on the remittance basis, he needs to segregate income and capital overseas if he is likely to want to remit funds to the UK. Remitting capital will not trigger an income tax charge (although it could trigger a capital gains tax charge if the employee has realised capital gains overseas). It is, however, for the employee to demonstrate that what he is remitting is capital. If no income has ever been paid into the relevant bank account it is easy to do this. Income means income arising after the employee became UK resident. Income earned before that date is capital for this purpose. If any income has been paid into the account, however, it becomes impossible in many, if not most, cases to demonstrate that what is being remitted is not that income. The Revenue's approach is to regard all remittances from such a mixed fund as income until the whole of the income content of the fund has been accounted for. The 'cessation of source' trick does not work for Schedule E income. Accordingly, once income has been paid into a mixed fund that fund is tainted until such income has either been remitted or can be shown to have been spent overseas. A gift overseas to a third party (including a relative or even the employee's spouse) will not give rise to a remittance even if the recipient brings the money into the UK (as it is not income in the hands of the recipient) provided that it can be shown that the gift is made overseas and that the gift is genuine. For the gift to be made overseas the money ought to be transferred from an overseas bank account of the donor to an overseas bank account of the donee.

Travel expenses

12.27   There are some special rules on travelling expenses. Where a person who is both resident and ordinarily resident in the UK has two or more employments and the duties of one of them are performed wholly or partly outside the UK, the expense of travel to or from the UK is treated as having been necessarily incurred in the performance of the duties which he is to perform at his destination [*ICTA 1988, s 193(5)(6)*]. In other words, travel from overseas where the employee was working under the overseas employment is treated as an expense of the UK employment and travel from the UK is treated as an expense of the overseas employment. The employee must have performed duties of one of his employments at the place from which he is travelling and must be going to the other country to perform duties of the other employment there [*ICTA 1988, s 193(5)(6)*]. If the duties are covered by a single global contract the expenses are allowable under general principles so this special rule is not needed. If the travel is partly for the purpose of performing the duties of the employment and partly for some other purpose the provision applies only to such part of the expenses as is properly attributable to the former purpose [*ICTA 1988, s 193(6)*]. The Revenue give as an example of another purpose a holiday, and say that apportionment is a matter of negotiation and will depend on the facts. Where a person is resident in the UK one purpose of travelling to the UK is normally to come home, which is clearly a non-employment purpose, but in practice the Revenue do not take this point as to do so would undermine the purpose of the relief.

12.28   Where an employee who is not domiciled in the UK is in receipt of emoluments for duties performed in the UK he is allowed a deduction in charging tax under Case I or II of Schedule E for the cost of:

(*a*)   any journey from his usual place of abode (i.e. his home country) to the UK in order to perform duties of the employment in the UK;

(*b*)   any journey from the UK after performing such duties here to his usual place of abode; and

(*c*)   if he is in the UK for a continuous period of 60 days or more, up to two return journeys in a tax year per person by his spouse or infant children between his normal place of abode and the place where he works in the UK, provided that the journey is either to accompany the employee at the beginning of that 60 day period or to visit him during it.

[*ICTA 1988, s 195(1)(5)(6)*].

12.29   There are a number of caveats to this basic rule. The expense must be met or reimbursed by the employer [*ICTA 1988, s 195(7)*]. A continuous period of 60 days means just that; strictly speaking a business trip or holiday overseas would break the period. However, the Revenue will ignore such days of absence on genuine business trips provided that at least 60 days are spent in the UK in the period, i.e. if the person is abroad for three days for business the continuous period would need to be 63 days including the business trip (Schedule E Manual, para SE 35050). A child includes a stepchild and an illegitimate child but not a person who is 18 or over at the beginning of the journey to the UK [*ICTA 1988, s 195(10)*]. The relief will still apply to the expense of the return trip if the child turns 18 whilst he is in the UK. A person's usual place of abode is the country outside the UK in which he normally lives [*ICTA 1988, s 195(9)*]. It is not necessary for him to have retained a residence there (Schedule E Manual, para SE 35040). In the case of a secondee it is likely to be the country from which he was seconded, although it is possible to envisage circumstances where that will not be the case.

12.30 The relief applies only to the costs of the journey. This would include costs of hotels and probably subsistence and hotels en route but would not cover board and lodging while in the UK (Schedule E Manual, para SE 35050).

12.31 The deduction applies only to journeys made within five years of the date that the employee first makes a qualifying arrival in the UK. This is normally the date he initially comes to the UK. However, this will be a qualifying arrival only if either:

(*a*)   he was not resident in the UK in either (not both) of the two tax years immediately preceding that in which the arrival occurs; or

(*b*)   he was not in the UK for any purpose (such as on holiday) at any time during the two years (periods of 365 days) immediately preceding the date of arrival.

[*ICTA 1988, s 195(2)(3)*].

A secondee will normally have no difficulty in meeting (*a*) above.

12.32 The normal UK rules on travel expenses apply where a person works partly overseas and partly in the UK. In particular, a deduction is allowed from salary for expenses of travelling which are attributable to the necessary attendance at any place of the employee in the performance of the duties of his employment and which are not expenses of ordinary commuting or private travel (*ICTA 1988, s 198(1A)*). The exclusion for ordinary commuting covers travel between the employee's home and a place which is a permanent workplace and that for private travel between the employee's home and a place which is not a workplace at all in relation to the employment (*ICTA 1988, Sch 12A para 2(1)–(3)*). The effect is that travel between an employee's home and a temporary workplace is deductible (whether or not the cost is borne by the employer). The legislation provides that a place cannot be a temporary workplace if the employee's attendance there is in the course of a period of continuous work at that place which either lasts more than 24 months or comprises almost all of the total period for which the employee is likely to hold the employment [*ICTA 1988, Sch 12A para 5(1)*]. A period of continuous work is a period over which, taken as a whole, the duties of the employment fall to be performed to a significant extent at that place [*ICTA 1988, Sch 12A para 5(2)*]. The Revenue have said that they regard duties as performed to a significant extent at a place if the employee spends 40 per cent or more of his working time at the place.

12.33 This can be a very significant relief for short-term secondees. If a person is sent to work for his employer's UK branch under a secondment of less than two years his place of work in the UK will be a temporary workplace and his travel expenses to the UK will be fully deductible without having to meet the restrictive conditions of *section 195.* Travel expenses normally includes accommodation and subsistence.

> 'Even where an employee stays away for some time and the travel expenses are deductible, the cost of meals and accommodation is part of the overall cost of the business travel'
>
> (Schedule E Manual, para SE 1815)

The Revenue give as a specific example:

> 'An employee of a German company is seconded to a temporary workplace in the UK for 15 months. He sells his flat in Germany and rents a flat in the UK. When he returns to Germany he will need to find himself a new place to live. The rent of the UK flat is attributable to the business travel and a deduction can be given for the cost.'
>
> (Schedule E Manual, para SE 1816)

Travel costs can also include other incidental costs that form an integral part of the cost of the business journey. This could include the cost of hiring a car and parking charges (Schedule E Manual, para SE 31820).

12.34   There is a major trap here. If the secondee becomes an employee not of a UK branch but of a UK subsidiary company his place of work in the UK will not qualify as a temporary workplace as it is his permanent workplace while in the subsidiary's employment. Accordingly, no deduction for the above expenses would be due.

Removal expenses

12.35   There are no special rules on removal costs where an employee moves from his home overseas to the UK. The normal rules apply. These allow a deduction for specific expenses up to a maximum of £8,000 provided that these expenses are paid for or reimbursed by the employer (or by a third party such as another group company). Although the specified expenses include travelling expenses, if travelling expenses qualify for relief under *ICTA 1988, s 195* (see 12.28–12.31) they are not eligible expenses under the removals legislation [*ICTA 1988, Sch 11A para 12(4)*]. The effect is that such expenses do not count towards the £8,000 limit on other expenses.

Other deductions

12.36   Where a person in receipt of foreign emoluments (see 12.10) makes payments corresponding to those in which the payments would have reduced his liability to income tax the Revenue can (and of course normally will) allow those payments as a deduction in computing the amount of the emoluments [*ICTA 1988, s 192(3)*]. The main, if not only, items this is nowadays likely to cover are contributions to overseas pension funds and interest paid under a foreign loan agreement. Pension scheme contributions are deductible only if the Revenue's Pension Schemes Office is provided with details of the scheme and takes the view that the benefit it provides corresponds to those under a UK approved scheme. They will not grant approval if the benefits are significantly better than those that can be provided under a UK scheme. The PSO no longer grants blanket approval in relation to such schemes. It needs to approve the payments in respect of each individual employee who comes to the UK and is a member of the scheme. The Revenue will allow a deduction for foreign interest payments only if the taxpayer has insufficient foreign income to cover the payments (Schedule E Manual, para SE 32665). The interest must of course also be for an allowable purpose.

Tax equalisation payments

12.37   When a multinational seconds an employee to the UK it normally makes available a tax equalisation plan. Tax equalisation aims to ensure that an employee sent to work in a foreign country pays no more (and sometimes no less) tax than he would have paid had he continued to work in his home country. The details of such plans vary. A payment to an employee (or direct to the Revenue) under a tax equalisation plan is income for UK tax purposes. If the payment relates to income taxable under Case I or II of Schedule E it is taxable in the UK (subject to the wording of any relevant double tax agreement), even if it is paid to the employee after he has returned home, as it is additional earnings for the period of UK residence. It is, however, taxable in the year in which the payment is made.

12.38   Where an employee has both Case II income (for work performed in the UK) and Case III income (remittances of earnings of a foreign employment) the Revenue consider that to the extent that the tax equalisation payment is to meet a tax liability in respect of the Case II earnings it is itself taxable under Case II. They do not accept that as the tax liability relates to the employee's overall taxable income it should be apportioned in proportion to such income. They feel so strongly about this that they have said that anyone who takes the contrary view will need to litigate the position (Tax Bulletin Issue 27, February 1997).

Share options

12.39   The special provisions in relation to share options normally apply only where the employee is taxable under Case I of Schedule E (i.e. he is both resident and ordinarily resident in the UK when the option is granted (or in some cases exercised)). If a person who is not UK resident and ordinarily resident is granted an option there will still be a tax charge on the value of the option at the time it is granted. This is normally very small. The value of an option depends on the view that a prospective purchaser would take of the likely value of the shares at the time the option comes to be exercised and his assessment of the risk that the then value might be below the option price.

Secondment from the UK

12.40   Secondment from the UK is of course secondment to another country. Except for very short term secondments the secondee is likely to cease to be UK resident and become a resident of the host country. In such circumstances he will leave the UK tax net and become enmeshed in that of the host country. Advice needs to be taken locally as to the tax position in the host country.

Loss of UK residence and ordinary residence

12.41   The basic rule is that a person will cease to be resident in the UK if he spends less than 90 days on average in the UK in subsequent tax years. He will cease to be ordinarily resident in the UK if he is non-UK resident for three consecutive years (IR20, paras 2.8 and 2.9). If at the time a person leaves the UK there is evidence to indicate that he is likely to be non-resident for the next three tax years the Revenue will provisionally treat him as non-UK resident from the time of his departure and will revisit the position after three years. If there is no such evidence they will provisionally regard him as remaining UK resident but will again review the position after three years and if they then decide that he ceased to be UK resident when he left will adjust his tax position with retrospective effect.

12.42   The UK cannot require a non-UK resident to make a return of non-UK income as the reaches of the UK tax system cannot stretch beyond the borders of this country. In the context of self-assessment it is for the taxpayer to take a view on his residence position. If he takes the view that he is non-resident and does not file UK tax returns there is not a lot that the Revenue can do about it while he is overseas. By the time he ultimately returns to the UK the evidence to establish his non-residence is likely to have become available.

12.43   There is a more generous residence rule where a person leaves the UK to work full time abroad provided that the following conditions are met (IR20, para 2.2).

(*a*)   His absence from the UK and his employment abroad span at least one complete tax year.

(*b*)   His visits to the UK do not exceed 182 days in any one tax year or 90 days a year on average over the period spent overseas.

The employee is treated as being both non-resident and non-ordinarily resident in the UK from the time he leaves the UK until the time that he returns.

12.44   It will be seen that the employee needs to leave the UK before the start of one tax year and not return (except for visits) until after the end of that year. Strictly the overseas employment also needs to continue. However, if the secondee is made redundant or leaves during the year abroad and takes another overseas employment the Revenue will normally apply this concessionary treatment. Indeed, they may be prepared to do so even if the employee returns to the UK between the jobs and looks for the new overseas job while he is here, if the time spent in the UK is short and there is a continuing intention to go overseas again (IR20, para 2.3).

12.45   The Revenue regard a person as working full-time abroad for this purpose (but not necessarily for other purposes) if the individual is putting in what a layman would clearly recognise as a full working week. IR20 (para 2.5) suggests that they look at a typical UK working week, but it is far more logical to look at the normal working week in the foreign country concerned. Where a job does not involve a formal pattern of hours they look at the nature of the job and take account of local conditions and practices in that particular occupation. Where a person has several part-time jobs abroad contemporaneously with the same group of companies they will normally aggregate the time and may be prepared to do this even where the companies are not connected (Tax Bulletin Issue 6, February 1993).

12.46   If a person is treated as non-UK resident under this rule and his spouse accompanies him overseas the spouse is regarded as non-UK resident as well (but obviously in applying the 182 and 90 day tests it is the spouse's visits not the employee's that are looked at (Extra-Statutory Concession (ESC) A78).

12.47   An employee who ceases to be UK resident will cease to be liable to UK income tax (except on UK source income) on income arising from the day that he leaves the UK (ESC A11). However, for capital gains tax purposes he remains resident until the following 5 April (i.e. he is UK resident for the whole of the year of departure) except where he was non-UK resident and ordinary resident for at least four of the previous seven tax years (ESC D2). In other words, for capital gains tax, split year treatment normally only applies where the individual originally lived overseas and came to the UK for a temporary period of up to three years.

12.48   Where a secondee will cease to be UK resident it needs to be borne in mind that the Schedule E rules take a two stage approach to taxing earnings. The person's status at the time the work is done determines taxability but once this has been done the income is taxed in the year in which the income is received. This means that if the secondee receives a bonus or commission after leaving the UK which relates to work done while he was UK resident that amount will be chargeable to UK tax, albeit that he is non-UK resident when he receives the payment – unless of course it is taken out of the scope of UK tax under a double tax agreement. Whilst not free from doubt, there is a good argument that in applying the OECD standard wording under the dependent personal services article (which deals with employment income) the test as to whether the UK can tax the income is applied by reference to the employee's presence in the UK during the tax year in which the remuneration is paid, rather than that in which it was earned. Other countries do not adopt the UK's two stage test so it is impractical to apply it in interpreting a double tax treaty between two countries.

12.49   If the secondment is for such a short period that the secondee will remain UK resident, earnings for the work performed in the other country will remain liable to UK tax but the employee will be entitled to claim double taxation relief for any foreign tax payable on those earnings. Where the overseas country is one which has a double tax agreement with the UK that agreement may well prohibit that country from taxing the salary (see 12.11). If it prohibits local taxation but such tax is nevertheless deducted at source the Revenue may well refuse to grant double tax relief. The correct procedure is for the employee to reclaim the tax from the overseas tax authority.

12.50   It should not be overlooked that there may be cases in which it is in the employee's interest to remain UK resident. For example, if he will work in several countries some of which have high tax rates it may be preferable to remain within the UK tax net and use the UK's double tax agreements to escape tax in the overseas countries. However, except in the case of seafarers who are entitled to a special foreign earnings deduction, this situation is unlikely to be common.

Pension contributions

12.51   If the secondee is a member of his employer's Revenue approved pension scheme he can remain a member of that pension scheme even if he will cease to be UK resident during his period overseas (IR booklet, 'Occupational pension scheme practice notes', IR12, para 15.6). He can remain a member of the scheme even if he is working for an overseas subsidiary or other associated company during the period of his secondment provided that:

(*a*)   either there is a definite expectation that the employee will return to the UK to take up employment with a scheme employer or to retire, or the employee's earnings remain chargeable to UK tax;

(*b*)   the UK employer continues to pay any contributions due in respect of the employee and is reimbursed by the overseas employer for such amounts;

(*c*)   the pensionable earnings are calculated by reference to similar employment in the UK; and

(*d*)   the period of service does not exceed 10 years (where there is more than one period of overseas service they must be aggregated).

(IR20, para 15.9.)

These conditions are easily met in the case of most secondees.

Travel expenses

12.52   Where a UK resident and ordinarily resident employee works in an employment carried on wholly outside the UK (the earnings from which are not foreign emoluments – see 12.10) he can deduct from the earnings from that employment the costs of travelling from the UK to take up the employment and of returning to the UK on its termination [*ICTA 1988, s 193(2)(3)*]. If board and lodging outside the UK is provided for him at the cost of his employer (or he incurs the cost and his employer reimburses it to him) no tax charge arises on the employee in respect of that cost [*ICTA 1988, s 193(2)(4)*]. If the expense is incurred partly for such a purpose and partly for some other purpose an apportionment must be made [*ICTA 1988, s 193(3)(4)*]. The relief for travel between employments where a person who has two employments, one in the UK and one elsewhere, is described at 12.27.

12.53   If a person has an office or employment, the duties of which are performed partly in the UK and partly elsewhere, no benefit in kind arises on a journey by the employee from any place in the UK to the place of performance of any of the duties outside the UK (or from the place of performance of those duties back to the UK) [*ICTA 1988, s 194(3)*].

12.54   Unlike under *section 193(2)* (see 12.51) the expenses must be borne (or reimbursed) by the employer [*ICTA 1988, s 194(1)*]. The employee must be resident and ordinarily resident in the UK. Although this is not specifically stated in the legislation, the relief is to be given in charging tax under Case I of Schedule E which can only apply where a person is both resident and ordinarily resident in the UK. The overseas duties concerned must be duties that can only be performed outside the UK and the journey must be made wholly and exclusively for the purpose of going to (or returning from) performing the duties [*ICTA 1988, s 194(4)*]. This is an anti-avoidance provision. Without it the employee could have taken a suitcase of work to the South of France and escape tax on the fare when that work could just as easily have been performed in the UK.

12.55   It should be noted that this relief will not apply if the employee has a separate employment for overseas work. The separate relief in *section 193* (see 12.51) will apply in such circumstances but it is less generous as it applies only to journeys at the beginning and end of the employment. This gap is filled by *ICTA 1988, s 194(5)*. This provides that where a person (who is UK resident and ordinarily resident) is absent from the UK for the purpose of performing the duties of one or more employments, no benefit charge will arise in respect of travel expenses of any journey by him from the place of performance of the duties outside the UK to any place in the UK, or of the return journey after such a trip. Again the overseas duties must be ones that can only be performed outside the UK [*ICTA 1988, s 194(6)*]. This will ensure that no benefit charge arises on, for example, weekend visits back to visit the employee's family provided that the employer is prepared to bear the cost of such trips.

12.56   Where an employee is absent from the UK for a continuous period of 60 days or more, for the purpose of performing the duties of one or more employments, no tax charge on the employee arises on travel expenses borne by his employer for a journey between any place in the UK and the place of performance of any of the overseas duties by either his spouse or child to accompany him at the beginning of the period of absence or to visit him during that period [*ICTA 1988, s 194(1)(2)*]. The exemption is limited to two return journeys per person in a tax year [*ICTA 1988, s 194(2)*]. A child includes a stepchild and an illegitimate child. The child must be 18 or over at the beginning of the outward journey from the UK [*ICTA 1988, s 194(2)*].

12.57   The Revenue have said that holidays taken abroad and weekends spent abroad do not interrupt a continuous period of absence for this purpose, even if the leave is taken at the beginning or end of the period of absence (Schedule E Manual, para SE 34060). It should particularly be noted that the two allowable visits is not per continuous period overseas but per tax year. Accordingly, if a person is seconded abroad from, say, 1 March to 31 May his family could visit him twice in the period 1 March to 5 April and a further two times in the period 6 April to 31 May without a benefit in kind charge arising. The Revenue tell their staff to interpret the place of performance of the overseas duties sensibly. They also indicate that if a person is working in, say, Paris a trip by his family to meet him in Nice would not qualify but a trip to Paris would qualify even if the family all then go on from Paris to Nice (the Paris to Nice leg would obviously not qualify) (Schedule E Manual, SE 34060).

12.58   *Section 194* actually refers to 'travel facilities' but does not define that expression. The Revenue say that it should be taken as covering fares and subsistence expenditure while travelling (Schedule E Manual, para SE 34130). They give as an example an individual who travels by train, eats meals on the train and stays overnight to break the journey. The cost of all three would qualify for the relief.

12.59   The normal relief for travelling and accommodation costs for 'detached duties', i.e. where a person is working at a temporary workplace for not more than 24 months, apply as much where the temporary workplace is outside the UK as they do to another UK location. This relief is described at 12.32–12.34 above. Similarly, the relief for removal costs described at 12.35 will apply where the removal is to a place outside the UK.

12.60   Where the secondment is for less than two years and the employer provides accommodation for the employee in the overseas location this should not give rise to a UK tax charge. This is because relief can be given for that accommodation under either *section 193(4)* (see 12.51) or *Schedule 12* (see 12.33) if the employee remains UK resident, and the overseas earnings will be outside the scope of UK tax if he does not.

National insurance

12.61   Although national insurance, like income tax, is administered by the Inland Revenue the rules are not identical. Liability to UK primary Class 1 national insurance (i.e. the employee's contributions) arises if a person is either resident, present, or ordinarily resident in the UK [*Social Security (Contributions) Regulations 2001, (SI 2001 No 1004), reg 145(1)(a)*]. If there are no primary contributions there are no secondary contributions (employer) either. If a liability to primary contributions arises then secondary contributions are payable only if the employer is either resident in the UK or has a place of business in the UK [*SI 2001 No 1004, reg 145(1)(b)*].

12.62   The Revenue tells its staff 'You should operate Residence Manual guidance in deciding whether a person is resident or ordinarily resident in the UK except that split year treatment should not be used for NICs' (National Insurance Manual, para 33021). On the face of it this should mean that the test for residence and ordinary residence is the same for both tax and national insurance. Unfortunately, the Residence Guide Manual does not say much about the meaning of residence and ordinary residence. There are, however, two Revenue leaflets, 'National insurance for employers of people working abroad' (NI132 – June 2001) and 'National insurance abroad – a guide for employers of employees from abroad' (CA76 – April 2001).

12.63   The first of these does not define residence but states that a person is ordinarily resident in a particular country if he normally lives there, apart from temporary or occasional absences, and has a settled and regular mode of life there. It says that the amount depends on individual circumstances, but factors to take into account are whether the person will be returning to the UK from time to time during the period of employment (the more frequent or longer the returns, the more likely that ordinary residence continues); what will be the purposes of return visits (visits to family who have remained at the person's home in the UK would indicate continued ordinary residence); whether the partner and/or children will also go abroad during the overseas employment; whether a home will be maintained in the UK during the absence (if so this points to continued ordinary residence); if a home is maintained in the UK whether it will be available for their use on return (indicative of continued ordinary residence); whether the person has lived in the UK for a substantial period (the longer the period the more likely that ordinary residence status will be maintained despite the period of employment abroad); and whether the person will return to the UK at the end of the period of employment abroad (if so, and the earlier the return, the more likely that ordinary residence status will be maintained in the UK). It should particularly be noted that there is no three year (or other period) time limit to these tests – in the past the Contributions Agency, which formerly administered national insurance, used a five year time limit. The coming to the UK leaflet does not define either residence or ordinary residence, but that is not surprising as these are not relevant tests where a person works in the UK, as he is clearly present here while he carries out that work.

12.64   The probability is that the test is broader than that used for income tax. For income tax purposes there is a statutory provision in relation to income tax under Schedule D (self-employment) or Schedule E (employment), namely that the question whether a person is in the UK for some temporary purpose only and not with a view to establishing his residence there is to be decided without regard to any living accommodation available in the UK for his use [*ICTA 1988, s 336(3)*]. In practice, the Revenue ignore such accommodation for all income tax purposes, but it appears from leaflet NI132 that they do not ignore it for national insurance purposes. Unfortunately it appears from the leaflet that there is no standard test; the Revenue will take a view individual by individual on a person's ordinary residence.

12.65   The general rule for secondees out of the UK is that there is a liability to Class 1 national insurance contributions on overseas earnings for up to 52 weeks if:

(*a*)   the employer has a place of business in the UK;

(*b*)   the employee is ordinarily resident in the UK; and

(*c*)   the employee was resident in the UK immediately before starting the overseas employment.

[*SI 2001 No 1004, reg 146 (1)(2)(a)*].

There is no liability on earnings after the first 52 weeks. The 52 week period is a continuous period. If a person returns to work in the UK and subsequently restarts overseas employment in the same fiscal year a new 52 week period starts. This basic rule is modified if the employee is working in a country in the European Economic Area (EEA) (see 12.69), or in a country with which the UK has a reciprocal agreement (see 12.74).

12.66   An employer is regarded as having a place of business in the UK if he occupies premises of which he is the lawful occupier, or if an employee or agent carries out any activity in the UK which furthers the employer's business (whether or not that activity is remunerated) (N1132). If a person works overseas for an overseas subsidiary of his UK employer the subsidiary may well not have a place of business in the UK. This will change the national insurance position as no Secondary Class 1 contributions will be payable. The Revenue say that the employee will still have a liability to pay primary contributions if he is ordinarily resident in the UK (National Insurance Manual, para 33021). They quote as authority *Social Security (Contributions) Regulations 2001 (SI 2001 No 1004), reg 145(1)(a)*. However, liability on contributions for employment outside the UK is covered by *reg 146* and that is stated to apply only where the employer has a place of business in the UK.

12.67   If he wishes, the employee can opt to pay Class 3 (voluntary) contributions after the end of the 52 week period. [*SI 2001 No 1004, reg 146(2)(b)*].

12.68   The general rule for secondees to the UK is that national insurance is payable on the UK earnings from the date the person comes to the UK. However, if he is neither UK ordinarily resident nor employed in the UK (i.e. by a UK company) but his employer's place of business is outside the UK and the employee works mainly outside the UK, national insurance is not payable on UK earnings in pursuance of that overseas employment [*SI 2001 No 1004, reg 145(2)*]. The effect of this provision is that there will be no UK national insurance liability for short business visits to the UK. This exemption applies for 52 weeks (assuming of course that the employee does not become ordinarily resident in the UK during this period). It should be noted that it will not automatically apply if the employer (which could well be the person who exercises control rather than the person with whom the employee has contracted) is a UK company. If it is the overseas company it does not matter if it has a place of business in the UK in addition to its overseas one (National Insurance Manual, para 33023).

12.69   Interestingly, the Revenue seem to allow the exemption even if the UK employment is with a different employer to the overseas one. They give as an example a doctor who works for a hospital in Egypt and takes a post for two years with a UK hospital to extend his experience but the Egyptian hospital keeps his job open. They accept that the work in the UK, albeit with a different employer, is 'in pursuance of employment' in Egypt (National Insurance Manual, para 33024). A secondee ought to be able to meet this test.

12.70   The rules in paras 12.64 to 12.68 do not apply where the secondee goes to or comes from another EEA State. This is because there is an *EC Regulation 1408/71* which provides (in *Article 6*) that it replaces bilateral agreements between Member States. This regulation was extended to cover all EEA States (other than Switzerland) from 1994 by a treaty between the EC and EFTA. The EEA consists of Austria, Belgium, Denmark, Finland, France, Germany, Greece, Iceland, Italy, Liechtenstein, Luxembourg, Netherlands, Norway, Portugal, the Republic of Ireland, Spain, Sweden and the UK (i.e. the EC plus Iceland, Liechtenstein and Norway). The *Regulation* applies only where the employee is an EEA national or a stateless person residing in an EEA country.

12.71   The *Regulation* provides that a person employed in an EEA State is liable to social security contributions only in the EEA country in which he works if his employer is resident in that country (*Article 13(2)(a)*). If his employer is resident in another EEA country (e.g. his home country) he is liable to social security contributions in his home country provided that the work in the host country is expected to last less than 12 months and the worker is not replacing another employee who has completed a tour of duty abroad (*Article 14(1)(a)(i)*). If due to unforeseen circumstances the period overseas is extended beyond 12 months this treatment will apply for up to a further 12 months.

12.72   Where a UK national is sent overseas the employer must obtain a form E101 from the Revenue (NICO International Services Office) which can then be produced to the social security authorities in the other country to show that there is a continuing liability to UK national insurance. When an EEA national comes to the UK he must produce a form E101 from his home country to show that he is liable to social security there. Where the period is extended a form E102 must be obtained from the Revenue (in the case of a secondment from the UK) or the corresponding social security authority (in the case of a secondment to the UK) and produced to the social security authorities in the host country before the expiry of the initial 12 month period. It is possible for countries to agree bilaterally to extend the home country liability (and host country exemption) beyond 12 months on a case by case basis. An application to do this needs to be made to NICO International Services Office. It is not normally possible to agree an extension to more than 5 years (National Insurance Manual, para 33011).

12.73   Where the secondment will initially be for a period of more than 12 months (or the employee replaces a previous employee and the combined posting will exceed 12 months) the host country is entitled to collect the social security contributions. However, the two countries concerned are empowered by *Article 17* to agree that the home country should be the one to collect the contributions. The Revenue have indicated that they will enter into such an agreement only where either:

(*a*)   the employee has specialist knowledge or skills;

(*b*)   the employer has specific objectives in the other EEA country for which the employee's specialist skills are required; or

(*c*)   it is in the employee's interest to remain UK insured.

(National Insurance Manual, para 33011.)

12.74   If an employee normally works in two or more EEA countries he will remain liable to social security contributions in his home State if:

(*a*)   he is habitually resident in that State; and

(*b*)   he works partly in that State (or works for several employees with a place of business in different States) (*Article 14(1)(b)(i)*).

He will be liable to social security contributions in the State in which his employer has its registered office or place of business (which probably means principal place of business within the EEA) if the employee does not live in any EEA State in which he works in the course of his employment (*Article 14(1)(b)(ii)*). There are some special rules for civil servants and diplomats (*Articles 13(2)(c) and 16*).

12.75   The UK has entered into reciprocal agreements (or Double Taxation Conventions) covering national insurance with Barbados, Bermuda, Canada, Cyprus, Guernsey, Isle of Man, Israel, Jamaica, Japan, Jersey, Korea, Malta, Mauritius, Philippines, Switzerland, Turkey, USA and Yugoslavia. It also has reciprocal agreements with all of the EEA countries other than Greece and Liechtenstein. Although these have been superceded by the EEA Regulations for EEA nationals such agreements will still be applicable if the secondee is a national of a non-EEA country.

12.76 Obviously the relevant agreement needs to be looked at. The general principal of such agreements is that a person should pay social security in the country in which he works. However, if a person is employed in the UK and is posted by his UK employer to work in the other country for a limited period (or sometimes if he will work in both countries for that limited period) the UK retains the taxing right. Similarly, if he is employed by a company in the other country and comes to the UK for a limited period the other country retains the taxing rights and national insurance is not payable. A form similar to the E101 must be obtained from the social security authorities in the country that claims the taxing rights. The limited periods are:

Up to 1 year:	Bermuda, Yugoslavia (including Bosnia and Herzegovina, Croatia, Slovenia and the former Republic of Macedonia)
2 years:	Israel, Mauritius, Switzerland
3 years:	Barbados, Cyprus, Guernsey, Jamaica, Jersey, Malta, Philippines, Turkey
4 years:	None
5 years:	Canada, Japan, Korea, USA

The agreement with the Isle of Man is limited and attributes liability to the country of residence.

12.77 It should particularly be noted that it is normally a condition of home country liability that the employee must work for an employer in his home country while he is in the host country and must have also worked for that same employer in his home country. This treatment cannot apply if, for example, a UK company recruits someone specifically to work for it in, say, the USA. The employee must have worked at least for a short period for the employer in the UK. If the employee is seconded to work for a local subsidiary he will have to pay local social security contributions.

13 Sheltering Income and Gains Overseas for UK Domiciled Individuals: Problems and Solutions

David Kilshaw BA (Oxon) and Carolyn Steppler MA DPhil (KPMG)

Introduction

13.1   United Kingdom taxpayers are not unique in their desire to shelter profits from the ravages of taxation. Unfortunately, although Parliament's fiscal sovereignty only extends to the United Kingdom, the two tenets on which it is based – personal presence of the taxpayer and location of assets – make it difficult for United Kingdom domiciled and resident individuals to shelter profits overseas. These difficulties are compounded by a substantial battery of anti-avoidance legislation.

13.2   This chapter considers the circumstances in which income and capital profits can be sheltered from tax on the assumption that the individual taxpayer is domiciled in the UK. It also considers some of the problems which must be overcome if the planning is to achieve its ultimate objective, the sheltering of income and gains overseas. There are in essence three elements in any individual's tax profile – his domicile, his residence and his ordinary residence status. A change in any one of these can alter the tax position. The chapter on tax planning for non-domiciled individuals considers the loss of the most durable of these factors. This chapter considers, where appropriate, how the abandonment of residence or ordinary residence (while retaining a UK domicile) can nevertheless achieve a tax saving. It is proposed first, however, to comment briefly on the concepts of domicile and residence.

Domicile

13.3   It is not appropriate to enter here into a lengthy discussion on domicile which, for present purposes, may be equated with an individual's permanent home. At the outset of any planning, an individual's domicile should be carefully reviewed. In both writers' experience it is not unusual for the most apparently quintessential of 'Englishmen' to have an overseas domicile. Given the tax savings available, this is always an avenue of enquiry worth pursuing.

Although in strict law an individual can only be domiciled in a territory subject to a single system of law, this chapter adopts the shorthand of the UK tax legislation and refers to a domicile in the United Kingdom (see, for example, *ICTA 1988, s 65(4)*).

Residence and ordinary residence

13.4   Despite their central impact on liability, there are no statutory definitions of either residence or ordinary residence. Instead, there is a largely unsatisfactory mixture of case law and Revenue practice. It would be beyond the scope of this chapter to consider the rules in detail, but it should be noted that while residence usually (but in the Revenue's view, not necessarily) requires physical presence in the UK in the tax year in question, an individual can (in the Revenue's view) be ordinarily resident in the UK even if he has not visited the UK at any time during the tax year.

13.5   The Inland Revenue regards ordinary residence as broadly equivalent to habitual residence and an individual as being ordinarily resident in the UK if he is resident there year after year. As ordinary residence can have a large bearing on a UK domiciled individual's ability to shelter profits, it can be important to determine the time when this status is lost or acquired. This can be difficult in practice, although guidance may be obtained from the Inland Revenue's booklet IR20.

Sheltering income from tax

Territorial limits

13.6   Lord Herschell summarised the territorial scope of income tax in the following terms:

> 'The Income Tax Acts . . . themselves impose a territorial limit, either that from which the taxable income is derived must be situate in the United Kingdom or the person whose income is to be taxed must be resident there' (*Colquhoun v Brooks HL 1889, 2 TC 490*).

This dual test highlights the main obstacle facing schemes designed to shelter income from tax. Not only must the source of the income always be considered but also an individual's residence and/or ordinary residence status. As one would anticipate, the planning opportunities increase as the fiscal connection with the United Kingdom decreases.

13.7   The following sections consider first the impact of the source doctrine and then discuss how the shedding of a resident or ordinarily resident status can bring with it the possibility of sheltering income from tax, notwithstanding the retention of a UK domicile. Finally, the role of trusts as a means of sheltering income is reviewed. It will be seen that Parliament has used the territorial scope of income tax to good effect and bolstered it when necessary with powerful anti-avoidance legislation, although tax planning opportunities remain.

UK source income

13.8   All individuals, regardless of their domicile or residence status, will (subject to the provisions of any applicable double tax treaty and to Inland Revenue concession) be liable to income tax on income arising from a source within the UK. In this context, reference should be made to the *Finance Act 1995, s 128* which places an upper limit on the UK tax liability of a non-resident person on most investment income. The 'doctrine of the source' has wide-ranging implications for those seeking to shelter profits from income tax; it means in particular that a UK domiciled individual (even if he is resident and/or ordinarily resident overseas) cannot shelter his UK source income from tax by the simple expedient of transferring it to an overseas structure (always assuming that he could in any event side-step the anti-avoidance legislation referred to at 13.26–13.32 below). Endeavours to shelter income overseas from tax are usually therefore directed to the shelter of overseas income. References in this chapter to 'overseas income' are to income from a source outside the UK.

13.9   In passing, however, it may be noted that, although UK source income cannot be totally sheltered from tax, by placing the source within an offshore structure, the effective tax rate can in some circumstances be lowered. Companies resident outside the United Kingdom are liable only at the basic rate [*ICTA 1988, s 1(2)*]. Tax on income arising from a source within the UK can thus be restricted (subject to the points mentioned below) if the income-producing asset is held within such a vehicle. One would in any given case have to take regard of the anti-avoidance legislation reviewed below and to ensure that such a company was not effectively managed and controlled from (and therefore resident in) the UK.

Resident and ordinarily resident individuals

13.10   The territorial limits of income tax mean that, regrettably, there is little scope for an individual who is domiciled and resident and ordinarily resident in the UK to shelter income by investing cash etc., in offshore bank accounts or otherwise holding income-producing assets in his own name outside the UK. All such individuals are liable to tax not only on UK source income but also on income derived from overseas sources.

Attempts to side-step this principle over the years have taken various forms, but have largely proved unsuccessful. Where there has been limited success, the legislature has usually moved swiftly to close the loophole once exposed.

13.11   For example, attempts to shelter income by transferring the ownership of the income-producing asset to an offshore company or trust will usually be negated by *ICTA 1988, s 739* (see 13.28–13.30). Another method of avoiding income tax which evolved was to transform the income into a capital receipt. To this end, schemes were marketed – particularly in the early 1980s – whereby income would be capitalised within an offshore fund. Such funds were typically operated in low tax jurisdictions and offered investors either shares or units in the fund at a price which mirrored the value of the funds' underlying assets, being income-producing securities. The income received within the fund was reinvested in further similar securities, the increased value of which would ultimately be reflected in the price paid to the investor on the disposal of his shares or units. The obvious advantage to the higher rate taxpayer was the conversion of what would otherwise then have been taxed as investment income into a capital gain.

It was to counter such schemes that anti-avoidance legislation was introduced, which is now found in *ICTA 1988, ss 757–764* and *Schs 27, 28*.

13.12   In brief, the offshore fund legislation applies where there is a disposal of an asset which constitutes a material interest in an offshore fund which is, or has at any material time been, a non-qualifying offshore fund. Where the legislation applies, the gain arising to a person resident or ordinarily resident in the United Kingdom (or trading in the United Kingdom through a branch or agency), at any time during the year of assessment in which the income gain arises, is treated as income arising at that time to the individual making the disposal and chargeable to income tax accordingly. 'Roll-up' funds can enable an individual to defer the tax bill until such time as the investor is in a lower tax bracket (e.g., on retirement). Assuming that the actual performance of the fund is as favourable as UK funds, a 'roll-up' fund can still therefore prove advantageous to individuals who are resident and ordinarily resident in the UK.

13.13   Despite such reversals, there remains some scope, albeit strictly limited, for UK resident and ordinarily resident individuals to shelter income from tax. As will be seen, placing the income within a UK trust can achieve a tax saving if the individual is willing to divest himself of all interest in that income. Similarly, emigration from the UK can provide an extremely effective way of sheltering income receipts from tax. This was illustrated by the case of *Reed v Clark (1985) 58 TC 528, Ch D*; a case which repays close analysis by those pursuing the emigration route. Emigration is usually linked with the sheltering of capital receipts, but can also provide a shelter for income.

Individuals who are not resident

13.14   The position is more promising for the UK domiciled individual who is not resident in the United Kingdom. An individual who is not resident in the United Kingdom is only liable to income tax on income which arises from a source within the United Kingdom or on profits from 'any trade, profession or vocation exercised within the United Kingdom'. [*ICTA 1988, s 18(1)*]. Such an individual will therefore not be liable to tax on overseas income and need not undertake any complicated planning to achieve this happy result.

13.15   The non-resident individual will be liable to tax on his trading profits if he carries on a trade in the United Kingdom, as indicated at 13.14. There is an established distinction between trading with and trading in the United Kingdom. In determining on which side of the line an activity falls, the courts will consider not only where the contracts are concluded (*Grainger & Son v Gough (1896) 3 TC 462, HL*) but also where 'the operation takes place from which the profits in substance arise' per Atkins LJ in *FL Smidth & Co v Greenwood (1922) 8 TC 193, HL* (and see *Firestone Tyre and Rubber Co v Llewellin (1957) 37 TC 111, HL*). A non-resident should, therefore, take care in the structuring of his operations. See also in this context *FA 1995, s 126*.

Individuals who are resident but not ordinarily resident

13.16   If a UK domiciled individual (provided he is also a Commonwealth citizen including a British subject or a citizen of the Republic of Ireland) is resident in but ordinarily resident outside the United Kingdom there are again limited tax planning possibilities. In addition to the use of trusts to shelter overseas income (see 13.23), such an individual will be able to take advantage of the 'remittance basis' of taxation, with the result that income arising from a Schedule D, Case IV or V source outside the United Kingdom will only be subject to UK tax if the income is 'received' in the United Kingdom. [*ICTA 1988, s 65*]. Such income can thus be retained outside the United Kingdom free of tax. Cases IV and V charge to tax income arising from securities outside the UK and 'possessions' (which would extend to a foreign trade) outside the UK respectively. An individual who is ordinarily resident outside the UK would thus be advised to retain income-producing investments (e.g., bank accounts) overseas and if he is trading, to establish a separate trade overseas. In this latter connection, consideration must be given to the case of *Ogilvie v Kitton (1908) 5 TC 338*, as the Revenue is reluctant to accept that a sole trader who is resident in the UK can carry on a trade in two distinct parts, one wholly overseas. In such cases, consideration should be given to conducting the UK trade through the medium of a partnership or company.

13.17   The definition of what constitutes a 'remittance' to the United Kingdom is wide. Nevertheless, there are circumstances in which the overseas income can be enjoyed in the United Kingdom without a tax charge. For example, if a source of income has ceased in an earlier year, it may be possible to remit the income to the UK in a later year; see *Bray v Best [1989] STC 159, HL*.

13.18   Similarly, income effectively alienated outside the United Kingdom (for example, by gift) can be remitted without a tax charge by the recipient; *Carter v Sharon (1936) 20 TC 229, KB*. Care must be taken where the gift is made between spouses, particularly if the recipient spends the gift on items such as household expenditure which the donor may enjoy: the Inland Revenue can be expected to look closely at such cases. In this context, reference should be made to the case of *Grimm v Newman [2002] STC 84*. This case serves as a reminder of the need for care in structuring remittances. The principle in *Carter v Sharon* would not extend, for example, to discharging a UK doctor's bill by payment into a Jersey bank account.

Where available the 'remittance' basis is an extremely effective form of shelter and reference should also be made to the chapter on non-domiciled individuals.

Schedule E planning

13.19   The remittance basis can also apply to emoluments from an employment, again providing a real opportunity to shelter income from tax. Where an individual who is ordinarily resident outside the UK intends to enter into an employment arrangement which includes an overseas element – for example, with a non-UK resident employer, with overseas duties – the position should always be carefully reviewed to ensure that, where appropriate, full advantage is taken of the remittance basis. In appropriate cases, consideration may be given to dual employment contracts with a view to enabling the emoluments for duties performed overseas to be more easily identified. For example, if a UK domiciled but not ordinarily resident individual is employed by a UK resident employer, his emoluments for duties performed in the UK will be taxed under Schedule E, Case II, whereas he will be taxed on the remittance basis under Case III in respect of that part of his emoluments attributable to his duties performed wholly abroad. Reference should also be made to SP5/84, 28 March 1984 in relation to the split between the two sets of duties. Consideration should also always be given to any relevant double tax treaty.

Sheltering income via trusts

13.20   The limited role of trusts in sheltering income can be attributed to three main factors: the doctrine of the source, the nature of the trust, and, the comprehensive anti-avoidance legislation. The major opportunities are available where it is sought to shelter overseas income in an offshore trust for the benefit of individuals other than the settlor and his spouse. Each of the factors will be reviewed in turn.

UK source income

13.21   As with individuals, trustees will be liable to tax on income from a source within the UK, regardless of their residence status. Trustees of a discretionary trust (as defined in *ICTA 1988, s 686*) will be liable to tax at the Schedule F trust rate or the rate applicable to trusts (unless exceptionally the trustees are non-resident and there are no UK beneficiaries when it appears that *FA 1995, s 128* exempts such trusts from any additional liability in respect of certain categories of 'excluded income' (primarily bank interest and dividends)). Accordingly, trusts are usually of assistance only in sheltering overseas income from tax, and even this is subject to the anti-avoidance legislation, which is discussed at 13.29–13.34.

Nature of the trust

13.22   As will be seen, it is only trusts which provide for the income to be accumulated or distributed at the discretion of the trustees which provide scope for sheltering income from tax.

Interest in possession trust

13.23   Where the trust is an interest in possession trust (that is, where a beneficiary is automatically entitled to receive the trust income) it is effectively ignored for income tax purposes. The Inland Revenue 'looks through' the trust and the income arising to the trustees is taxed as part of the total income of the beneficiary (*Archer-Shee v Baker (1927) 11 TC 749, HL*). Although the trustees may be taxable to the extent that the income is actually received by them, this is merely in a representative capacity on behalf of the beneficiary.

Discretionary trusts

13.24   Discretionary trusts, which for present purposes may be taken to include accumulation and maintenance trusts for children until the beneficiaries become entitled to a vested interest, provide a vehicle by which an individual can divest himself of his income while retaining (under a discretionary trust) the ability to enjoy it, or a benefit provided from it, at some future date. In the absence of specific anti-avoidance legislation, such a trust would therefore provide the perfect means of sheltering income from tax. While a UK resident beneficiary would be liable to tax on income distributions made to him (under Schedule D, Case V in the case of an overseas trust), such a charge could be avoided by accumulating the income and making an appointment of capital.

13.25   It is to negate the possibility of an individual restructuring his ownership of income-producing assets in this way that two sets of anti-avoidance legislation were enacted. The legislation is wide-ranging and its scope is considered below. Nevertheless, there are, as will be seen, gaps in and restrictions on its scope and discretionary trusts can still assist UK domiciled individuals in achieving income tax savings.

The anti-avoidance provisions

13.26   The anti-avoidance provisions are to be found in *ICTA 1988, Part XV* ('the settlement code') and, secondly, in *ICTA 1988, ss 739–746*. The provisions are not limited to formal trusts as such. The *Part XV* provisions include any 'disposition, trust, covenant, agreement, arrangement or transfer of assets' [*ICTA 1988, s 660G*] and *ICTA 1988, ss 739, 740* ('Transfer of Assets Abroad') will apply not only to the use of a trust to shelter profits, but also (*inter alia*) an overseas company or partnership.

IRC v Brackett (1986) 60 TC 134, Ch D is an example of the very wide ambit of *ICTA 1988, s 739*; in this case it was held that a contract of employment with an overseas company could trigger the provisions in *section 739*.

The Part XV provisions

13.27   The settlement code is wide-ranging. In *IRC v Countess of Kenmare HL 1957, 37 TC 383* Viscount Simonds said:

> 'The language of [*ICTA 1988, s 672*] and particularly of [*ICTA 1988, s 681(i)(a)*] makes it clear beyond all doubt that any settlement, wherever made and whatever foreign element might be imported by the residence of the settlor or the trustees or the forum of administration, is caught by its provisions if the income arises in the United Kingdom'.

The provisions operate primarily where the settlor or his spouse (but not a widow(er)) retains an interest under the terms of the trust. They also apply where a minor unmarried child of the settlor receives a benefit from the trust (see, for example, *Butler v Wildin [1989] STC 22*). See also in the case of bare trusts the provisions introduced by *FA 1999, s 64*. The circumstances in which a settlor will be found to have retained an interest under a trust are very wide and extend not only to the case where the settlor is a named beneficiary but also, for example, where he benefits under a resulting trust.

Where the provisions of 'the settlement code' apply, the broad effect is to treat the income arising within the trust as taxable in the hands of the settlor rather than of any other person. The practical result is that a UK resident individual cannot shelter even overseas income by placing the source in trust so long as he wishes to continue to enjoy, or have the possibility of enjoying, this income.

ICTA 1988, s 739

13.28   The intention of *section 739* is clear from the wording in *subsection (1)* which provides that the purpose of the section is to prevent:

> 'the avoiding by individuals ordinarily resident in the United Kingdom of liability to income tax by means of transfers of assets by virtue or in consequence of which, either alone or in conjunction with associated operations, income becomes payable to persons resident or domiciled outside the United Kingdom'.

The scope of *section 739* is extended by the supporting sections; for example, a 'transfer of assets' includes the creation of rights [*ICTA 1988, s 742(9)*] with the result that the section extends, for example, to the incorporation of a foreign company and the subscription for its shares.

Section 739 operates by providing that where an individual who is ordinarily resident in the UK has, in consequence of the transfer, power to enjoy (regard being had to the substantial result and effect of the transfer) the income of the overseas person, he is treated for income tax purposes as though the income were his, and is assessable to tax under Case VI of Schedule D. The circumstances in which an individual has the 'power to enjoy' income is, for example, wide enough to include both actual and potential future receipts and capital sums.

Section 739 thus negates the ability of an individual to shelter income by placing it within a discretionary trust of which he is a beneficiary. Moreover, *section 739* would extend not only to income arising to the trustees but also to any income in an underlying company formed by the trustees. The *section* is thus a major obstacle to individuals who are ordinarily resident in the UK and who are seeking to shelter income from tax.

Avoiding the ambit of section 739

13.29 Nevertheless, despite the fact that *section 739* is an anti-avoidance provision and therefore given a wide construction by the courts, there are limitations on its scope which can provide practical planning possibilities. The *section* only applies where the individual with the power to enjoy the income or who is in receipt of capital is ordinarily resident in the UK; an individual will not fall within the ambit of the *section* if he is merely resident in the UK. The *section* also has no application in respect of overseas income where the individual is resident outside the UK. Reference should also be made to the interpretation published in the Inland Revenue Tax Bulletin Issue 40 April 1999; this suggests limitations on *s 739* which may not be justified in law.

Section 739 and *section 740* (as to which, see below) do not apply where the individual can satisfy the Commissioners of Inland Revenue that either:

(*a*) tax avoidance was not one of the purposes for which the transfer or any associated operations were effected; or

(*b*) the transfer and the associated operations were bona fide commercial transactions not designed for the purpose of avoiding liability to taxation.

IRC v Willoughby (1995) 70 TC 57 also discussed the scope of these provisions and suggests that *section 739* will not apply where the tax legislation already contains a specific provision (in that case the offshore roll-up legislation) directed at the tax planning in question.

The difficulty of falling within these 'defence' provisions is not to be underestimated, although two recent decisions have offered some encouragement to taxpayers. In *Beneficiary v IRC [1999] STC (SCD) 134* and *Carvill v IRC [2000] STC (SCD) 143*, the Special Commissioners decided that the question of whether there was tax avoidance is a subjective one. 'Purpose is not effect and in our view it is essential to look into the minds of the actors to discover their purpose' *1999 STC (SCD)* at page 143. The circumstances and intention of the parties will be of prime importance. Documentary evidence will also be critical.

These cases are also encouraging for the proposition that if the transfer (and any associated operations) are tax mitigation rather than tax avoidance, the defence should apply.

Less encouraging for the taxpayer is the debate on the meaning of the phrase 'bona fide commercial transactions' within the context of *section 741(b)*. The Inland Revenue are of the view that this phrase is taken to apply only to the furtherance of trade or business and not to the making or managing of investments. This is a highly debatable view but one for which there is some support in *Carvill v IRC*. If this view ultimately proved to be correct, it would be another problem in the attempt to shelter investment income from tax.

The Inland Revenue moved swiftly to close another 'crack' in *section 739* which had been raised by the *Willoughby* case: the *Finance Act 1997* made it clear that *section 739* applies even if the individual was not ordinarily resident in the United Kingdom at the time when the transfer of assets was made. The *Finance Act 1997* change applies irrespective of when the transfer took place, but applies only to income arising on or after 26 November 1996.

ICTA 1988, s 740

13.30   In *Vestey v IRC (1979) 54 TC 503*, the House of Lords decided *section 739* only applied to the original transfer (and possibly also to individuals who procured or were associated with the original transfer; see also here the discussion in *Carvill v IRC [2000] STC (SCD) 143* at page 163). *Section 740* was enacted to close the resulting opportunity. *Section 740* provides that where, in consequence of a transfer of assets made at any time, income becomes payable to a person resident or domiciled outside the United Kingdom and an ordinarily resident individual receives a benefit provided out of assets which are available as a result of the transfer, that individual is liable to tax under Schedule D, Case VI to the extent that the value of the benefit can be matched with the income which has arisen to the non-resident or non-domiciled person.

Tax planning for beneficiaries

13.31   *Section 740* would therefore clearly apply to an overseas trust. However, in circumstances where the settlor and his spouse are excluded from benefit, no income tax charge will arise until a beneficiary receives a 'benefit' from the trust, which is defined to include 'a payment of any kind'. [*ICTA 1988, s 742(9)*]. *Section 740* thus permits the opportunity to defer the tax charge. Any individual who is domiciled and resident in the UK could thus transfer monies to overseas trustees to invest outside the UK for the benefit of his children. No UK income tax would be payable until the children received the benefit from the trust, and the gross receipts could thus be reinvested for greater capital growth.

Moreover, the profits arising within the trust can often be enjoyed without triggering the full tax liability. Thus, if the trustees make an interest-free loan to a beneficiary, the tax charge will probably be based on the amount of interest which would have been charged by the trustees if they had made the loan to an unconnected party on a commercial basis. It should be noted, however, that the legislation is silent on how the value of a 'benefit' is to be calculated and it is arguable that there is no 'benefit' where the loan is not for a fixed period and repayable on demand (but see 13.41). *Section 740(1)(b)* provides that the benefit must be provided 'out of assets' and it may also be that any advantage which does not diminish the value of the fund cannot be a 'benefit' for these purposes.

The Inland Revenue does not regard the conferring of an interest under a settlement (e.g. the appointment of a life interest) as a 'benefit' as it is not provided out of the available assets.

13.32   Income which arises within the offshore structure can only support an income tax charge in relation to a particular beneficiary if it can be directly or indirectly used for that beneficiary's benefit (that is, if it is 'relevant income' in relation to him; *section 740(3)*). A trust can thus be structured so that beneficiaries who are ordinarily resident in the UK cannot benefit from the income, but would be possible recipients of capital appointments made at the discretion of the trustees. In this way, while such individuals could receive capital payments from the trustees there would be no 'relevant income' to frank these and *section 740* would not be applicable. Such a restructuring of the trust instrument, with the effective creation of separate trusts of income and capital, would, however, require careful drafting.

13.33   The income could also be accumulated within the trust and distributed tax free if the beneficiaries of the trust emigrated. A charge under *section 740* can only arise if the recipient of the 'benefit' is ordinarily resident in the UK. It appears from the interpretation mentioned in 13.29 above that it may be possible, however, to 'wash' the available income by a prior payment to a beneficiary who is ordinarily resident outside the UK, followed by a distribution to an ordinarily resident beneficiary.

13.34   The above advantages arise where the source of the trust income is located outside the UK. If the income arising within the trust has a UK source, the advantages of deferral considered above are likely to be outweighed by an increased overall tax rate. In general terms, it is not prudent to hold UK source income within an accumulation and maintenance (or discretionary) offshore trust from which the settlor is excluded. The disadvantage arises because no credit will be given for tax which has been charged on the UK source income (see Notes of Meeting of the Law Society and the Revenue, 8 June 1981, paragraph 15). The position may be contrasted with that contained in *ICTA 1988, s 743* which applies only to *ICTA 1988, s 739*, where the settlor retains an interest under the trust.

In such a situation it would usually have been preferable for UK resident trustees to have been appointed, where the income could have been capitalised and paid to the beneficiary without a further tax charge.

Where the children are minors, the provisions of *ICTA 1988, s 660B* ('Payments to unmarried minor children of settlor') should always be considered in relation to the above planning, irrespective of the location of the trust.

Sheltering capital gains from tax

13.35   Until the advent of the *Finance Act 1991*, there were more solutions than problems in the context of sheltering capital gains from tax. These solutions invariably involved the use of trusts. At a stroke, *FA 1991* removed many of the solutions offered by trusts and taxpayers now have to consider other tax planning techniques, such as emigration. However, the introduction in *FA 1998* of taper relief (which in many cases can promise a tax rate of 10 per cent) also offers an attractive solution. The following paragraphs consider the possibilities available to an UK domiciled individual who is anxious to realise a capital profit tax free.

The impact of residence

13.36   For such an individual, the main restriction on CGT planning opportunities is the possession of a resident or ordinarily resident status. If an individual is resident or ordinarily resident in the UK in any part of a year of assessment (6 April to 5 April) he will be liable to CGT in respect of chargeable gains accruing to him in that year, irrespective of where the asset which gave rise to the gain was situated. [*TCGA 1992, ss 2(1), 12*]. Residence and ordinary residence have the same meanings as for income tax. [*TCGA 1992, s 9(1)*].

It is thus not possible for a UK domiciled individual to shelter assets from CGT by the simple expedient of holding them physically outside the UK. This may be contrasted with the remittance basis available to the individual's non–UK domiciled counterpart. Tax planning for UK domiciled individuals therefore centres on either placing the individual outside the scope of the CGT net or transferring the ownership of the assets to persons who are themselves resident and ordinarily resident outside the UK. The former is achieved by emigration; the latter is achieved by the employment of companies and trusts.

Emigration

13.37   The period overseas must now normally extend to five complete tax years. The relevant provisions are to be found in *TCGA 1992, s 10A* which should be studied closely by anyone considering the emigration route.

Emigration must also now normally take place in the tax year before the disposal: except on rare circumstances, it is not possible to split the tax year by concession into a resident period and a non-resident period. An individual who wishes to emigrate to avoid a CGT liability on the sale of a private company may seek to address this problem by making the original disposal by way of an exchange for (say) loan notes in the purchaser (pursuant to *TCGA 1992, s 135*). Extreme caution is required: the Inland Revenue has been known in such cases to refuse a clearance under *TCGA 1992, s 138*.

The 'five-year' test does not apply for income tax purposes and strategies to turn a capital profit into an income receipt are becoming increasingly common. The simple step of taking a tax free dividend while offshore, instead of making a capital disposal while within the five-year regime, can (with careful planning) be adapted so that not only the dividend is received tax free but a capital loss is generated to set against a prior capital gain. Similarly, *section 10A(10)* expressly provides that the provision is 'without prejudice to any right to claim relief in accordance with any double taxation relief arrangements'. The practice has been established, therefore, of individuals seeking to relocate to Belgium (or another country with which the UK has an appropriate tax treaty) and relying on the treaty to make a tax free disposal without remaining outside the UK for five years. Again, care is required.

The view has become commonly held that emigration to Belgium for a single year will suffice: this seems overly ambitious given (as will usually be the case) that the individual, in order to rely on the treaty, must show that his 'permanent' home is in Belgium. This route will also require the individual to dispose of (or at least let on a long lease) his UK home.

Section 10A operates by taxing any gains made in the period of the overseas stay as accruing to the taxpayer in the year of return. The provision does not, however, extend to most assets acquired while outside the UK. This may again provide planning opportunities.

13.38   Even if an individual successfully emigrates, the CGT saving would not be achieved to the extent that he continues to fall within the ambit of *TCGA 1992, s 10*. This section provides that where such an individual carries on a trade, profession or vocation in the UK through a branch or agency (as defined in *section 10(6)*) he will be liable to CGT on the disposal of assets which are situated in the UK and which are used in or for the purposes of the profit generating activities.

Prior to 14 March 1989, the impact of this provision could have been avoided by the expedient of physically removing the asset overseas prior to disposal, thereby sheltering the gain overseas. *FA 1989, s 127* (now *TCGA 1992, s 25*) countered this avoidance technique by making the occasion of the removal of the asset from the jurisdiction a deemed disposal at market value, triggering an immediate tax charge.

Nevertheless, the teeth of this provision can often be drawn by the taxpayer ceasing to carry on the trade prior to his emigration. If required, the trade could be transferred to a company incorporated for this purpose, the individual retaining the assets pregnant with gain in his own name until emigration.

Sheltering capital gains via trusts

13.39   Once offering much opportunity, offshore trusts now offer limited scope for individuals seeking to avoid a liability to CGT. The opportunities were reduced further by the *Finance Act 1998*.

Reference should be made to the earlier editions of *Tolley's International Tax Planning* for a fuller explanation of the enduring saga of the CGT treatment of offshore trusts and for a detailed review of the regime which existed during 1991–1998. The following paragraphs focus mainly on the present position. An offshore trust for these purposes is one the general administration of which is ordinarily carried on outside the UK by trustees who (or a majority thereof) are not resident and not ordinarily resident in the UK. [*TCGA 1992, s 69*]. Such trusts do not pay capital gains tax (unless exceptionally the trust is a trading trust *within TCGA 1992, s 10*).

As the trustees themselves are outside the scope of capital gains tax, anti-avoidance legislation exists. As indicated above, this legislation was re-enforced in 1991 and again in 1998.

The most significant change for planning purposes was that introduced by the *Finance Act 1991* and now found in *TCGA 1992, s 86*. The essential effect of this provision is to render an offshore trust under which the 'settlor' retains an interest (for example, as a discretionary beneficiary) ineffective as any gains accruing to the trustees are treated as the settlor's as and when they arise.

A settlor (being any person from whom the settled property, or part of the settled property originated) will have an interest if the trust fund or the income thereof can be paid to, or applied for the benefit of, a widely defined class of persons. Already wide enough to extend to trusts for the settlor, the settlor's spouse and children (and spouses), the *Finance Act 1998* has extended the provision to include trusts for grandchildren and their spouses. 'Defined persons' also includes a company controlled by 'defined persons' or a company which is itself associated with such a controlled company. Trusts created before 17 March 1998 for the benefit of grandchildren and spouses (but no other class of defined persons) are outside the scope of the 'settlor' charge unless tainting occurs.

The width of this provision is apparent at once. The opportunities, such as they are, arise from a close scrutiny of the legislation. For example, the 'settlor charge' only applies in a year of assessment for part of which the settlor is resident or ordinarily resident in the United Kingdom. It would thus be possible for a settlor to create an offshore trust for his children while he is resident and ordinarily resident outside the United Kingdom with a view to achieving a deferral of CGT liability. While the trust would come within the scope of the anti-avoidance provisions for any year in which the settlor became resident or ordinarily resident in the UK, the trust would not be caught by the legislation after the settlor's death and a valuable shelter can thus be created where an individual can temporarily shed his residence status. There would, however, be little advantage in his placing the assets in trust for his own benefit (even though the 'settlor charge' would not be applicable) as he would not be liable to CGT on a sale in any event because of his tax status.

Offshore trusts are thus most likely to be employed by UK domiciled individuals either to shelter gains for the benefit of persons who do not fall within the class of 'defined persons' (see above), or for post-death tax planning. The settlor charge does not apply where a trust is set up by a will or where the settlor dies during the year of assessment. Nephews and nieces or parents are not, for example, 'defined persons'. Trust instruments will require careful drafting to ensure that a 'defined person' cannot inadvertently creep within the ambit of the trust.

If the 'settlor charge' is not applicable, the offshore trust will fall within the capital payments regime regulated by *TCGA 1992, s 87*. In essence, this provides that there is not an immediate CGT charge when the trustees dispose of an asset. Instead, the gains are accumulated within the trust and used to support a CGT charge when a 'capital payment' (broadly, any benefit) is made to an individual who is domiciled and resident or ordinarily resident in the United Kingdom.

This opportunity to defer a CGT bill must be viewed in the light of the fact that there are increasingly few trusts which will be able to benefit from it and also in light of the supplementary charge (discussed below).

Prior to the *Finance Act 1998*, offshore trusts created prior to 19 March 1991 in which the settlor retained an interest (as defined) could also continue to benefit from a CGT deferral (i.e., to fall within the capital payments regime) provided that the trust was not 'tainted'. The circumstances in which a trust could be 'tainted' (in which event the gains would be taxed on the settlor as they arose) were specified in *Sch 5 para 9*; the most common instance of 'tainting' was the provision of further property to the trust.

The tax deferral opportunity offered by pre-March 1991 offshore trusts was removed by the *Finance Act 1998*. The settlor of a pre-1991 settlement is now automatically liable to CGT on an arising basis on trust gains made from 6 April 1999 if the settlor, his spouse, children or companies controlled by any of them are beneficiaries. The settlor may thus be liable even if he is excluded from benefit. Certain 'protected settlements' are excluded from this charge but the opportunity this presents is a narrow one and likely to be of limited application in practice.

A settlement will be 'protected' (and as such enable to continue to benefit from the capital payment regime under *section 87*) if it is restructured to exclude the settlor and certain other defined beneficiaries. The beneficiaries of the restructured trust must be restricted to minor children of the settlor (and, the Inland Revenue has confirmed, grandchildren), unborn children of the settlor, future spouse of the children, future spouse of the settlor and persons outside the class of 'defined persons'. Reference should be made to *Sch 5 para 10A* for a fuller definition.

The limited opportunity this presents becomes apparent when one realises that a child, if he or she is to be included as a beneficiary, must be under the age of 18 and must be excluded on attaining majority. Moreover a 'protected settlement' will become a 'qualifying settlement' (i.e., one within the *section 86* regime) if the trust is 'tainted'. 'Tainting' for these purposes is defined in *Sch 5 para 9(3)–(6A)*: the definition is essentially the familiar one which used to (but no longer does) apply to trusts created before 19 March 1991.

The supplementary charge

13.40   Even if a trust offers the opportunity of a CGT deferral, because it is one of the few not now within the ambit of *TCGA 1992, s 86*, this brings with it the possible problem of an increased charge when the beneficiary of the trust receives a capital payment.

The aim of the 'supplementary charge' is to make it less attractive to use offshore trusts to defer a capital gains tax liability by imposing an increased charge on the beneficiary when the funds eventually leave the tax-free shelter which is the trust.

The supplementary charge which was introduced by *FA 1991, s 90* and *Schedule 17* and is now found in *TCGA 1992, ss 91–95*, applies to capital payments made by non-resident trustees on or after 6 April 1992.

In essence, tax payable by a beneficiary in respect of gains attributed to him is increased by an amount equal to the interest which would have been yielded if simple interest of 10 per cent per annum had been payable on an amount equivalent to the tax during the 'chargeable period'. [*TCGA 1992, s 91(3)*]. The chargeable period is defined in *section 91(4)*.

For those paying tax at a rate of 40 per cent the maximum effective rate of tax on chargeable gains will (at present rates) be 64 per cent. The Treasury is empowered to change the rate of the deemed interest charge by statutory instrument; it has not done so since the new provisions were introduced.

There is no deemed interest charge if a gain is distributed to a beneficiary in the year in which it is realised by the trustees or in the subsequent year. The provisions therefore still allow one year's deferral of tax without penalty. A distribution in any later year will attract a charge of 10 per cent per annum with no allowance for the first year. The minimum charge is therefore 20 per cent. Capital payments are effectively matched with outstanding trust gains on a first in first out basis.

The 'supplementary charge' can only apply where there is a 'capital payment' and so planning designed to negate the existence of a 'capital payment' will be of importance (see below). In any given case, it will also be necessary to consider whether the impact of the 'supplementary charge' can be matched by returns on the investment of the gross funds in the trust prior to a distribution.

Capital payments

13.41   The tax charge under *section 87* and supplementary charge can only bite if the beneficiary receives a 'capital payment'.

TCGA 1992, s 97 provides that a 'capital payment' in the case of a UK resident recipient is any payment which is not chargeable to income tax in the recipient's hands. For a recipient who is neither resident nor ordinarily resident in the UK it is any payment received otherwise than as income.

References to a payment include references to the transfer of an asset, the conferring of any benefit and any occasion when a beneficiary becomes absolutely entitled to trust property as against the trustees. Where the 'capital payment' is an outright transfer of cash, the tax charge will be levied by reference to the actual amount of money paid. Where the 'capital payment' comprises the conferring of any other benefit, the value of the receipt for CGT purposes is taken to be the value of the benefit conferred by it.

A capital payment is treated as received by a beneficiary if it is received by the beneficiary directly or indirectly, if it is applied directly or indirectly by the trustees in payment of a debt of the beneficiary or otherwise applied for his benefit or if it is received by a third person at the beneficiary's direction.

TCGA 1992, s 97(1)(b) makes it clear that a capital payment does not include a payment under a transaction entered into at arm's length.

A number of tax planning opportunities have evolved to enable funds to be extracted from an offshore trust without triggering the capital payments charge. As these will become of less significance post the *Finance Act 1998* changes, they are not rehearsed here; some of the main opportunities were discussed in the earlier editions of this book. The Court of Appeal decision in *Billingham v Cooper [2001] STC 1177* has effectively put an end to one such planning opportunity. The Court agreed that not only was an interest free loan, revocable on demand, a 'capital payment', but that the value of the benefit can be computed by reference to the period over which the loan was outstanding.

Planning opportunities may remain. The trustees could consider making a loan at a commercial rate of interest but omit to collect the interest. The failure to collect the interest may in itself be a benefit and hence a 'capital payment' but it is arguable that it has no or, no substantial, value as the debt has not been waived.

A further solution to 'wash-out' the stockpiled gains in offshore trusts may also have been inadvertently provided by the Inland Revenue. Normally, if assets were moved from an existing trust to a new trust, the stockpiled gains (or a proportion of them corresponding to the amount of assets transferred) would be transferred to the new trust by virtue of the operation of *Section 90* of *TCGA 1992*.

However, if the trustees of the original trust were first to borrow funds from a bank, the provisions of *TCGA 1992, s 4B* will apply (transfers of value by trustees linked with trustee borrowing). Where this is the case, it would appear that the application of *section 90* is precluded by *section 90(5)*. As a consequence, the stockpiled gains can be left behind in the old settlement. The funds will be in the new trust, available for distribution to the UK resident and domiciled beneficiaries but with no available stockpiled gains to 'frank' them as capital payments.

The non-domiciled settlor

13.42   If the settlor of an offshore trust was at the time of its creation, and remains, non-domiciled, his position is far more favourable and the non-domiciled settlor (and any non-domiciled beneficiary) can receive distributions from the trust without a CGT liability.

Prior to the *Finance Act 1998* changes, the protection offered by the umbrella of a non-domiciled trust extended even further. If the settlor was non-domiciled, then under the former provisions, any distribution to any beneficiary would be outside the scope of CGT. Gains made on or after 17 March 1998, from a trust of which the settlor is non-domiciled, however, will be taxed under *section 87* where capital payments are made to beneficiaries who are UK resident and domiciled. The order and form of distributions will thus be of prime importance in these cases.

Other vehicles

13.43　Given the depth of anti-avoidance legislation which now applies to offshore trusts, the individual seeking to shelter his offshore gain must look to other vehicles. Several opportunities exist, but none are without difficulty.

The use of an offshore company is one such vehicle on the basis that if the company is not resident or trading in the United Kingdom, it will not be subject to CGT. Again, however, the Inland Revenue has a number of possibilities for challenging such planning. First, the Inland Revenue may challenge the residence status of the company. A company will be resident in the UK if it is incorporated in or managed and controlled from the UK. There is a substantial body of case law on the meaning of this latter phrase; see in particular *De Beers Consolidated Mines Ltd v Howe (1906) 5 TC 198, HL* and *Unit Construction Co Ltd v Bullock (1959) 38 TC 712, HL*. The Inland Revenue has indicated (see SP1/90) that where a dominant UK resident shareholder effectively runs a company, the company will be resident in the UK for these purposes notwithstanding that formal directors may have been appointed who are resident in an offshore jurisdiction. In many instances therefore a company used to shelter assets overseas may in fact be UK resident. This would render it largely ineffective for tax purposes, as the company itself would be liable to corporation tax on chargeable gains and a further tax charge would arise on the extraction of the profits. The holding of assets via a UK resident company enables profits to be sheltered from the highest rate of CGT but only at the cost of a subsequent tax bill.

Even if the company is non-UK resident, the provisions of *TCGA 1992, s 13* will operate in most cases to attribute the gain made by the company to the UK resident and domiciled shareholder, thus negating any planning. *Section 13* provides that the gains arising to the offshore company are to be attributed to 'participators' in the company, that term taking its definition from *ICTA 1988, s 417*. The amount of the gain that is attributed to each participator is the amount that corresponds to that participator's interest in the company. The interests of all participators in the company will be taken into account in assessing what is a just and reasonable proportion of the chargeable gains that should be attributed to any one participator. However, *section 13* may be side-stepped if the company is situated in a jurisdiction with a suitable double tax treaty, as treaty protection applies both to the company and to the shareholders under *section 13*, except from 20 March 2000, where trustees are the shareholders/participators. [*TCGA 1992, s 79B* introduced by *FA 2000, s 94*].

The use of offshore companies may, however, become more prevalent following two recent changes. First, the section does not apply where the amount falling to be apportioned to a participator and persons connected with him does not exceed one tenth of the gain. This change (the limit was previously 5 per cent) was introduced by *FA 2001* with effect for chargeable gains accruing after 6 March 2001. Second, the introduction of CGT taper relief for shareholdings in investment companies. A detailed consideration of taper relief is beyond the scope of this chapter. However, for present purposes, it should be noted that certain shareholdings can qualify for business asset taper and, where they do so, the tax rate can (after a specified period of ownership, the duration of which the Inland Revenue keeps changing) be as low as 10 per cent.

Importantly, for present purposes business asset taper relief is available for shareholdings in investment companies where an individual is an employee or officer (which can include a non-executive director) of the company and does not have a 'material interest' in the company (*TCGA 1992, Sch A1 para 6*). 'Material interest' is widely defined as possession or control of more than 10 per cent of any of the issued shares; of any class of issued shares; of voting rights; of the right to profits available for distribution; or of rights to assets on a liquidation.

The ability to create an offshore company to allow investments to be realised tax free, with only a 10 per cent tax rate on an ultimate disposal of shares in the company, has thus the potential to become a real solution to those seeking to shelter gains overseas.

Offshore bonds (being in the usual case a single premium non-qualifying life assurance policy) have also been advanced as a viable alternative for individuals seeking to shelter profits offshore. Their main attraction is that they convert future gain into income, thereby avoiding an immediate CGT charge and providing the platform for a tax deferral and future planning. Investors can withdraw tax free up to five per cent of their original capital for 20 years. [*ICTA 1988, ss 540, 542, 545, 546*].

UK trusts

13.44   Trusts with UK resident trustees offer little scope for sheltering gains overseas. This is partly because, as UK residents, the trustees are themselves liable to CGT [*TCGA 1992, s 2(1)*] and partly because of the anti-avoidance provisions contained in *TCGA 1992, s 77*. These are similar (but narrower in scope) to the *TCGA 1992, s 86, Sch 5* provisions discussed above and provide that if a settlor or his spouse retain an interest under the settlement, the trust gains are treated as accruing to the settlor and taxed in his hands. The provisions do not apply if the settlor is not resident and ordinarily resident in the UK for a given year or if the settlor dies during the year.

If *section 77* does not apply, limited scope is available for tax planning. Trustees of trusts, under which neither the settlor nor his spouse have an interest, are only liable to CGT at a rate of 34 per cent. It is therefore possible to shelter assets, irrespective of their location, from the higher rate of CGT by placing them in an appropriate trust if the settlor is prepared to divest himself of any interest in those assets.

Moving offshore

13.45   In addition to finding a suitable vehicle to shelter the gain once the asset is offshore, there are also problems in moving an asset into an offshore structure without triggering a tax charge.

Unless the asset is an exempt asset (such as cash) or there are available losses (and in this context *TCGA 1992, s 18(3)* should always be borne in mind), a CGT charge is likely to be triggered on the transfer to an offshore trust or person. The transfer will normally be a deemed disposal at market value.

If a trust is exported, the trustees are deemed to dispose of and reacquire the settled property on export. [*TCGA 1992, s 80*]. The practice had developed for UK trustees holding quoted investments to seek to side-step the 'export charge' by selling the shares in the market and then exporting the trust while holding cash. Within 30 days of the export, the same shares would be repurchased. There is a persuasive argument that in such a case the 'bed and breakfasting' matching rule (*TCGA 1992, s 106A(5)*) operates to nullify the gains that would otherwise have arisen on emigration. In the April 2001 edition of Tax Bulletin, the Inland Revenue seek to refute this analysis.

Particular care is also required where a UK domiciled individual wishes to place land or any property deriving its value from land (e.g. a shareholding in a company deriving its value directly or indirectly from land) offshore, due to the provisions of *ICTA 1988, s 776*. This section is enacted to 'prevent the avoidance of tax by persons concerned with land or the development of land' and where applicable its effect is to subject any gain of a capital nature to income tax, thereby removing the possibility of sheltering the profit offshore pursuant to the provisions of *TCGA 1992, s 87*. The section would, for example, usually negate the possibility of an individual who acquired land for onward sale at a profit from transferring the land to an offshore trust for a sale by the trustees, as the profit on the ultimate sale by the trustees would fall to be taxed on the individual pursuant to *ICTA 1988, s 776(5)*. If, in contrast, the individual's own acquisition of land did not fall within the circumstances specified in *section 776(2)* (e.g. because he inherited it), it is thought that the transfer by way of gift into an offshore trust would also fall outside the ambit of *section 776*, with the result that the trustees could sell the land to the ultimate purchaser without an immediate tax liability (assuming that the trust was drafted for a class of beneficiaries who did not constitute 'defined persons').

Conclusion

13.46   Sheltering income and gains overseas remains difficult. Opportunities exist, but careful planning and execution is required to take advantage of them.

14 Tax Havens: A Comparative Study

Ian Ferrier

Introduction

14.1   The tax haven is a creature of the twentieth century, and began to be used extensively because of the high levels of tax which prevailed after the First World War.

Use by individuals

14.2   For many years, it was primarily wealthy individuals who sought to minimise tax by transferring their assets abroad. Those who did so included such luminaries as Rudyard Kipling (see *Bambridge v IRC (1955) 36 TC 313, HL*) and a naval hero (see *Admiral Earl Beatty's Executors v IRC (1940) 23 TC 574*).

14.3   Legislation to counter such transfers commenced with *FA 1936, s 18* (see now *ICTA 1988, s 739*). The operation of the section could be draconian. A warning to would-be tax avoiders was issued by Lord Greene, MR in *Lord Howard de Walden v IRC (1941) 25 TC 121, 134, CA*:

> 'For years a battle of manoeuvre has been waged between the legislature and those who are minded to throw the burden of taxation off their own shoulders on to those of their fellow subjects. In that battle the legislature has often been worsted by the skill, determination and resourcefulness of its opponents, of whom the present Appellant has not been the least successful. It would not shock us in the least to find that the legislature has determined to put an end to the struggle by imposing the severest of penalties. It scarcely lies in the mouth of the taxpayer who plays with fire to complain of burnt fingers'.

Although Lord Greene's words, uttered in the heat of the Second World War, represent perhaps an extreme position, they still serve as a salutary warning to anyone contemplating the use of a tax haven.

14.4   The pendulum swung back to the taxpayer in *Vestey v IRC (1979) 54 TC 503, HL*, in which the operation of *section 739* was described by Lord Wilberforce as unjust, arbitrary and unconstitutional and a previous decision of the House in *Congreve v IRC (1948) 30 TC 163, HL* was overruled. The lacuna in the legislation thus created was filled by *section 740*, which allows a charge on individuals other than the transferor who receive benefits from the transfer.

14.5   The Revenue continues to be active in exploiting *section 739*. It attempted to use it in relation to a personal portfolio bond taken out by an expatriate living in Hong Kong as provision for his retirement. This appeared to the Lords to be a perfectly legitimate exercise in tax planning expressly authorised by Parliament (see *IRC v Willoughby (1997) 70 TC 57, HL*), but it has been brought within the tax net by *ICTA 1988, s 553C*, inserted by *FA 1998, s 89*.

Use by companies

14.6   The use of tax havens by the corporate sector was for a long time not so prominent as their use by individuals. The difference in marginal tax rates was, in any case, not so great. However, where a tax haven built up expertise in a particular area, as, for example, with insurance in Bermuda, international companies increasingly set up subsidiaries there to benefit from the beneficial tax status available.

14.7   Counteracting legislation was introduced in *FA 1984* [see now *ICTA 1988, ss 747–756* and *Schs 24–26*]. This imposes a charge on the profits of a controlled foreign company levied on its parent where it is located in a territory with a lower level of taxation than the UK, unless the foreign company pursues an acceptable distribution policy. To ease the burden of compliance, the Revenue issues from time to time a list of countries which are considered to be excluded from the legislation. A full list was published in a Press Release of 5 October 1993, and this has been periodically amended, as necessary. Some countries are wholly excluded and others are excluded subject to qualifications. For example, the US is excluded save for domestic international sales corporations. It goes without saying that the countries usually regarded as tax havens do not figure on the list.

14.8   Another area of possible tax avoidance is the sale of goods or services at artificial prices between associated companies. This was formerly dealt with by provisions in *ICTA 1988, ss 770–774* concerning sales at an undervalue or overvalue, but this has largely been superseded by *Sch 28AA*, inserted in 1998. The Schedule is based on an Organisation for Economic Cooperation and Development (OECD) Model and attacks provisions made between associated persons other than at arm's length.

Preliminary considerations

14.9   Before using a tax haven, it is desirable to give thought to whether it is necessary. The taxation of individuals and companies in the UK has decreased dramatically over the past 20 years to the extent that the UK itself has become something of a tax haven. Also, the advent of a Labour government has so far left unaffected if not totally unscathed such tools of tax planning as the potentially exempt transfer for inheritance tax and reinvestment relief for capital gains tax. Income tax at a top rate of 40 per cent is still far from negligible, but routes exist for mitigating this, depending on the objectives of the individual concerned.

14.10 If it is considered appropriate to take the offshore tax haven route, the next point to consider is the basic structure to be adopted. In many cases this will comprise a settlement in one jurisdiction which subscribes for shares in a company, usually in another, which in turn holds the settlor's assets located within the UK. The advantage of this structure is that the settlement, which may be discretionary in form with a letter of wishes from the settlor, could be protected from inconvenient scrutiny since a company never dies and so there is never any occasion, for example, to apply for probate in England, at which point an enquiry regarding inheritance tax might become relevant.

Tax havens – desiderata

14.11 A primary consideration in the choice of a tax haven is political stability. No one would wish to involve themselves or their assets in a risky situation, however great the apparent tax advantages.

14.12 Closely allied to this is the rule of law, in the broadest sense. A country under a dictatorial regime may appear to offer stability over a long period, but the price to be paid for this could be a sudden revolutionary change with consequent danger to property rights.

14.13 It will usually be desirable to choose a jurisdiction where English law operates, with its historic division into common law and equity, so facilitating the dual structure alluded to above. The British Commonwealth now has over two score members and there is also a significant number of residual colonial territories. As well as law, the English language is part of their common heritage. This also applies to the greatest economy in the world, the United States, although the US is not usually considered as a tax haven. Within the federal entity there are 50 state jurisdictions, each with a varying structure of law, which may offer particular opportunities. For example, Delaware has long been a favourable location for the incorporation of companies.

14.14 It is also important to be assured of adequate local expertise in administering whatever structure is set up. The size of the activity in the trust or corporate area will usually be an indication of this. This issue is addressed below in the detailed review. Once a broad selection is made, the final choice can be governed in the light of the detailed services offered by the particular location and those operating within it. As in other spheres, cheapness must be carefully balanced against quality.

14.15 In recent years, the tax haven has broadened its scope to become a financial haven. One particular area of concern for high net worth individuals (HINWIs) who are professional people is the increasing litigiosity of our society. Someone must be to blame for every misfortune and indemnity insurance that is totally satisfactory may be either unavailable or cripplingly expensive. In such a case, a bank account or settlement in an appropriate locality could be a prudent provision against calamity.

14.16   Sometimes there have been attempts to exploit tax havens through double tax treaties (see, for example, *Padmore v IRC (1989) 62 TC 352, CA*). It was possible through the use of such treaties for a company, settlement or individual to enjoy a dual resident status, with beneficial fiscal consequences. These have now virtually been eliminated so far as the UK is concerned by counteracting legislation. In any case, there are few such treaties with the leading tax havens.

14.17   An individual may wish to establish domicile in a tax haven for inheritance tax purposes. The field here is rather narrower, unless there is some pre-existing connection. The Isle of Man is rather cold, the Channel Islands are more congenial. Monaco is even more so, but is rather small (see, for example, Luciano Pavarotti's difficulty in persuading the Italian authorities that a two bedroom flat there was his principal private residence). On the whole the Caribbean, perhaps particularly the Bahamas, offers the best alternative in this context.

Tax havens in detail

14.18   For the UK taxpayer, tax havens with a background of English common law and trust law will tend to be preferable. The closest to Britain geographically are the three dependencies of the Isle of Man, the Channel Islands and Gibraltar.

The Isle of Man

14.19   Once under the rule of Norway, the Isle of Man was acquired by Parliament from the Stanley family in 1765. It retained its ancient legislature, the House of Keys, and has more recently acquired its own chief minister and government. In view of possible European Union measures against tax havens, the House of Keys has debated a potential move to full independence from Britain. Tax rates are low, with a top rate on individuals, companies and trusts of 20 per cent. A duty of £600 is charged on companies incorporated in the Isle of Man which trade and are controlled outside the island. There is a vigorous financial sector, including 60 licensed banks and 80 investment businesses, regulated by a Financial Supervision Commission. There is a compensation fund to protect investors, under the Commission.

The Channel Islands

14.20   The Channel Islands comprise two main jurisdictions, Jersey and Guernsey. They are the last remains of the once extensive English possessions in France and owe allegiance to the Queen as successor to the Dukes of Normandy. Jersey and Guernsey each have internal self-government, but are subject to some measure of British authority through the Privy Council. Jersey is the larger island. Income tax is levied at 20 per cent, but there is no value added tax. The financial services industry is huge, contributing more than half of GDP. There are about 80 banks from 16 countries with deposits of over £100 billion and over 30,000 companies are registered. Foreign-owned companies enjoy exemption from tax on their trading profits, unless the trade is carried on through an established place of business in the island. An annual fee of £600 is charged to such companies. The tax and financial regimes are similar in Guernsey (and its dependency Alderney) and over 70 banks operate. The little island of Sark is governed by a feudal seigneur. It was noted for a time for a device known as the 'Sark lark' which is now obsolescent.

Gibraltar

14.21   Gibraltar was acquired by conquest from Spain under the Treaty of Utrecht (1713). Its colonial status is entrenched by the treaty provision that it will revert to Spain if Britain ever relinquishes sovereignty. There is constant friction between Britain and Spain over Gibraltar, but Britain has promised to respect the wishes of the people of Gibraltar, who voted overwhelmingly in 1967 to retain the British connection. There have been signs of a wish by the British authorities to appease Spain on this issue, but any move to dilute or abandon sovereignty over Gibraltar is certain to meet fierce opposition both locally and in Britain. Gibraltar has been active in the offshore business for some time. In *Eilbeck v Rawling (1981) 54 TC 101*, heard in the Lords along with *Ramsay*, an unsuccessful capital gains tax avoidance scheme, depended on a sum of money being 'blasted into space' from a Gibraltar settlement to a Jersey settlement. Nevertheless, Gibraltar has continued to expand as an offshore financial centre, albeit on a smaller scale than the Isle of Man or the Channel Islands. Recent figures showed 25 banks and two building societies operating there. Some Spanish banks have established offices in Gibraltar.

14.22   There also exist a group of tax havens in the British West Indies. These are small islands acquired over a period of two centuries by settlement and conquest. Decolonisation resulted in fragmentation, a process which seems even now not to have reached an end. An attempted West Indies Federation soon collapsed because of perceived domination by Jamaica. Lacking natural resources, the islands have been eager to acquire offshore financial business, which they have done with varying degrees of success. Some are still colonies, others have obtained independence, though usually with the Queen as head of state. Generally, those which have continued as colonies appear to have achieved greater success, possibly because of the lesser likelihood of misgovernment under the supervision of a British governor.

Bermuda

14.23   Bermuda is located to the northeast of the Caribbean islands, some 600 miles distant from the mainland of the United States. It was colonised as long ago as 1613, and continues to be a colony, independence having been rejected by a large majority in a referendum in 1995. Its balmy climate has long made tourism its most important industry, but it has also become an offshore financial centre with tax exemption facilities. There are about 9,000 exempted companies. Bermuda has become a preferred location for offshore insurance companies, to such effect that a territory with a population of 60,000 is now the world's third largest insurance market after London and New York.

Cayman Islands

14.24   An even more spectacular success has been achieved by the Cayman Islands. Colonised in the seventeenth century, they were administered from Jamaica, but opted to remain a British colony when Jamaica obtained independence in 1962. Since then, a group of islands with a total population of under 40,000 has developed as an offshore financial centre to such an extent that it has been described as the world's third largest after New York and London. It has representation from over 60 countries through 570 banks and trust companies, of which 30 operate domestically. In addition, there are 500 licensed insurance companies and 60,000 registered companies, almost all offshore. A stock exchange and a monetary authority were inaugurated in 1997. This unprecedented success has been assured by a complete absence of direct taxation.

Bahamas

14.25   The largest in extent though not in population of the Caribbean tax havens is the Bahamas, which stretch about 400 miles south-east of the Florida Coast. It has had independence since 1973, with the Queen as head of state. Tourism is the most important industry, but financial business produces about 20 per cent of GDP. Over 400 banks and trust companies are licensed, about half being branches of foreign companies. There is no direct taxation. Ship registration is also an important activity, with over 27 million tonnes registered, a figure exceeded only by Panama and Liberia.

Other tax havens

14.26   The other Caribbean tax havens are smaller. Many of the islands are eager to develop such business, but the competition is intense. The following may merit consideration.

Antigua

14.27   This is an independent country with the Queen as head of state. It has developed an offshore banking sector with nearly 20 banks registered and operating, but tourism remains by far the most important industry.

Barbados

14.28   One of the earliest British colonies to have its own legislature (1639), it has developed continuously until the present day, when it has the same constitutional status as Antigua. It is much larger in population than Antigua (300,000 as against 100,000) and the offshore sector includes 3,400 international business companies, 2,900 foreign sales corporations, 350 exempt insurance companies and 45 offshore banks. There is a stock exchange which participates in the Caribbean regional exchange.

British Virgin Islands

14.29   As befits a group of islands with a total population of 20,000, the British Virgin Islands remains a colony. Financial services have now sur-passed tourism as the largest industry. Over 350,000 international business companies are registered in the BVI. The British Virgin Islands are adjacent to the much larger and more populous (but less prosperous) Virgin Islands of the United States and the US dollar is the unit of currency.

St Kitts and Nevis

14.30   This tiny group of islands with a population of 40,000 illustrates the fissiparous tendencies of the Caribbean islands. Anguilla broke away in 1969 and is still a colony. The other two achieved independence under the Crown in 1983. There have recently been moves for Nevis (population 9,000) to secede from the federation. Despite this political turbulence, Nevis has developed a tax haven sector, with 9,000 offshore businesses registered.

Turks and Caicos Islands

14.31   This small group, geographically an extension of the Bahamas, became a separate colony in 1973 after periods of association with the Bahamas and Jamaica. It achieved unwelcome prominence when its Chief Minister was arrested in Miami in connection with drug trafficking, follow-ing which there was a period of closer British government surveillance. Nevertheless it continues to be a factor in international business planning. It has four commercial banks and offshore finance is stated to be a major industry.

14.32   Other tax havens, outside the British or British Commonwealth aegis, are difficult to classify, but several merit mention.

Switzerland

14.33   While perhaps not strictly a tax haven, Switzerland has long been a refuge for the funds of the wealthy. This arises partly from the stability of its currency, which over the decades has steadily appreciated against sterling, and partly from the complete secrecy surrounding banking operations, although the numbered account has been abolished. Of the population of 7 million, well over a million are foreign nationals, most of them workers with temporary residence permits. The sturdy independence which has characterised the Swiss since the days of William Tell has extended to a refusal to enter the European Union.

Andorra

14.34   High in the Pyrenees, Andorra is under the joint suzerainty of the President of the French Republic and the Spanish Bishop of Urgel, but it has a constitution empowering it to conduct its own affairs, with consultation on matters affecting France or Spain. Although tourism is the main industry, there is a substantial banking sector with tax haven status.

Monaco

14.35   Monaco is perhaps the smallest tax haven, with an area of less than 500 acres, but it attracts the wealthy because of its pleasant location and climate. Over a thousand yachts are registered. The population is 30,000, of whom only 7,000 are native Monegasques. For most purposes (other than tax) Monaco can be regarded as part of France. Its constitutional status rests on the rule of the House of Grimaldi, whose control dates back to 1297.

Liechtenstein

14.36   Liechtenstein is larger than Monaco (60 square miles) but has a similar population, which includes 12,000 resident foreigners. Located between Switzerland and Austria, its early history connected it to the latter, but since the First World War its major links have been with Switzerland. It is a constitutional monarchy. Low taxes and strict bank secrecy laws have made it a successful offshore financial centre. The 'anstalt' enjoys many of the characteristics of an English trust, and is targeted by UK anti-avoidance laws.

Liberia

14.37   Liberia is an example of how tax haven business can be carried on in the most discouraging circumstances. Originally a colony of emancipated American slaves, Liberia's governing elite was overthrown in a bloody revolution in 1980 led by Master-Sergeant Doe. He was killed in 1990, since when civil war has raged. The Liberian company has long been popular in offshore tax planning because of the low fees charged and minimal supervision. Bearer shares are the norm. This business is presently carried on through the Liberian embassy in Washington. Liberia is also a major flag of convenience, with 60 million tonnes registered.

Panama

14.38   Panama was almost a creation of the US, having been encouraged to secede from Colombia to facilitate the building of the Panama Canal. The power of the US was demonstrated as recently as 1990 when the President of Panama was seized and removed to Miami for trial on drug dealing charges. Nevertheless, Panama has now taken control of the Canal. It has a large banking sector, with over 100 banks, which have deposits of $25 billion (of which $16 billion are offshore). Panama also figures importantly in the flag of convenience business, with nearly 100 million tonnes registered.

Conclusion: words of warning

14.39   Quite apart from the hostile attitude to tax havens evinced by Lord Greene in his remarks cited at the beginning of this chapter, and possible action against them by the European Union, there are two dark shadows hanging over the use of tax havens.

14.40   The first is the illegal drugs industry, which is estimated to have an annual turnover of $600 billion, more than the gross national product of most countries. Heroin moves westwards from the Far East to Europe, cocaine north from Latin America to North America and Europe. Although both these trails are beset by criminality of all kinds, it is in the Caribbean that tax havens are most liable to be drawn in, particularly in the laundering of the proceeds of the trade. However, investors in any tax haven must be aware of the potential risks involved in guilt by association. It is essential to be able to demonstrate the innocent provenance of any funds which have been placed there and the absence of any subsequent contamination.

14.41   The second is an apparently increasing tendency by the Inland Revenue to take criminal action against those involved in tax haven activities. This is exemplified by *R v Charlton [1996] STC 1418, CA*, in which a tax adviser and his professional associates were convicted of the common law offence of cheating the public revenue and sent to jail. The charges concerned the purchase of commodities from overseas suppliers and their routing to the UK through a Jersey company, and the application of the Jersey company's funds to the purchase of properties in Spain. The result of the case caused great concern to professional bodies both because of the inordinate length of the trial (six months) and the possibility that a naive jury (and even judge) could be bamboozled into regarding as criminal activities which were perfectly normal tax planning. Unfortunately, the sheer volume of material made it impossible to conduct an adequate review of the case.

14.42   The golden rule is that all tax advice must be tendered to a client on a basis of total transparency, that is that all details could be disclosed to the Revenue if necessary without any possible imputation of dishonesty. In the past this would have been sufficient to ensure immunity from prosecution, but this can no longer be asserted with total confidence.

15 The Taxation of UK Source Income in the Hands of Non-Residents

John Dixon and Phil Barrett
(Ernst & Young)

Introduction

15.1   The purpose of this chapter is to analyse the circumstances in which a non-resident individual or company can be liable to tax in respect of UK source income, and if this is the case, the mechanisms available to the UK Revenue for collecting that tax.

The basic charge

Land

15.2   A non-resident is liable to tax under Schedule A on rents or receipts arising in respect of land in the UK. [*ICTA 1988, s 15*].

Public revenue dividends

15.3   It used to be the case that non-residents were charged in respect of all profits arising from public revenue dividends payable in the UK under Schedule C. However, by virtue of *FA 1996, s 79*, the charge to tax under Schedule C was abolished and replaced with a charge to tax under Schedule D, for the purposes of income tax for 1996/97 and subsequent years of assessment, and for the purposes of a corporation tax for accounting periods ending after 31 March 1996.

Trades and professions

15.4   A non-resident is charged to tax under Case I (trade) and Case II (profession or vocation) provided that the trade, profession or vocation is exercised 'within the UK'. [*ICTA 1988, ss 18(3)* and *18(1)(a)(iii)*].

Interest

15.5   A non-resident is liable to tax under Case III of Schedule D in respect of interest of money, whether annual or short, or other annuities, discounts or annual payments (*ICTA 1988, s 18(3)*) to the extent that such interest, annuity or annual payment has a UK 'source'.

Other income

15.6   Similarly, any other annual profit or gain not falling under Cases I, II or III of Schedule D is potentially taxable in the hands of a non-resident under Case VI of Schedule D, provided that the annual profit or gain has a UK 'source'.

Employments

15.7   A non-resident is charged with respect to emoluments from any office or employment in respect of duties performed in the UK under Case II of Schedule E. [*ICTA 1988, s 19(1)*].

Dividends

15.8   A non-resident is liable to tax in respect of dividends and other distributions from companies resident in the UK under Schedule F. [*ICTA 1988, s 20*].

Capital gains

15.9   A non-resident is liable to tax on any gain realised on the disposal of assets used for the purpose of a UK trade. [*TCGA 1992, s 10*].

New rules were included in the *FA 1998* which could result in a non-UK resident, returning to the UK, being subject to capital gains tax on disposal of assets owned prior to becoming non-resident.

Having summarised the basis of the charge, we will examine the various types of income and gain in more detail.

Rates of tax

15.10   Non-resident individuals are liable to UK tax on all UK source income with a few exceptions. A non-resident company, to the extent that it conducts a trade in the UK through a branch or agency, is subject to corporation tax without reliance on the small companies rate. [*ICTA 1988, s 13*]. A non-resident company that does not trade in the UK through a branch or agency is subject to income tax at the basic rate only on income arising to it from a UK source.

Companies resident in certain jurisdictions can invoke the small companies rate of corporation tax by taking advantage of the non-discrimination article of a suitable tax treaty. (ICAEW Technical Release TR 500 Taxline 1991/7).

Personal allowances

15.11   Personal allowances are generally not available to non-residents [*ICTA 1988, s 278*], but are available to:

(*a*)   Commonwealth citizens,

(*b*)   EEA nationals,

(*c*)   Isle of Man and Channel Islands residents,

(*d*)   certain Crown servants and their dependants,

(*e*)   people living abroad for certain health reasons,

(*f*)   residents of countries with a suitable double tax agreement with the UK.

Land

15.12   A non-resident individual or company is liable to income tax (companies at the basic rate only) on the annual profit or gains arising from any business conducted from the exploitation of land in the UK or any interest or rights over land in the UK. The salient features of the regime are:

(*a*)   the profits or gains of a Schedule A business are calculated on Case I principles [*section 21A*],

(*b*)   income from the right to use caravans and houseboats that are only used at one location are deemed to be income from an interest in land [*section 15(3)*],

(*c*)   income from furnished and holiday lettings is taxed under Schedule A and not case VI,

(*d*)   with effect from April 1995, all interest paid is deductible in computing the net profits that accrue in respect of UK land – prior to 5 April 1995, interest was only deductible if it was UK source or if paid to a UK bank and if certain conditions as to the period of letting were met.

15.13   In respect of payments made before 6 April 1996, the position was that rents paid directly by a tenant to a non-resident landlord were subject to a withholding requirement imposed by *ICTA 1988, s 43*, but there was no such withholding requirement if rents were paid to an agent who was assessable in the name of the non-resident landlord. For 1996/1997 and subsequent years new rules were introduced by *ICTA 1988, s 42A* for the charging of non-residents. *Section 42A* leaves the actual charging, assessment, collection and recovery of tax mechanisms to regulations which were issued as the *Taxation of Income from Land (Non residents) Regulations 1995* (*SI 1995 No 2902*), which were made on 10 November 1995.

15.14   The regulations deal with the provision for the charging, assessment, collection and recovery of tax from 'prescribed persons'. In most cases, a 'prescribed person' will be as follows.

(*a*)   A person issued with a notice by the Inland Revenue. That person must either be the person who has the obligation to make payments to the non-resident [*ICTA 1988, s 42A(2)(a)*] or any other person who acts on behalf of the non-resident 'in connection with the management or administration' of his Schedule A business. The notice issued by the Revenue can be issued in respect of the whole or part of the business of the non-resident.

(*b*)   If no notice is issued by the Revenue in respect of a particular business or part of the business of the non-resident landlord, and there is a person whose 'usual place of abode' (it is curious that the Revenue should retain this phraseology rather than use the term resident) is in the UK who acts as an agent in respect of that business or part and has power to receive income in respect of that business or part, or has control over the direction of that income, then that person will be a 'prescribed person' unless his activity on behalf of the non-resident is confined to the provision of legal advice or legal services. If there is more than one person who can be such a 'prescribed person', then the regulations spell out a procedure for nominating the particular person who will be responsible for the administration of the regime. The procedure, detailed in *regs 3(4)* and *4* of the *Regulation* envisages (although the wording of the term 'last agent' in *reg 4(1)(c)* is obscure) that if there is more than one person who is an agent and has power to receive income, the prescribed person is the agent who elects with the last agent, or failing such an election the last agent.

(*c*)   If there is no person who is a prescribed person within (*b*) above, then the tenant can be a 'prescribed person' where the tenant is liable to pay to the non-resident in respect of his occupation of the particular premises in question sums exceeding £5,200 per annum (proportionately reduced for lettings of part of the year).

The 'prescribed person' is required by the regulations to register with the Inland Revenue within a 30-day period following the time when he fell to be characterised as a 'prescribed person'.

15.15   There are special rules for partnerships and agents who have more than one branch.

The provisions in the regulations dealing with the payment and recovery of tax distinguish between prescribed persons who are tenants and prescribed persons who are agents. The tenant (or more accurately the person who falls within *ICTA 1988, s 42A(2)(a)* as being the person by whom sums are payable to the non-resident), is required to calculate on a quarterly basis the amount of tax which is or may become chargeable in respect of the business or part in respect of which the person is a prescribed person. The calculation is to be made at the basic rate on all the income payable by him in the quarter to the non-resident or paid to a person other than the non-resident where such payment is not likely to be a deductible expense. No such calculation is required to be made in respect of income in respect of which the non-resident is liable to corporation tax.

The key feature to note about the requirements to calculate and pay income tax that fall on the tenant, is that no deduction can be made for expenses.

15.16   As far as the obligations on an agent who is a prescribed person is concerned, regard should be had to *para 9* of the regulation. The agent is required to calculate the tax at the basic rate on the income received by the prescribed person in the quarter concerned, or the income which was under the power and direction of that person, after deduction for expenses, and which was either paid by the prescribed person or at his direction net of amounts which are likely to be deductible for the purposes of computing net income for UK tax purposes.

There are detailed requirements in the regulations for returns to be filed on a quarterly and annual basis by the prescribed person.

It is possible, however, for the non-resident to apply to the Revenue to disapply the withholding requirement on the tenant/agent detailed above. Detailed information [*regulation 17*] needs to be provided and certain undertakings given.

Trading in the UK

15.17   In the absence of a double tax agreement a non-resident is liable to UK tax if he conducts a trade 'within' the UK. Non-resident companies are liable to income tax at the basic rate, if they conduct a trade within the UK, but instead to corporation tax if they conduct a trade within the UK through a branch or agency. Non-resident individuals are liable to income tax.

15.18   The question of whether and when a non-resident conducts a trade 'within' the UK can, as a matter of practice, be a difficult one and much will depend on the precise mechanics by which the trade is conducted. There are a number of cases on this area of UK law some of which are quite lengthy and many of which are very old (the majority were heard before 1930). These cases offer indications as to which factors are relevant in determining when a trade is conducted within the UK. Ultimately, each case will depend on its own precise facts and therefore it is difficult to determine which combination of factors, for example, trade contracts, profit origins, agents, delivery etc., will be decisive. As the Lord Chancellor explained in *Maclaine v Eccott (10 TC 481)*: '. . . it is undesirable to attempt to lay down any exhaustive test of which constitutes such an exercise of trade'. What appears to be fairly well established is that a distinction can be drawn between trading with and trading within the UK. It is only the latter which will precipitate a UK tax exposure for the non-resident. This distinction was first addressed by Asquith QC in *Grainger & Son v Gough ((1895) 3 TC 311)*: '. . . M. Roederer does not exercise a trade within this country. He may carry on a trade with this country without carrying it on within it'.

15.19   How do we determine whether a trade is conducted within the UK as opposed to with the UK? Probably the most important factor in this connection is the location where the profit earning contract is made. Often quoted in this connection is Brett LJ in *Erichsen v Last ((1881) 1 TC 351; affd (1881) 4 TC 422)*:

> '. . . whenever profitable contracts are habitually made in England by or for foreigners with persons in England, because they are in England, to do something for or supply something to those persons, such foreigners are exercising a profitable trade in England, even though everything to be done by them in order to fulfil the contract is done abroad. The profits arise to them from the contract which they make . . . the contract is made in England with him in England, and it is in respect of such a contract that the profit is came.'

As the Master of the Rolls, Lord Esher put it in *Werle & Co v Colquhoun ((1888) 2 TC 402)* '. . . the contract is the very foundation of trade. It is the trade really.' (*Pommery and Greno v Apthorpe ((1886) 2 TC 182)*), confirms that even if an agent acts as an errand boy communicating the non-resident's acceptance of an order to the UK client, a contract was made in the UK.

15.20   There are, however, limitations to this principle. In *Grainger & Sons v Gough*, Lord Watson said:

> 'When a trade is carried on in a foreign country, and British customers not only purchase but take delivery there, I do not think that the employment of an English agent to collect (occasionally) and remit the debts due to him by those purchasers can be regarded as an exercise of his trade in this country by the foreign merchant.'

Graingers were agents for L. Roederer's Champagne, soliciting in the custom of clients, whose orders when received, were transmitted to Roederer at Rheims, who exercised his discretion as to fulfilment of orders. If he accepted the order, he delivered the wine at the customer's cost and risk to the client in England and invoiced them in his name. The customers frequently remitted money directly to Roederer abroad but occasionally debts were collected by the agents. Asquith QC said:

> 'No contract for the sale of his wine is made in England by Grainger & Son. They have no power to bind him to a contract of sale by anything they do here. The contract is only completed when it is accepted in France.'

Lord Herschell agreed and added:

'An order given to a merchant for the supply of goods does not of itself create an obligation. Until something is done by the person receiving the order, which amounts to an acceptance, there is no contract . . . the appellants . . . have no authority to so do.'

15.21   The place of execution of contract is not, however, decisive in determining whether trade is conducted within the UK. The lack of contract execution in the UK does not automatically mean trading with as opposed to trading within. As Atkin LJ said in *Smidth & Co v Greenwood ((1921) 8 TC 193)*:

'The question is not whether respondents carry on business in this country. It is whether they exercise a trade in the country so that profits accrue to them from the trade so exercised . . . I think that the question is, where do the operations take place from which profits in substance arise?'

Lord Radcliffe agreed in *Firestone Tyre & Rubber Co v Llewellin ((1956) 37 TC 111)*:

'. . . it cannot mean more than the law requires that the place of sale will not be the determining factor if there are other circumstances present that outweigh its importance.'

15.22   Furthermore, the employment by the non-resident of a UK agent or UK based employee does not automatically constitute trading within the UK. If an agent makes the contract with the client in the UK, this is evidence that the principal is trading within the UK. However, if he is used as an accessory, the non-resident does not automatically exercise a trade within the UK provided that the substance of the profits arise abroad. In *Smidth v Greenwood* an employee of the non-resident firm was used to court clients, who were then referred to the non-resident to make the contract abroad. The employee also supervised construction work at the clients' sites after the contracts had been signed. As the Master of the Rolls said: '*Mr Greenwood Robinson gives substantial help in the carrying out of the respondent's contracts, but he does not and cannot conclude any contracts*'. There must, however, be a limitation to this principle. If all the terms are negotiated by the agent and the contract is simply signed abroad, the Revenue is likely to take the case strongly that a trade is being exercised within the UK.

15.23   It will be appreciated that there are, as explained above, numerous cases on a question of whether a trade is exercised in the UK. In the analysis above, some of the more important themes have been discussed, but the analysis is by no means exhaustive. What is clear is that there is no categoric rule which determines when a trade is exercised within the UK or not and in any particular case it will be the actual combination of factors present in that case which will determine whether a trade is exercised within the UK. Some of the more important themes, however, can be summarised as follows:

(1)   On a contract for the sale of goods, it is likely to be the place where the contract is made which is the prime factor which determines whether the trade is exercised within the UK or not.

(2) On a contract for the supply of services, however, the position is less clear and it may be the place where the services are performed which is relevant.

(3) If the sale contract is made outside the UK, the trade may nevertheless be exercised within the UK if the profits still in substance arise here.

(4) The question of whether the money is received in the UK is not directly relevant.

(5) The employment of an agent or employee in the UK should not of itself result in a UK tax liability on trading profits.

(6) The purchase of goods in the UK should not of itself give rise to a trade exercised within the UK.

(7) The use of an agent to communicate acceptances of orders in the UK is likely to result in a UK trade, unless other strong factors suggest a trade conducted with the UK.

15.24 The rules dealing with the collection of income tax and capital gains tax from non-residents for the year 1996/1997 onwards, and for corporation tax purposes in relation to accounting periods beginning after 31 March 1996, can be found in *sections 126* and *127* and *Schedule 23* of *FA 1995*. For prior periods, regard should be had to *sections 78–82* of the *Taxes Management Act 1970*.

15.25 In this chapter, we will deal, in the main, with the new rules. Under these provisions, certain obligations are placed on the 'UK representative' of a non-resident person.

Who is the UK representative? A UK representative is a person who:

(*a*) is a branch or agency of the non-resident within the meaning of *TMA1970, s 118 [FA 1995, s 126(8)]*. Thus, the UK representative must be a factorship, agency, receivership, branch or management of the non-resident person;

(*b*) the non-resident must conduct a trade, profession or vocation within the UK through the branch or agency [*FA 1995, s 126(2)*]; and

(*c*) income from the trade profession or vocation must arise directly or indirectly through or from that branch or agency. [*FA 1995, s 126(2)(a)*].

A person can only be a UK representative in respect of:

(i) income from a trade profession or vocation that arises through the branch or agent;

(ii) income from property or rights used or held by or for the branch or agent; and

(iii) gains on the disposal of assets held by the branch or agent.

There are certain special provisions for partnerships.

15.26   A person will not, however, be a non-resident's UK representative [*FA 1995, s 127*] in relation to amounts which arise in the following ways.

(*a*)   By reference to transactions conducted as an agent but not on a regular basis for the non-resident.

(*b*)   In relation to transactions carried out through a broker where that broker was carrying on the business of a broker, the particular transaction in question was carried out by the broker on behalf of the non-resident in the ordinary course of that business, the remuneration which the broker received for the provision of the services to the non-resident in respect of the transaction in question was at a rate which is not less than is customary for that class of business and the broker is not in any other respect treated as being a UK representative. [*FA 1995, s 127(2)*]. Unfortunately, the term 'broker' is not defined in the legislation and one must have regard to the normal meaning of that term. Useful comment on the meaning of this term can be found in *Fleming v London Produce Co Ltd (1968) 44 TC 582.*

(*c*)   From investment transactions carried out through an investment manager where:

   (i)   the transaction was carried out on behalf of the non-resident by a person who at the time was carrying on a business of providing investment management services;

   (ii)   the transaction was carried out in the ordinary course of that business;

   (iii)   the manager when he acted on behalf of the non-resident in relation to the transaction did so in an independent capacity;

   (iv)   the remuneration which the manager received for the provision to the non-resident of the investment management services in question was at a rate which was not less than that which would have been customary for that class of business; and

   (v)   the non-resident does not otherwise fall to be treated as having the manager as his UK representative.

15.27   There are detailed provisions in *section 127* which restrict the exemption from UK representative status for the investment manager when he is entitled beneficially to a proportion of the income of a non-resident. Investment transactions, defined in *section 127(12)* are transactions, shares, stocks etc., but not futures contracts or options relating to land.

The obligations that are imposed on the UK representative are detailed in *FA 1995, Sch 23*. In broad terms all of the provisions of the *Taxes Acts* and the *TCGA 1992* dealing with the assessment of collection and recovery of tax apply to the UK representative. In addition there are additional reporting requirements.

15.28   The question of any UK tax liability on trading profits accruing to a non-resident may, of course, be affected by the terms of an applicable double taxation agreement that would generally provide that the non-resident will only in fact be chargeable if he conducts a trade in the UK through a 'permanent establishment'.

Foreign partnerships trading in the UK

15.29   As part of the move towards self-assessment in the UK, the treatment of partnerships resident outside the UK have undergone change. New rules were introduced from 1995/96 for partnerships set up and commenced after 5 April 1994 and from 1997/98 for all other partnerships.

New rules

15.30   Under the rules introduced, where a partnership is controlled outside the UK, and thus resident outside the UK, the profits of a non-resident partner are now computed under *ICTA 1988, section 111* as if the partnership were an individual not resident in the UK. The effect of this, where the partnership carries on a trade partly in the UK and partly outside the UK is to restrict the charge on the non-resident to his share of the profits of the part trade carried on in the UK. Where an individual member of the partnership becomes or ceases to be resident in the UK, the deemed trade carried on by a partner individually is treated as having ceased and a new trade commenced. There is no effect on the trade carried on by the partnership but the individual partner is taxed on worldwide profits during the period of UK residence and UK profits only for the period of non-residence. [*ICTA 1988, s 112(1B)*]. A UK resident partner who is not domiciled in the UK or who is a Commonwealth citizen or citizen of the Republic of Ireland not ordinarily resident in the UK continues to be assessed under Schedule D, Case V on the remittance basis. [*ICTA 1988, s 112(1B)*].

Interest, annuities and annual payments

15.31   As detailed above, a non-resident is liable to tax under Schedule D, Case III in respect of 'UK source' interest annuities and annual payments. The limitation of the basis of charge to 'UK source items' requires some explanation.

Case III [*ICTA 1988, s 18(3)*] charges tax in respect of such amounts 'whether such payment is payable within or out of the UK . . .' and contains no such limitation as to the source of the payment. Indeed, *ICTA 1988, s 18(1)(a)*, whilst limiting the charge to tax in respect of annual profits or gains received by the non-UK resident to income from 'property whatever in the UK' [*section 18(1)(a)(iii)*], contains no such limitation for 'interest of money, annuities and other annual profits or gains not charged under Schedule A, C or E . . .'. As Lord Hailsham said in the case of *Westminster*

Bank Executor and Trustee Co (Channel Islands) Ltd v National Bank of Greece SA (1970) 46 TC 472 at page *492*:

> 'Read out of context these words would appear to be wide enough to charge income even of residents outside the UK even from property outside the UK. But it is clear that they cannot be so read . . .'.

Lord Hailsham in the *Greek Bank* case imposed a territorial limitation following *Colquhoun v Brooks (1889) 2 TC 490*. 'The income tax acts, however, themselves, impose a territorial limit, either that from which the taxable income is derived must be situate in the UK or the person whose income is to be taxed must be resident of there.' (Lord Herschell at page *499*).

Thus, following the *Greek Bank* case and *Colquhoun*, interest annuities and other annual payments will be charged in the hands of the non-resident if the source of the property or obligation from which the income is derived is situate in the UK.

It is at this point that academic opinion, and judicial comment, becomes less certain as to the criteria that should be established in determining whether the property or obligation in a particular case is a situate within or without the UK. As a matter of practice, some reliance can be placed on the Inland Revenue statement which appears in Tax Bulletin Issue 9, details of which are given below.

15.32   The Revenue view on the location of the source for interest is based on the case of *Westminster Bank Executor and Trustee Co (Channel Islands) Ltd v National Bank of Greece SA (1970) 46 TC 472* – the *Greek Bank* case. The factors considered relevant in that case (leading to the conclusion that the income involved did not have a UK source) were:

(*a*)   there was an obligation undertaken by a principal debtor which was a foreign corporation;

(*b*)   the obligation was guaranteed by another foreign corporation with no place of business in the UK;

(*c*)   the obligation was secured on land and public revenues outside the UK; and

(*d*)   funds for payments by the principal debtor of principal or interest to residents outside Greece would have been provided by either a remittance from Greece or funds remitted by debtors from abroad (even though a cheque might be drawn in London).

15.33   Although the *Greek Bank* case was concerned with income which turned out not to have a UK source, the Revenue stated that inferences can be drawn from that case about the factors which would support the existence of a UK source, the most important of which are:

(*a*)   the residence of the debtor, i.e., the place in which the debt will be enforced;

(*b*)   the source from which interest is paid;

(*c*)   where the interest is paid; and

(*d*)   the nature and location of the security for the debt.

If all of these are located in the UK then it is likely that the interest will have a UK source.

Whilst the Revenue said it was not possible for them to comment individually in advance on the many cases in which the location of the source of interest may be relevant, since the precise tax consequences depend on all the factors and on exactly how the transactions are in fact carried out, they hoped that the summary of their views would assist practitioners and their clients in determining for themselves where the source of interest with which they may be concerned is located.

15.34   It will be appreciated that because of the nature of the issue any statement as to the criteria that should be applied in determining the source of interest will give rise to ambiguity and uncertainty where the precise circumstances in question do not match the exact criteria detailed in such a statement. Despite this inherent uncertainty, the Revenue statement can be welcomed as a reasonable attempt to outline the more important criteria in determining the source of interest, although the basis of some of those criteria must be subject to question. Specifically, the question of where the interest is paid would, arguably, be irrelevant in determining the source because of the fact that the definition of Case III in *ICTA 1988, s 18* places no reliance on the question of where payment is made envisaging payments made within and without of the UK. The use of the residency of the debtor as being an important determinant factor has basis in law in the context of simple contract debts (that is contract debts which are not specialty debts) (see *New York Life Insurance Co v Public Trustee [1924] 2 CH 101*; *IRC v Viscount Broome's Executors (1935) 19 TC 667* and *Kwok Chi Leung Karl v Comr of Estate Duty [1988] 1 WLR 1035*). In the context of specialty debts, however, a strong case can be made that the residency of the debtor has no application.

The mechanism by which tax is collected in respect of interest paid to a non-resident, together with annuities and other annual payments, is by withholding under *ICTA 1988, s 349*.

Obviously, provisions of a double tax agreement may affect the question of any liability to tax in respect of such income.

Other income

15.35   In addition to income from a trade, profession or vocation and income from interest annuities and other annual payments and discounts, there are of course other types of income that may be received by a non-resident that may be paid from or in respect of or in connection with the UK where the question of UK tax needs to be considered. Strictly a non-resident, in addition to being liable to tax in the manner detailed above, is liable to tax in respect of other annual profits or gains not falling under any other case of Schedule D and not charged for tax under Schedules A, C or E, under Schedule D, Case VI. Here, the limitation contained in *ICTA 1988, s 18 (1)(a)(iii)* is directly in point in that the profit or gain must accrue or arise in respect of property 'in' the UK.

Typically such income may be payments for the use of or in respect of:

- patent,
- trademark,
- copyright,
- registered designs,
- public lending rights,
- know-how,
- other miscellaneous receipts.

Putting aside the question of whether any receipt is income or capital (not the subject of this chapter), there can be considerable uncertainty in dealing with the question of how such receipts should be taxed and how such tax should be collected. This can particularly be the case where payments are made in respect of a bundle of rights, but conceptually difficulties extend to the basic principles and how they apply to payments in respect of such rights.

Copyright

15.36   A non-resident who receives a payment for the right to use a copyright can, in principle, fall to be taxed under Case I (trade), Case II (profession), Case III (annual payment) or Case VI. A payment which is an annual payment is unlikely to be a trading or professional receipt (as they must be pure profit income – *IRC v Whiteworth Park Co Ltd (1958) 38 TC 531*) but could be taxed, potentially, under Case VI (see *Asher v London Film Productions SA 22 ATC 432*). In either case, whether an assessment is levied under Case III or Case VI, there must be property situate in the UK, and there is little guidance as to the circumstances which determine when copyright is so situate. For capital gains tax purposes legislative guidance can be found in *TCGA 1992, s 275*, but for income tax purposes the only assistance can be found in the case of *Jarvis v Curtis Brown (1929) 14 TC 744*. This seems to suggest that copyright exists in the UK if it is enforceable in the UK. This would mirror the capital gains definition.

The mechanism for collection of tax falls into two distinct areas being:

(*a*)   potential collection from UK representatives by virtue of the arrangements detailed above,

(*b*)   withholding under *ICTA 1988, s 536*.

The withholding provisions provide that where the usual place of abode of the owner of a copyright is outside the UK, basic rate income tax is deductible from any copyright royalty paid to him from the UK and must be accounted for by the payer to the Inland Revenue. Royalties or sums paid in respect of copies of works which are shown on a claim to have been exported from the UK for distribution abroad may be paid gross. [*ICTA 1988, section 536(2)*]. Payments of royalties to a non-resident professional author are not subject to deduction of tax at source under these provisions (see the Parliamentary written answer in Hansard Vol 791, Col 31, of 10 November 1969).

Patents

15.37   Similar principles apply in the context of payments for the use of a patent.

Following *English, Scottish and Australian Bank Ltd v IRC [1932] AC 238*, a patent is situate in the country in which it is registered. It may well be the case, however, that the source of a royalty for the use of a patent may be other than the place of registration, and the case of *International Combustion Ltd v IRC (1932) 16 TC 532* illustrates this particular point. Unfortunately, *International Combustion* does not take us very far in determining precisely what criteria should be applied in determining where property which gives rise to a patent royalty is situate. Indeed, Rowlatt J recognised at page *539* the difficulty of this issue.

Payments of royalties in respect of the use of a patent which are UK 'source' are subject to withholding requirements under *ICTA 1988, ss 348* and *349*.

15.38   In respect of other miscellaneous receipts, trademark royalties, know-how payments etc., there is little guidance as to the criteria that should be applied in determining source. Withholding requirements are contained in the legislation in *ICTA 1988, ss 348* and *349* to the extent that the payments represent annual payments. Care should in this context be taken concerning *ICTA 1988, s 349(1)(b)*. This applies a withholding requirement on 'any royalty or other sum paid in respect of the user of a patent'. The term 'any royalty' here applies to patent royalties only and not other periodic payments that may commercially be called a 'royalty'. *Section 537* applies in respect of public lending rights where the owner is abroad, and *section 537B* in respect of design royalties where the owner is abroad. It is generally recognised, however, that this legislation represents only a machinery for the collection of tax as opposed to legislation which imposes a tax charge.

15.39   It will be seen from the above that if a liability to tax arises in respect of this type of income the mechanism of collection is usually by way of with-holding basic rate income tax. In order for the payer to pay at a reduced treaty rate of withholding advance clearance needs to be obtained from the Inland Revenue (see *SI 1970 No 488*). Care needs to be taken in order to 'fit' the particular income in question within the terms of the applicable double tax agreement and ensure that there are no treaty shopping or other restrictions that can deny treaty relief. In the case of 'interest' or other royalties for specific intellectual property this is generally (although not always) not a problem as this will usually be a comprehensive 'interest' or 'royalty' article in the applicable treaty. It will be appreciated from the above analysis, however, that there is a class of payments, 'annual payments' that are subject to withholding requirements in the UK but which do not necessarily fit into the definition of 'royalties' in the applicable treaty. In these cases reliance may need to be placed either on the 'business profits' article or the 'other income' article of the treaty to protect the non-resident from a UK tax exposure.

Dividends

15.40   Dividends from UK companies are taxed under Schedule F. [*ICTA 1988, s 20*].

Non-resident companies which receive dividends from UK companies are not subject to any further taxation liability in respect of the dividend income. In the case of individuals, regard needs to be paid to *ICTA 1988, ss 231, 232* and *233*. In addition, *F(No 2)A 1997, s 30* is relevant for dividends paid on or after April 1999. This *section* provides that there will be no entitlements to have excess tax credits repaid, unless provided for in the terms of a relevant double taxation agreement. Regard should also be paid to the limitation provisions contained in *FA 1995, s 128*.

Employment income

15.41   Non-residents who perform duties in the UK are liable to tax in respect of that income under Case II of Schedule E.

By virtue of *section 132(2)*, where an office or employment is in substance one the duties of which fall to be performed outside the UK, then duties performed in the UK, which are incidental to the performance of other duties, are treated as being performed outside of the UK. The question of whether duties are so incidental are discussed in paragraphs 5.7 and 5.8 of the Inland Revenue booklet IR20, and further comment in this connection can be found in the case of *Robson v Dixon (1972) 48 TC 527*.

The question of the circumstances in which an individual would be liable to UK tax under Case II would also be affected, of course, by the provision of any relevant double tax agreement between the UK and the country of residency of the individual concerned.

The usual mechanism for the collection of tax on employment income is of course PAYE.

15.42   In the context of foreign individuals who come to work in the UK on a temporary basis and are subject to tax under Case II of Schedule E, there are certain features of the PAYE regime that require explanation. The case of *Clark v Oceanic Contractors Inc (1980) 56 TC 183* established that only employers with a sufficient presence in the UK can be required to operate PAYE. Per Lord Scarman 'the only critical factor, so far as collection is concerned, is whether in the circumstances it can be made effective. A trading presence in the UK will suffice'. This basic principle has, however, been modified by changes in *ICTA 1988 (sections 203B–E)* which both replaced the rules for 'intermediate employers' in *reg 4* of the *PAYE Regulations (SI 1993 No 744)*, and extended the scope of PAYE.

It should be noted that *regs 102* and *104* of the *PAYE Regulations* provide procedures whereby PAYE can be recovered directly from an employee on a quarterly basis, where 'the Inspector is of the opinion that deduction of tax by reference to the tax tables is impracticable'. Such procedures (direct collection) may be applied where the Inspector does not consider that an overseas employer has sufficient presence in the UK for it to be required to operate PAYE, and the statutory provisions referred to below do not apply.

15.43   *ICTA 1988, s 203C* applies where an employee 'works for' (i.e., in the course of carrying out any of the duties of his employment) a person other than his employer, and the PAYE regulations do not apply to the person making payments to the employee, or to the employer, if payments are made by an intermediary of the employer. Where PAYE is not deducted or accounted for by the person making the payments to the employee, then the person for whom the employee 'works' (i.e., other than his employer) is required to operate the PAYE system in respect of payments of remuneration made to the employee.

This provision typically covers the situation where the services of an employee of an overseas company are provided to a UK person, perhaps a member of the same group as the employing company, by way of secondment. Whether the payments are made to the employee by the employer, or by any other intermediary of the employer, the party to which the services are provided must operate PAYE. However, the legislation is silent on the mechanism by which the PAYE is funded, where payments are made to the employee directly by the overseas employer.

15.44   *ICTA 1988, s 203D* applies in relation to an employee who is either not resident, or if resident, not ordinarily resident, in the UK and such an employee has both UK and overseas duties of employment. The employer may apply to the Revenue for a direction that PAYE be applied only to a specific proportion of the individual's remuneration, representing the proportion in respect of UK duties chargeable under Case II. In the absence of obtaining such a direction, the legislation imposes an obligation for PAYE to be operated on the whole of the employee's remuneration, i.e., including that for overseas duties. This legislation applies where there is an overseas or UK employer: however, if an employee is resident, part of the income from employment should be paid directly offshore.

This provision was enacted in light of the decision of *IRC v Herd [1993] STC 436* which had suggested that PAYE need not be operated where only part of a payment to an employee constitutes assessable emoluments. The amount of income paid in, or remitted to, the UK should also be considered, as such amounts would also form part of a resident employee's taxable income under Case III of Schedule E.

15.45   In relation to 'inbound' employees, the guidance provided by the *Employers Guide to PAYE* confirms that PAYE must be operated in respect of all employees working at a UK branch or office of any overseas business (presumably on the basis that the employer would then have a sufficient UK presence). Moreover, PAYE is required to be operated in respect of all employees 'who work under the general control and management of a business in the UK or the UK branch or office of an overseas business. The concern in the UK who is using the employee's services must operate PAYE as if it was the employer'.

Whilst this guidance is clearly based upon *section 203C*, it is interesting that the wording 'general control and management' is used. This wording, taken from the now repealed *reg 4* of the *PAYE Regulations*, is not repeated in *section 203C*. Rather, *section 203C* uses the wording 'works for'.

The guidance confirms that there is an obligation to operate PAYE whether the employee is paid by the UK concern or the overseas concern – if part of the employee's income is paid from overseas, then it is up to the UK concern to obtain the necessary details to operate PAYE.

Where employees are sent to the UK by an overseas business, and it is not considered that they are working under the UK concern's day-to-day control or management, then the UK concern is requested to provide details to its PAYE office. Pending the agreement of the tax office otherwise, PAYE should be operated in the normal way.

15.46   The Revenue guidance outlines the procedures in order to request a direction to apply PAYE to only part of an employee's remuneration, where *section 203D* is relevant. Moreover, they invite applications to 'relax' normal PAYE requirements, where it is considered that the dependent personal services article of a double taxation treaty is in point to exempt the employee from UK income tax in respect of his remuneration. This is known as a 'Short Term Business Visitors' agreement which allows the Revenue to grant an exemption from the operation of PAYE in return for an annual statement from the employer for each visitor to the UK, detailing evidence to support the claim under a relevant double taxation agreement.

In practice, it would usually be desirable for new 'inbound' employees to complete Form P86 ('arrival in the UK') to support any applications to mitigate PAYE. In most cases, the Revenue will require the completion of this form anyway in order to determine the residence of the individual and to determine an appropriate notice of coding for them. Care should be taken when the employee completes this form to ensure that their determined residence status does not conflict with any application for a ruling under *section 203D*.

Capital gains

15.47   A non-resident is subject to capital gains tax to the extent that:

(*a*)   he carries on a trade in the UK through a branch or agency;

(*b*)   he disposes of assets situated in the UK which are used in or for the purposes of the trade at or before the time when the capital gain accrued; or

(*c*)   he disposes of assets situated in the UK and used or held for the purposes of the branch or agency at or before the time of disposal or disposed of assets acquired for use by or for the purposes of the branch or agency.

In addition, new rules were introduced in the *FA 1998*, now contained in *TCGA 1992, s 10A* such that individuals who leave the UK on or after 17 March 1998 and who have been both;

(*a*)   resident in the UK for tax purposes during any part of the seven tax years of assessment immediately preceding the year at departure; and

(*b*)   non-resident for less than five complete tax years commencing with the year after departure from the UK

will be treated as remaining liable to capital gains tax on assets which were owned at the date of departure.

Limitation on tax liability

15.48   The *Finance Act 1995* provides new rules which give a legislative 'ceiling' to the UK income tax and corporation tax due on non-residents.

16 UK Self-Assessment for Non-Resident Individuals and Trustees

Andrew Roycroft ATII
(Solicitor)

Introduction and overview

16.1   Chapter 15 sets out the circumstances in which non-UK resident individuals and trustees are subject to UK taxation in respect of UK source income. This chapter deals with the rules for collecting that tax from such non-UK residents under the system of 'self-assessment', which came into force for years of assessment 1996/1997 onwards.

16.2   The main principles of the self-assessment regime apply equally to UK residents and non-UK residents alike. Under this regime, taxpayers are obliged to notify the Inland Revenue of their chargeability to income tax or capital gains tax. Then, if specifically required by the Inland Revenue to do so, they must file a tax return. Although this tax return must include a 'self-assessment' of the taxpayer's tax liability, an individual need not include a self-assessment if that tax return is filed early enough (in most cases by September 30 following the end of the year of assessment in question). Instead of judging the accuracy of each and every tax return and assessing the tax due, the Inland Revenue concentrates its efforts on enquiring into the accuracy of a limited number of tax returns. This power to enquire into tax returns is a distinctive feature of the self-assessment regime. Although some cases will be selected for enquiry on a random basis, an enquiry is more likely to occur where there is a significant tax risk or there is a suspicion that something is wrong.

16.3   The Inland Revenue no longer issues partnership assessments. Under self-assessment, each partner is only liable for tax on his share of the partnership profits, which must be included in his own personal tax return. These figures are taken from a partnership statement which each partnership must deliver to the Inland Revenue, along with a partnership return.

16.4   Another major change is the introduction of a system of 'payments on account', whereby individuals must make two payments on account of their liability to income tax for the year of assessment. The first payment being due by 31 January which falls during the year of assessment in question and the second being due by 31 July following the end of the year of assessment. As both payments are based on the previous year's tax liability, a balancing (re)payment must be made by 31 January following the end of the year of assessment.

16.5   Other changes to the tax system were introduced to coincide with the introduction of self-assessment. Of particular relevance to non-residents are the changes to the rules for collecting and recovering tax from UK representatives of non-UK residents, which impose joint responsibility on the non-UK resident and the UK representative for complying with all aspects of self-assessment. Also of importance are the new regime for taxing property income of non-residents, the new computational rules for non-resident partners, for non-UK residents carrying on a business in the UK and the statutory limit on the income tax liability of non-UK residents. As these substantive changes are discussed in other chapters of this book, the focus here will be to set out the basic compliance obligations referred to in the previous paragraphs, as amended or imposed by the self-assessment regime.

The obligation to notify the Inland Revenue of chargeability to tax

16.6   For years of assessment 1995/1996 onwards, every person who is chargeable to income tax or capital gains tax for any year of assessment must notify the Inland Revenue that he is so chargeable. The notice must be made to an officer of the Board within six months of the end of the year of assessment in question. The maximum penalty for failing to give such notice is the amount of tax for which the person is ultimately liable and which is unpaid at 31 January following the year of assessment in question. [*TMA 1970, s 7(1), (8)*].

16.7   No notice need be given by a taxpayer who has received a notice from the Inland Revenue requiring him to make and deliver a tax return for the year of assessment in question. Nor need any notice be given if the taxpayer has no chargeable gains and his total income for the year of assessment in question consists of income from the following sources:

(*a*)   a source all payments of (or on account of) income from which (along with all income which does not consist of payments) has been taken into account in the making of deductions or repayments of tax under the PAYE scheme;

(*b*)   a source all income from which has been or will be taken into account either in determining that person's liability to tax or in the making of deductions or repayments of tax under the PAYE scheme;

(*c*)   a source all income from which is income on which the recipient could not be liable to tax under a self-assessment made in respect of the year of assessment;

(*d*)   a source all income from which is income from which income tax has been deducted;

(*e*)   a source all income from which is income from or on which income tax is treated as having been deducted or paid;

(*f*)   a source all income from which is income chargeable under schedule F.

A source will only qualify under headings (*d*) to (*f*) if the recipient is only liable to tax at the lower or basic rate of tax. [*TMA 1970, s 7(1)(b), (3) to (7)*].

16.8   It will be appreciated that the effect of these rules will, in most cases, be to limit the obligation to notify the Inland Revenue of chargeability to cases where the Inland Revenue has not issued a tax return and the tax-payer is either (*a*) in receipt of income from which tax has not been deducted at source, or (*b*) a higher rate taxpayer in receipt of investment income.

The obligation to file a tax return

16.9   An officer of the Board may give a notice to a person, requiring that person to make and deliver to the officer a return containing such informa-tion as may be reasonably required for the purpose of establishing the amounts in which that person is chargeable to income tax and capital gains tax for the year of assessment and the amount payable by that person by way of income tax for that year. [*TMA 1970, s 8(1)(a)*].

16.10   The return must include a declaration by the person making it that it is, to the best of his knowledge, correct and complete and must be accom-panied by such accounts, statements and documents (e.g. dividend vouchers, SC60s etc.), relating to information contained in the return, as may reason-ably be so required. In practice, the Inland Revenue only looks for separate accounts to accompany the return for large or complex businesses. For most businesses it will be sufficient to include standardised accounts information in the relevant boxes on the return. Different information, accounts and statements can be required for different periods or in relation to different descriptions of sources of income or in relation to different descriptions of person. [*TMA 1970, s 8(1)(b), (2), (3) and (4)*].

16.11   As a practical matter, the Inland Revenue will accept a 'best esti-mate' of information which cannot be finalised in time to submit the return. The correct figure should be notified to the Inland Revenue without delay, together with an amended self-assessment. The Inland Revenue has con-firmed that they will not send back a return that does not have an adequate explanation for why provisional or estimated figures are needed or does not give a date for the supply of final figures. The omission of that information will, however, be a factor which the Inland Revenue will take into account in order to decide whether to open an enquiry into the return. The Inland Revenue takes the view that the use of provisional or estimated figures may result in an incorrect return, for which a penalty may be charged if the tax-payer did not take reasonable care when he calculated the figures or if final figures could have been obtained before the return was sent to the Revenue. [Tax Bulletin Issue 57, January 2002].

16.12   Although the return must be delivered by 31 January following the end of the year of assessment in question, submitting it on or before 30 September following the end of the year of assessment in question avoids the need to include a self-assessment (see 16.17 below). If the notice requiring the person to make the return is not given until after 31 October following the end of the year of assessment in question, the deadline for filing the return is extended to three months from the giving of the notice to make the return. Failure to deliver a return by these deadlines can lead both to the Inland Revenue making a determination of the tax due from the taxpayer (see 16.47 below) and to penalties being imposed (see 16.50 below). [*TMA 1970, s 8(1A)*].

16.13   In the Revenue's view, the return will only be filed on time of it is 'in the hands of' the officer of the Board on or before the deadline. However, it will normally accept that the return is filed on time if it is clear that the taxpayer has taken steps to ensure that it would be received in time but for some reason it is delayed thereafter. An example would be a post office delay. For returns filed on 31 January 2001, the Inland Revenue have confirmed that any return which was found in the tax office post box before 7:30 am on 1 February 2001 would be treated as put there before midnight on 31 January 2001. Such a return would, therefore, be regarded as filed on time. Likewise, following the Special Commissioners decision in *Steeden v Carver (Inspector of Taxes) [1999] STC (SCD) 283*, the taxpayer would have a reasonable excuse for not delivering his tax return on time, provided the return was found in the tax office post box by 7:30 am on 2 February 2001. In the latter case, no late filing penalty would be levied. However, because the return was, technically, filed late, the period within which the Inland Revenue had to enquire into that return was extended to the quarter day following the first anniversary of the day on which the return was actually filed. This gave the Inland Revenue almost three months more time in which to launch an enquiry than if the return was found in the tax office post box by 7:30 am on 1 February 2001. [Tax Bulletin Issue 44, December 1999].

16.14   The notice requiring the person to make the return can also require the return to include particulars of any assets acquired by the person on whom the notice was served in the period specified in the notice. This can include particulars of the person from whom the asset was acquired and the consideration for the acquisition. However, no particulars can be required of assets acquired before 6 April 1965. Nor can particulars be required of:

(*a*)   assets exempted from capital gains tax by *sections 51(1)* (rights to winnings from pool bettings, lotteries or games with prizes), *121* (government non-marketable securities), *263* (passenger vehicles), *268* (decorations for valour or gallant conduct) or *269* (foreign currency for personal expenditure) of the *Taxation of Chargeable Gains Act 1992*;

(*b*)   tangible movable property where the consideration for its acquisition was £6,000 or less and which is not within the exceptions listed in *section 262(6)* of the *Taxation of Chargeable Gains Act 1992* (terminal markets and currency); or

(*c*)   trading stock (as defined in *section 100(2)* of the *Income and Corporation Taxes Act 1988*). [*TMA 1970, s 12(2), (3)*].

16.15 Persons who carry on a trade, profession or vocation in partnership are, additionally, required to include each amount which is stated in the partnership statement (as to which see 16.35 below) to be his share of the income, loss, tax, credit or charge for the period in respect of which the partnership statement is made. [*TMA 1970, s 8(1B)*].

16.16 Identical provisions apply to trustees, requiring them to submit tax returns for the purpose of establishing the amounts in which the trustees, the settlors and the beneficiaries of a settlement are chargeable to income tax and capital gains tax. A single notice can be given to any one trustee or separate notices can be given to each trustee or to such trustee as the officer of the Board thinks fit. [*TMA 1970, s 8A*].

The obligation to include a self-assessment

16.17 In addition to the information stated in 16.10–16.15 above, a tax return made by an individual or a trustee must include a 'self-assessment' unless the return is delivered to the Inland Revenue on or before the 30 September following the end of the year of assessment in question. If the notice requiring the return to be made is not given by 31 July following the end of the year of assessment in question, the obligation to include a self-assessment can be avoided by submitting the tax return within two months of the date when the notice requiring the return was given. [*TMA 1970, s 9(1), (2)*].

16.18 A self-assessment comprises two elements. Firstly, an assessment of the amounts in which the person making the return is chargeable to income tax and capital gains tax for the year of assessment. This must be based on the information contained in the return and take into account any relief allowance or claim which is included in the return. Secondly, an assessment of the amount payable by the person by way of income tax, i.e., the difference between the amount in which he is assessed to tax and the amount of any tax deducted at source and any tax credits. [*TMA 1970, s 9(1)(a)(b)*].

16.19 Where the person submits a tax return before the above time limits, the officer of the Board must make an assessment (based on the information contained in the return) on behalf of the taxpayer, which will constitute the taxpayer's self-assessment. Such an assessment does not require the officer to make any judgment as to the accuracy of the figures contained in the return. It is a purely computational task, leaving him free to open an enquiry into the return at a later stage. In any other case where the taxpayer fails to include a self-assessment, it is within the discretion of the officer of the Board to make such an assessment or to make a determination (see 16.47 below). [*TMA 1970, s 9(2), (3)*].

Claims and elections

16.20 Where a person is required to make and deliver a tax return, any claims which that person wishes to make should be included in that return.

This only applies to claims which could be included in the return and does not apply to claims which fall to be taken into account in making deductions or repayments of tax under the PAYE scheme. Nor does this apply where a specific provision of the *Taxes Acts* provides otherwise, e.g. carry-back claims. It is sufficient that the claim be included by virtue of an amendment of the tax return. Furthermore, a supplementary claim may be made if the claimant subsequently discovers that an error or mistake has been made in the claim (provided that the supplementary claim is made within the time allowed for making the original claim). [*TMA 1970, s 42(1), (2), (3), (9)*].

16.21   The claim must be made within five years of the 31 January next following the year of assessment to which it relates. Any claim for a relief, an allowance or a repayment must be for an amount which is quantified at the time when the claim is made. Although it is not possible to make a provisional claim for an estimated amount, the taxpayer may include estimated figures in a return (see 16.11 above). Again, this does not apply to claims which fall to be taken into account in making deductions or repayments of tax under the PAYE scheme. [*TMA 1970, ss 42(1A), (3) and 43(1))*].

16.22   Claims under any of the provisions specified in *TMA 1970, s 42(7)* must, in the case of a trade, profession or business carried on by persons in partnership, be included in the partnership return so far as possible. [*TMA 1970, s 42(6)(a)*].

16.23   *Schedule 1A* to the *Taxes Management Act 1970* sets out the procedure for making claims which are not made in the taxpayer's tax return, e.g. carry-back claims and claims to alter PAYE coding. The rules require that the claim must be in such form as the Board may determine (which form may require, amongst other things, such information as is reasonably required for the purpose of determining whether, and if so, the extent to which the claim is correct and also the delivery, with the claim, of such accounts, statements and documents, relating to information contained in the claim as are reasonably required for that purpose) along with a declaration that all the particulars given in the form are correctly stated to the best of the information and belief of the person making the claim. In the case of a claim made by or on behalf of a person who is not resident in the United Kingdom (or who claims to be not resident), an officer of the Board may require a statement or declaration in support of the claim to be made by affidavit. The same requirement may be imposed in relation to a claim made by or on behalf of a person who is not ordinarily resident, who claims to be not ordinarily resident, who is not domiciled or who claims to be not domiciled in the United Kingdom. The Inland Revenue has powers to enquire into a claim and to call for documents for the purposes of such an enquiry. The taxpayer must keep such records as may be requisite for the purpose of enabling him to make a correct and complete claim and must preserve those records until the Inland Revenue has completed any enquiry into the claim. If no such enquiry is opened, the duty is to preserve the records until the Inland Revenue no longer has power to enquire into the claim (broadly the quarter day next following the first anniversary of the day on which the claim was made). Both the Inland

Revenue and the taxpayer are entitled to amend claims. In the case of the Inland Revenue, the power is to amend the claim to correct obvious errors and mistakes (which must be exercised within nine months of the claim being made). The taxpayer can amend a claim at any time within the twelve months following its submission, provided an enquiry has not been opened into the claim. An enquiry will be completed when an officer of the Board issues a closure notice, which must either state the officer's opinion that no amendment of the claim is required or if, in the officer's opinion, the claim is insufficient or excessive, amend the claim so as to make good or eliminate the deficiency or excess. Within 30 days after the issue of the closure notice the officer will give effect to any such amendment by making such adjustment as may be necessary (e.g. by way of assessment on the claimant, by discharge of tax or by repayment of tax). The taxpayer has thirty days from the issue of the closure notice to bring an appeal. An extended time limit of three months applies in respect of certain matters, including appeals against any question arising under *section 278* of the *Income and Corporation Taxes Act 1988* (personal reliefs for non-residents) and appeals against any question of residence, ordinary residence or domicile.

16.24   These provisions mirror the provisions which permit the Inland Revenue to enquire into (and call for documents for the purposes of an enquiry into) a tax return, which require the taxpayer to preserve records relating to his tax return and which permit the amendment of tax returns (see 16.65 *et seq* below).

Partnerships: the obligation to deliver a partnership return

16.25   Officers of the Board have two powers to require persons who are carrying on a trade, profession or vocation in partnership to make and deliver a return. The purpose of such a return is threefold. Firstly, to establish the amount in which each partner is chargeable to income tax for any year of assessment. Secondly, to establish the amount payable by way of income tax by each partner and, finally, to establish the amount in which each partner is chargeable to corporation tax for any period. An officer of the Board is entitled to exercise either power, or both together.

16.26   The first power is to give a notice to the partners generally. The notice will require that such person as is identified in accordance with rules given with the notice (or a successor of his) make and deliver in respect of the period specified in the notice a return containing such information as may reasonably be required by the officer for the above purposes. The notice can also require that the return be accompanied with such accounts, statements and documents relating to the information contained in the return as may reasonably be required. [*TMA 1970, s 12AA(1), (2)*].

16.27   The second power is to give a notice to any one partner (or a successor of his) requiring him to make and deliver in respect of the period specified in the notice a return containing such information as may reasonably be required for the above purposes. Again the notice may require that the return be accompanied by such accounts, statements and documents relating to information contained in the return as may be reasonably required. The officer has discretion to give such notices to any one partner, separate notices to each partner or to such partners as the officer thinks fit. [*TMA 1970, s 12AA(1), (3)*].

16.28 Where the partner who is required to make and deliver the return is no longer available, a successor may be nominated to make and deliver the return. The nomination must be made by a majority of the persons who were partners at any time during the period for which the return was required (including the personal representatives of such persons) and only takes effect when notice of the nomination is given to an officer of the Board. Although the nomination can be revoked, the revocation does not take effect until notice has been given to an officer of the Board. In the absence of such a nomination, the identity of the successor with responsibility for making and delivering the return will depend upon which power the officer of the Board has exercised to require the making of the return. If the return has been required under the officer's power to give a notice to the partners generally (i.e. the first power, referred to at 16.26 above), the successor will be such partner as is identified in accordance with the rules set out in the notice. If the return has been required under the officer's power to give a notice to a particular partner (i.e. the second power, referred to at 16.27 above), the successor will be such partner as is nominated for the purpose by an officer of the Board. [*TMA 1970, s 12AA(11)–(13)*].

16.29 Whichever power the officer has exercised to require a partnership return to be made, that return must contain the following:

(*a*) a declaration of the name, residence (in the case of a company, its registered office) and tax reference of each of the persons who have been partners for the whole or part of the relevant period; and

(*b*) a declaration by the person making the return that it is, to the best of his knowledge, correct and complete. [*TMA 1970, s 12AA(6), (10)*].

16.30 In addition, the notice requiring the return to be made can also require that the following particulars be included in the return:

(*a*) the particulars which would have been required to be provided in respect of any disposal of partnership property during the period as if the partnership were liable to tax on chargeable gains accruing on the disposal; and

(*b*) particulars of any assets acquired by the person on whom the notice was served in the period specified by the notice requiring the return (including particulars of the person from whom the asset was acquired).

16.31 As with the requirement that an individual's return should include particulars of assets acquired in the period specified by the notice (see 16.14

above), the particulars which a partnership return can be required to include does not extend to particulars of assets acquired before 6 April 1965 or particulars of the assets listed at 16.14 (*a*) to (*c*) above. [*TMA 1970, s 12AA(7)*].

16.32   As is the case with an individual's tax return, the notice can require the partnership tax return to include different information, accounts and statements for different periods. It can also require the partnership tax return to include different information, accounts and statements in relation to different descriptions of source of income. Different information, accounts and statements can also be required in relation to different descriptions of partnerships. [*TMA 1970, s 12AA(8), (9)*].

16.33   In the case of a partnership which includes at least one individual, the partnership return must be delivered by 31 January following the end of the fiscal year in question. The partnership return may be submitted later if the notice requiring the return to be made is not given until after 31 October following the end of the year of assessment in question, in which case, the partnership return must be submitted within three months of the day on which the notice is given. [*TMA 1970, s 12AA(4)*].

16.34   In the case of a partnership which includes at least one company, the partnership return must be delivered by the first anniversary of the period in respect of which the return is required to be made. Again, the partnership return may be submitted later, if the notice requiring the return to be made is not given within nine months of the end of the period in respect of which the partnership return is required to be made. In which case, the partnership return must be submitted within three months of the day in which the notice is given. [*TMA 1970, s 12AA(5)*].

Partnerships: the obligation to include a partnership statement

16.35   Although a partnership return will not include a self-assessment, it must include a partnership statement, i.e. a statement of the following amounts:

(*a*)   the amount of income or loss from each source which has accrued to or been sustained by the partnership for each period of account ending in the period for which the return is made;

(*b*)   the amount of the consideration which has accrued to the partnership in respect of each disposal of partnership property during that period;

(*c*)   each amount of income tax which has been deducted or treated as deducted from any income of the partnership (or treated as paid on any such income) for that period;

(*d*)   the amount of each tax credit which has accrued to the partnership for that period;

(*e*)   the amount of each charge which was a charge on the income of the partnership for that period;

(*f*)   in the case of each of the partners, his share of that income, loss, consideration, tax, credit or charge.

[*TMA 1970, s 12AB(1)*].

16.36   The amounts stated in the partnership statement must be based on the information contained in the partnership return and must take into account any relief or allowance in respect of which a claim under any of the provisions listed in *TMA 1970, s 42(7)* has been included in the return. [*TMA 1970, s 12AB(1), (5)*].

Electronic filing of tax returns

16.37   It is possible to comply with the obligation to file certain tax returns by transmitting the information in question electronically. This is possible for personal tax returns, trustee's tax return and partnership returns (i.e. those required under *sections 8, 8A* and *12AA* of the *Taxes Management Act 1970*), but only if the notice requiring the return to be filed was given after 1 March 1997. The notice requiring such a return to be delivered may state that any document which is required to be delivered with the return (the 'supporting documents') may also be transmitted electronically. In which case, the taxpayer may also fulfil this obligation by transmitting the information electronically. Alternatively, the taxpayer may choose to file the tax return electronically and deliver the supporting documents in the normal way. In which case, the taxpayer has until the last day for the delivery of the return to deliver the supporting documents. Any information which is accepted for electronic lodgement will, generally, have the same status as information in documents which are delivered by post. In particular, both the Inland Revenue and the taxpayer will have the same rights to enquire into the information, make amendments etc. as they have in relation to information contained in returns etc. delivered by post (as to which, see 16.65 *et seq* below). However, as will be seen, hard copies of the information which is accepted for electronic lodgement must be made and authenticated. It is these hard copies which are treated, for the purposes of any proceedings before the General or Special Commissioners or certain other tribunals, as if they were the tax return etc. which was required to be delivered. [*TMA 1970, Sch 3A, paras 2, 3, 10* and *11* and *SI 1997 No 57*].

16.38   Although filing a tax return (and any supporting documents which the taxpayer chooses to file electronically) in this way dispenses with the need to sign the tax return or to include certain declarations or certificates (e.g. the declaration that the return is to the best of his knowledge correct and complete), this does not absolve the taxpayer from the consequences of failing to file a return which is correct and complete. As will be seen, the hard copy of the information which is transmitted electronically must be endorsed with a declaration that the hard copy is to the best of the knowledge of the person concerned correct and complete. Furthermore, the tax return (and any supporting documents which the taxpayer chooses to file electronically) will not be regarded as delivered or made until the end of the day on which the last of four conditions are met. [*TMA 1970, Sch 3A, paras 1(4), (5), 3(5)* and *8(2)*]

16.39   The first condition is that the electronic transmission must be made by a person approved by the Board of Inland Revenue. *Schedule 3A* of the *Taxes Management Act 1970* contains detailed provisions dealing with the procedure by which a person may seek approval for the purpose of transmitting information on his own behalf or on behalf of another person or persons (including provision for a person whose application is refused or whose approval is withdrawn to appeal to the Special Commissioners). [*TMA 1970, Sch 3A, para 4*].

16.40   The second condition is that the person who makes the transmission must comply with any requirements, as to the manner in which transmissions are to be made by him, of which he is notified by the Board of Inland Revenue. These may include requirements as to the hardware to be used, type of hardware to be used, software to be used or type of software to be used to make transmissions or a description of transmissions. [*TMA 1970, Sch 3A, para 5*].

16.41   The third condition is that the transmission must signify, in a manner approved by the Board of Inland Revenue, that before the transmission was made a hard copy of the information proposed to be transmitted was made and authenticated in accordance with certain requirements. Those requirements are that the hard copy must be made under arrangements designed to ensure that the information contained in that hard copy is the information in fact transmitted. To be authenticated, the hard copy of a tax return must be endorsed with a declaration that the hard copy is to the best of the knowledge of the 'relevant person' correct and complete. Any other hard copy document must be signed by the relevant person. In either case, the relevant person is the person who would have been required to make the declaration or sign the document in question, if it had not been delivered electronically. [*TMA 1970, Sch 3A, paras 6* and *8*].

16.42   The final condition is that the information transmitted is accepted for electronic lodgement under a procedure selected by the Board of Inland Revenue. [*TMA 1970, Sch 3A, para 7*].

16.43   Finance Act 1999 gave the Commissioners of Inland Revenue power to make regulations to facilitate the use of electronic communications for delivering information relating to taxation and making payments of tax. Although the provisions which the Inland Revenue can include in such regulations are extensive, only one set of regulations has been issued to date. [*FA 1999, s 132*].

16.44   These regulations permit the Board of Inland Revenue to use electronic communications in connection with the delivery of an individual's tax return or a trustee's return or in connection with the making of any payment or repayment of tax or other sums in connection with the operation of *sections 8, 9* or *9A* of the *Taxes Management Act 1970*. By contrast, anyone else (e.g. taxpayers) can only use electronic communications in connection with these matters if the taxpayer satisfies three conditions. Firstly, the taxpayer must be permitted to use electronic communications. Such permission must take the form of an authorisation given by means of a direction of the Board of Inland Revenue. The Revenue have issued a direction that this may take the form of a form 64-8 signed by the taxpayer or by means of an on-line authorisation given by the taxpayer on the government gateway website (www.gateway.gov.uk). Secondly, that person must use an approved method. In particular, the method must be an approved method for authenticating the identity of the sender of the communication. The method must also be an approved method of electronic communications and an approved method for authenticating any information delivered by means of electronic communications. Thirdly, any information or payment sent by means of electronic communications is in an approved form. Details of the methods, form and software products which are approved can be found on the Inland Revenue's website (www.inlandrevenue.gov.uk). Finally, the person must maintain such records (in a written or electronic form) as may be specified in a general or specific direction given by the Board of Inland Revenue. The Inland Revenue have issued a direction requiring that an agent who delivers information on behalf of another person must make a copy of the information before it is sent and authenticate that copy, by means of a signature confirming that the information is correct to the best of the taxpayer's knowledge and belief. Information delivered in this way will be treated as delivered on the day on which the last of these conditions (along with those imposed by any other applicable enactments and specific or general direction given by the Board of Inland Revenue) is satisfied. [*SI 2000 No 945, regs 2, 3* and *5(2)*].

16.45 Although information which is delivered by means of electronic communications will be treated as having been duly delivered if all of the conditions referred to above are satisfied (along with any others imposed by any other applicable enactments and specific or general direction given by the Board of Inland Revenue), the information contained on the computer system maintained by or on behalf of the Commissioners of Inland Revenue will be presumed to be correct unless the contrary is proved. Thus, questions as to the identity of the sender or recipient of information, as to the information or payments delivered, as to the content of any information delivered by means of electronic communications will be presumed to be as recorded on that computer system unless the contrary is proved. A print-out of any electronic communication which is recorded on that computer system will be presumed to constitute the entirety of the electronic communication recorded on that computer system, provided it is certified by an officer of the Board. Again this is subject to contrary proof, although any document purporting to be such a certificate will be presumed to be such a certificate unless the contrary is proved. [*SI 2000 No 945, regs 5 to 10*].

16.46   By way of an incentive to use electronic communication, the Inland Revenue made a payment of £10 to any individual who made and delivered his personal tax return for year of assessment 1999/2000 using electronic communications. To receive this discount (which was credited to the individual's tax account shortly after the 31 January filing date), at least one of any payments which the individual was liable to pay by way of income tax for that year of assessment had to be made by a form of electronic payment specified by the Inland Revenue. This incentive payment could be withdrawn if an officer of the Board considered that one or more conditions which the Inland Revenue had specified were not met and, if already paid, the incentive payment could be recovered from the individual as if it were an amount of income tax repaid to that individual which ought not to have been repaid to him. [*FA 2000, s 143* and *SI 2001 No 56*].

Consequences of a failure to deliver a tax return: determinations of tax

16.47   Where a person who has received a notice requiring him to make and deliver a return fails to do so by the filing date, an officer of the Board may make a determination of the amounts in which that person is chargeable to income tax and capital gains tax and of the amount which is payable by him by way of income tax for that year of assessment. [*TMA 1970, s 28C(1), (1A)*].

16.48   The officer's determination must be to the best of his information and belief and, until superseded by a self-assessment, will have the same effect as a self-assessment. Notice of the determination must be served on the taxpayer, stating the date on which it is issued. [*TMA 1970, s 28C(1A), (2), (3)*].

16.49   The officer has five years from the deadline for delivering the tax return in which to make such a determination, and the taxpayer has twelve months from the date of issue of a determination in which to make and deliver a self-assessment, which will supersede the determination for all purposes (including any recovery proceedings already commenced). [*TMA 1970, s 28C(5)*].

Consequences of a failure to deliver a tax return: fixed and tax geared penalties

16.50   A fixed penalty of £100 is payable if the taxpayer fails to file a tax return by the deadline for doing so. Additionally, an officer of the Board can apply to the General or Special Commissioners for a direction imposing a further penalty of £60 per day to be levied for each day that the failure to deliver the return continues after the date on which the taxpayer is notified of the direction. Such daily penalties are intended to be used where the fixed penalties are not regarded as a sufficient deterrent, such as in cases where the tax at risk is believed to be significant. If no such application is made during the six months following the deadline for filing the return, a further £100 penalty will be imposed if the return is not filed within that six-month period. [*TMA 1970, s 93(1)–(4)*].

16.51   If the taxpayer has not filed the return within one year of the deadline for filing the return, a tax geared penalty will be imposed of up to the amount of tax which would have been shown had the return been filed. [*TMA 1970, s 93(5)*].

16.52   The total penalties which can be imposed on the taxpayer are capped at the amount of tax which would have been shown had the return been filed. This cap does not apply to the £60 daily penalties. [*TMA 1970, s 93(7)*].

16.53   The taxpayer is entitled to appeal to the Commissioners against any penalty. The Commissioners may set aside the penalty if it appears to them that throughout the period of default (i.e. the period from the deadline for filing the return until the date on which it is actually delivered) the taxpayer had a reasonable excuse for not delivering the return. [*TMA 1970, s 93(8), (10)*].

Consequences of a failure to deliver a partnership return: fixed and daily penalties

16.54   If a partner has been required to deliver a partnership return and neither he nor his successor delivers that return by the deadline for doing so, a £100 penalty will be imposed on each person who was a partner at any time during the period for which the return was required. [*TMA 1970, s 93A(1), (2), (8)*].

16.55   An officer of the Board can apply to the General or Special Commissioners for a direction imposing a further penalty of £60 per day to be levied for each day that the failure to deliver the partnership return continues after the date on which the partner required to deliver the return (or his successor) is notified of the direction. If no such application is made within the six months following the deadline for filing the return a further £100 penalty will be imposed on each person who was a partner at any time during the period for which the return was required. This further £100 penalty will only be imposed if the return is not filed within six months of the deadline for filing. [*TMA 1970, s 93A(3), (4)*].

16.56   There are no tax geared penalties for failing to deliver a partnership return. Any such penalties will only arise as a result of the failure by individual partners to include their share of the partnership profits etc. on their personal tax returns.

16.57   Although each partner is entitled to appeal against any such penalty, the partner who was obliged to deliver the return is responsible for bringing a composite appeal against any penalty imposed as respects two or more partners in respect of the same failure to deliver a return. The Commissioners will only set aside the penalty if it appears to them that throughout the period of default (i.e. the period from the deadline for filing the return until the date on which it is actually delivered) the person required to deliver the return had a reasonable excuse for failing to do so. [*TMA 1970, s 93A(6)–(8)*].

Tax geared penalties for incorrect and uncorrected tax returns

16.58   A tax geared penalty will be imposed on a person who fraudulently or negligently:

(*a*)   delivers an incorrect return;

(*b*)   makes an incorrect return, statement or declaration in connection with any claim for any allowance, deduction or relief in respect of income tax or capital gains tax; or

(*c*)   submits any incorrect accounts in connection with the ascertainment of his liability to income tax or capital gains tax.

[*TMA 1970, s 95(1)*].

16.59   Such a penalty will also be imposed if it comes to the taxpayer's notice that a return, statement, declaration or accounts made or submitted by him were incorrect and he does not remedy the error without unreasonable delay. [*TMA 1970, s 97*].

16.60   In either case, the maximum penalty is the difference between the amount of income tax and capital gains tax payable by that person for the year of assessment in question and the amount which would have been payable if the return etc. which he submitted had been correct. [*TMA 1970, s 95(2)*].

Tax geared penalties for incorrect and uncorrected partnership returns

16.61   A tax geared penalty will be imposed where a partner fraudulently or negligently:

(*a*)   delivers an incorrect partnership return;

(*b*)   makes an incorrect statement or declaration in connection with a partnership return; or

(*c*)   submits to an officer of the Board any incorrect accounts in connection with a partnership return.

[*TMA 1970, s 95A(1)*].

16.62 Such a penalty will also be imposed if such an error is attributable to fraudulent or negligent conduct on the part of that partner. A penalty will also be imposed if it comes to the partner's notice that a return, statement, declaration or accounts made or submitted by him were incorrect and he does not remedy the error without unreasonable delay. [*TMA 1970, ss 95A(1)* and *97*].

16.63 In such cases, the maximum penalty which can be imposed on each person who was a partner at any time during the period in respect of which the return was made is the difference between the amount of income tax payable by him for the period in respect of which the return was made and the amount that would have been payable if the return etc. which he submitted had been correct. [*TMA 1970, s 95A(2)*].

16.64 As with appeals against penalties for the failure to deliver a partnership return, an appeal against any of the above penalties must be made as a composite appeal by the partner responsible for submitting the partnership return, if the penalty is determined as regards two or more partners in respect of the same return etc. [*TMA 1970, s 95A(3)*].

Taxpayer's right to amend a tax return

16.65 Individuals and trustees are entitled to amend their tax returns in any way, provided they do so by notice to an officer of the Board of the Inland Revenue not more than 12 months after the filing date for the return (as to which, see 16.12 above). As the taxpayer's self-assessment is treated as part of his tax return, this power extends to amending both the return and the accompanying self-assessment. Any amendments which the taxpayer wishes to make after this period has expired can only be made by means of an 'error or mistake' claim. [*TMA 1970, ss 9(3A)* and *9ZA*].

16.66 Although the taxpayer may amend his tax return when an enquiry into that return is in progress (as to which see 16.73 below), that amendment does not restrict the scope of the enquiry. However, it may be taken into account, together with any matters arising, in the enquiry. Furthermore, insofar as it affects the amount stated in the self-assessment as the amount of tax payable, the amendment will not take effect while the enquiry is in progress (i.e. the period beginning on the day on which notice of enquiry is given and ending with the day on which the enquiry is completed). Nor will it take effect at the end of the enquiry, if the officer states (in the closure notice) that he has taken the amendment into account and either the amendment has been taken into account in formulating the amendments contained in the closure notice or the officer's conclusion is that the amendment is incorrect. Otherwise, the amendment will take effect when the closure notice is issued. [*TMA 1970, s 9B(1)–(4)*].

Officer's power to amend a tax return (without commencing an enquiry)

16.67   The officer's power to amend the tax return of an individual or a trustee, without launching a formal enquiry (as to which see 16.73 below), is limited to correcting obvious errors or mistakes in the return (whether errors of principle, arithmetical mistakes or otherwise). This does not involve the officer forming a judgment as to the accuracy of the information contained in the return. This power can only be exercised by giving notice to the taxpayer within nine months of the day on which the return was delivered. Where the correction is required in consequence of an amendment of the return made by the taxpayer, (under the power referred to at 16.65 above), this nine month period runs from the day on which the taxpayer's amendment is made. Any correction made by the officer under this power will, however, have no effect, if the taxpayer gives notice rejecting that correction. Such notice of rejection must be given, within 30 days of the date of issue of the notice of correction, to the officer by whom the notice of correction was given. The effect of this power to reject a correction is that taxpayers have absolute freedom to reverse any change made by the officer to correct a purported obvious error or mistake, thereby forcing the officer to either abandon his position or open a formal enquiry into the return. As with the taxpayer's right to amend the return, this power extends to both the return and the associated self-assessment. [*TMA 1970, ss 9(3A)* and *9ZB*]

Partner's right to amend a partnership return

16.68   The partner who made and delivered a partnership return may amend that return, as may his successor. In either case, the amendment must be by notice to an officer of the Board no later than 12 months after the filing date for the partnership return (see 16.33 and 16.34 above). The officer must, by notice to each of the partners, amend each partner's tax return so as to give effect to the amendment of the partnership return. [*TMA 1970, s 12ABA*].

16.69   Although a partner may amend the partnership return when an enquiry is in progress into that partnership return (see 16.79 below), that amendment does not restrict the scope of the enquiry. However, it may be taken into account, together with any matters arising, in the enquiry. Furthermore, insofar as it affects any amount stated in the partnership statement, the amendment (along with any amendments to the partners' personal tax returns, to give effect to it) will not take effect while the enquiry is in progress (i.e. the period beginning on the day on which notice of enquiry is given and ending with the day on which the enquiry is completed). Nor will the amendment to the partnership return take effect at the end of the enquiry, if the officer states (in the closure notice) that he has taken the amendment into account and either the amendment has been taken into account in formulating the amendments contained in the closure notice or the officer's conclusion is that the amendment is incorrect. Otherwise, the amendment will take effect when the closure notice is issued (at which point, the partners' personal tax returns will be amended to give effect to the amendment to the partnership tax return). [*TMA 1970, s 12AD(1)–(5)*].

16.70   In certain situations, the *Tax Acts* allow alternative methods to be used for bringing amounts into charge to tax, i.e. in computing profits chargeable to tax under Case I or II of Schedule D or as amounts within Case III, IV or V of Schedule D. Where a partnership return is made using one of those methods, but could have been made using an alternative method, the officer may determine which of the alternative methods is to be used. Such a determination is final and conclusive, for the purposes of any enquiry into the return, as to the basis of charge to be used. Nor may it be questioned on an appeal under *section 31* of the *Taxes Management Act 1970*. [*TMA 1970, ss 12AE(1), (2)* and *31(3)*].

16.71   In contrast to an enquiry into a personal or trustee tax return, the officer has no power to amend the partnership return during the course of an enquiry other than to correct obvious errors or mistakes (see 16.72 above). Instead, if there is a concern as to a possible loss of tax to the Crown, the officer can consider exercising his right to amend the personal tax returns of one or more of the partners (see 16.77).

Officer's power to amend a partnership return (without commencing an enquiry)

16.72   Although an officer of the Board has power to amend a partnership return, that power is limited to amending the return so as to correct obvious errors or mistakes in the return (whether errors of principle, arithmetical mistakes or otherwise). This does not involve the officer forming a judgment as to the accuracy of the information contained in the return. This power can only be exercised by giving notice to the partner who made and delivered the return, or his successor. That notice must be given within nine months of the day on which the return was delivered. Where the correction is required in consequence of an amendment of the return made by the taxpayer (under the power referred to at 16.68 above), this nine month period runs from the day on which the taxpayer's amendment is made. The officer must, by notice to each of the partners, amend each partner's tax return so as to give effect to the correction of the partnership return. Any correction made by the officer under this power will, however, have no effect, if the person to whom notice of such correction was given (or his successor) gives notice rejecting that correction. Such notice of rejection must be given, within 30 days of the date of issue of the notice of correction, to the officer by whom the notice of correction was given. The effect of this power to reject a correction is that taxpayers have absolute freedom to reverse any change made by the officer to correct a purported obvious error or mistake, thereby forcing the officer to either abandon his position or open a formal enquiry into the return. [*TMA 1970, s 12ABB*].

Officer's power to enquire into personal and trustee tax returns

16.73   An officer of the Board is entitled to enquire into any individual or trustee's tax return, provided he gives notice of his intention to do so, within 'the time allowed', to the person whose return it is. The time allowed depends upon whether the tax return was filed after the filing date. If the tax return was delivered on or before the filing date for that tax return (see 16.12 above), the officer has 12 months from that filing date to give the taxpayer notice of his intention to enquire into that return. If the return was delivered after that filing date, the officer has up to and including the quarter day next following the first anniversary of the day on which the return was filed, to give the taxpayer notice of his intention to enquire into that return (the quarter days being 31 January, 30 April, 31 July and 31 October). The time within which the officer must give such a notice is extended where the individual or trustee amends the tax return pursuant to the power at 16.65 above. In such a case, the officer has until up to and including the quarter day next following the first anniversary of the day on which the amendment was made, to give the taxpayer notice of his intention to enquire into that return. In the case of each of these deadlines, the requirement is that the taxpayer must have received the notice by the deadline in question. As a result of adverse decisions of the Special Commissioners on this point (*Wing Hung Lai v Bale (Inspector of Taxes) [1999] STC (SCD) 238* and *Holly v Inspector of Taxes [2000] STC (SCD) 50*), the Inland Revenue have accepted that there are doubts as to the validity of enquiry notices which were issued on or about 30 January 1999 in respect of 1996/97 tax returns. The Inland Revenue's procedures for handling such enquiries is set out in the April 2000 special edition of the Tax Bulletin. It is not, of course, open to a taxpayer to merely deny, without evidence, that he ever received the notice of enquiry, as notices given by post will, unless the contrary is proved, be deemed to be served within a specified number of days of posting. In the case of notices given by first class mail, this will be the second working day after posting and, in the case of notices given by second class mail, this will be the fourth working day after posting. In the cases before the Special Commissioners, the Inland Revenue issued the notice so close to the deadline for giving these notices that they could not rely on the deeming provisions to establish that they had been received by the taxpayers in question. Accordingly, these decisions are only likely to assist taxpayers in relation to notices which are issued close to the deadline for giving a notice of enquiry. [*TMA 1970, s 9A(1), (2), (6)*].

16.74   Although the power can only be exercised once in relation to any return or amendment, it can extend to anything contained in the return, or required to be contained in the return. This includes any claim or election included in the return. There is one exception to this rule, which limits the scope of an enquiry. This exception applies where notice of enquiry is given as a result of an amendment of the return by the taxpayer (i.e. under the power at 16.65 above). Such an enquiry will be limited to matters to which the amendment relates (or which are affected by the amendment), but only if the notice was given outside the normal time limit for beginning an enquiry (see 16.73 above) or an enquiry into the return has been completed. [*TMA 1970, s 9A(3), (4), (5)*].

16.75   Once an enquiry has commenced, no aspect of the taxpayer's tax liability for the period covered by the return is finalised until the enquiry is completed. One issue which can cause an enquiry to remain 'open' for a significant time is a valuation issue. Agreeing a valuation for capital gains tax purposes can cause an enquiry to remain open long after the 12 months deadline for starting an enquiry referred to above. The Inland Revenue have issued a statement of practice (SP1/99) which confirms that where an enquiry remains open after the expiry of that deadline solely because of an unagreed valuation for capital gains tax purposes, the Inland Revenue will not raise further enquiries into matters unrelated to the valuation or the capital gains tax computation. This should provide taxpayers with a degree of certainty in relation to matters unrelated to the valuation which remain at issue, at least once the deadline for raising an enquiry has passed. This practice will not prevent the Inland Revenue from raising further enquiries into matters unrelated to the valuation, however, if the circumstances are such that an officer of the Board could have a made a discovery assessment. Nor will it fetter the Inland Revenue's right to ask further questions or make further enquiries on matters connected with or consequential to the valuation, even if those questions or enquiries were not raised when the valuation was first referred to the Inland Revenue's shares valuation division or the valuation office agency.

16.76   Although the Inland Revenue does select some cases for enquiry on a random basis, many are selected either because there is significant tax at risk or because there is a suspicion that something is wrong. Such suspicion may arise because of information provided by third parties.

Officer's power to amend self-assessment during an enquiry

16.77   An officer can amend the taxpayer's self-assessment where an enquiry is in progress (i.e. during the period beginning with the day on which notice of enquiry is given and ending with the day on which the enquiry is completed), but only if he forms the opinion that the amount stated in the self-assessment contained in the return as the amount of tax payable is insufficient and, furthermore, that unless the assessment is immediately amended there is likely to be a loss of tax to the Crown. The amendment of the assessment, to make good the deficiency, must be made by notice to the taxpayer. Any appeal against such an amendment will not be heard and determined until the enquiry is complete. Where the scope of the officer's enquiry is limited as a result of the provisions discussed at 16.74

above (i.e., certain enquiries into amendments made by taxpayers), the officer's power to amend the assessment is limited to an amendment to make good the deficiency attributable to the taxpayer's amendment. [*TMA 1970, ss 9C(1)–(4)* and *31(2)*].

16.78   In certain situations, the *Tax Acts* allow alternative methods to be used for bringing amounts into charge to tax, i.e. in computing profits chargeable to tax under Case I or II of Schedule D or as amounts within Case III, IV or V of Schedule D. Where a return is made using one of those methods, but could have been made using an alternative method, the officer may determine which of the alternative methods is to be used. Such a determination is final and conclusive, for the purposes of any enquiry into the return, as to the basis of charge to be used. Nor may it be questioned on an appeal under *section 31* of the *Taxes Management Act 1970*. [*TMA 1970, ss 9D(1), (2)* and *31(3)*].

Officer's power to enquire into partnership returns

16.79   An officer of the Board is entitled to enquire into any partnership return, provided he gives notice of his intention to do so, within 'the time allowed', to the partner who made and delivered the return (or his successor). The time allowed depends upon whether the partnership return was filed after the filing date. If the tax return was delivered on or before the filing date for that tax return (see 16.33 and 16.34 above), the officer has 12 months from that filing date to give the partner (or his successor) notice of his intention to enquire into that partnership return. If the partnership return was delivered after that filing date, the officer has up to and including the quarter day next following the first anniversary of the day on which the partnership return was filed, to give the taxpayer notice of his intention to enquire into that return (the quarter days being 31 January, 30 April, 31 July and 31 October). The time within which the officer must give such a notice is extended where the partnership return is amended pursuant to the power at 16.68 above. In such a case, the officer has until up to and including the quarter day next following the first anniversary of the day on which the amendment was made, to give the partner (or his successor) notice of his intention to enquire into that partnership return. In the case of each of these deadlines, the requirement is that the taxpayer must have received the notice by the deadline in question. As a result of adverse decisions of the Special Commissioners on this point (*Wing Hung Lai v Bale (Inspector of Taxes) [1999] STC (SCD) 238* and *Holly v Inspector of Taxes [2000] STC (SCD) 50*), the Inland Revenue have accepted that there are doubts as to the validity of enquiry notices which were issued on or about 30 January 1999 in respect of 1996/97 tax returns. The Inland Revenue's procedures for handling such enquiries is set out in the April 2000 special edition of the Tax Bulletin. It is not, of course, open to a partner to merely deny, without evidence, that he ever received the notice of enquiry, as notices given by post will, unless the contrary is proved, be deemed to be served within a specified number of days of posting. In the case of notices given by first class mail, this will be the second working day after posting and, in the case of notices given by second class mail, this will be the fourth working day after posting. In the cases before the Special Commissioners, the Inland Revenue issued the notice so close to the deadline for giving these notices that they could not rely on the deeming provisions to establish that they had been received by the taxpayers in question. Accordingly, these decisions are only likely to assist partners in relation to notices which are issued close to the deadline for giving a notice of enquiry. [*TMA 1970, s 12AC(1), (2), (7)*].

The giving of notice of enquiry into a partnership return also has the effect of beginning an enquiry into the personal and corporate tax returns of each partner who, at that time, has made a tax return or, at a subsequent time, makes such a return. [*TMA 1970, s 12AC(6)*].

16.80   Although the power can only be exercised once in relation to any partnership return or amendment, it can extend to anything contained in the partnership return, or required to be contained in the partnership return. This includes any claim or election included in the partnership return. There is one exception to this rule, which limits the scope of an enquiry. This exception applies where notice of enquiry is given as a result of an amendment of the partnership return by a partner (i.e. under the power at 16.68 above). Such an enquiry will be limited to matters to which the amendment relates (or which are affected by the amendment), but only if the notice was given outside the normal time limit for beginning an enquiry (see 16.79 above) or an enquiry into the return has been completed. [*TMA 1970, s 12AC(3), (4), (5)*].

16.81   Once an enquiry has commenced, no aspect of the partners' tax liability for the period covered by the return is finalised until the enquiry is completed. One issue which can cause an enquiry to remain 'open' for a significant time is a valuation issue. Agreeing a valuation for capital gains tax purposes can cause an enquiry to remain open long after the 12 months deadline for starting an enquiry referred to above. The Inland Revenue have issued a statement of practice (SP1/99) which confirms that where an enquiry remains open after the expiry of that deadline solely because of an unagreed valuation for capital gains tax purposes, the Inland Revenue will not raise further enquiries into matters unrelated to the valuation or the capital gains tax computation. As noted above, this should provide taxpayers with a degree of certainty in relation to matters unrelated to the valuation which remains at issue, at least once the deadline for raising an enquiry has passed. This practice will not prevent the Inland Revenue from raising further enquiries into matters unrelated to the valuation, however, if the circumstances are such that an officer of the Board could have made a discovery assessment. Nor will it fetter the Inland Revenue's right to ask further questions or make further enquiries on matters connected with or consequential to the valuation, even if those questions or enquiries were not raised when the valuation was first referred to the Inland Revenue's shares valuation division or the valuation office agency.

The Inland Revenue's power to call for documents etc. for the purposes of an enquiry

16.82   An officer of the Board who has given notice of an enquiry into a tax return, amendment etc., may also require the taxpayer to produce to the officer such documents as the officer may reasonably require for the purpose of determining whether and, if so, the extent to which the return is incorrect or incomplete or the amendment is incorrect. This power can be exercised either at the same time as giving the taxpayer notice of the enquiry or subsequently. However, the officer can only require the taxpayer to produce documents which are in the taxpayer's possession or power. The notice requiring production of the documents must be in writing and it must specify the time, being not less than 30 days, which the taxpayer has to produce the documents. In *Self-assessed v Inspector of Taxes (SpC 207) [1999] STC (SCD) 253*, the Special Commissioners have held that the 30-day period runs from receipt of the notice by the taxpayer, not from the date on which the notice was issued. The Inland Revenue will, however, be able to rely on statutory presumptions as to the date on which notices given by post are deemed to be served. Unless the contrary is proved, notices given by first class mail will be presumed to have been received by the second working day after posting and notices given by second class mail will be presumed to be received by the fourth working day after posting. [*TMA 1970, s 19A(1), (2)(a)* and *Interpretation Act 1978, s 7*].

16.83   In addition to requiring the production of documents, the notice can require the taxpayer to furnish such accounts or particulars as the officer may reasonably require for the purpose of determining whether and, if so, the extent to which the return is incorrect or incomplete or the amendment is incorrect. The Inland Revenue regards this as entitling officers to require taxpayers to give a detailed factual account of how an entry in a return is made up. Although it does not confer a power on the Inland Revenue to require the taxpayer to attend an interview, the Inland Revenue regard this as an effective way of resolving an enquiry. [*TMA 1970, s 19A(2)(b)*].

16.84   An officer may also require the taxpayer to produce to the officer such documents as the officer may reasonably require for the purpose of making a determination (see 16.47 above). Again, the notice may also require the taxpayer to furnish such accounts or particulars as the officer may reasonably require for the same purpose. The notice must be in writing, must specify the time (at least 30 days) which the taxpayer has to comply and can only require the taxpayer to produce documents which are in his possession or power. [*TMA 1970, s 19A(2A)*].

16.85   The taxpayer may produce copies instead of original documents provided the copies are photographic (or otherwise by way of facsimile). In which case, the officer may, by notice, require the original to be produced for inspection by him. Such a notice must be in writing and specify the time which the taxpayer has (at least 30 days) to produce the original for inspection. [*TMA 1970, s 19A(3)*].

16.86   The officer may take copies of or make extracts from any documents produced to him, but cannot require the taxpayer to produce documents (or furnish particulars) relating to the conduct of any pending appeal by him. [*TMA 1970, s 19A(4), (5)*].

16.87   The taxpayer may appeal to the Commissioners against any require-ment that he produce documents or furnish accounts or particulars, but only has 30 days from the date on which the notice is given in which to bring this appeal. Such an appeal is dealt with in the same way as an appeal against an assessment to tax, except that the Commissioners' task is to determine whether it appears to them that the production of the documents or the fur-nishing of the accounts/particulars was reasonably required by the officer for the above purposes. To the extent that the Commissioners agree that the documents etc. were reasonably required, the Commissioners will confirm the notice. In which case, the taxpayer has a further 30 days from the deter-mination of the appeal in which to comply with the notice (as confirmed by the Commissioners). The decision of the Commissioners is final and con-clusive. [*TMA 1970, s 19A(6)–(11)*].

16.88   The initial penalty for failing to comply with a notice requiring a tax-payer to produce documents or furnish accounts/particulars is £50. A further penalty of £30 per day or £150 per day can be imposed for each day that the failure continues after the imposition of the initial penalty. Although the £30 daily penalty can be imposed by an officer of the Board, the £150 penalty can only be imposed by the Commissioners. Neither penalty can be imposed after the failure has been remedied. Nor will they be imposed in cases where it is genuinely impossible, for whatever reason, to comply with the notice. A tax-payer will only be penalised for failing to produce records which do not exist under the provision referred to at 16.98 below. [*TMA 1970, s 97AA*].

Enquiries: referring questions to the Special Commissioners

16.89   During the course of an enquiry into a tax return, questions may arise in connection with the subject-matter of that enquiry. Such questions may arise in connection with the subject-matter of an enquiry into an indi-vidual's tax return, a trustee's tax return or a partnership return. Any such question may be referred to the Special Commissioners for their determina-tion, provided a notice of referral is given, in writing, to the Special Commissioners. As that notice must be given jointly by the taxpayer (i.e. either the person to whom the notice of enquiry was given or, in the case of an enquiry into a partnership return, his successor) and an officer of the Board, this procedure is only available where both the taxpayer and the Inland Revenue agree that the question should be referred to the Special Commissioners. [*TMA 1970, s 28ZA(1), (2)*].

16.90   The determination of a question referred to the Special Com-missioners is binding on the parties to the referral, in the same way (and to the same extent) as a decision on a preliminary issue in an appeal. Furthermore, the officer must take the determination into account in reaching his conclusions on the enquiry and in formulating any amendments of the return required to give effect to those conclusions. Nor may the right of appeal, against an amendment to a self-assessment etc., under *section 31(1)(a), (b)* or *(c)* of the *Taxes Management Act 1970*, be exercised so as to reopen any question determined by the Special Commissioners. Such a determination may only be reopened to the extent (if any) that it could have been reopened if it had been determined as a preliminary issue in that appeal. The procedure for handling such referrals, including appeals to the High Court, is set out in regulations made by statutory instrument. [*TMA 1970, ss 28ZC* and *28ZE(1), (2), (3)*].

16.91   There is no restriction on the number of notices of referral which may be given in relation to any enquiry, but each notice of referral must specify the question, or questions, being referred. Furthermore, the question must be referred at a time when the enquiry is in progress, i.e. during the period beginning with the day on which notice of enquiry is given and ending with the day on which the enquiry is completed. [*TMA 1970, s 28ZA(3), (4), (5)*].

16.92   The effect of referring a question to the Special Commissioners is to prevent the enquiry from being closed, because while proceedings on a referral are in progress in relation to an enquiry, no closure notice can be given in relation to that enquiry and no application may be made for a direction to give such a closure notice. Either party may, however, withdraw a notice of referral. As soon as the notice of referral is withdrawn, the proceedings on the referral will no longer be in progress in relation to the enquiry and, so, the prohibition on a closure notice being given or applied for ends. Likewise, the prohibition on a closure notice being given or applied for will end when the question(s) have been finally determined by the Special Commissioners (such a determination is only final when there is no possibility of it being varied or set aside, disregarding any power to give permission to appeal out of time). [*TMA 1970, ss 28ZD(1), (2), (3)* and *28ZB(1)*]

16.93   To withdraw a notice of referral, a party must give a notice of withdrawal, in writing, to both the other party and the Special Commissioners. Furthermore, that notice of withdrawal must be given before the first hearing by the Special Commissioners in relation to the referral. [*TMA 1970, s 28ZB(2)*].

Completion of an enquiry into a personal tax return or a trustee tax return

16.94   An enquiry into a personal or a trustee tax return will only be completed when an officer of the Board informs the taxpayer (i.e. the person to whom notice of enquiry was given), by notice, that he has completed his enquiries and states his conclusions. That notice is a 'closure notice' and must either state that, in the officer's opinion no amendment of the return is required or make the amendments of the return required to give effect to his conclusions. Although the closure notice only takes effect when it is issued, the taxpayer has the right to apply to the Commissioners for a direction requiring an officer of the Board to issue a closure notice within a specified time. The Commissioners hearing the application (which will be heard and determined in the same way as an appeal) are required to give the direction applied for, unless they are satisfied that there are reasonable grounds for not issuing a closure notice within a specified period. [*TMA 1970, s 28A(1)–(6)*].

Completion of an enquiry into a partnership tax return

16.95   An enquiry into a partnership return will only be completed when an officer of the Board informs the taxpayer (i.e. the person to whom notice of enquiry was given, or his successor), by notice, that he has completed his enquiries and states his conclusions. That notice is a 'closure notice' and must either state that, in the officer's opinion no amendment of the partnership return is required or make the amendments of the partnership return required to give effect to his conclusions. If the notice makes such amendments, the officer must also, by notice to each of the partners, amend the partner's tax return so as to give effect to the amendments of the partnership return. Although the closure notice only takes effect when it is issued, the taxpayer (again, the person to whom notice of enquiry was given, or his successor) has the right to apply to the Commissioners for a direction requiring an officer of the Board to issue a closure notice within a specified time. The Commissioners hearing the application (which will be heard and determined in the same way as an appeal) are required to give the direction applied for, unless they are satisfied that there are reasonable grounds for not issuing a closure notice within a specified period. [*TMA 1970, s 28B(1)–(7)*].

Completion of an enquiry into a claim

16.96   Certain claims may not be made in a tax return, but made separately. In such a case, there is a separate power to enquire into the claim (see 16.23 above). Such an enquiry will only be completed when an officer of the Board informs the claimant (in the case of a partnership claim, this means the person who made the claim or his successor), by notice, that he has completed his enquiries and states his conclusions. That notice is a 'closure notice' and its contents will differ according to the nature of the enquiry. If the enquiry is into a claim for discharge or prepayment of tax, the closure notice must either state that in the officer's opinion no amendment of the claim is required or, if in the officer's opinion the claim is insufficient or excessive, amend the claim so as to make good or eliminate the deficiency or excess. In the case of an enquiry into any other claim, the closure notice must either allow the claim or disallow the claim, wholly or to such extent as appears to the officer appropriate. [*TMA 1970, Sch 1A, para 7(1)–(3), (8)*]

16.97   Although the closure notice only takes effect when it is issued, the claimant has the right to apply to the Commissioners for a direction requiring an officer of the Board to issue a closure notice within a specified time. The Commissioners hearing the application (which will be heard and determined in the same way as an appeal) are required to give the direction applied for, unless they are satisfied that there are reasonable grounds for not issuing a closure notice within a specified period. [*TMA 1970, Sch 1A, para 7(4)–(7)*].

The obligation to keep and preserve adequate records

16.98   Any person who is required to make and deliver a tax return must keep such records as may be requisite for the purpose of enabling him to make and deliver a correct and complete return. Those records must also be preserved until at least the 31 January following the end of the year of assessment for which the return is made. In the case of a person carrying on a trade, profession or business (whether alone or in partnership), the records must be preserved until at least the fifth anniversary of the 31 January following the end of the year of assessment for which the return is made. [*TMA 1970, s 12B(1)(a), (2)*].

16.99   Where enquiries are made into a return (or an amendment is made by an officer of the Board), the records in question must, additionally, be preserved until the officer has, by notice, informed the taxpayer that he has completed his enquiries and stated his conclusions as to the amount of tax which should have been contained in the taxpayer's self-assessment or (as the case may be) partnership statement. [*TMA 1970, s 12B(1)(b)(i) and (2)*].

16.100   In any event the records must be preserved until the date on which an officer of the Board no longer has power to make enquiries into the return (see 16.73 above). [*TMA 1970, s 12B(1)(b)(ii)*].

16.101   If the officer of the Board does not give a notice requiring a taxpayer to make and deliver a return until after the dates referred to above, the taxpayer's only obligation is to preserve any records which he has in his possession at the time that the notice requiring him to make the return is given. [*TMA 1970, s 12B(2A)*].

16.102   The records which persons carrying on a trade, profession or business (whether alone or in partnership) are required to keep and preserve include records (such as accounts, books, deeds, contracts, vouchers and receipts) of:

(*a*)   all amounts received and expended in the course of the trade, profession or business;

(*b*)   the matters in respect of which the receipts and expenditure took place; and

(*c*)   all sales and purchases made in the course of any trade involving dealing in goods.

For this purpose, the letting of property is treated as carrying on a trade. [*TMA 1970, s 12B(3)(6)*].

16.103   It is sufficient, in the case of most records, to preserve the information contained in them. However, originals of the following records must be kept:

(*a*)   dividend vouchers and certificates of tax deducted at source;

(*b*)   certificates given to subcontractors under the subcontractors in the construction industry scheme;

(*c*)   records requisite for making a correct and complete claim in respect of (or return relating to) tax which has been paid under the laws of a territory outside the United Kingdom.

Copies of documents other than (*a*) to (*c*) above are admissible in evidence in any proceedings before the Commissioners to the same extent as the original records would have been. [*TMA 1970, s 12B(4)(4A)*].

16.104   The maximum penalty for failing to keep or preserve the requisite records is £3,000. No penalty can be imposed if the failure is to keep or preserve records which are requisite only for the purposes of claims, elections or notices which are not included in the tax return. Nor will a penalty be imposed for failure to keep and preserve dividend vouchers or certificates of tax deducted at source if the officer of the Board is satisfied that any facts which he reasonably requires to be proved (and which would have been proved by those records) are proved by other documentary evidence furnished to him. In practice, penalties are only likely to be imposed once taxpayers and advisers have had a reasonable period in which to assimilate Inland Revenue guidance as to what records should be kept. A failure to keep records will also be taken into account in determining other penalties (e.g. for delivering an incorrect return). [*TMA 1970, s 12B(5)–(5B)*].

Payment of tax

Due date for payment

16.105   A person will usually have to pay any income tax and capital gains tax liability for any year of assessment by the 31 January following the year of assessment in question. This will be the deadline even if the tax is as set out in a self-assessment which supersedes a determination (see 16.49 above). This corresponds to the deadline for filing the relevant tax return. There are a number of exceptions to this rule. [*TMA 1970, s 59B(4)*].

16.106   The first exception is where a person who has complied with his obligation to notify the Inland Revenue of his chargeability to income tax or capital gains tax within the time prescribed does not receive a notice requiring him to deliver a tax return until after 31 October following the end of the year of assessment in question. In such a case, that person has three months from the day on which the notice in question was given to pay his income tax and capital gains tax liability for the year in question. Again, this corresponds to the deadline for filing the tax return where the notice requiring it to be delivered is late. [*TMA 1970, s 59B(3)*].

16.107   The second exception is where tax has to be paid (or repaid) following the amendment or correction of a self-assessment. The date on which the tax has to be paid or repaid depends upon the precise circumstances in which the self-assessment is amended or corrected (e.g. whether the amendment or correction is made by the taxpayer or the Inland Revenue) and the reader is referred to *Schedule 3ZA* of the *Taxes Management Act 1970*, where these rules are set out in detail. In broad terms, these rules provide for such tax to be payable/repayable within 30 days of the date on which the relevant notice of amendment, correction, closure etc., was given. In each case, these rules only override the deadlines set out above if they provide for a later deadline than the rules set out above. [*TMA 1970, s 59B(5)* and *Sch 3ZA*].

16.108   The final exception relates to tax which is payable by virtue of an assessment which is not a self-assessment (e.g. a discovery assessment). This tax is payable within 30 days of the day on which the notice of assessment is given. [*TMA 1970, s 59B(6)*].

16.109   Where the tax return in question shows an amount of tax as being repayable to the taxpayer, the deadline for making that repayment will generally be the same as the deadline which would have applied if the return had shown an amount as being payable by the taxpayer. However, if the return in question is the subject of an Inland Revenue enquiry, no repayment need be made until the enquiry is completed. In such a case, the officer of the Board may make the repayment on a provisional basis, to such extent as he thinks fit. [*TMA 1970, s 59B(3), (4A), (5)*].

16.110   The amount of tax payable (or repayable) by the relevant deadline will be the difference between the amount of income tax and capital gains tax contained in the person's self-assessment for the year of assessment and the following amounts:

(*a*)   the payments on account made by him in respect of that year of assessment (see 16.115); and

(*b*)   the amount of income tax which, in respect of that year of assessment, has been deducted at source. [*TMA 1970, s 59B(1)*].

16.111   Amounts deducted at source under the PAYE scheme in respect of prior year tax liabilities are not treated as income tax which has been deducted at source in the year in which it is actually deducted. However, amounts to be deducted in future years under that scheme in respect of the current year of assessment are treated as deducted at source in respect of the current year of assessment, as are tax credits in respect of dividends received by the taxpayer. [*TMA 1970, s 59B(2)*].

Surcharge for late payment

16.112   Income or capital gains tax not paid within 28 days of the relevant deadline, as determined above, attracts a surcharge equal to five per cent of the unpaid tax. To avoid this surcharge, the tax must be paid by the end of that 28th day. The High Court held, in *Thompson v Minzly [2002] STC 450*, that it was not sufficient for the taxpayer to pay the penalty during the 29th day. A further surcharge of five per cent of the unpaid tax will be levied if the tax is not paid within six months of the deadline, as determined above. Any unpaid tax which has been taken into account in determining a penalty for failure to notify the Inland Revenue of chargeability to tax (see 16.6 above), failure to deliver a return within a year of the filing deadline (see 16.51 above) or the submission of an incorrect return, partnership statement or accounts (see 16.54, 16.55 and 16.58) is not taken into account in computing these surcharges. [*TMA 1970, s 59C(1)–(4)*].

16.113   These surcharges can be imposed by an officer of the Board, who must serve notice of the imposition of the surcharge, stating the day on which it is issued and the time for appealing against the imposition of the surcharge. On appeal to the Commissioners, the surcharge may be set aside if it appears to the Commissioners that, throughout the period of default, the taxpayer had a reasonable excuse for not paying the tax. Inability to pay the tax is not a reasonable excuse for non-payment. The Commissioners of Inland Revenue also have discretion to mitigate any surcharge imposed, to stay or compound proceedings for the recovery of any such surcharge or, after judgment, to further mitigate or entirely remit the surcharge. As a matter of practice, any surcharge or interest for late payment of tax will be waived to the extent that it arises because of a delay attributable to the Inland Revenue failing to notify the taxpayer of the tax due in time for that tax to be paid. [*TMA 1970, s 59C(5), (7)–(11)*].

Interest in respect of late paid tax

16.114   Interest is payable in respect of late paid tax from the due date for payment (in the case of tax arising from amendments of a self-assessment and discovery assessments, this is the filing date for the relevant year) until it is actually paid. It is also payable on an unpaid surcharge and runs from 30 days after the date on which the surcharge is imposed until payment. Overpaid tax also attracts interest from the Inland Revenue. [*TMA 1970, ss 59C(6) and 86*].

Payments on account

16.115 A person who is assessed to income tax in respect of a year of assessment must make two payments on account of his liability to income tax (including Class 4 national insurance contributions) for that year of assessment, but only if all of the following conditions are met.

16.116 Firstly, the amount of his liability for the immediately preceding year of assessment must have exceeded the amount of income tax which has been deducted at source in respect of that year of assessment. The amount of income tax which has been deducted at source will include dividend tax credits and income tax deducted at source under the PAYE scheme in respect of that year of assessment, even if it is not to be deducted until the following year. However, income tax deducted under the PAYE scheme during that year of assessment will not be included for this purpose if it is deducted in respect of the prior year of assessment. [*TMA 1970, s 59A(1)(a), (b), (8)*].

16.117 Secondly, the amount of that excess must exceed a *de minimis* level prescribed by regulations. For 1996/1997 onwards, the amount has been set at £500. [*TMA 1970, s 59A(1)(c)* and *SI 1996 No 1654, reg 3*].

16.118 Finally, the amount of that excess must be more than 20 per cent (or such other proportion as may be prescribed by regulations) of the persons income tax liability for the year of assessment. [*TMA 1970, s 59A(1)(d)* and *SI 1996 No 1654, reg 4*].

16.119 Two payments on account will be due, each being 50 per cent of the excess of the income tax liability for the preceding year (including Class 4 national insurance contributions) over the income tax deducted at source in respect of that year. The first payment on account will be due by 31 January in the year of assessment in question and the second will be due by 31 July following the year of assessment in question. Late paid payments on account attract the surcharges and interest referred to at 16.112–16.114. [*TMA 1970, s 59A(2)*].

Claims to eliminate or reduce payments on account

16.120 A taxpayer is entitled to make a claim discharging him from the obligation to make a payment on account in respect of any year of assessment. The claim must be made by 31 January following the end of the year of assessment in question and must state his belief that he will either not be assessed to income tax for that year or that the amount in which he will be so assessed will not exceed the amount of income tax deducted at source. It must also state his grounds for that belief. [*TMA 1970, s 59A(3)*].

16.121 Alternatively, the taxpayer may choose to make a claim requiring each of the payments on account to be reduced. Again, the claim must be made by 31 January following the end of the year of assessment in question and must state the taxpayer's belief as to the amount by which his income tax liability for the year will exceed the amount of tax deducted at source. The taxpayer's grounds for that belief must also be stated in the claim. [*TMA 1970, s 59A(4)*].

16.122   As the Inland Revenue has no power to reject such a claim, there is a penalty for fraudulently or negligently making an incorrect statement in connection with either type of claim. The maximum penalty is the difference between the payments on account which would have been made if the taxpayer had made a correct statement and the payments on account which the taxpayer actually made. Such penalties are not intended to be imposed in cases where the taxpayer has acted in good faith but got the numbers wrong. They are intended to prevent gross and persistent abuse of the right to reduce payments on account. The Inland Revenue will look to see if there is a significant difference between the tax ultimately shown as due on the self-assessment and the amount of the payments on account for that year. Persistent claims excessively reducing payments on account will be penalised. Interest will be payable by the taxpayer, regardless of whether the error is fraudulent or negligent. [*TMA 1970, s 59A(6)*].

16.123   Officers of the board are also empowered to direct that the obligation to make payments on account shall not apply to any person specified in the direction. [*TMA 1970, s 59A(9)*].

Other adjustments to payments on account

16.124   If a taxpayer is assessed to tax on or before a payment on account is due to be made or his assessment to tax is amended after the date on which a payment on account is due to be made, the amount of the payment on accounts due to be made are deemed always to have been the amounts which would have been due on the basis of that (amended) assessment. [*TMA 1970, s 59A(4A)*].

16.125   The same is true if a discovery assessment is made. The amount of the payments on account due are, retrospectively, increased to the amount due on the basis of the tax shown in the discovery assessment. [*TMA 1970, s 59A(4B)*].

16.126   In both cases, this will have implications for the taxpayer, in terms of interest for late payment of tax.

17 Use of Trusts in International Tax Planning

Andrew Penney BA Hons TEP
(Solicitor) (Partner, Speechly Bircham, London)

Introduction

17.1   The modern trust, as it evolved during the last decades of the 20th century, has become a sophisticated and flexible vehicle for holding private wealth. There are non-tax reasons (mainly family and asset protection issues) for creating a trust and where the proposed settlor and beneficiaries are in the same jurisdiction, there will be domestic tax issues which determine if a trust is a useful vehicle and, if it is, how it should be structured. The aim of this chapter is to examine when a trust may be useful in planning for individuals/families with cross border tax issues. A comprehensive review is impossible in a chapter of this length so the points of principle are illustrated with examples from the tax regimes of the USA, UK, Canada, South Africa and France using law in force at 1 January 2002.

What are the uses of trusts in international tax planning?

17.2   There are really three main applications for trusts in this context:

1.   making tax efficient provision for families across international borders. One of the most significant trends in wealth planning over the last 25 years has been the increasing mobility of families and the ability of tax planners to arbitrage the tax planning anomalies which exist in the applicable tax regimes;

2.   providing tax efficient pre-immigration vehicles for individuals/families moving to a new jurisdiction; and

3.   providing tax efficient vehicles for investing in another jurisdiction be the investment in business, real estate or a portfolio of securities.

General principles

17.3   The effective use of trusts in international tax planning involves the ability to take advantage of (or arbitrage) different rules and concepts used to tax trusts in different jurisdictions.

The settlor of the trust

17.4   The domicile or residence status of the settlor is a crucial determinant as to the opportunities available. If the settlor is located in a different jurisdiction to that where the beneficiaries reside then there is usually considerable scope to achieve tax deferral or even avoidance.

In most jurisdictions it makes a significant difference if the settlor is dead – it is impossible to apportion or attribute income or gains to a dead settlor and trusts created by dead settlors are, therefore, more favourably taxed.

The jurisdiction where the beneficiaries reside may have legislation which confers favoured (grandfathered) status on trusts which are set up prior to a certain date when legislative rules changed adversely or were set up prior to the settlor/beneficiary becoming a tax resident of that jurisdiction (or a certain number of years before his acquiring that status).

Type of trust

17.5   Some regimes provide different tax regimes for trusts which are either discretionary or fixed. For example, the UK has a more favourable inheritance tax (IHT) regime for fixed interest trusts. It is, however, possible to draw a trust which qualifies as a fixed interest under the UK regime (for example, an interest in possession subject to an overriding power of appointment) that would be regarded as a discretionary trust in another jurisdiction such as the USA. Advantage can be taken of this.

Many jurisdictions draw a distinction between revocable and irrevocable trusts.

Location of beneficiaries

17.6   If all beneficiaries are subject to a worldwide basis of taxation in the same jurisdiction (for example, all are US citizens or all are UK domiciliaries/residents), this presents less scope for planning than with a more geographically disparate group of beneficiaries. For example, it is often possible to distribute taxable accumulated income/gains to non-residents of the high tax regime, which requires a computation of such a taxable residue leaving tax free capital available for distribution to the residents of the high tax regime. Such a strategy is likely to work best where the beneficial class includes one or more persons who are residents of a tax haven or jurisdiction which does not tax income and gains on a worldwide basis.

Location of trustees

17.7   In the past, the tax planner's usual objective was to try and have the trust resident in a neutral low tax jurisdiction even if it involved paying some sort of excise tax or incurring a capital gains tax (CGT) disposal to get the assets there.

With an increasing panoply of anti-avoidance legislation, 'offshore' is becoming less attractive. The UK, the USA (specifically Delaware) and New Zealand (amongst others) are all examples of onshore high tax jurisdictions which offer attractive regimes for establishing trusts with zero rates of local taxation provided that neither the settlors, beneficiaries nor the immediate assets are located there (it would be common to hold a portfolio of stocks through an intermediate holding vehicle).

In addition, there is scope to locate trustees in a jurisdiction where it is possible to utilise a double tax treaty with the jurisdiction where the settlor/beneficiaries are located in such a way as to protect the assets from taxation in the country where the settlor/beneficiaries reside.

Cross border family provision

17.8   The best way to illustrate the principles described above is by means of a case study. Take the example of a settlor resident in the UK but with beneficiaries resident in, for example, the USA, Canada, South Africa and France. Assume the settlor wishes to make a gift of £5 million in cash (so there is no UK CGT issue) with two objectives; firstly, the transfer of wealth free of gift or estate taxes either during the settlor's lifetime or on his death; and, secondly, the trust to be invested in such a way that taxation of income and gains is at least deferred until assets are distributed to beneficiaries.

USA beneficiaries

17.9   The idea is to create a trust without UK liabilities being incurred but, for US purposes, the trust falls to be classified as a foreign grantor trust. For US federal tax purposes, all trusts are 'foreign trusts' unless a US court is able to supervise primary supervision over the trust administration (the 'court test') *and* one or more US persons have the authority to control all substantial decisions (the 'control test'). For US purposes, a trust will be a grantor trust if the settlor retains incidents of ownership or control such as a general power of appointment, the ability to control the designation of beneficiaries or timing of distributions (amongst other things). The grantor is assessed on the distributable net income of a US grantor trust and distributions from such a trust are treated as gifts from the grantor. However, a 'foreign trust' can only be a foreign grantor trust under Internal Revenue Code (IRC) *section 672(f)* if the grantor has direct power to revoke the trust or the only permissible beneficiaries are the grantor and his spouse during their lifetime. In addition, certain pre-September 1995 foreign trusts that qualified as foreign grantor trusts under *IRC s 676 or 677* were 'grandfathered' and still have favoured status. The benefit of having foreign grantor trust status is that so long as the trust has non-US income and gains, there is no US tax on the receipt by the trustees of such income and gains and tax free distributions can be made to US beneficiaries. Such distributions are treated as foreign gifts so there is a reporting requirement (but no tax) if they exceed $100,000 in any year.

The position for our UK resident settlor with US beneficiaries depends on whether the settlor is UK domiciled or not. A non-UK domiciliary can create a foreign discretionary trust of which they and their spouse are the only beneficiaries during the settlor's lifetime. It is not possible for a UK domiciliary to create such a trust without incurring lifetime inheritance tax at 20 per cent (to the extent the gift into trust is above the nil-rate band). A UK domiciliary could create an interest in possession trust for themselves and their spouse which could be structured as a foreign grantor trust but it would still form part of the settlor's estate for UK IHT. Moreover, the UK domiciled settlor would be taxed on all income and gains on an arising basis whether the trust was onshore (*ICTA 1988, Pt XV* and *TCGA 1992, s 77*) or offshore (*ICTA 1988, s 739* and *TCGA 1992, s 86*).

By contrast a UK domiciliary can create a revocable trust. *Section 5(2)* of *IHTA 1984* makes it clear that even if the settlor has retained a power of revocation (akin to a general power of appointment) over the trust, the assets should not remain part of their estate if they are otherwise excluded from benefit. Therefore, a UK domiciled settlor can create an interest in possession trust for their US children which also confers an overriding power of appointment exercisable by the trustees to achieve flexibility and a power of revocation exercisable by the settlor to achieve foreign grantor trust status for US purposes. A gift to such a trust should constitute a potentially exempt transfer for UK IHT, which will, therefore, fall out of account if the settlor lives for seven years. At the time of writing we have the anomalous and, in the writer's view, incorrectly decided decision of *Melville v IRC [2001] STC 1271* which means that a power of revocation is treated as a separate asset for UK inheritance tax purposes and would, therefore, result in the entire value of the trust fund forming part of the settlor's estate. This does not square with *IHTA 1984, s 5(2)* but it should be possible to circumvent the *Melville* decision by having the settlor's power of revocation subject to the consent of someone who is regarded as a 'non-adverse party' for US purposes such as the trustees or the protector, etc. The real problem with revocable trusts created by UK domiciliaries is that whether the trust is set up onshore (in which case *ICTA 1988, Pt XV* and *TCGA 1992, s 77* are relevant) or offshore the UK (in which case *ICTA 1988, s 739* and *TCGA 1992, s 86* are in point) anti-avoidance legislation will assess income and gains of the trustees on the settlor. This is the case regardless of whether the trust excludes the settlor and his spouse from benefit – if the trust is revocable the settlor can always recover the assets and so is regarded as capable of benefiting.

The result is that it is very difficult for a UK domiciliary to plan tax efficiently for children in the US. The solution is probably to purchase offshore variable life insurance – equivalent to the UK single premium bond but qualifying under *IRC s 7702* to meet the US requirements of insurance for tax purposes. Such products provide for a tax free build up of income and gains within the policy and if the policy is held by an irrevocable onshore or offshore trust from which the settlor and his spouse are excluded, then with the absence of gains at trust level (all gains will be realised in the underlying policy), this will prevent *de facto* taxation of the UK settlor. If the trust is off-shore the UK, *TCGA 1992, s 86* is still applicable but there will be no gains realised at trust level and apportionment of policy gains is not permitted.

A non-domiciliary can use either of the alternatives described above (whilst being aware of *Melville* issues with a revocable trust).

Canadian beneficiaries

17.10   Canada has draconian rules for the taxation of offshore trusts set up for Canadian resident beneficiaries by a Canadian resident settlor (the latter term has an extended definition which is explained in more detail below). However, where a foreign discretionary trust is genuinely established by a non-Canadian resident for the benefit of Canadian resident beneficiaries:

(*a*)   income and gains received by the foreign trustees are free of Canadian tax as they arise; and

(*b*)   distributions of income, capital gains or original capital from the trustees to Canadian resident beneficiaries are free of Canadian tax in the hands of the beneficiaries (although it is understood that they are subject to reporting requirements).

Thus, for a UK resident parent with Canadian resident children, it is relatively easy to achieve this tax nirvana. However, there are some pitfalls.

The trust needs to be discretionary for Canadian purposes. A fixed interest trust is treated by Canadian tax laws as a non-resident company and a Canadian resident beneficiary with a beneficial interest of 10 per cent or more is required to include his share of passive foreign investment income in his tax return. While this presents no difficulty for a non-domiciled UK resident settlor (e.g., a Canadian *émigré*), for a UK domiciled or deemed domiciled person, a gift to a fully discretionary trust would trigger UK IHT at 20 per cent. The objective must be, therefore, to create a hybrid trust which counts as discretionary for Canadian purposes but whose funding is capable of qualifying as a potentially exempt transfer for UK IHT purposes. An interest in possession trust subject to an overriding flexible power of appointment would suffice from the UK viewpoint.

If the settlor is domiciled for ordinary purposes in the UK, any foreign trust he creates for the benefit of his children or grandchildren would be subject to *section 86* of *TCGA 1992* i.e., capital gains will be assessed on the settlor as they arise regardless of whether the settlor and their spouse are excluded from benefit or, indeed, whether there are any UK resident beneficiaries.

The only obvious way to circumvent this is to utilise an offshore single premium insurance bond product which qualifies as insurance for UK tax
purposes (life assurance at least 101 per cent of premium). These products
restrict investments to a broad range of onshore and offshore collective
investment funds but switching funds within the policy does not result in a
capital gain at trust level, which can then be attributed to the settlor.
Moreover, it is possible to extract 5 per cent of the initial premium each year
by way of a tax free withdrawal which would then be available for distribution on a tax free basis to the Canadian resident beneficiaries. These
products are becoming more flexible in the terms of the ability to roll over
the policy value and extract larger amounts under the tax free withdrawal
facility. As an alternative to the single premium bond, the trustees might
consider investing in a collective investment fund onshore or offshore. While
this would avoid individual changes in investments, giving rise to a gain
being assessed on the settlor, there would be no facility for tax free withdrawals, i.e., a redemption of units to provide cash for distribution *would*
give rise to a capital gain assessed on the settlor.

The status of the settlor is crucial, not only from a UK perspective, but also
in Canada where the rules are in a state of change. The current rules (which
will apply until at least 1 January 2003) are those contained in *Section 94
Income Tax Act* (Canada). In broad terms, in order to fall outside the
favourable Canadian tax treatment described above (with the result that the
trust is deemed resident and therefore taxable in Canada) it is necessary that:

(*a*)   the settlor has been resident in Canada for a cumulative period of five
years during his lifetime before the relevant tax year;

(*b*)   the settlor has been resident in Canada at some time in the 18 months
before the relevant tax year;

(*c*)   the beneficiaries include (or are capable of including) the settlor and
persons related to him; and

(*d*)   at least one of the beneficiaries (or persons capable of being added as
beneficiaries) is a Canadian resident.

Only if all these tests are satisfied would the trust be regarded as Canadian
resident, regardless of where it is actually resident. If the proposed changes
are enacted with effect from the 2003 tax year, the trust will be deemed
Canadian resident (and, therefore, subject to Canadian tax on worldwide
income and gains) if either:

(i)   a Canadian resident (for the relevant tax year) directly or indirectly
transfers or loans property to the trust in such a way as to increase the
fair market value of the trust fund. The term Canadian resident here
includes companies, partnerships or trusts as well as individuals, but
the individual must have been resident for five years; or

(ii) the trust has a Canadian resident beneficiary and the settlor either is,
or has been, resident at some time during his life for five years; has not
been outside Canada for five years at the time he transfers or loans

property to the trust and returns to Canada within five years of the contribution. It is proposed that a 'wait and see' rule applies to retroactively tax trusts that fall into this category.

It will be noted that the proposed rules are a significant extension (they deem resident trusts created by a Canadian settlor which have no Canadian beneficiaries) but would not affect the attractive treatment of trusts established by genuine foreign settlors or long term *émigrés* from Canada.

South African beneficiaries

17.11   The objective from the South African beneficiaries' viewpoint is for assets to be held in an irrevocable discretionary trust. Again, a distinction needs to be drawn between a UK resident non-domiciled settlor (a South African *émigré*) and a UK domiciled and resident settlor. The former can readily create an offshore discretionary trust in this situation. The latter, however, cannot without:

(*a*)   20 per cent lifetime IHT; and

(*b*)   taxation to settlor of trust gains under *TCGA 1992, s 86* whether the settlor is a beneficiary or not.

All considerations discussed above in relation to US and Canadian beneficiaries, therefore, apply to a UK domiciled and resident settlor with South African beneficiaries. Again, a single insurance premium bond is probably the only viable solution to *section 86*. The IHT point can be addressed by using an interest in possession trust on the basis that no income will arise from the insurance policy to flow through to the South African resident beneficiary.

Reverting to the more likely scenario of a UK resident but non-domiciled settlor establishing an irrevocable discretionary trust. From the South African point of view, income received by the trustees will not be taxed in South Africa until it is distributed to a South African resident beneficiary under *section 25B(2)* of the *South African Income Tax Act (ITA) 1962* (as amended). Accumulated income is also now liable as well as current year income (*section 25B(2)(A)*, inserted with effect from 1 March 2001). There have been two important changes to South African rules in this area recently.

1.   Prior to the amendment of the definition of 'income' in 2000 (the abolition of the source basis of taxation), only income of the trust which was sourced in South Africa or deemed sourced there and was distributed to South African resident beneficiaries in the year it accrued, was taxable in South Africa.

2.   Prior to 1 March 2001, South African resident beneficiaries had no liabilities to South African income tax on the distribution of capital which represented income accumulated in previous years. New *section 25B(2)(A)* means it now retains the character of income and is taxable.

With regard to capital gains, *ITA sch 8, para 80(3)* was introduced in late 2001 to deal with the taxation of capital distributions from offshore trusts and to mirror the provisions of *ITA, s 25B(2)(A)* described above in relation to income distributions from offshore trusts. If a capital distribution from a non-resident trust to a South African beneficiary comprises capital gains realised by the trustees in either the current or previous tax years or comprises an asset pregnant with gain, then the resulting gains are taxable in South Africa in the hands of a beneficiary at rates of up to 42 per cent on one quarter of the capital gain, i.e., an effective top rate of 10.5 per cent. While this is not particularly onerous it should be remembered that until very recently there was no capital gains tax in South Africa.

It is worth noting that if the trustees make loans, this will still avoid both income tax and CGT but only if prior exchange control approval is sought by providing Form E to the receiving bank. In addition, there must be some prospect for the beneficiary being able to repay the loan to the trustee.

French beneficiaries

17.12   The problem with trusts with French beneficiaries is that the trust concept is unknown to the civil law regime. As a result there is no certainty as to the tax treatment. Nevertheless, it is contended that if a French resident individual is simply a potential beneficiary of an irrevocable discretionary trust governed by the laws of a suitable Anglo Saxon jurisdiction with trustees and administration outside France, then the receipt of income and realisation of capital gains by those trustees will not, in itself, give rise to tax liability in France, i.e., there is a deferral of tax.

If the settlor is a UK resident but non-domiciled person (perhaps a French *émigré*) then the creation of the irrevocable discretionary trust in a tax haven jurisdiction presents no UK IHT or CGT issues. However, the same cannot be said for a UK resident and domiciled person who has French resident beneficiaries. The difficulties in this latter case are two-fold.

1.   The funding of an irrevocable discretionary trust will give rise to a 20 per cent lifetime IHT charge in the hands of a UK domiciliary or deemed domiciliary. It might be thought that using a flexible interest in possession trust with overriding power of appointment could circumvent this. The problem here, however, is that the French authorities may regard the interest in possession as akin to a usufruct interest. The concern is that the value of the trust property would be subject to wealth tax assessment on the French resident with the life interest and the French resident beneficiary would be subject to income tax on anything they received from the foreign trust, be it income or capital. The uncertainty this presents causes problems under the French self-assessment system. Perhaps a better solution would be to use an irrevocable discretionary trust but to have the UK domiciled settlor retain a power to direct trust assets after three

months (relying on the *Melville* decision). This should work for French purposes and avoid the UK 20 per cent IHT charge but on the death of the UK domiciled settlor, the assets will still be part of his estate for UK IHT.

2.   The second problem is that any trust created by a UK domiciliary is caught by *TCGA 1992, s 86* with the result that gains realised by the trustees will be assessed on the settlor regardless of whether the settlor and their spouse are excluded from benefit and despite whether there are any UK resident beneficiaries. As already mentioned in the context of US and Canadian beneficiaries, the way around this is probably to use some form of single premium insurance product. Although a product which qualifies as insurance for UK tax purposes would avoid the *section 86* problem (because no gains arise at trust level or in a form that can be apportioned to trust level), it is unlikely it will be recognised as a valid insurance policy in France. At the time of writing it is understood that the French authorities effectively ignore the EU *Third Life Directive* and will only afford favourable tax treatment to life products issued by French insurance companies – denying such recognition to insurance products issued by other EU life insurance companies. Thus, what would otherwise be tax free withdrawals from a Dublin or Luxembourg single premium policy held by a suitable trust, would still be regarded as taxable income in the hands of a French resident beneficiary.

Turning to the French tax consequences of a distribution from a foreign irrevocable discretionary trust established by a foreign citizen resident outside France, there are four issues to be concerned with.

Whether the French Revenue will respect the trust concept

17.13   The French Revenue may unilaterally determine that the trust concept is incomprehensible to civil law and determine that any sum which benefits a taxpayer is part of an elaborate bank deposit arrangement. In recent years there has been an increasing amount of French jurisprudence which recognises the effect of trusts (*Ganay* in 1970, the *Caron* decision in 1985 and *Ziezeniss* in 1996). In addition, in July 1985 France signed (but to date has not ratified) the Hague Convention on Recognition of Trusts. Accordingly, the approach of disregarding trusts is gradually giving way to a more reasoned approach based on legal analysis. Nevertheless, such analysis is likely to be tainted by the anti-tax haven hysteria engendered by the Paris based OECD. There is likely to be a more measured approach to trusts established in non-tax haven jurisdictions such as within the states of the US, provinces of Canada or England and Wales.

Impact of Article 123A of French General Tax Code

17.14   This legislation was enacted in 1999 and is aimed at taxing the income of a foreign fiducie in the hands of a French resident beneficiary, even if it is not distributed to them, provided that they *hold* 'directly or indirectly at least 10 per cent of the fiducie'. This is the case even where the fiducie is the subject of a privileged tax regime. The report of the National Assembly which led to the adoption of this legislation stated on page 210 that:

> 'The aim is to apprehend all structures likely to be liable for revenue duty that have an autonomous existence in relation to the natural and legal persons who hold them directly or indirectly.'

It is believed that the beneficiary of an irrevocable discretionary trust will not be treated as 'holding it directly or indirectly'. Page 211 of the above mentioned report acknowledges that an irrevocable trust leads to permanent relinquishment by the settlor of the assets placed in trust. The beneficiary is not a party to this act of relinquishment and often knows nothing about the trust for years afterwards. They cannot be said to be holding assets just because another person (the settlor) has relinquished them, unless the French authorities can prove that they have title to, or actual possession of, those assets. In a discretionary trust situation, it is the trustee who decides the distribution or retention of the capital and income.

Article 2228 of the Civil Code provides additional support by stating:

> 'possession is the holding or use of a thing or the right which we have or which we exercise ourselves, or through someone else who has it or exercises it on our behalf.'

The term holding (*détention*) means actual power over an asset in terms of possession. In the context of an irrevocable discretionary trust, the assets are in the hands of the trustee who exercises powers on his own behalf. This is in contrast to the 'fiducie' who acts on behalf of the real owner. The term use (*jouissance*) denotes more than *de facto* power or control – rather the exercise of a right or prerogative, which can asserted in a court if necessary. The beneficiary of a discretionary trust can only require a trustee to apply the trust instrument and consider the objects of his discretion: the beneficiary cannot compel a distribution and so has no prerogative against the trustee. A beneficiary cannot, simply because he has received distributions in the past demand further distributions.

Taxation of distributions

17.15   In the absence of a double tax treaty the French resident beneficiary is taxed under *Article 120-9* of the General Tax Code at ordinary income tax rates on any actual distributions received as if it were a dividend without tax credit. The top marginal rate is currently 54 per cent but CSG/CRDS may be imposed on top. In the circumstances it may be better to plan the distributions when the beneficiary is not French resident.

In this context the use of a Canadian trust to effect distributions is still believed to be valuable. Under the French/Canadian double tax treaty, a trust is treated as a person fully entitled to treaty benefits. The French Revenue cannot disregard a Canadian resident trust. A distribution of capital from a Canadian trust to a French resident beneficiary will not be caught by *Article 120-9* and taxed as income. The usual rule in the absence of a treaty is that all trust distributions are treated as income. It will need to be shown that the distribution from the Canadian trust to the French beneficiary is not a gift under Canadian rules otherwise there is a danger that the French Revenue would seek to levy French gift tax at the highest applicable rate. It is understood that Canada treats transfers of income from tax haven trusts to Canadian trusts as a resettlement of capital for Canadian tax purposes and, on this basis, the French/Canadian treaty offers scope for useful conduit planning in routing distributions to French resident beneficiaries.

Death of a beneficiary

17.16   As beneficiaries have neither ownership nor possession, death should not result in trust property being returned to the beneficiary's patrimony and being subject to French estate tax. If the trustees subsequently decided to terminate the trust and distribute assets to French heirs/legatees, then the French Revenue would impose income tax under *Article 120–9* or gift tax under *Article 750b* as if the payment was a deferred distribution of a gift made by the settlor (at rates up to 60 per cent for non-related persons).

Pre-immigration planning

17.17   In addition to cross border family provision, one of the main uses of trusts in international tax planning is when planning to assist the tax efficient structuring of assets for individuals who intend to become resident in a new jurisdiction. The trust provides a vehicle in which to place pre-residency capital and to shelter income and gains arising on that capital from taxation in a new country as well as protecting it from death taxes. Again, this principal is best illustrated by examples comparing and contrasting the different regimes.

USA

17.18   Since the enactment of the *US Foreign Trust Tax Compliance Act* in 1996, the use of a foreign trust as a pre-US immigration vehicle has been severely curtailed. This legislation provided that if a person established a non-US trust less than five years before becoming a US tax resident (usually 1 January in the year of arrival), the trust would be treated as established on the date when they became US tax resident. It would, in other words, be treated as a grantor trust and completely transparent from the US income tax viewpoint providing no shelter from tax on income/capital gains arising to the trustees.

If a person moving to the US has significant pre-residency capital and wishes to shelter the income and capital gains arising on it from US income tax while they are US resident, the only option is to subscribe the capital before they become resident to an offshore insurance company in exchange for the issue of a variable annuity contract or, better still, a variable life insurance contract capable of complying with *IRC s 7702* (the definition of life insurance for US tax purposes). In contrast to a UK single premium insurance bond, such policies involve a high level of life insurance which adds to the cost (in the region of 0.5 per cent per annum of the premium subscribed, although possibly less on large contracts). The advantage of these variable life insurance contracts include:

1.   Tax free build up of income and gains on investment assets held in a segregated account on the insurance company's balance sheet.

2.   Ability to surrender the policy tax free on leaving the US.

3.   On certain contracts which are funded by multiple premiums over a period of up to seven years (known as Non Modified Endowment contracts) there is the ability to access funds tax free and interest free while in the US by means of a policy loan. It is understood the period of funding can be reduced in certain circumstances to four and a half years.

4.   In comparison with US onshore products, much lower administrative charges and the ability to access a much wider range of investment products (including offshore hedge funds) but always subject to strict investor control and investment diversification requirements.

It may be attractive to hold a variable insurance policy via an offshore trust because if the trust is funded, and the policy established, prior to the individual becoming US tax resident, the individual is able to remove the value of the pre-residency capital from their estate for US gift tax and estate tax purposes without incurring US gift tax. The definition of US residence for estate and gift tax purposes (and generation skipping tax 'GST') differs than that for income tax because it involves the individual being a domiciliary of the US, i.e., establishing the US as their permanent home.

If the offshore insurance product is in place before the individual becomes US tax resident for income tax purposes then this will also avoid liability to 1 per cent excise tax. However, it has to be remembered that the normal rule is that an individual is US tax resident from 1 January (even if they moved in the middle of the following summer) unless they can show that they have a closer connection with a tax home elsewhere. (In which event they will only become US tax resident from the date they moved unless they spent more than ten days in the US before moving, in which case the exception cannot apply.) Normally, therefore, it is safer to plan on the basis that the individual will become US tax resident on the 1 January preceding their move to the US.

Apart from acting as a vehicle to protect insurance policy assets from US estate tax, a trust established before becoming US resident may prove an attractive long term estate planning vehicle. If all the settlor's heirs are US citizens or residents, such a trust might conveniently be established in a state which has abolished the rule against perpetuities, e.g., Delaware. As a domestic trust it will avoid the onerous 'throwback' rules associated with the offshore accumulation of income but is capable of conferring freedom from estate and gift tax and GST as long as the assets remain in trust. An attractive idea should the proposed abolition of those taxes in 2010 prove short-lived.

A trust established prior to becoming US resident may also be attractive for non-US heirs. If the trust is drawn in such a way that no US citizen or resident may benefit from it, the trust will not be a grantor trust for US income tax purposes. Depending upon the tax regime in the jurisdiction where the heirs are resident, this may prove a particularly attractive vehicle for avoiding taxation in the country where the heirs reside. For example, prior to implementation of the proposed changes to the Canadian regime applicable to foreign trusts, due to take effect on 1 January 2003, a person who has left Canada (having paid departure tax) – possibly moving to the UK or Ireland for a period prior to taking up long term permanent residence in the US – might take advantage of the period in Europe to establish an offshore trust for the benefit of their Canadian children and grandchildren (on the basis that all US citizens and residents are exchanged).

Aside from these limited uses, a trust is unlikely to be much benefit in pre-US immigration tax planning.

United Kingdom

17.19   A distinction has to be drawn between a returning UK expatriate, who has probably never shed his UK domicile of origin and a non-UK domiciliary, probably a foreign national moving to the UK for the first time. The best strategy for the former is to uplift CGT base costs prior to becoming UK resident again and to seek out a tax efficient investment vehicle. This might be a single premium insurance bond which permits tax free build up and tax free withdrawals or, alternatively, a collective investment umbrella fund to maximise CGT non-business taper relief. If a trust is utilised for IHT planning, the considerations are the same as for any other UK domiciliary/resident.

In relation to a non-domiciled person, although they will be able to take advantage of the favourable remittance basis of taxation by establishing separate capital, income and capital gains bank accounts, the use of a trust confers three distinct advantages.

Permanent protection from IHT

17.20   At the time of writing a non-domiciliary establishing a trust before they have been UK resident for 17 UK tax years, is able to obtain permanent protection from IHT for non-UK situs assets. This means there will be no charge to IHT on the death of the settlor or any person holding an interest in possession (life interest) under the trust. Similarly, the trust is not subject to the IHT regime applicable to discretionary trusts (ten-year anniversary charges and entry and exit charges) except in respect of UK situs assets. It is still possible to shelter UK assets from IHT by owning them through an underlying offshore holding company or, if this is inappropriate for some reason, (for example, in the case of real estate occupied by the settlor) by the use of debt instruments as explained below.

This favourable regime may change. On the face of it, the IHT reservation of benefit rules introduced by *FA 1986, s 102*, applied equally to domiciled and non-domiciled persons, so that if a non-domiciliary made a gift to a trust but remained a beneficiary of that trust, then *prima facie*, they have reserved a benefit in the assets gifted and they would remain comprised in their estate. Shortly after *FA 1986* was enacted, the Inland Revenue indicated that they would not seek to apply this legislation to non-domiciliaries – there were practical issues in relation to trusts set up many years before by persons who, at that time, had no intention of moving to the UK. The Capital Taxes Office has recently been consulting on the impact of restricting this concessionary treatment, so that once a non-domiciled settlor became deemed domiciled (when they have been UK tax resident for 17 out of the last 20 tax years), if they are still a beneficiary at that time, then reservation of benefit would be treated as applying to the trust from that date. It is unclear at the time of writing whether this change will be introduced.

Freedom from CGT

17.21   A non-domiciled UK resident who is able to take advantage of the remittance basis of taxation without a trust is liable to CGT on UK source gains as they arise and on foreign source gains which are remitted to the UK. By contrast, if assets are held through a trust then both UK and foreign source capital gains can be distributed by the trustees to the UK resident non-domiciled beneficiary free of CGT. The position will only change if the settlor became domiciled in the UK in the ordinary sense (as opposed to becoming deemed domiciled under the 17-year rule applicable only for IHT).

Administrative advantage

17.22   A wealthy UK resident non-domicilary can make his life administratively easier by employing a professional trustee to deal, on their behalf, with the burden of complying with the remittance basis of taxation.

One of the most practical uses of a trust in this context is that it acts as a vehicle for the purchase of a home. If a non-domiciled resident buys UK real estate in their own name for personal occupation and dies owning the property, it will be subject to IHT regardless of whether they are non-domiciled, deemed domiciled or domiciled in the ordinary sense at the date of their death. This is because the UK reserves the right to tax UK situs assets on the death of the owner. If, however, the property is instead purchased by a trust with the entire purchase price borrowed from the non-domiciled settlor and the debt is documented by a deed (a specialty debt) which is kept offshore, it is possible to convert the UK situs property (the house) into a non-UK situs asset (the debt). Before the settlor has been resident in the UK for 17 years, the specialty debt should be gifted to a second trust. To protect any increase in the value of the property for IHT purposes, interest should be accrued but not paid on the loan during the life of the settlor. Income tax will only be payable as and when interest is paid after the settlor's death. This strategy for a UK resident non-domiciliary acquiring UK residential property avoids the difficulties and dangers associated with purchasing the property through an offshore company underlying the trust. Following the House of Lords decision in the case of *R v Allen (No 2) [2001] STC 1537*, there is a substantial risk of the Inland Revenue assessing the occupant of property owned by an offshore company as a shadow director of the company on the benefit in kind which the Revenue considers that rent free occupation confers. (See *ICTA 1988, ss 145–146*.)

Canada

17.23   Canada has a special regime for five-year immigration trusts. This enables a person intending to become a Canadian tax resident (or who has recently become Canadian tax resident) to transfer pre-residency capital to an offshore trust and shelter income and gains arising on that pre-residency capital from Canadian tax for five years. Canadian residence involves physical presence in Canada for 183 days or more in a calendar year *or* spending a lesser period but satisfying a 'facts and circumstances' test which involves considering a number of factors including availability of personal residence, location of dependants and social and economic ties.

If advantage is not taken of this opportunity, Canada taxes residents (with rate variations between the provinces) on worldwide income and gains from the date of arrival at rates of up to 50 per cent on income and 24 per cent on capital gains. The five-year trust will be treated as Canadian resident and taxable in Canada at the settlor's top marginal tax rate from the beginning of the tax year in which the settlor's fifth anniversary as a Canadian resident occurs. Effective strategies for deferring the onset of Canadian taxation in this situation are few.

A five-year trust can be utilised as part of a long term international tax planning strategy. For example, an individual might leave the UK with assets pregnant with latent capital gain and transfer them into a Canadian five-year trust. Having ceased to be UK tax resident, the assets can be realised in the five-year trust at a time when the settlor is Canadian resident (free of all tax) and when the five-year period is up the settlor might move to the US having taken steps to 'wrap' the assets in the five-year trust in a form of US qualified variable life insurance. A similar strategy might be employed by a US visa resident (not a US citizen or green card holder) who leaves the US with highly appreciated stock, realising it within a five-year trust while Canadian resident and subsequently leaves Canada for his ultimate home in Europe.

South Africa

17.24   South Africa is not a major destination for new migrants due to the weak currency and personal security issues. However, for a person planning to move permanently to South Africa and able to offload pre-residency capital into an irrevocable discretionary trust before becoming a South African resident, such a course of action would place those assets outside the scope of South African estate tax and would not be subject to donations tax (effectively gift tax). (Although it would be necessary to check this did not give rise to any gift tax implications in the jurisdiction the new migrant was moving from (in case they was still subject to capital taxation in that jurisdiction).) For example, a UK domiciliary remains subject to UK IHT for three years after departure. Many other jurisdictions such as Germany have a longer period of residual liability after departure. To the extent it is possible to place assets in an irrevocable discretionary trust before becoming South African resident, then this should effectively shelter those assets from South African income tax and capital gains tax unless, or until, a payment is received either by the settlor or another beneficiary in South Africa.

France

17.25   If assets are settled in an irrevocable discretionary trust prior to becoming French tax resident, it should be possible to obtain deferral from French taxation on income/gains arising on pre-French residency capital within the trust. The reason why a discretionary trust is helpful in this situation has already been discussed in 17.7 above, although from that discussion it will be appreciated that this strategy presents difficulties to a UK domiciliary/resident or a US citizen.

Pre-immigration planning in other jurisdictions

17.26   The use of a trust in pre-residency planning is useful in many other jurisdictions, particularly those Latin American countries which still have a territorial system of taxation such as Brazil. However, under IMF pressure many Latin American countries have adopted 'black list' regimes outlawing the holding of investments in blacklisted tax havens. This has encouraged the use of onshore trusts discussed later in this chapter.

Structuring of inward investment

17.27   This section concerns the person who is not resident or domiciled in a country but who wishes to invest in that country perhaps because it is more politically or economically stable than his home country, or has a stronger currency or simply as part of an asset diversification strategy.

The issue in this situation is how to structure the investment to protect it from local tax. As the investor is not resident in the country they are investing in, the most likely taxes with which they will be concerned are:

(*a*)   withholding tax on income (as opposed to income tax);

(*b*)   any special capital gains taxes applicable to foreign investors (the main example of this is the Foreign Investment in Real Property Tax in the US known as FIRPTA which is a capital gains tax on US real estate and is virtually impossible to avoid); and

(*c*)   inheritance taxes on the death of the investor: many high tax jurisdictions impose death taxes on assets such as real estate, shares, bonds or even cash deposits which are physically situated in their jurisdiction.

Inward investors often make use of trusts to try and mitigate these taxes. A trust resident in a tax haven or low tax jurisdiction will not be of assistance in reducing withholding tax. Withholding tax is best reduced or eliminated by the investor entity, be it an individual, trust or company situated in a jurisdiction which has a suitable double tax treaty with a jurisdiction in which the investment is located. By contrast trusts are more effective in avoiding inheritance or estate taxes, which would otherwise be incurred, if the investment was held directly by the individual investor at the time of his death. An irrevocable trust will not come to an end unexpectedly and in that sense provides the perpetual existence which a corporate entity is also able to offer. Whether the investor should use a trust or a body corporate or a partnership or some combination of these entities depends upon their own personal tax status and estate planning objectives. Reference has been made below to issues which arise with assets in specific jurisdictions.

US assets

17.28   It is very common for wealthy non-US investors (non-resident aliens 'NRAs') to want to hold US equities. US equities represent 60 per cent of world equity market capitalisation, provide US dollar currency exposure and include world-leading businesses. A portfolio of US equities is, however, subject to US estate tax on the death of the NRA holder, as is US real estate and household contents and a US incorporated trade or business – all by virtue of *IRC ss 2101–2108*. By contrast, general deposit accounts, government and corporate bonds and life insurance proceeds are excluded from the estate tax charge. Partnerships are not black and white. Where estate tax is payable, the unified credit exclusion for non-resident aliens is just $60,000 (by contrast to a US citizen who in 2002 has a $1 million unified credit exclusion). The top rate of tax increases rapidly to 50 per cent in 2002 but this will fall to 45 per cent by 2009 and estate tax will be abolished altogether by 2010 under current law. However, there is every likelihood that further changes will be made to the estate tax regime before then and most US tax advisers indicate that long term planning to counter estate tax should continue. The objective is to invest through some form of perpetual entity. The US estate tax treatment of partnerships and other 'pass through' entities being uncertain, the trust has been the favoured vehicle for estate tax protection.

With regards to an irrevocable discretionary trust (typically offshore), often investors from civil law countries are not familiar with the trust concept or the trust needs to be structured as a foreign grantor trust because there are US beneficiaries who are to inherit on the death of the NRA investor. An irrevocable trust will result in the throwback rules applying to accumulated income and gains in the trust. However, while a revocable trust may meet the investor's personal and income tax objectives it will not, in itself, provide estate tax protection.

A revocable trust holding either an offshore company or some other separate juridical entity which elects for corporate status on IRS Form 8832 under the Entity Classification or 'Check the Box' regulations (for example, a Scottish limited partnership or Dutch CV) may also be utilised to provide US estate tax protection. In this situation the revocable trust operates as a Will substitute and the corporate entity provides estate tax protection. If this structure is used, and where there are US heirs, it is important to remember that there is no automatic re-basing of the underlying US equities or other US situs property for US capital gains purposes on the death of the investor. It is, therefore, important to sell and re-purchase securities on a regular basis to 'step up' the capital gains base cost of the assets. Failure to do this would result in any US resident heirs having to pay capital gains tax when they sell the assets after inheriting them. It should be noted that under *IRC s 1441*, dividend withholding tax will be imposed on dividends paid to offshore companies and trusts in the absence of a suitable double tax treaty.

To avoid payment of back up withholding tax at 31 per cent on the sale proceeds of investments it is necessary for the offshore bank trustee to have Qualified Intermediary status and to subject itself to regular IRS audit or comply with the new W8 reporting regime. The latter involves certifying under penalty of perjury the identity of the owner of the US securities and that the owner is not a US taxpayer.

UK assets

17.29 Very similar considerations apply to UK situs equities and real estate held by a foreign investor. On the death of the non-UK domiciled non-resident investor, if the assets are held directly, a 40 per cent IHT charge applies to the extent the value of the assets exceeds the IHT nil-rate band, currently £242,000. However, if the assets are held through an irrevocable trust settled by the non-UK domiciled non-resident, this will not, of itself, remove the IHT charge. A discretionary trust is potentially subject to periodic charges to IHT in respect of UK situs assets on every tenth anniversary of the trust with exit charges at other times. A life interest (interest in possession) trust is subject to IHT on the death of the life tenant to the extent that UK assets are held. This charge can only be avoided by interposing an offshore company between the trust and the assets. Indeed, the inward investor might simply utilise an offshore company without a shareholder trust. While this will be sufficient from a UK point of view, whether it is the correct approach overall will depend on the tax regime to which the investor is subject and whether he wants the offshore company in his estate or not. With UK equities, dividend income is more significant than with US equities.

There is no withholding tax in the UK as such but all dividends carry a 10 per cent non-recoverable dividend tax credit. No use can be made of this unless the shareholding entity is in a suitable double tax treaty jurisdiction. With regard to real estate, provided the investor remains non-UK resident or the property is let commercially, there is no UK tax problem with holding real estate through a non-resident company which, again, can be held directly or by a trust as required by the investor's personal situation. This will protect the value of the land from UK IHT but rental income is potentially subject to 20 per cent income tax which should be deducted by the tenant at source unless application is made under the Non-Resident Landlords Scheme for payment gross. This scheme involves giving an undertaking to comply with the procedure to pay taxes which are due. Income tax on rental income can be mitigated if the property is acquired with the aid of a borrowing, interest on such a loan is deductible in computing the income tax on rental income. Unlike the US, the UK does not currently seek to tax non-residents on capital gains arising on UK assets.

Canadian/Australian assets

17.30 By contrast to the three jurisdictions discussed already, Canada and Australia do not have an estate tax for inward investors to worry about, so a trust is not needed to mitigate local tax liabilities although it may be relevant to the investor's home country.

South African assets

17.31 This is less of an issue as South Africa's exchange control system and long term currency depreciation have reduced the attractions of inward investment. However, like the US and the UK, South Africa imposes estate tax on South African assets and imposes withholding tax on South African source income. An irrevocable discretionary trust should be effective in protecting South African real estate or South African equities from the estate tax. South Africa has a number of double tax treaties relating to its estate tax and these treaties may, where the investor is resident in a treaty partner country, relieve South African situs assets from local estate taxation on the death of the investor on the basis that they are subject to estate taxes in their home country. This avoids the need for bespoke planning in situations where all a trust would do is remove the local liability but leave the investor exposed to IHT/estate tax in their home country. This is just as true with South African investments as it is in the US and UK.

French assets

17.32 France has similar issues to the US and UK in relation to French real estate and French equities in that these are subject to French inheritance tax on the death of a foreign investor. Moreover, private international law principles mean that real estate is always subject to the succession laws of the country in which it is situated. This is particularly relevant in a civil law country, such as France, which does not have freedom of testamentary disposition. In common with other civil law countries, France has a system of reserved shares for children which can cause a number of problems where the investor dies leaving minor children without a suitable marriage contract to protect the position of the widow or widower. Regrettably, as France does not recognise trusts, the trust is unlikely to be the most reliable way of avoiding either the succession problems referred to above or liability to French estate tax. In the case of real estate, the succession law problem is best avoided by purchasing the property through a French incorporated company such as a *Société Civile Immobilière* – a form of transparent company similar to a partnership. This converts the real estate into personal property which will then be governed by the law of succession of the deceased shareholder's domicile.

Use of onshore trusts

17.33 Up until now this chapter has focused on the use of the traditional offshore trust: established under the laws of traditional zero tax jurisdictions such as Bermuda, Cayman, the Bahamas, the Channel Islands or Isle of Man and administered there or possibly in Switzerland. This industry which began in a modest way after World War II expanded enormously in the 1980s and matured in the 1990s. By the end of the 20th Century it was under pressure from three sources:

1. Anti-avoidance legislation in the US, Canada and the UK (amongst other places) made it very difficult for individuals who were tax resident and domiciled in those jurisdictions without international family connections to obtain any meaningful legitimate tax advantage from offshore trusts.

2. Money laundering legislation adopted by G7 governments, initially to deal with terrorism and drug trafficking, has been expanded to cover

all crimes including tax evasion. G7 governments are under pressure to increase the supply and quality of public services (e.g., health, education and infrastructure) but are faced with an inability to raise the overall level of taxes. As a result they have sought to improve the efficiency of tax collection and reduced the scope to arbitrage different tax regimes. The OECD initiative against harmful tax competition, the EU initiative on tax harmonisation and the Financial Action Tax Force initiative on money laundering have all combined to put pressure on traditional offshore jurisdictions who, under threat of sanctions, have been forced to adopt bureaucratic and expensive regulatory procedures, which inevitably reduces the profitability of offshore businesses and reduces their attraction to potential users. While clearly the curtailment of terrorism and drug trafficking (and indeed other crimes) is to be encouraged, evidence suggests that financial institutions in the G7 countries are used as much, if not more, for handling the proceeds of crimes than the tightly regulated offshore locations.

3.   Emerging markets such as Eastern Europe, Latin America and South East Asia which have been the great growth engines for the offshore industry as enormous personal wealth has been created in the hands of relatively few families. However, under pressure from world economic cycles and dependent on IMF assistance to bail out failing banking systems, these jurisdictions are increasingly being forced to move from territorial systems of taxation to taxing their residents on a basis of worldwide income. In so doing to improve the efficiency of tax collection by adopting anti-avoidance legislation.

In response to the above, tax planners have looked to onshore jurisdictions and double tax treaties to develop a new range of strategies. Onshore jurisdictions, which have especially attractive tax regimes applicable to domestic trusts established by foreigners, are described below.

USA

17.34   Certain US states have modified their trust laws to make themselves significantly more attractive to the international community. Although states such as Alaska, Colorado, South Dakota, Wyoming and Nevada have enacted features into their state laws which are worthy of consideration, Delaware stands out as the state which has done most to develop an attractive range of products for the international community. Particular features of Delaware legislation include:

(*a*)   perpetual trusts: Delaware has no rule against perpetuities so trusts can go on forever;

(*b*)   Delaware follows the prudent investor rule;

(*c*)   unlike, say, New York, in Delaware investment management can be delegated to someone other than the trustee to improve investment flexibility and in many cases performance;

(*d*)   asset protection laws exist to safeguard trust assets from creditors of the settlor even if the settlor is still a beneficiary; and

(*e*)   unlike New York, trust administration is not court supervised and as a result is cheaper.

The biggest concern for international clients when establishing a US domestic trust with US trustees and subject to the jurisdiction of a US court, is the loss of confidentiality and the potential to be caught up in the complexity of the US tax regime. In fact the tax rules are not unattractive:

(i)   A non-US person (referred to earlier in this chapter as a non-resident alien or NRA) can make lifetime gifts of US equities/bonds to a Delaware trust free of gift tax. The trust fund will not be subject to US estate tax or GST on the settlor's death. This is attractive not only to a NRA seeking investment exposure to US equity markets but also a NRA who has US children/grandchildren as beneficiaries. If structured as a Delaware perpetual trust, then, potentially, the assets can remain in trust free of US gift and estate tax on a permanent basis, generating income from capital that would otherwise have been lost in US estate tax.

(ii)   Even if the NRA settlor does not have US beneficiaries, the Delaware perpetual trust achieves many of the same objectives as a traditional offshore trust without having the tax haven taint. (A particular problem for residents of jurisdictions such as Mexico, Venezuela or Argentina which have adopted tax haven black list legislation.)

(iii)   A NRA settlor can use a Delaware perpetual trust as an alternative to an offshore trust as a pre-immigration vehicle. It is important that the transfer into trust is structured as a completed gift and occurs before the settlor becomes US resident for gift and estate tax purposes but this does not rule out the possibility of the settlor gaining access to income or capital distributions from the trustees.

(iv)   If structured so that a non-US person (perhaps a Protector) has control over one or more 'substantial decisions', then the trust will be a foreign trust for US purposes, and because both the settlor and beneficiaries are NRAs, then the Delaware trustees should not be liable to US federal income tax or Delaware state income tax on income/gains accruing to the trust. The Delaware 'foreign trust' may be one of the most exciting new developments on the international trust scene.

UK

17.35   UK trusts have certain limitations as to a substitute for an offshore trust. A non-UK domiciled/non-resident individual can establish a trust under the laws of England and Wales with UK professional trustees (lawyers, accountants or bank trust companies) and such a trust will be afforded the following favourable tax treatment.

(*a*)   A discretionary trust can be funded free of IHT and may continue for up to 80 years (the maximum fixed perpetuity period permitted) free of IHT provided that no UK situs assets are held in the trust fund or, if there are UK situs assets, they are held through an underlying off-shore company or other foreign vehicle to change their situs. In this situation, the settlor's death will be a non-event for IHT.

(*b*)   The trustee can realise capital gains free of CGT by virtue of the special exemption in *TCGA 1992, s 69(2)* for professional trustees.

(*c*)   Income will still be subject to income tax at, currently, 34 per cent unless there is at least one non-UK resident trustee (a Swiss, Singapore or New Zealand trustee may be suitable) in which case no income tax is payable. [*FA 1989, s 110*].

Income tax need not be a concern if the only trust asset is non-income producing such as a single premium insurance bond, non-distributing offshore collective fund or even an offshore company. A second non-resident trustee can always be appointed when it is proposed to make a distribution which would constitute an income receipt in the hands of the trustees.

With reference to Latin American clients affected by anti-tax haven black list legislation, one common solution has been to establish a revocable UK resident discretionary trust which, in turn, incorporates a Scottish limited company and a Delaware LLC. The former acting as a 1 per cent general partner and the latter acting as 99 per cent partner funded by the trust joined together in a Scottish limited partnership under the *1907 Limited Partnerships Act*. The Scottish limited partnership, unlike its English counterpart, has a separate legal personality under Scots law and, therefore, as a matter of private international law, is a suitable substitute to an offshore company as a vehicle for holding a US equity portfolio. This is reinforced by submitting 'Check the Box' elections to the IRS to elect the partnership as having corporate status for US tax purposes but with the Delaware limited partner electing for pass through status. This structure replicates the revocable offshore trust with underlying BVI company – so popular in the past with Latin American clients. Having said all that, at the end of 2001, Mexico was in the throes of passing legislation which requires all foreign entities directly or indirectly held for Mexican residents to pay tax at a minimum level (proposed to be 16 per cent at the time of writing) if the foreign entity is not to be subject to full reporting and hence taxation in Mexico.

Canada

17.36   Certain Canadian provinces, notably Prince Edward Island, New Brunswick and Nova Scotia have passed legislation permitting the incorporation of Canadian trust companies which operate through foreign branches, typically in tax haven locations. Provided such trust companies do not undertake trust business with Canadian settlors or beneficiaries, they only pay tax in Canada on their own profits, i.e., the income and gains of trusts which they administer are free of Canadian tax and not subject to any form of reporting in Canada. Such arrangements can lend a veneer of respectability to what is to all intents and purposes an offshore trust.

New Zealand

17.37   New Zealand has developed its own approach to the taxation of trusts based, not on the residence of the trustee or beneficiaries, but on the source of the trust fund – taxability in New Zealand depends on whether the settlor is a New Zealand resident. On the basis the settlor is not a New Zealand resident, the trust is only taxable on New Zealand source income regardless of whether one or all of the trustees or, one or all of the beneficiaries are New Zealand tax resident (*Income Tax Act 1964*, *s HH4(3B)*)). The New Zealand resident beneficiary is, of course, taxable on any income they receive from the trust. Non-New Zealand beneficiaries receiving distributions from the trust would, however, only have suffered New Zealand tax on New Zealand source income and no tax at all on capital gains (regardless of source) as New Zealand only taxes capital gains arising on New Zealand businesses. Thus, in relation to a portfolio of international bonds and securities, income and gains can roll-up free of New Zealand tax in the hands of the New Zealand trustees and on distribution to the non-New Zealand beneficiaries.

Under New Zealand law, trusts established by non-New Zealand resident settlors, with or without New Zealand trustees, are termed 'foreign trusts' but are not deemed non-resident by the legislation. Trust residence has no meaning in the *Income Tax Act 1964* – it is the residence of the settlor which determines whether a trust is foreign or domestic. This means that a 'foreign trust' with New Zealand trustees can take advantage of New Zealand's network of double tax treaties. In some circumstances this can relieve income and gains from taxation in the source country (without taxation in New Zealand) so long as it can be shown that the trustees are resident in New Zealand for the purposes of the treaty. This is discussed further later on.

Overall, therefore, a New Zealand foreign trust is an attractive alternative to an offshore tax haven trust achieving many of the same advantages for international clients but without the stigma associated with a tax haven structure. It also has asset protection and pre-immigration advantages for those intending to migrate to New Zealand. It is, however, important to avoid owning a New Zealand business or performing contracts in connection with a foreign business in New Zealand.

Singapore

17.38   Singapore, like New Zealand, has a legal system based on English common law and rules of equity. There is no separate regime for the taxation of trusts: a Singapore corporate trustee would simply pay corporate rate income tax (currently 24.5 per cent top rate) on trust income sourced in, or brought into, Singapore. By keeping foreign source income offshore Singapore, tax is legitimately avoided and can be distributed to non-Singapore beneficiaries tax free. Singapore based beneficiaries get a credit on distribution under an imputation system which usually gives rise to a repayment claim (the top rate of personal income tax in Singapore of 26 per cent only applies to those earning more than US$250,000 per annum). Trusts established by a non-Singapore resident settlor for non-Singapore resident beneficiaries with non-Singapore assets can easily avoid paying Singapore tax, including the estate duty which applies on the death of a Singapore domiciliary or, indeed, any individual owning Singapore situs assets.

A Singapore incorporated company, if managed and controlled outside Singapore, is regarded as non-resident there and is, therefore, only subject to tax on Singapore sourced income. However, a non-resident company such as this cannot take advantage of Singapore's network of double tax treaties. These are only available to Singapore resident companies, i.e., companies managed and controlled in Singapore and which pay the corporate rate of income tax up to 24.5 per cent.

Use of double tax treaties

17.39   There is no guidance in the OECD Model and Commentary on the application of double tax conventions to trusts, trustees or beneficiaries: the convention applies to 'residents' of one or both contracting states. Treaties to which the US and Canada are party usually state that trusts where either the trustee or beneficiary has paid tax, will constitute residents. However, in the absence of significant case law on this topic, the only guidance comes from academic work such as '*The Treatment of Trusts Under the OECD Model Convention*' [1989] BTR41-60 and 65–102.

Trusts give rise to significant international tax issues.

(*a*)   A trust may hold assets in different jurisdictions giving rise to income and/or capital gains.

(*b*)   A trust may have three different trustees all of whom may be resident in different jurisdictions.

(*c*)   Beneficiaries may be resident in different jurisdictions.

Notwithstanding this complexity, the application of a treaty can only be properly considered by looking at each income source in the hands of the trustees (wherever they are as a single continuing body of persons treated as being resident), and then looking at the treatment of that income in the hands of each individual beneficiary (wherever he may reside and depending on whether the income source changes character on distribution by the trustees). The issues to be considered in such an analysis are as follows:

(i)   Distinction has to be made between bare trusts (and possibly life interest trusts) where the beneficiary is entitled to the income and the situation where the income can be retained and accumulated by the trustee. There is a case for ignoring the trust for the purposes of the Model Convention in the former case.

(ii)   A discretionary or accumulation trust is undoubtedly a person for the purposes of *Article 3* of the Model Convention, but it is necessary to look at the individual trustees as a single continuing body of persons: it is not acceptable to have three trustees, each resident in different jurisdictions. Usually a trust is resident where it is effectively managed.

(iii)   Discretionary and accumulating trusts are the beneficial owners of dividends, interest and royalties for the purposes of *Articles 10–12* of the Model Convention.

(iv)   Except in the case of bare trusts, the trustee is the alienator for the purposes of *Article 13* dealing with capital gains. This should be contrasted with the situation where the beneficiary alienates his trust interest. There can be opportunities for tax avoidance in this latter situation where the trust owns land in a different jurisdiction to that where the beneficiary resides.

(v)   When the discretionary/accumulation trustees decide to make a distribution of income, either that income retains its original character as dividends, income or royalties under *Articles 10–12* or it changes character and becomes 'other income' for the purposes of *Article 21* of the Model Convention. *Article 21* income is always taxable in the hands of the beneficiary for Convention purposes. This would seem to be the better analysis but the position is not free from doubt.

It will be appreciated from the above that the international tax issues associated with trusts give scope for both double taxation and tax avoidance. In the absence of any OECD guidelines on trust issues, the resulting uncertainties will only be resolved on a case by case basis.

Some practical illustrations will show how treaties can be utilised to the taxpayer's advantage in the international private client context.

USA

17.40   Traditionally, Latin American investors purchased US real estate either directly through a BVI company or through a US subsidiary of a BVI company, the structure ultimately being owned through a tax haven trust. If the land was held directly by the BVI company it was subject to US income tax and possibly Branch Profits Tax in respect of income and capital gains tax/FIRPTA on disposal. By contrast, if the BVI company is migrated or continued into a Delaware LLC with the US real estate transferred down to a US subsidiary and this structure is transferred into a Scottish limited partnership (as described in 17.27 above) which utilises the US/UK double tax treaty or a Dutch CV (partnership) utilising the

US/Netherlands treaty then it may be possible to avoid US Branch Profits Tax and capital gains tax. A reorganisation is required involving Form 8832 'Check the Box' election. The Dutch CV or Scottish partnership will ultimately be owned by a UK trust (with a foreign co-trustee). The key to the success of this structure is the double tax treaty containing exchange of information provisions which permits an election under *IRC s 897i* which removes the FIRPTA liability. A rare example of the US permitting treaty shopping!

UK

17.41   As has already been seen in 17.7 above, it is very difficult for a UK domiciled settlor to establish a trust for children in, for example, the USA, Canada, South Africa or many other jurisdictions. One of the main problems is the application of *TCGA 1992, s 86* which taxes the settlor on capital gains realised in the trust regardless of whether he is a beneficiary.

Article 13(4) of the UK/Mauritius (or UK/New Zealand) treaty, provides that gains arising on disposal of, for example, a securities portfolio, are taxable only in Mauritius/New Zealand if the alienator is resident there. On the face of it, therefore, if the UK domiciled settlor establishes a trust in Mauritius/New Zealand (or it is possible to transfer a tax haven trust there), he might avoid being taxed on the gains under *section 86*. Unfortunately, the effect of the Court of Appeal decision in the case of *Bricom Holidays Ltd v IRC [1997] STC 1179* which concerned controlled foreign company provisions which, like *TCGA 1992, ss 86–87* involved an assumption as to UK residence, means there is a statutory computation of hypothetical gains which are then imputed to the UK person. This displaces the alienator's treaty residence for the purposes of the UK anti-avoidance legislation. This applies to gains realised by non-resident trusts either within *section 86*, settlor interested charge or within *section 87*. *Section 87* applies where the settlor is dead or where the beneficiaries are not close relatives of the settlor (outside the definition of defined persons for *section 86*) or where the settlor is non domiciled but the beneficiaries are UK domiciled. The only glimmer of hope is to bring the trusteeship back from Mauritius/New Zealand to the UK before the end of the UK tax year in which the gains are realised. In this situation, *sections 86–87* cannot apply and treaty protection cannot be denied on Bricom grounds. However, care must be taken to avoid dual residence and to avoid a UK CGT charge, it will be necessary to argue that the treaty overrides *TCGA 1992, s 77* and the ordinary UK charge to CGT on UK resident trustees.

The UK/Canada treaty will also have the same effect; additionally there is a base cost uplift for CGT purposes on the trustees becoming Canadian resident which would restrict Canadian tax to gains accruing after the trust became Canadian resident. (New Zealand and Mauritius have no CGT applied to portfolio assets.) There may, however, be traps in the *Canadian Foreign Affiliate Passive Income* regime.

Canada

17.42   Normally, *Section 94* of the *Income Tax Act* (Canada) prevents Canadian residents creating offshore trusts and the Foreign Accrual Property Income rules (FAPI) prevent Canadian residents accumulating wealth in offshore companies. However, if a Canadian resident is trading internationally – for example, buying materials in Europe and selling them to customers in Latin America (where no part of the trading takes place in Canada) – then there may be scope to escape the application of the FAPI rules, provided a treaty protected structure is created.

There is a very favourable double tax treaty between Canada and Barbados. If the Canadian resident is able to arrange for a non-Canadian resident family friend or relative to create a trust for a nominal amount (a few thousand dollars) and that trust forms a Barbados International Business Corporation, then that company may undertake the non-Canadian trading. The Barbados company will be subject to tax in Barbados at a nominal rate (2.5 per cent) but this should prevent the income of the trust being subject to FAPI rules because the income of the underlying company is active business income. The income can, in effect, be accumulated in the Barbados corporation or, if it is surplus to the reinvestment needs of the business, it can be distributed by capital distribution to the Canadian resident on a tax free basis under the principles outlined earlier in this chapter.

France

17.43   Treaties may also be of assistance for trusts with French beneficiaries. In 17.11 above under the subheading 'Taxation of Distributions', reference was made to the Canadian/French treaty and the use of a Canadian conduit trust to route income distributions from an offshore trust to French beneficiaries – although clearly the French gift tax implications have to be considered.

Conclusion

17.44   The purpose of this chapter has been to illustrate the main uses of trusts in international tax planning as opposed to purely domestic tax planning and as distinct from the non-tax uses of trusts.

In this context, the offshore trust has traditionally been useful in tax planning for families spread across international borders who have been able to 'arbitrage' differences in tax systems. Trusts have also been useful in pre-immigration planning and for cross border investment. This subject is vast and in the space available merely illustrates the potential with a few examples of outbound planning for a UK settlor with 'foreign' beneficiaries. A similar length chapter could be written for almost every other jurisdiction but hopefully some of the opportunities, limitations and pitfalls have been highlighted.

As the advantages of offshore trusts have been circumscribed by anti-avoidance legislation and international initiatives on money laundering/tax harmonisation, practitioners have begun to focus on the uses of the trusts in mainstream onshore centres for international tax planning and the opportunities which can be derived from suitable double tax treaties. It remains to be seen how this will develop.

Index

Introduction. The index covers Chapters 1 to 17. Index entries are to paragraph numbers, but in the Appendices, entries are to Appendix numbers e.g. in the form 2:1, which is Appendix 1 in Chapter 2. Alphabetical arrangement is word-by-word, where a group of letters followed by a space is filed before the same group of letters followed by a letter, e.g. 'Tax havens' will appear before 'Taxable persons'.

Index

Clarke: Offshore Tax Planning Eighth Edition

Giles Clarke, MA, PhD, FTII, Barrister

Offshore Tax Planning is the essential guide to successful planning through offshore trusts and companies. It also focuses on the tax treatment of foreign domiciliaries. For all taxation advisers, accountants and lawyers with international clients this is the indispensable guide to understanding the legislation, opportunities and pitfalls associated with offshore tax planning.

The eighth edition of **Offshore Tax Planning** has been revised to take account of recent developments. It will ensure that you are fully abreast of all the relevant issues.

The book is divided into seven parts each dealing with a different aspect of offshore tax planning and takes you straight to the area you need guidance on immediately:

- Fiscal Connection
- UK Domiciliaries
- Non-domiciliaries
- Practical Issues
- Anti-Avoidance Legislation
- Sheltering Business Profits
- Migration

Offshore Tax Planning is a must have for you in your day-to-day offshore tax planning work.

Published: October 2001   **Format:** Soft Cover   **Price:** £89.95   **ISBN:** 0 406 93909 8   **Product code:** COT8

How To Order

To order, please contact LexisNexis Butterworths Tolley
Customer Service Dept: **LexisNexis Butterworths Tolley,**
FREEPOST SEA 4177, Croydon, Surrey CR9 5WZ
Telephone: **020 8662 2000**   Fax: **020 8662 2012**

Butterworths Tolley, 35 Chancery Lane, London WC2A 1EL
A division of Reed Elsevier (UK) Ltd
Registered office   25 Victoria Street   London SW1H OEX
Registered in England number 2746621
VAT Registered No. GB 730 8595 20

Tax Direct is the ultimate online service that provides you with instant access to the most authoritative information ... all via the internet.
For more information on all of our products, please visit our website at www.butterworths.com